T0354280

BUILDINGS MUST DIE

THE MIT PRESS
CAMBRIDGE, MASSACHUSETTS
LONDON, ENGLAND

STEPHEN CAIRNS   JANE M. JACOBS

BUILDINGS
MUST DIE
A PERVERSE
VIEW OF
ARCHITECTURE

First MIT Press paperback edition, 2017

This book was set in Helvetica Neue Pro by the MIT Press.
Printed and bound in the United States of America.

Library of Congress Cataloging-in-Publication Data

Cairns, Stephen, author.
Buildings must die : a perverse view of architecture /
By Stephen Cairns and Jane M. Jacobs.
pages cm
Includes bibliographical references and index.
ISBN 978-0-262-02693-2 (hardcover : alk. paper)
        978-0-262-53471-0 (paperback)
1. Architecture. 2. Building materials—Deterioration.
3. Creation (Literary, artistic, etc.)—Social aspects.
I. Jacobs, Jane M. (Jane Margaret), 1958– author. II. Title.
NA2540.C32 2014
720.1—dc23
2013028480

10   9   8   7   6   5   4   3

FOR MAE

CONTENTS

ACKNOWLEDGMENTS

In the alchemy at the heart of any book are the many who contribute ingredients, whether encouragement, information, leads, references, critique. We would like to thank those many who contributed.

Adrian Forty allowed us to read sections of the manuscript for his book *Concrete and Culture* in advance of its publication. Paul Walker offered valuable suggestions on the history of Gothic revival in New Zealand. Ian Lochhead generously allowed us to read his unpublished paper on George Gilbert Scott's first design for Christchurch Cathedral. François Roche spent time with us talking through his Bangkok museum project, and many other things on the way. Andrew Johnson gave freely of his expertise on urban shrines in Bangkok. Katherine Gibson and Andrew Hui read and commented on early drafts. We thank Liang-Ping Yen and Nan-wei Wu for taking photographs of the Paper Dome church in Puli, Taiwan, and interviewing Meei-Ya Chen, Deputy Director of the Newhomeland Foundation. We also thank Meei-Ya Chen for taking the time to offer her views on the amazing history of the Paper Dome building. Richie Carroll of the Glasgow Housing Association was similarly generous and helped facilitate our work at Red Road.

Many other people generously gave us access to photographs from their private collections. Keith Lynch allowed us to reproduce his image of the immediate aftermath of the February 2011 earthquake in Christchurch. Chris Leslie allowed us to use his evocative photographs of Red Road. Flickr users— Klaus Bergheimer, Stéphane Plapied, Florian Blümm, Jonathan Burr, and Boris Hamilton—were responsive and enthusiastic about the project and allowed us to reproduce visual results from their intrepid travels. Pansit Torsuwan gave us access to his renderings of the Sathorn Tower project. Stewart Brand allowed us to reproduce his recycling image. Shigeru Ban gave us access and insight into his new Cardboard Cathedral project in Christchurch. Marcus Trimble reflected on his experience when visiting the moving remnants of the Takatori Church in Kobe. Miki Uono, in Toyo Ito's office, and Darko Radović were important allies in sourcing original images for the U-House project.

We would also like to acknowledge the image librarians at the Haas Family Arts Library at Yale University, the Museum of Modern Art, Canadian

Centre for Architecture, Manchester Local Image Collection, Alexander Turnbull Library, The Royal Academy of Arts London, The John Soane Museum, Royal Institute of British Architects, and Fondazione MAXXI Centre for their prompt and helpful responses to our queries.

Important aspects of this book were seeded in a generous grant from the UK's Arts and Humanities Research Council (AHRC). That funding allowed us to begin looking closely at the sublime hulk that was the Red Road flats in Glasgow, which even in its decrepit state remained home to so many. We thank those at Red Road for their generous help. In this early work we were pleased to have Ignaz Strebel on the team, along with Paul Anderson, Emma Bush, and Nigel Peake. Many other colleagues in the UK alternately put up with and enthused along with us in these early hesitant observations. Miles Glendinning, Richard Williams, Andrew Patrizio, and Eric Laurier were especially supportive.

Later, in Singapore, the fledgling environments of the Singapore-ETH Centre's Future Cities Laboratory and the Yale-NUS College offered stimulating settings for the drafting of the manuscript. Here we were pleased to have new colleagues such as Matthias Berger and Dirk Hebel, who invited us to present our work in his Constructing Waste seminar.

Roger Conover's early insights on our proposal were energizing and formative. We thank him for that and his subsequent trust. Gillian Beaumont and Matthew Abbate were thoughtful and careful editors.

To all these people we offer warm thanks. We alone (together) take responsibility for the many loose threads that dangle around the edges of this book.

As with most books, writing them takes time. And in that time other things happen. For us, the full gamut: international relocations, bereavements, birthdays, anniversaries, illnesses. Lorelei has been a patient and quizzical witness to our toils. To her we offer special appreciation.

Singapore
March 31, 2013

x

INTRODUCTION: A FEELING FOR THE INERT

This feeling for the inert has a special significance in our age,
in which the obverse of the capitalist drive to produce
ever more new objects is a growing mountain of useless waste,
used cars, out-of-date computers, etc., like the famous
resting place for old aircraft in the Mojave desert. In these
piles of stuff, one can perceive the capitalist drive at rest.
SLAVOJ ŽIŽEK (2003b, 14)
....

Death is that putrefaction, that stench ... which is at once the
source and the repulsive condition of *life*.
GEORGES BATAILLE (1991, 80)
....

Whoever must be a creator always annihilates.
FRIEDRICH NIETZSCHE (1968, 59)

ENDINGS

To assert that a living organism—be it human, animal, or vegetable—must die is an obvious truth. Life by definition is finite; death is inevitable. Is not death, along with taxes, as Benjamin Franklin famously claimed, the only certainty guaranteed to human life? Do we not, deep down, know that Freud was right when he proposed the now famous death instinct, "the task of which is to lead organic life back into the inanimate state"? We certainly get the gist when Woody Allen quips: "I am not afraid of death, I just don't want to be there when it happens."

Buildings, although inanimate, are often assumed to have "life." And it is the architect, through the art of design, who is the authorized conceiver and creator of that life. As a profession and discipline, architecture's identity is grounded in this creative act. Its extension into metaphors of building life and life-giving are clues to just how deep architecture's natalist vein runs. Invested as it is in creating ("life"), what is architecture's relationship to the processes of wasting, deterioration, destruction, and "death," to which buildings are inevitably subject?

This book offers a "perverse" view of architecture by focusing on these other processes. This is the shadow story of architecture's natalism. It is a story currently underdeveloped in architecture's sense of itself, yet it forms a necessary part of how architecture and architects are in the world. What would it mean for architecture to cultivate a sensitivity to how buildings waste, deteriorate, and die, what Žižek calls "a feeling for the inert" (2003b, 14)? We argue that developing receptiveness toward the negative realms of wasting and death is profoundly important for contemporary architecture. It has implications for the interrelated realms of architectural design, everyday human conduct, and wider processes of world-making at various scales. Death, destruction, and deterioration represent the negative, anxiety-inducing flip side to a range of enduring and sometimes contradictory assumptions about built architecture's defining attributes: its material durability, its creative genesis, its productive utility, its aesthetic value.

1

Our approach to uncovering this shadow story is both theoretical and empirical. We draw on a range of theoretical and philosophical propositions relevant to making sense of processes of wasting and destruction. We also attend to specific instances of building decay, deterioration, and destruction: some designed and others unintended, some lamented and others celebrated. By exposing architecture to these counterforces we do not seek to debunk the creativity, or imaginative inventiveness, of architectural design. We do not merely confront the vitality of design with the entropy of endings. Rather, we aspire to enrich the category of design through an expanded ethical horizon that encompasses a fuller and more complex view of architecture's "life" and "death." As architectural historian James Stevens Curl notes, "[l]ife spent without any contemplation of death is a denial of life, since death is the logical and inevitable end for us all" (Curl 1993, 1).

A MEMENTO MORI FOR ARCHITECTURE

In part our book is a memento mori for architecture: an architectural equivalent of the iconographic skulls, rotten fruit, hourglasses, and trails of smoke that began to populate many paintings from the Renaissance onward. Those motifs prompted the viewer to contemplate their mortality. They whispered to mortal viewers: "Remember, you must die." For rotten fruit we substitute spalling concrete, peeling paint, and moldering surfaces. For skulls we substitute earthquake-shattered churches, demolished brutalist office blocks, and crumbling housing estates. For hourglasses and trails of smoke we substitute obsolete buildings whose usefulness has long since been eclipsed by economic circumstance. Borrowing from the traditions of art, we too whisper: "Remember, buildings must die."

We do not document the decay and destruction of buildings so that it might be tabled as evidence of architecture's inadequacies. We do not insist, for example, that the excesses of design be curbed by the practicalities of weatherproofing against decay, although this is a well-rehearsed theme in literature on architecture and building. Nor do we moralistically admonish architecture for its tendency to inject life into its creations by anthropomorphizing them, although we do reflect upon the consequences of such projections. The content of this book looks awry at standard architectural concerns such as what comprises good form, what generates effective function and utility, and how architecture might best add positive value to the world. It does so not to kill architecture off. We broach these negative states of buildings in order that architecture might live better with the malforming and deforming facts of its existence. So, we offer this reflection on the decay and destruction of buildings not as a death sentence for architecture, but as a path to a new way for it to be in the world.

2

The shifting function and form of memento mori in the field of visual arts guides our own reflections on architecture, and two instances are usefully illustrative. Nicolas Poussin's painting *Et in Arcadia Ego* (1637–1638) features four youthful figures—three men and a woman—grouped around a tomb set against an Arcadian landscape of rolling hills and cloudy skies. The tomb is unadorned save an inscription that says: "Et in Arcadia Ego." One of the figures kneels on the ground and traces the inscription with his finger, as if to decipher its meaning. Another is turned away from the tomb and, facing the woman, seems to be relaying to her the inscription's message. She stands upright and listens in still contemplation. The fourth figure, to the left of the group, leans against the tomb and looks quietly down. As Erwin Panofsky suggests, in a famous essay, "[i]t is as though the youthful people, all silent, were listening to or pondering over this imaginary message of a former fellow being: 'I, too, lived in Arcadia, where you now live; I, too, enjoyed the pleasures which you now enjoy; and yet I am dead and buried'" (Panofsky 1963, 224).

Panofsky credits Nicolas Poussin's painting with an "entirely new idea" regarding mortality. On viewing the painting, Panofsky argues, we "instantly perceive a strange ambiguous feeling which suggests both a mournful anticipation of man's inevitable destiny and an intense consciousness of the sweetness of life" (Panofsky 1963, 224). While Poussin remains within the traditional conventions for the depiction of death, he also breaks with those conventions. This is not merely a "dramatic encounter with Death." Nor are there present conventional tokens of the memento mori—skull, hourglass, and so on. Instead the youthful figures engage knowingly and reflectively with the tomb as an artifact of death. Poussin's portrayal of the contemplation of mortality transforms "a mere memento mori into the revelation of a metaphysical principle which connects the present and the future with the past." As Panofsky argues, this transformation "overthrows the limits of individuality" and reaches out to a broader understanding of "Life … as transitory yet blessed with indestructible beauty and felicity." This perspective in turn changes the status of death: "'Death' is seen as a preserver as well as a destroyer" (Panofsky 1963, 240). The entire scene, while engagingly intimate, opens to a cosmic fact:

> From this emerges the magnificent conception of cyclical progression which subordinates the existence of individuals to the inexorable laws of cosmic principles, both natural and moral, endowing every stage of this existence, however transitory, with a substantial value of its own. (Panofsky 1963, 240)

We might demur, as did art critic T. J. Clark, that Panofsky's reading is "a bit too abstract and redemptive" in tone (Clark 2006, 96). Be that as it may, it discerns an innovation in the artistic interpretation of the memento mori tradition.

3

In Poussin's painting, the memento mori is more than a symbolic, iconographic device. It offers an open conception of the cyclical character of existence, inaugurating a "dialectical" account of life and death in which the "human agent reaches out again to contain" the forces of death (Clark 2006, 97).

This theme of human agency with respect to death's inevitability is well expressed by another instance of memento mori in fine art. The composition of Hans Holbein's painting *The Ambassadors* (1533) appears simple and clear. Two figures—the eponymous ambassadors—stand in an interior space almost symmetrically on either side of the picture plane, confidently addressing the viewer. They lean stiffly against a set of shelves upon which are arranged the instruments of knowledge contemporary to their times, such as globes, sundials, and various astronomical instruments. The figures are crisply rendered against the richly textured dark green brocade backcloth, and a Turkish carpet that drapes over the shelf. The composition, and the viewer's gaze, are disturbed by a gray shape that cuts diagonally through the shallow perspective space of the picture, conspicuous yet indistinct. The viewer can make sense of it only if they stand in just the right spot, which is to the lower left of the painting. From that viewing point the indistinct shape is foreshortened, and reveals itself to be a human skull: an encoded memento mori.

Jacques Lacan discusses Holbein's memento mori in his Seminar XI. Lacan was fascinated by the visual ambiguity in the painting—comparing it to Salvador Dalí's melting pocket watches and Giuseppe Arcimboldo's portraits composed of painted flowers, fish, and assorted vegetables. More conventionally, Holbein might have rendered the skull discreetly on the shelf alongside the globes, sundials, and instruments. Rather, he chose to present it anamorphically, in the same picture plane, but according to its own distinct visual logic. This rendering demands an intensified attention from the viewer. While the ambassadors and their accouterments are presented self-evidently, it is only on second or third viewing that the skull emerges from its anamorphic distortion. Standing in front of the painting for the first time, the viewer can stare directly at death without recognizing it. Holbein's anamorphic skull undermines the illusion of a world singularly legible by way of perspective space.[1] The skull does not establish a wholly other kind of space, but lies "immanent in the geometral dimension" of the painting. In doing so the memento mori "complements what geometral researches into perspective allow to escape" (Lacan 1981, 87).

We expand upon the memento mori tradition in the dialectical spirit of Panofsky's Poussin and with the immanent perspectival distortions of Lacan's Holbein. In doing so we take up the still largely unaddressed challenge laid at the feet of architecture in 1990 by philosopher Jacques Derrida in his provocative "Letter to Peter Eisenman," where he asked what might bring architecture back to "the experience of 'its own' ruin?" The letter was nothing less than a memento mori to the profession, insisting that architecture

> carries within itself the traces of its future destruction, the already past future, future perfect, of its ruin … it is haunted, indeed signed, by the spectral silhouette of this ruin, at work even in the pedestal of its stone, in its metal or its glass. (Derrida 1990, 11)

Our extended memento mori is animated by the spirit of these architectural "hauntings." We scrutinize various instances, both major and minor, of building "deaths": spectacular demolitions and collapses as well as more minor instances of water staining, spalling, and moldering. We dwell on these deforming and devaluing conditions not to say "we told you so" or "this ends too soon," but to allow architecture to better be with the inevitable fate of its creations.

GATHERINGS

This is a book about architecture, but it is written with the benefit and risk of an interdisciplinary perspective that includes scholarship from architectural theory, material and building science, economics, history, geography, urban planning, organization studies, and beyond. None of these perspectives agrees about what architecture is. Some see it as an elaboration of built form as governed by autonomous procedures and formal protocols, some as professional practice, some as a disciplinary area, others as an expression of wider social, political, and economic parameters. This book traverses through each of these manifestations of architecture. In this regard our book inquires into those discourses of architecture that codify the terms of reference, and delimit what can be said and done in the name of architecture. For all of this ranging, central to our understanding of architecture, and what is at stake in the writing of this book, is the idea of architectural design. We follow our diverse trajectories through architecture, guided by a commitment to say something back to the discourse and practice of architectural design. We are not alone in our turn to the perverse side of the built. For example, urban studies are also meditating on what Stephen Graham (2004a, 170) has called the city's "dark terrain … where urban destruction, devastation, de-generation, de-modernization and annihilation haunt dreams of urban modernity and development."

5

In many situations death and deterioration are not some perversion of the logic of life, they are lived with routinely and actively. For example, rapidly urbanizing cities of the so-called Global South are often overwhelmed by an entirely different aesthetics, what Hecker (2010, 265) dubs "the apocalyptic sublime." This is the aesthetics of precarity that, in architectural terms, manifests as deteriorating infrastructures, incomplete new builds and failing or destroyed old builds, as well as creatively formed informalities. This aesthetic has acquired a popular charm of late, often documented in glossy, high-circulation magazines such as *Time*, *National Geographic*, and *Newsweek*. Incorporated into this emergent documentation of deterioration are the carcass landscapes of deindustrialization: from Wang Bing's haunting record of a Chinese postindustrial landscape in *Tie Xi Qu: West of the Tracks* (2003), to Thomas Jorion's photographs of ruined and abandoned buildings, to the recent spate of coffee-table books on a Detroit variously understood as "lost," "disassembled," or in "ruins."[2] The thirst for what some have dubbed "ruin porn" is undeniable. We regard "ruin porn" as a variant of art's "dramatic encounter with Death" (Panofsky 1963, 240). It has a shocking but ultimately dulling effect, and does not, in the end, promote a more sustained contemplation of the inevitable place of decay, undoing, and destruction in creativity and life.

Our survey of buildings, architecture, and death cannot claim to be comprehensive. There are many ways in which buildings meet their end that we have not considered. Our partial offering dovetails with the complementary scholarship on other such endings. The destruction of buildings through war and terrorism is perhaps the most obvious omission from the pages to follow.[3] Such destructions are willful, self-conscious, and terror-filled. Our book, in contrast, offers an account of the often slower entropic processes that press upon buildings of all kinds. Such processes may precede moments of willful destruction, such as building demolition, but for the most part the deteriorations that we chart in the pages to follow are not associated with any one willful agent of destruction. That the processes we are interested in are often so indistinct and diffuse merely shrouds an issue of profound significance for architecture and the built environment.

This book also travels in the wake of other contributions on building destruction.[4] To this like scholarship we seek to add a theoretical discussion that draws out the wider consequences of such processes for the profession and discipline of architecture.

Recent scholarship in what has come to be known as waste studies has offered a central starting point for our work. This scholarship addresses the many ways objects transit between the categories of value and waste. A number of recent collections in this field offered theoretical scaffolding as we picked across the many instances of buildings decaying and ending.[5] Within art theory we found inspirational ideas in the scholarship on iconoclasm as well as the concern with entropy among the twentieth-century avant-garde.[6] Within geography we benefited from resonant scholarship on the materiality and experience of ruins.[7] Much of the parallel thinking within architecture we discuss at greater length in the pages to follow, but there are two books we would mention here.[8] Although we are not concerned with the practicalities of building maintenance, an early example of such scholarship articulates well our starting point. This was Banister Fletcher's 1872 book *Dilapidations*. A largely practical guide for architects and surveyors, it starts with a question that resonates with our own curiosity: "When one considers the numerous arts and sciences that the professional man must have at least some acquaintance with, a list of which the reader will find given at some length by that grand old writer, Vitruvius … is it to be wondered at, that dilapidations are not more studied?" (Fletcher 1872, 1). Some hundred years later, Kevin Lynch's (1990) *Wasting Away* began the job of answering this question, a line of inquiry truncated by his untimely death. Our book again takes up this question and inquires further into these often discarded aspects of architecture.

We are indebted to these and other fellow-travelers, past and present, whose lack of fear of the negative (waste, destruction, death) spurred us on into this *subterranea*. Like Baudelaire's *chiffonier* or "rag-picker" we have scavenged through the ruins and rubble of built commodity production in order to develop a feeling for the inert of our own architectural times. We have sought out the trash of social theory and its litter of architectural asides. Garbologists like William Rathje, whose life's work sought to understand modern society through its discards, offered us a model for our work.[9] We too try to track that which architecture has excluded from its sense of itself, as well as the actual rubble it produces. We do so in order to argue for the positive value for architecture of tarrying with the negative.

STRUCTURE OF THE BOOK

We hope this book will offer an innovative treatment of a relatively underexplored area. As part of our effort we seek to advance an extended theoretical position on the relationship between architecture and value that productively draws on theories of wasting. This more theoretically oriented aspect of the book unfolds in the first four, and last chapters. The current chapter is a scene-setter, and offers some of the key intellectual coordinates for the reflections that follow. The second chapter, "Design, Creativity, and Architecture's Natalism," develops the premise of the book by scrutinizing architecture's relationship to the idea of creativity. It inquires historically into how architecture came to be invested in a particular kind of pragmatic creativity as its central disciplinary trait. We suggest that this disciplinary investment manifests as a form of natalism in which creativity is metaphorically figured as the birth of buildings subsequently given vital characteristics. The limitations of this metaphor have profound consequences for architectural practice. These limitations are given some context in our third chapter, "Terminal Literacy," where we tease out a minor thread in recent architectural theory that consciously engages with issues of waste, deterioration, and

7

death. The chapter examines key terminology in this terminal literacy, such as "junk," "dross," "subtraction," "event," and "wasting." The fourth chapter, "Toward a General Economy of Architecture," broadens our scope by engaging with conceptual vocabularies that have informed debates on death and deterioration in the fields of philosophy, cultural studies, and economics. The title of the chapter is adapted from Georges Bataille's suggestive concept of a "general economy," with its emphasis on unproductive excess, death, and decay.

The central part of the book consists of five, more empirically focused, chapters that examine overlapping processes of building deterioration, destruction, and decay. We look at the ways in which such endings are managed and resisted through technical terminologies, bureaucratic vocabularies, and public spectacles. And we uncover the various, but all too rare, ways in which architecture has embraced such inevitabilities. These chapters take as their starting point keywords such as "decay," "obsolescence," "disaster," "ruin," and "demolition." We do not imagine that these keywords describe discrete and self-sufficient categories. An obsolete structure, for example, could well be in a ruinous state because subject to decay and partial demolition. Nor do these keywords always imply each other in expected ways. Ruins are not always obsolete. Demolitions do not always follow decay. Rather, these terms overlap, interpenetrate, and overdetermine each other. In doing so they give rise to strange and ambivalent categories that we examine and seek to understand: hyperpatina and bioreceptivity, instant obsolescence and "carcasses of flux," acts of God and "weak architectures," functional ruins and the aesthetics of decay, not to forget architectural murders and suicides.

Along the way, we look at the work of diverse architects such as Eero Saarinen, Shigeru Ban, Cedric Price, Carlo Scarpa, Gigon and Guyer, François Roche, Minsuk Cho, Rem Koolhaas, Arata Isozaki, and Toyo Ito, among others. We encounter diverse sites, including Kobe (Japan), Puli (Taiwan), New York and Moline (USA), Paris (France), Christchurch (New Zealand), London, Manchester, and Glasgow (UK), Jakarta (Indonesia), Donguan (China), and Bangkok (Thailand). As the case material accretes, we hope that the theoretical and synoptic chapters will be drawn into a conversation that bears on the question of architecture and death, and its wider consequences for creativity and design.

8

DESIGN, CREATIVITY, AND ARCHITECTURE'S NATALISM

ARCHITECTURE'S LIFE

Buildings are inorganic and inanimate. Yet they are routinely said to function like living organisms. Architecture deploys a range of metaphorical conventions to invest buildings with life. Building structures are referred to as "sinews" and "bones"; walls are likened to biological "membranes" or "skins" that may even "breathe"; windows and doors are understood as sensory apertures that "see," "smell," and "hear"; some spaces are thought of as "cellular," others as "flowing"; and ornamental markings are characterized as "tattoos" or "cosmetic layers." Building geometries are animated by "bending," "twisting," and "folding," while the conception of spaces that facilitate movement—corridors, staircases, vestibules—as "circulation" is so engrained in architectural thinking that its derivation from human physiology, and the circulation of bodily fluids, is long forgotten.[1] Buildings are ascribed life not only through bodily metaphors. They are also thought to have many of the higher qualities of humankind. Frank Lloyd Wright and Le Corbusier imbued architecture with "spirit." Many, from John Ruskin to Aldo Rossi and Charles Moore, have believed in architecture's ability to hold and disseminate "memory."[2]

There are even those who think buildings have a kind of agency, or at the very least a capacity to adapt to changing circumstances through time. Stewart Brand famously referred to this as architecture's ability to "learn" (Brand 1995). A more recent information technology turn in architectural design means that buildings now, quite literally, have artificial intelligence. As early as 1984 New York real estate agents were reportedly extolling the virtues of a new generation of buildings that could, as smart building advocate James Sinopoli (2010, 8) put it, "almost think for themselves." Jean Nouvelle's Arab World Institute building in Paris gave powerful and poetic expression to this promise of an intelligent building. Its façade was composed of thousands of wired mechanical apertures that opened and closed automatically in response to shifts in external light levels.

The current integration of computer-based telecommunications and sensing systems has given buildings the capacity to survey and monitor their users' movements; to manage their own heating, ventilation, air conditioning and lighting systems; to adjust the flows of electricity, water, data; and to detect smoke, CO_2, and other contaminants. As telecommunications and sensing systems become more deeply integrated into the fabric of buildings, so critics have begun to diagnose the complex "panoptic" (Foucault 1980; Lyon 2006) and "oligoptic" (Latour 2005) character of the intelligences that result, and the potential threats they pose to human autonomy.

The incorporation of principles of synthetic biology into architectural design and fabrication has further extended its lifelikeness. Scientific insights into the behavior of metals, alloys, ceramics, and concrete, combined with synthetic reproductions of protocells and biological systems, has offered new pathways for architectural design and building engineering. For example, self-healing and even self-generating materials promise an architecture that might, for example, be biologically programmed to sequester its own carbon emissions: detecting the CO_2 it emits, then actively absorbing the emissions back into its own fabric (see chapter 5). Whereas architecture was once ascribed life metaphorically, these newly sentient, intelligent, and self-generating cyborg buildings seem literally to pulse with (artificial) life.

Earlier anthropomorphic metaphors for architecture were, then, prescient. That anthropomorphic thread stretches back to Vitruvius's likening of the parts of a building to the human figure. Alberti, Palladio, and Michelangelo extended this tradition in the Renaissance (Wittkower 1971). Anthropomorphism of various kinds has also informed the rhetoric and design practices of modernists, postmodernists, arts and crafts proponents, and phenomenologists alike. Indeed, Suzanne Preston Blier, drawing evidence from her study of non-Western vernacular building traditions, goes so far as to claim that anthropomorphism is "one of architecture's universals" (1987, 118).

Architecture's anthropomorphism complements, and is complicated by, an equally long-standing biomorphism. A wide range of biological phenomena—flora, fauna, and whole ecological systems—have been taken as inspiration for, or models of, architecture. This again is a tradition that stretches back to Vitruvius, who observed that "primitive man" imitated "the nests of swallows and the way they built" (Vitruvius 1960, 38 [book II, chapter 1, i]). The German art historian Wilhelm Worringer's account of the history of aesthetics notes that such "primitive" and "organic" expression later gave way to the "super-organic" northern European Gothic, which was "unconcerned with organic life" and followed lines that were "dead in themselves" (Worringer 1920, 47). Within more contemporary architectural expression, the biomorphic spans from the quirky to the innovative.

12

We might think here of the Reverend J. G. Wood's (1875) *Homes without Hands*, which offered a description of how animals design and build shelters. More centrally, there are those who have argued that architecture has taken or should take inspiration from biomorphic structures. Banister Fletcher (1897), for example, turned the entire history of architecture arboreal in his famous "Tree of Architecture" illustration. Similarly, D'Arcy Thompson's *On Growth and Form* proposed that the form of an object was a diagram of the forces nature "impressed upon it" (Thompson 1961, 11).[3] In the latter part of the twentieth century, the often idiosyncratic biologism evident in Thompson's work found more subtle expression in mainstream architectures, be it in the high-tech conventions of modernism or the later biomimetic forms of architects like Future Systems, Richard Rogers, and Norman Foster. Contemporary experiments in biomimetic architecture—such as Steffen Reichert and Achim Menges's HygroScope project, or Philippe Rahm's work on biochemical processes—reach toward less static and formal interactions between materials, gases, liquids, and surrounding atmospheres, although it remains to be seen whether architecture will succumb entirely to what Deleuze once called the "animalizing" of the line (Deleuze 2003, 33).[4]

If architecture is invested with life—a living, breathing, sentient existence, with a spirit and a memory, a capacity to learn, and even a rudimentary facility to think for itself—what of its death? How is the inevitability of death figured and managed in the rich narrative of life that attaches to architecture? In Gruber's careful overview of the primary historical threads of contemporary biomimetics in architecture, the "death of buildings" is given a single paragraph (Gruber 2011, 141). Similarly, Thompson focuses only on "organic growth," and openly admits that he is not interested in the question of deterioration and "the long battle against the cold darkness which is death" (Thompson 1961, 9). "Death," we might also note, merits but a single reference in Wood's *Homes without Hands* (1875, 125).

Only occasionally does architectural discourse acknowledge the potential threats to the "life" of buildings. Dealing with such threats is more usually understood to be the responsibility of building science or building regulation. Buildings can be subject to contamination by dampness and mold, and harbor rodents, roaches, and disease. They can be afflicted with "sick building syndrome." More rarely, buildings can be regarded as being "in pain" or as "wounded" through deliberate acts of vandalism, terrorism, or war.[5] Even in these instances, as Michael Guggenheim notes in his review of writing in professional architectural journals, architecture has quick recourse to the metaphorics of surgery, healing, and recuperation. Buildings threatened with death must be "reanimated," "reborn" so that they might enjoy a "new life." Buildings are even endowed with immune systems. Architect Arthur Cotton Moore has reflected that building a new addition in a conversion project is "like an organ transplant," and often "the old building wants to reject it" (cited in Guggenheim 2011, 23). The life story of a much-loved building is sometimes recounted in "biographical" terms and, on occasion, the demise of such a building is accompanied by an "obituary" (Harris 1999). And a subcultural appreciation for the ephemerality of built form can be discerned in the work of architects like Cedric Price and Toyo Ito (some of which we discuss in subsequent chapters). But what of the vast bulk of those ordinary buildings that are routinely demolished? Does this constitute murder? What if the state of a building was such that it appeared to be begging for its end? Would demolition constitute euthanasia? In fact, architecture's investment in the metaphor of life begins to lose credibility at the point when, through illness, willful destruction, or decrepitude, its end comes into view. The finitude of architectural life, be it pitiless and mechanical or mitigated by eschatological hope, may well be captured in these metaphorics, but they tell us little about what end conditions might mean for architectural theory and practice.

FACING DEATH

While the death of organic forms of life is inevitable, in human culture this does not lead to simple acceptance. Different branches of culture—religion, philosophy, literature and art—have generated complex accounts and rich forms of expression that variously dramatize, assuage, or otherwise negotiate death.[6] In the European Middle Ages, death was, in Philippe Ariès's view, "tamed" (Ariès 1974). As everyday life was conducted in the "shadow" of death, life itself was contemplated with a "resigned yet peaceful cohabitation with 'tame' death" (Bauman 1992, 97). Ariès's conceptualization of a premodern view proposes a foundational distinction between life and death, with the former being associated with health, goodness, and salvation, and the latter with sickness, evil, and sin. Today, we are perhaps more in tune with the medicalized conception of death, as encapsulated by physiologist Claude Bernard who, in 1876, pronounced that "[t]hese ideas of a struggle between opposing agents, of an antagonism between life and death, between health and sickness, inanimate and living nature, have had their day." In place of the life-and-death antagonism, Bernard proposed a universal and rational conceptualization of life and death as a "continuity of phenomena" marked by an "imperceptible gradation and harmony" (cited in Canguilhem 1991, 33). The sharp division that Ariès diagnosed in premodern European culture was, at that nineteenth-century moment, replaced by a continuity linking life to death. For sociologist Zygmunt Bauman this medicalization of death inaugurated a profound repression of death in life. He offers his own memento mori in response: "Without mortality, no history, no culture—no humanity" (Bauman 1992, 7).

14

More recently, this kind of universalist proclamation has been supported by a growing scholarship on non-Western conceptualizations of death. Building on an ethnographic tradition reaching back over two hundred years, contemporary scholarship—on such places as Sudan, Trobriand Islands, Cheyenne reservations in North America, Hokkaido in Japan—shows the diverse practices of grieving and mourning, burial, and commemoration in non-Western contexts. This scholarship affirms the remarkable diversity of mortuary rituals, and the consistent importance given to death in human society. As Robben suggests, "mortuary rituals are a true cultural universal that show people's resistance to accepting biological death as a self-contained event" (Robben 2004, 9).

The phenomenon of death is carefully held, framed, and mediated in varying ways in all cultures, and this has been the case throughout human history. The rich variety of ways in which humans face and mark death is a testament to a deep sensitivity to death's inevitability, be it understood as brutal annihilation and destruction of consciousness or, more commonly, the transformative threshold to another existence. Indeed, a more restricted functional view would cast religion, philosophy, literature and art as offering "solutions" precisely to the inevitability of death. This negotiation of death acknowledges, in turn, the aging process and the full complexity of the life cycle, and is seen as part and parcel of a healthy attitude to life itself.

As James Stevens Curl has shown, architectures of death, such as tombs, sepulchers, and memorials, play their part in this wider human history of dealing with death (Curl 1993, 2002). But there is a significant absence of this rich legacy of thinking about death in architecture, suggesting that it has a diminished, impoverished, and extremely partial view of its existence. Architecture lives on in fantasies of creativity and durability—so much so that a proclamation like "Buildings must die" provokes a double take, momentary incredulity, or even mild shock. Sensitivity to a building's end and an understanding of the conditions that attach to such an end—wasting, obsolescence, decay, decrepitude, ruination— is less developed in architecture. The investigation into matters of architecture's endings that will unfold in the pages that follow is premised on our belief that the processes of deterioration, wasting, and death are powerfully significant to a wide range of contemporary debates, not least the pressing questions of creativity and environmental sustainability.

FOUNDATIONS OF CREATIVITY
Architecture's repression of death is, we have suggested, reflected in the partial metaphor of life in which the discipline has invested. Understanding architecture's resistance to end conditions requires an appreciation of the circumstances by which the life metaphor came to be attached to architecture and integrated

into its disciplinary self-image. Central to this process was the concept of creativity as the faculty by which life is begotten, actualized, or brought into being. So, we begin our inquiry into architectural endings by way of a seeming detour: an investigation into the way architecture and creativity came to be so closely associated. Under what terms and within what parameters was architectural creativity forged? To what extent is this history still central to architectural identity and practice? We ask these questions because to understand architecture's trouble with death, we must understand the deep entwinement between the persistent metaphoric of life, the investment in creativity, and the nature of design practice.

A recent issue of the *Guardian* featured interviews with a diverse group of "artists": singers, stage and film directors, composers, poets, writers, and a lone architect. Headlined "Top artists reveal how to find creative inspiration," the piece reported in detail on the various *modi operandi*—techniques, habits, routines, manners, quirks, tactics—that characterized the creative practices of each interview respondent. Despite the variety of answers, respondents deployed a remarkably consistent vocabulary of creativity. The artists reported a relatively coherent range of techniques that mingled the ordinary (cultivating daily habits like walking the dog, getting up early, practicing, and imbibing coffee, tea, and assorted other stimulants) with the not-so-ordinary (taking chance and play seriously, inducing daydreams, and defamiliarizing the habitual and conventional). They also reported on doing different kinds of analytical research that depended on more systematic or scientific ways of seeing, allied with the sheer hard graft of making, rehearsing, and practicing. Almost all respondents accepted the premise that their creative work involved a search for inspiration, powered by imagination.

Inspiration and imagination are key terms in the history of aesthetics and the theory of creativity, being associated with Plato and Kant, respectively. Creativity, for Plato, involves inspiration literally ("inspiration," from *spirare*—to breathe—and related to "spirit"). The inspired artist is breathed upon by the gods or muses and then creates, with little conscious sense or control over their actions. Plato thought of inspiration as producing a kind of derangement in the creative practitioner. Kant goes along with Plato, although for him the imagination is an enabling faculty for the creative act. The imagination is triggered by genius innate to the artist, and this allows the faculties of imagination and understanding to interact in a playful way, ungoverned by rules. This formulation enabled Kant to make a distinction between a kind of creativity that emerges from imitation and a more radical creativity that brings new worlds into being. Creativity, in this view, is independent of conditioning protocols, rules, and procedures, and relies on the consciousness of the artist. The external agents—gods or muses—who deliver

16

inspiration in Plato's account are internalized within the consciousness of the creative subject. Kant also breaks with Plato in his proposition of a nonimitative form of creativity. It is the creative subject who makes the rules for his or her work, setting the terms of medium and significance according to an imagination in free play with the faculty of understanding. Kant sees in creativity a capacity to stimulate spontaneous leaps of imagination that generate unique aesthetic insights that eclipse the limitations of imitation.[7]

Historically speaking, these generalized philosophical formulations of creativity were realized in discipline-specific ways. Creativity for a musician means something different from what it means for a film director, or a sculptor. In architecture there are many forces that press heavily upon the ways in which creativity is realized: the materiality of buildings (stone, brick, timber, glass, steel, concrete); the physical forces that control their statics; the processes by which they are assembled (construction, structures, and technology); what users need; and, of course, what the client wants. It is no surprise to find that in the *Guardian*'s inquiry into contemporary creative practices it was the architect alone who ascribed his creativity to factors such as utility, buildability, and productivity as well as more typical factors like inspiration and imagination.[8]

CREATING DESIGN

Architecture's investment in the idea of creativity, as the faculty that purportedly spawns life, was formalized in the Renaissance. At that time the term "creativity" was first applied to artistic conception to suggest a parallel to Godly creation (Ackerman 1972, 242). The term *disegno*, meaning design through the practice of drawing, encapsulates this important development. We would like to linger on the technique and art of drawing because architectural design originated in (and sustains itself through) the act of drawing. Drawing offers a window onto the way in which creativity is embedded within architecture's disciplinary imaginary. The idea of creative practice that drawing—as *disegno*/design—instilled in architecture also directly implicated the idea of life, and the rich cluster of themes related to begetting life such as conception, birth, generation, speculation, and invention. This vocabulary has been deployed to powerful effect in the discipline ever since.

17

While drawings were an important aspect of architectural practice in medieval times, they primarily took the form of templates that transmitted preexisting geometric formulae for the layout of buildings (Harvey 1972). The architectural task in the medieval context involved the construction of buildings according to a set of received proportional relationships and constructional techniques which, although gradually modified and adapted over time, were understood to be essentially stable, fixed, and predetermined (Kostof 1977, 87–89). Master tradesmen, usually stonemasons, were charged with the setting-out of these proportions, as "[o]nly these masters, whose careers had begun by patrimony or by pupilage, possessed the special skills in geometrical setting-up which enabled the essential working drawings to be made" (Harvey 1972, 104). The training and authorizing body that sanctioned architectural practice was the Lodge. It was this institution that ensured, with great secrecy, that the geometric formulae of the trade were transmitted to approved initiates.

The most important and prominent drawings in medieval architectural practice were inscribed directly either into the surface of the building site or into the fabric of the building itself (Harvey 1972, 104; Kostof 1977, 87). As these drawings were inscribed with a metallic stylus—an instrument having the characteristics of both a chisel and a pen—they would have had a direct and tactile quality, closer to stereotomy than to modern architectural drawing. To modern eyes, the mason's stylus represents the commingling of distinctive categories: the intellectual labor involved in conceiving and developing architectural ideas and the manual labor involved in materializing those ideas. This commingling was reflected in the way the spaces for the production of drawing and the building site were organized in medieval architectural practice. The drawing and cutting of templates were done in the tracery house or Lodge located on the construction site itself. As a consequence there was—quite literally—very little space between the intellectual conception of the architecture and the manual labor of its fabrication. The act of building and its orchestration were almost indistinguishable (Kostof 1977, 89).

During the Renaissance the integration of intellectual and manual labor began to be teased apart in the name of a grand and unified art practice in which architecture held a central place. The conception of architectural ideas came to be distinguished from the practices of construction, and was formalized as "the art of design," the unifying principle for painting, sculpture, and architecture (Wilkinson 1977, 134). The catalyst for this new disciplinary alliance was the notion of *disegno*. While *disegno* is usually rendered in English as "drawing" or "design," the term had wider and more intellectual connotations. As Giorgio Vasari put it in 1568: "*Disegno* is an apparent expression and declaration of the *concetto* [or judgment] that is held in the mind of that which, to say the same thing, has been imagined in the intellect and fabricated in the *idea*" (Vasari 1991). *Disegno* was an intellectual practice, quite distinct from medieval drawing, and as the "father" of the arts—painting, sculpture, architecture—it served as a common foundation that set them apart from the crafts. Art historian Ernst Gombrich, for example, distinguishes between medieval drawing, which was characterized by the "firm line that testifies to the mastery of ... craft," and *disegno*, which relied instead on a tentative, repetitive, and exploratory line involving "correc-

18

tions, adjustments, adaptation." Design drawing, in this modern sense, offered the architect "the means to probe reality and to wrestle with the particular." It is the emergence of drawing as an investigative medium that facilitates innovation, invention, and the conception of architectural "ideas" (Gombrich 1960, 173).

This did not mean that classical theory, principally delivered through Vitruvius's *Ten Books of Architecture*, was simply overturned. Architecture's ancient anthropomorphic principles—the proportional system of the human body and its role as a guide for the formal organization of architecture—remained relevant for Renaissance architects and theorists. Figures such as Alberti and Francesco di Giorgio Martini, Sebastiano Serlio, Palladio, Giacomo Vignola, Vincenzo Scamozzi, and Filarete all sought to develop the new principles of *disegno* while reconciling them to classical theories of anthropomorphic proportion. But their reinterpretation of Vitruvius positioned anew the figure of the architect, now the conceiver of architectural ideas rather than the mere transmitter of building conventions.[9] As Françoise Choay shows, the collective writing of such architects began to form an autonomous discursive apparatus, or textual "foundation" that supported the conception of architectural ideas and the construction of "new and unknown forms of space" (Choay 1997, 6).

The general picture of baroque, rococo, and Enlightenment aesthetic theory is one of a fracturing and subsequent rationalization of the great artistic unity that the Renaissance had bequeathed. This process was underpinned by an emergence of philosophical aesthetics, and was, in the later eighteenth century, played out against a growing tension between empiricist interest in sentiment, feeling, and subjectivity, and rationalist concern for the maintenance and further codification of universal principles of taste.[10] The attempted formalization of a "system of the arts" during the Enlightenment generated an interest in the specific characteristics of each of the arts and the distinctions between them. As a consequence, the arts were increasingly rationalized according to the different senses they were thought to address. This meant that boundaries between the arts came to be more intensively scrutinized than ever.[11]

In this intellectual context, architecture's long-standing disciplinary responsibility to materiality, utility, function, and productivity complicated its standing in the emerging category of "fine" arts. The all-too-evident responsibility architecture had to utility and productivity marked it out from other fine arts, which sought, by Kant's formulation, no such use value and instead exploited a "free beauty" in order to realize embodied "purposiveness without purpose." Kant (1987 [1790]) later designated the aesthetic effects of those practices that, like architecture, tended toward utilitarian as "adherent beauty." In his aesthetic system, architecture was invested in purposiveness *with* purpose.[12] The outlines of architecture's distinctive creative, life-giving principle began to take modern shape. As it had always constructed its identity as an art by an appeal to function, need, and productivity—even if aesthetic pleasure was a consequence of this—architecture struggled to establish for itself a pure pleasure-inducing principle. As a consequence architecture was doomed to occupy a lowly rank in the aesthetic system. Kant's formulation of architectural creativity was, and remains today, a powerful sign of its relative lack of prestige in the context of those fine or liberal arts that were unencumbered by the duty of purpose.[13]

REINVENTING ARCHITECTURAL CREATIVITY

Architecture's loyalty to the Renaissance ideals is relatively easy to identify in the work of heroic masters and ordinary practitioners alike throughout the twentieth century. Le Corbusier, while most popularly associated with a rationally motivated architecture, was a powerful advocate of creativity in architectural design. Indeed, in his hands, architectural creativity takes on a blatant natalism. As Flora Samuel notes, "Le Corbusier was fond of using procreative imagery when talking about his own creative processes" (2004, 159). For example, Le Corbusier's own description of the three-stage design process of the chapel of Notre-Dame du Haut at Ronchamp involved "integrating with the site" then, after "incubation," a "'spontaneous birth' ... of the whole work, all at once, at a stroke," followed by "the slow execution of the drawings, the design, the plans and the construction itself" (cited in Pauly 1997, 71–72).[14] This natalized creativity was not always appreciated. While reveling in the poetics and emotional experiences that the Ronchamp chapel evoked, James Stirling concluded that it lacked "an appeal to the intellect" or the possibility of "intellectual participation," and offered "nothing to analyze or stimulate curiosity." For Stirling this building emerged from a populist, sensate, and picturesque impulse. It did not embody a proper modernist attitude to creativity grounded in a rigorous intellectual alignment of a building's technologies, spatial organization, materials, and forms of construction. Stirling's notion of architectural creativity insists on the "fusion of art and technology," and reasserts what he calls "the Victorian idea of progress as the invention and perfection of man's tools and equipment" (Stirling 1956, 161).

In his book *Architecture in the Age of Divided Representation: The Question of Creativity in the Shadow of Production*, Dalibor Vesely (2004) offers a more contemporary, phenomenological account of design that navigates between the natalism of Le Corbusier and the normative technical aesthetics of mid-century Stirling. Vesely, like Alberto Pérez-Gómez (1983) before him, wrestles with the legacy of the Renaissance *disegno* ideal, its subsequent rationalization in the Enlightenment, and its instrumentalization in modernism. His project is forthrightly critical, and seeks to discern and reinstate what he regards as an authentic kind of creativity. The difficulty with the concept of creativity that has been bequeathed to contemporary architecture, Vesely argues, is that the drive for originality leads to "isolation from the world that we all, in one way or another, share" (Vesely 2004, 13). As is announced in the ominous subtitle of his book, Vesely laments the threat to architectural creativity that comes in the wake of the instrumentalizing of design through rationalized systems of production. Production, for Vesely, interrupts authentically creative practice by establishing "an autonomous domain of reality" (Vesely 2004, 21). Authentic creativity is, by contrast, a kind of participatory practice "always situated within a particular communicative context from which it grows and in which the creative results participate." The "essence" of creativity lies in a kind of circular co-constitution of the human world. For Vesely this links to the wider theme of representation, including drawing—not Renaissance *disegno*, but the classical notion of *poiesis*. Drawing as *poiesis*, he suggests, "more or less coincides with the essential nature of making, and in particular with the making of our world." *Poiesis*, in this original Greek sense, is the "bringing into being of something that did not previously exist … a creative step that transforms the open field of creative possibilities into a representation articulated by gesture, word, image, or concept" (Vesely 2004, 14–15).

Others go so far as to claim a neurological basis for architecture's creativity. Harry Francis Mallgrave (2010), in his book *The Architect's Brain: Neuroscience, Creativity, and Architecture*, is intrigued by the promise of neuroscience to unlock the secrets of "such enigmatic issues as the designer's creativity." He argues that "[b]ecoming more fully aware of the extent of our biological complication, whose underpinnings reach deeply into the sensory-emotive world that we daily inhabit, is simply a first step in the process" (Mallgrave 2010, 5). Mallgrave adopts neuroscientist Gregory Berns's idea that creativity is a capacity to generate associated metaphors, suggesting that "creative individuals demonstrate a 'flatter associative hierarchy,'" by which he means that "during the creative process they recruit input from more spatially distributed areas of the brain" (Mallgrave 2010, 173). Mallgrave turns to Marco Frascari's (2003) discussion of Venetian architect Carlo Scarpa as evidence of this hard-wired creativity. According to Frascari, Scarpa "worked entirely through a synesthetic process that entailed, on the same page of sketches, different colors and styles of drawing with different media." These diverse media formed "bundles of intertwined sensory perceptions" that, Frascari argues, underpinned Scarpa's design process. This "joining of the information received by one sense to a perception in another sense," Frascari concludes, "is the essence of the architectural thinking." Frascari draws out the synesthetic dimensions of design, suggesting that by "moving away from medieval tracing floors to paper," architectural drawings "have evolved in a specific manifestation of non-verbal thinking" that functions as "aromatic-chromatic-visual tools to flavor buildings." Design drawings are not "transparent notations but synesthetic images" that mix "factual lines and non-factual demonstrations" (2003, 3). In this view, Frascari chimes with Hubert Damisch, who observed that Scarpa's drawings had a "demonstrative power," a "power of persuasion and evocation" (Damisch 1985, 209). (See chapter 5, where we discuss Scarpa's design for the Banca Popolare in Verona.)

Clearly the discipline and profession of architecture has undergone profound transformations since that figure of the architect-as-conceiver emerged in the Renaissance. The tensions embodied by utilitarian forms of creativity and the Kantian concept of "adherent beauty" became more intensely felt within the discipline as buildings became more technologically sophisticated, expensive to produce, and enmeshed in increasingly complex urban systems. As Bruno Latour (2009, 2) has observed, the term "design" has had an "extraordinary career" in recent years, rapidly growing in "comprehension" and "extension." On the one hand, more elements of any one object, are understood to be designed (comprehension); on the other, constellations of objects, systems, networks are assembled at ever larger scales no longer by mere calculation, engineering, or management but also by design (extension). The term "design" can now be applied to everything "from the details of daily objects to cities, landscapes, nations, cultures, bodies, genes, and ... to nature itself" (Latour 2009, 2). The long-held aspiration in architecture to design both at "the scale of the spoon and the city"[15] predisposes the discipline to such comprehension and expansion. Architects today spread their energies thinly, functioning as bureaucrats, business people, organization experts, managers of resources, and facilitators of social spaces. What it means to be an architectural creative practitioner is vastly more complex than it used to be. This stretches not only architects' competencies but also the public's belief in the idea of architect as creative practitioner.

We can also think of intellectual stances within the discipline that have, in one way or another, played down, complicated, or sidestepped overtly natalist models of creativity. Architectural investment in replicable forms is one such instance. The primary thrust of orthodox modernism, as we saw in Stirling's critique of Le Corbusier's Ronchamp chapel, emphasized technological solutions and industrial forms of production whose value lay in a generic repeatability. For example, with modernist mass housing solutions, architects invoked a form of invention that emerged from the interface of art and technology, underscored by an ethic of rationality, and deployed in pursuit of an ideal of efficient, universal provision. Similarly, postwar Italian rationalism promoted architectural types that eschewed difference in the name of a hyper-coherent serial repetition in urban morphology. An entirely different challenge to architecture's creative natalism resides in its long-standing, though awkward, relationship to vernacular building traditions, which stand as a testament to the values of skill and craft in architectural design. Those traditions have informed various arts and crafts movements within architecture that celebrate, in the words of William Morris, "the products" and "the producers of ordinary beauty" (Morris [1888] 1902, 209). A related challenge to the natalist conception of architectural creativity was expressed in the work of Alison and Peter Smithson, which valued found conditions.[16] As Adam Caruso explains in his essay "The Tyranny of the New," the "perpetual novelty" of technologically inspired design was seen as a threat to the "cultural continuity" needed for a creativity grounded in "collective action" (1998, 25). A similarly distributed notion of architectural creativity is also found in Venturi, Scott Brown, and Izenour's (1977) hymn to "ugly and ordinary architecture" found in *Learning from Las Vegas*.[17] This new architectural openness to the already existing displaces dogmatic forms of inspiration, and gestures toward a creativity grounded in what Lévi-Strauss referred to as the "science of the concrete." This view of architectural creativity as a relational aesthetic has informed a wide range of recent theoretical formulations, including bricolage, radical eclecticism, ad hocism, postmodern quotation, retrofitting and reuse, generic urbanism, and the open city.[18] Each of these formulations complicates and enriches the historical legacy of architectural design.

For all the caution we must exercise around thick and complex terms like "creativity," many historical and social scientific studies of the profession show that the Renaissance conception of *disegno*, and the associated values of creativity and invention, retain a powerful hold on the disciplinary imaginary.[19] The tropes of creativity, invention, and even the explicit natalism that find expression in Le Corbusier's reflections on design pervade ordinary architectural practice too. A well-known study conducted by sociologist D. W. MacKinnon (1970) in the 1960s administered the Gottschaldt Figure Test to architects and found most had scores that "fell shortly below those of artists."[20] The study also showed that, of the architects surveyed, between 60 and 100 percent were "intuitive perceivers" (those who concentrate on possibilities of things perceived) as opposed to "sense perceivers" (those who concentrate on things as they are). Judith Blau's (1987) survey of over 400 architects showed that 98 percent felt creativity was the distinctive feature of architecture, and 80 percent said they wanted more opportunities to work in the early parts of a design project where most creative energy is typically invested.

This view is affirmed again in Imrie and Street's (2011) more recent study on the role of regulation in architectural design. Their survey of architects in London showed that a majority (64 percent) expressed "ambivalent feelings" about design codes, seeing them as "curtailing architects' creativity," as "tying down

23

architectural freedom," as "stifling," "burdening," "straitjacketing," or "strangling" creativity (Imrie and Street 2011, 17).

From the Renaissance onward the discipline of architecture secured design as its disciplinary prerogative, its distinctive mark, its unique claim to status among the arts and professions. This variant of creativity shares a common heritage with the fine arts, has been nourished by contemporaneous philosophical debates on the nature of creativity, and is deeply indebted to the vocabulary of inspiration and imagination. Indeed, the cultivation of design remains, to this day, centrally placed in professionally accredited (AIA, RIBA, UIA) training regimes for architects throughout the world. But architecture's concept of creativity is also quite distinctive, both in the way it has taken shape and how it has been practiced. The themes of creativity, originality, and imagination have had to be constantly negotiated in and through architecture's entanglement in the contingencies of building fabrication, economics, function, occupation, and productivity. The complexity and sheer messiness involved in getting buildings built, having them usefully occupied and integrated into domestic and wider political economies, has meant that architectural creativity could never simply be understood in idealist terms.

LATENT FEELINGS

Architecture's persistent natalism comes from this foundational link to creativity by design, a link that has been rehearsed, modified, and reasserted throughout the history of the discipline. But in this entanglement of creation and creativity, when does the discipline ruminate on the finitude of the created work? Where are its treatises on afterlives, wasting, deterioration and destruction? When does architecture allow itself to tarry with the negative? How does it manage the hauntings that entropy necessarily visits upon all creative practices? These questions serve to orient this book. To date they have only tentatively been posed, and even more rarely addressed in a sustained way. One of our objectives in this book is to draw together those moments when these negative conditions were seen and taken seriously by architecture. Although we claim some novelty with respect to this project, from the early days of a professionalized discipline there have been signs of an architecture of the negative. We finish this chapter by revisiting two early instances of this latent sign of architecture's feeling for the inert in the architectural writings of two Renaissance scholars: Filarete and Francesco di Giorgio. Both these scholars hold a relatively marginal place in the historiography of architecture's origins. Their interpretations of Vitruvius have been positioned as less refined, more folk knowledge than rational scholarship, corrupt and even erroneous (Rykwert 1981b, 79). Nonetheless, their accounts of architecture offer suggestive deviations that remind us that death and dying have, from the beginning, resided inside architecture's self-image.

In the years between 1461 and 1464 the architect, sculptor, and writer Antonio Averlino, otherwise known as Filarete, wrote a substantial treatise on architecture.[21] As we have seen, Filarete was among a significant group of Renaissance architects and writers who were central to theorizing *disegno* and the reinterpretation of classical architectural theory. Filarete is especially interesting for us because he was, by his own admission, the least scholarly of the Renaissance architectural theorists.[22] His theory of architecture parallels many of the concerns of his contemporaries, including the proposition that in architectural creativity, building design and the body (assumed to be male) needed to be closely linked: "[T]he building is given form and substance by analogy with the members and form of man." Filarete elaborated this formal analogy in some detail, reflecting on the arrangement of passages, entrances and exits, all to be "formed and arranged according to their origins" in an analogy to the ideal man (Filarete 1965, 12 [book I, folio 6r]). He is in this sense part of the natalist tradition of architecture. Filarete also wrote in a more direct and exaggerated style than the more sober and controlled Alberti and Francesco di Giorgio (Kruft 1994, 55), and through his frankness we start to see a glimpse of an early architectural feeling for the inert.

Filarete pushed the formal analogy between building and body to its literal extremes, and in doing so complicated it in three ways. First, he explored what an ideal body might be. If proper architecture should replicate the proportional structure of the perfect body, then logic determined that other kinds of imperfect bodies, those of "dwarfs and overly large men and giants," for example, must be excluded. Filarete went into a peculiar and rather lengthy aside about the birth of giants, whom he saw as the result of miscegenetic unions (between women and giants) and a "travesty of nature" not to be adapted or mimicked in architecture. For Filarete such aberrant offspring served as a warning to architectural progenitors of the possibility of bad births. His goal was not simply an architecture that was properly proportioned, but also a godly architecture that understood how to manage its relationship with clients and others.[23]

> The building is conceived in this manner. Since no one can conceive himself without a woman, by another simile, the building cannot be conceived by one man alone. As it cannot be done without woman, so he who wishes to build needs an architect. He conceives it with him and then the architect carries it. (Filarete 1965, 15 [book II, folio 7v])

Secondly, Filarete elaborated the idea of creation as procreation. He suggested that if a building were based on the proportions of a body, it must also be like a "living man," for which the (feminine) architect and (masculine) client were the progenitors.

25

When the architect has given birth he becomes the mother of the building. Before the architect gives birth, he should dream about his conception, think about it, and turn it over in his mind in many ways for seven to nine months, just as a woman carries her child in her body from seven to nine months. He should also make various drawings of this conception that he has made with the patron, according to his own desires. A woman can do nothing without the man, so the architect is the mother to carry this conception. When he has pondered and considered and thought [about it] in many ways, he then ought to choose, [according to his own desires], what seems most suitable and most beautiful to him according to the terms of the patron. When this birth is accomplished, that is, when he has made, in wood, a small relief design of its final form, measured and proportioned to the finished building, then he shows it to the father. (Filarete 1965, 15–16 [book II, folio 7v])

Already we can see how Filarete's robust theorization of architectural creativity took natalist metaphorics to extremes. Yet in this extreme thinking he offers us some suggestive complications of the natalist emphasis. For example, he argued that a building, like a man, "must eat in order to live." Similarly, he talked of the ways in which architecture "sickens or dies." And, as modern conservation architects delight in telling us, he also talked of how buildings "are sometimes cured of … sickness by a good doctor." He said all of this knowing there would be doubting voices:

You can say that a building does not sicken and die like a man. I say to you that a building does just that, for it sickens when it does not eat, that is, when it is not maintained and begins to fall off little by little exactly as man [does] when he goes without food, and finally falls dead. This is exactly what the building does. (Filarete 1965, 12 [book 1, folio 6r])

You need to maintain it continually and to guard it from corruption and too much fatigue, because, as man becomes thin and ill from too much fatigue, so [does] the building. Through corruption, the body of the building rots like that of man. Through excess it is ruined and dies like man. (Filarete 1965, 13 [book 1, folio 6r])

While Filarete placed architecture into a life cycle that ended in death, his contemporary Francesco di Giorgio put death at the core of at least one of his accounts of the birth of architecture's ancient orders. Francesco was a painter-cum-architect-cum-military-engineer. He produced what has been dubbed a "corrupt pastiche" of Vitruvius in a treatise published in two different forms between 1480 and 1490 (Hersey 1989, 79). Among other things, and following Vitruvius, Francesco's carefully illustrated treatise addressed the origin of the Corinthian order. Vitruvius sought to raise architecture to the level of knowledge or *scientia*, and did so by showing it to be a mathematical art with proportions derived from those of the ("well-shaped") human body (Onians 1988, 33–34). His account of the Doric and Ionic orders was couched largely in this language of proportion, and operated as a set of instructions for building. It was only when he accounted for the later, Corinthian order that Vitruvius detoured into a set of origin narratives. The Doric order, he proposed, was derived from male proportions and associated with the Dorian warrior invaders: "Thus the Doric column, as used in buildings, began to exhibit the proportions, strength, and beauty of the body of a man" (Vitruvius 1960, 103 [book IV, chapter 1, vi]). In contrast, the Ionic order was derived from the female form, captured in the more slender proportions and in ornamentation reflecting curls of hair and the folds of matronly robes. In both cases we have no sense as to whether the bodies that offered up their proportions were alive or dead; we know only that they were properly formed. We do know, however, that the Doric and Ionic orders were described by Vitruvius first through the language of ratio and form, and were only later given a historicized origin by way of an aside written to serve his explanation for the origins of the novel, because more slim and ornamented, Corinthian order. As Joseph Rykwert (1996, 317) has noted, Vitruvius saw the Corinthian order as "procreated" by the older two: "she was their child."[24]

This natalist structure sits in sharp contrast to the deceased state of the human figure at the center of the legend about the origins of the Corinthian order. That origin story involved a maiden who died and whose burial site established the unique combination of elements that gave rise to the proportions and ornament of the Corinthian order. As Vitruvius recounts:

> A freeborn maiden of Corinth, just of marriageable age, was attacked by an illness and passed away. After her burial, her nurse, collecting a few little things which used to give the girl pleasure while she was alive, put them in a basket, carried it to the tomb, and laid it on top thereof, covering it with a roof-tile so that the things might last longer in the open air. This basket happened to be placed just above the root of an acanthus. The acanthus root, … when springtime came round put forth leaves and stalks in the middle, and the stalks, growing up along with sides of the basket, and pressed out by the corners of the tile through the compulsion of its weight, were forced to bend into volutes at the outer edges.
>
> Just then Callimachus, whom the Athenians called [Catatechnos] for the refinement and delicacy of his artistic work, passed by this tomb and observed the basket with the tender young leaves growing round it. Delighted with the novel style and form, he built up some columns after that pattern for the Corinthians, determined their symmetrical proportions, and established from that time forth the rules to be followed in finished works of the Corinthian order. (Vitruvius 1960, 104–106 [book IV, chapter 1, ix–x])

In this version of the legend, Vitruvius placed the dead girl as mere ground from which the form and ornament of the Corinthian column sprung. Francesco di Giorgio's reiteration of this story positioned the dead girl quite differently:

27

> In a garden which had much pleased her in her lifetime, her nurse, having arranged and composed the body in a pyramidal basket full of earth, brought her to the tomb, and set the coffin-basket on top of it. (Francesco cited in Rykwert 1981b, 80)

The story then reverts to form: a tile was placed on top of the basket, the basket was accidentally placed over the soon-to-sprout acanthus, the acanthus sprouted through the basket and beneath the tile. The composition was encountered by Callimachus, judged pleasing, and translated into architecture. As George Hersey (1989, 80) notes, in Francesco's alternative version, Vitruvius's basket of personal effects placed on the girl's tomb "is turned into a basket-sarcophagus for the girl herself."

Francesco di Giorgio's account of this order (and others) carried not the enlivened proportions of the human body, but an imprisoned corpse. For Francesco, death lay at the core of architecture's birth. Rykwert speculates as to the drive behind this perversion of the original story. On the one hand he wonders if Francesco's account arose from "a basic consciousness of man's immortality as a sublime reenactment of the death and resurrection of seed, of plants?" On the other, he observes that it may have been an unconscious reference to an Egyptian death rite in which reed-and-earth columns were placed beside the mummified body. Whatever the determining origins of this legend, we might note that Francesco's interpretation offered up the column not as a memorial to a life lived, but as the making of architectural permanence in death. Perhaps the Egyptian reverberation in Francesco's account was not a forgotten architectural type, but the proverb "Man is afraid of time, but time is afraid of the pyramids." As philosopher of death Alphonso Lingis (1989, 185) notes, "[l]ife consigns itself to be interred and monumentalized, held in reserve in the constructions of inertia." Georges Bataille even goes so far as to suggest that the static authority of architecture looms up against the "unquiet elements" of life: "man," he quips, "would seem to represent merely an intermediary stage within the morphological development between monkey and building" (Bataille et al. 1995, 35).

The temporal contradiction that ties architecture's inertia to human impermanence is no more clearly expressed than in ancient architecture's entanglement with sacrifice. Sacrifice is the giving up of life to a deity, but it belongs to the realms of continuity: the destruction of the victim grants divine grace and the perpetuation of life. George Hersey refers to sacrifice as the lost meaning of classical architecture. For Hersey, the form and nomenclature of the classical orders are haunted by the ambivalent potency of sacrifice. Columnal forms reflect ropes and trusses, the exuviae of bird beaks, skulls, teeth, horns and bones, rills and guttae for flowing blood or wine or honey, and shadows that represent "vapors ... dense with the tiny mote-like souls of the dead" (Hersey 1989, 22–23).

As he concludes: "This sense of the architectural ornament is very different from the urge to beauty" (1989, 150). It was such death-bound meaning that was drained from architecture by the rationalist etiologies produced in the Renaissance and reiterated thereafter. One such reiteration was in Hegel's philosophy of aesthetics, published after his death in 1835, which set reason above art and used architecture as the illustrative edifice. As Denis Hollier observed, Hegel created a tomb for architectural creativity: "Architecture is something appearing in the place of death, to point out its presence and to cover it up: the victory of death and the victory over death" (Hollier 1989, 6). Drawing on Bataille, Hollier goes further, arguing that architecture is "a petrification of the organism that is reduced in advance to its skeleton … [it] retains of man only what death has no hold on" (Hollier 1989, 55).

Like Filarete, Francesco di Giorgio, and Hersey, we wish to acknowledge architecture's extreme perversions. In what follows we seek to throw architecture with all of its own force toward its end. In doing so we speak against architecture's natalist fantasy of itself and its delusions of permanence, and for an architecture that tarries with deformation, decay, deterioration, devaluation, and destruction. As building scientist Steven Groák (1992, 105) notes, there is no way of calculating a building's lifetime, although there is immense value in thinking about time in building affairs. This turns us toward an architecture that does not cringe at death in order to save itself from destruction, but can bear death and may even be preserved by way of it. This is an architecture that knows that no physical object lasts forever, and that the durable category is a class of value with no members.

TERMINAL LITERACY: DROSS, RUST, AND OTHER ARCHITECTURAL JUNK

We have claimed that architecture's sense of itself is built on repressing a set of necessary negative conditions: devaluation, decomposition, and destruction. But this is not entirely fair. Throughout the history of architecture there have been latent recognitions of these deathly destinies: what we might think of as architecture's hidden feeling for the inert. It is useful to look more carefully at these recognitions, to gather them up so that we might benefit from their cumulative effect. Perhaps if they were more consciously coded, symbolized, and articulated they might better contribute to a new literacy with respect to architectural death. They might provide the idioms from which architecture might derive a necessary terminal literacy. Here we activate a broad sense of literacy, which goes beyond the acquisition of the skill of reading and writing, and refers instead to the possession of more generally necessary skills of discernment (Williams 1976, 188). Nowadays we expect and aspire to such literacies, be they "cultural," "emotional," "infrastructural," "urban," "economic," or "digital," to name but a few. Literacy in this broader sense is about being fluent in the idioms of a particular cultural or specialist field. We would like to suggest that it also means having the capacity to think self-reflexively about the ideological underpinnings of particular media and systems of representation, concerns of specific relevance to architecture. In what follows we begin the task of building a terminal literacy for architecture. We do so by teasing out instances of architecture's engagement with the conditions of its devaluation, decomposition, and destruction. Our survey is more indicative than exhaustive, and is designed to establish the basis for the lengthier explorations and reflections in the remainder of the book.

As we made our own pathway through architecture's previous engagements with terminal conditions, two framing concepts were useful: matter and mattering. The positive and negative states of architecture (manifest in the conception and destruction of buildings) are realized by way of two interrelated conditions. One is to do with matter: architecture's materialization and the necessary fate

31

of dematerialization. The other is to do with mattering: architecture's value and the necessary processes of revaluation. Let us take the condition of matter first. Architecture exists vitally in the realm of concept, but it is also true that for most architects a fundamental satisfaction is found when their concepts are realized in built form. Disciplinary convention tends to hold that the materialization of a design in built form (involving as it does practical compromises and creative opportunities) is the very first step in the wasting away of the architectural concept. And, given the proclivities of nature and other forces, things get much worse. As built form, architecture will inevitably start to decay and deform. A building's durability depends upon a series of post-construction actions that will offset or incorporate such facts. This might include maintenance regimes that ensure things literally hold together as they were intended to, or it might entail symbolic or aesthetic work that reclaims a disorderly building as a picturesque ruin; and there are other possibilities. This is the materialist idiom of architectural endings. Let us turn now to the condition of mattering. By this we mean to draw attention to the ways in which buildings are valued. This value can operate in the realm of taste and attachment (the meaning value of buildings). It can also operate in terms of how buildings are embedded in cycles of economic value creation. Both systems of mattering can impact directly on architecture's ability to realize itself materially, and the conditions under which it stays put once realized. We need only think of how buildings both loved and unloved fall foul of economic cycles of disinvestment and reinvestment, a theme we return to later in the book. The fate of a materialized object is unavoidably linked to processes of valuation, be they economic, social, or cultural. It is also important to grasp that it is impossible to keep fates of matter and fates of mattering apart—together they lay the basis for the idioms of architectural endings surveyed below.

THIS WILL KILL THAT

One of the best-known pronouncements of a death sentence for building and architecture is found in Victor Hugo's novel *Notre-Dame de Paris* ([1831] 2001, 471) when the archdeacon of the cathedral holds a book up to the edifice and declares, "This will kill that." This literary incident has received much attention from architectural critics, reminding us that such threats are not taken lightly.

The setting for this famous declaration is a moment when the archdeacon of Notre-Dame, Claude Frollo, reflects on the relative value of the cathedral as an architectural edifice to God's word as opposed to a newly printed folio near at hand:

> The archdeacon gazed at the gigantic edifice for some time in silence, then extending his right hand, with a sigh, towards the printed book which lay open on the table, and his left towards Notre-Dame, and turning a sad glance

from the book to the church, —"Alas," he said, "this will kill that." ... "Alas! alas! small things come at the end of great things; a tooth triumphs over a mass. The Nile rat kills the crocodile, the swordfish kills the whale, the book will kill the edifice." (Hugo 2001, 439)

Hugo's narrator goes on to explain the thought behind the Archdeacon's words. Architecture, he explains, once served as the "great handwriting of the human race," its "great book of humanity" (456). The development of the Gutenberg printing press in mid-fifteenth-century Europe, and the mass production of books it gave rise to, changed all that. The press's system of movable and reusable metal type was supplemented by new oil-based pigments and inks, fed by lighter and more plentiful paper, and embedded in newly efficient systems of organized labor. Never before had texts been so quickly, easily, and cheaply reproduced. This innovation meant that printed materials were rapidly disseminated throughout Europe and, as time went on, beyond. Printing technology, in the words of Hugo's narrator, was to "change the form" and "mode of expression" of human thought.

In the face of mechanically printed books, buildings appeared limited as a communicative medium. This was especially evident in the case of the cathedral, which had once enjoyed a privileged role as an instrument of public communication. The mechanically printed book rendered the cathedral—for all the beauty and power of its stone sculptures, stained-glass windows, flying buttresses, and soaring spaces—inflexible and unresponsive. Umberto Eco (1996) goes so far as to liken the medieval cathedral to "a sort of permanent and unchangeable TV program that was supposed to tell people everything indispensable for their everyday lives as well as for their eternal salvation." In comparison the book was a responsive, catalytic and animating medium of public communication. For Eco, book printing was a basic precondition of the modern notion of the public. It underpinned the rise of modern democratic practices, and provided a powerfully mobile repository for the protocols and findings of scientific inquiry. The book, through its reproducibility, came to achieve a durability that surpassed that of the architectural edifice. The development of the printing press quickly saw the brittle and elitist architectural "book of stone" make way for the ephemeral and democratic "book of paper." "One can demolish a mass; how can one extirpate ubiquity?" Hugo's narrator concludes (Hugo 2001, 462). Architecture may be durable, but the ever-reprintable book is deathless.

Hugo is not broaching merely the death of buildings, but the death of architecture itself. Architecture, in his telling, "wither[s] away little by little," its "sap departing," becoming "lifeless and bare." This is not an instant or spectacular death. Nor is it, evidently, a material death. Notre-Dame remains on its site on the Île de la Cité to this day. In Paris, as elsewhere, architecture continues to be practiced, and buildings continue to be constructed. These seemingly self-evident counterfacts are, however, in the eyes of Hugo's narrator, merely more evidence of architecture's demise as the principal nexus of collective human expression. Up until the time of the mass-produced book, all great thoughts and human creativity, Hugo's narrator argues, were put into stone and, so expressed, joyously shared in architecture's solidity and durability. But after the book, collective forms of expression abandon the sluggish and expensive built form of architecture for other media. Architecture after the printing revolution no longer serves as society's dominant communicative medium. Its debasement starts with the Gothic cathedral itself, which suffers "injuries" of all kinds as artistic creativity ebbs away from it; sculptors are replaced by stonecutters, decorators succeeded by mere glaziers, and artists substituted by workmen. We are offered evidence of this architectural "death" in Hugo's description of the urban fabric around Notre-Dame. Paris, his narrator laments, boasts too many architectural copies or "revivals," while other buildings are stripped back to mere "geometry." The proliferation of building types—"the palace of a king, a chamber of communes, a town-hall, a college, a riding-school, an academy, a warehouse, a court-house, a museum, a barracks, a sepulcher, a temple, or a theater"—each speaking to the complexifying social order, offer insufficient purpose for a true architecture (Hugo 2001, 340: see also Vidler 1977, 114; 1987, 1–4). Hugo openly mocks Paris's revivalist architecture. The church of Sainte-Geneviève (remodeled as the Pantheon), for example, is described as "the finest Savoy cake that has ever been made in stone," and the Palace of the Legion of Honor is a "very distinguished bit of pastry." Other buildings too are reviled for looking like "an English jockey cap" (the now demolished wheat market), or "two huge clarinets" (the towers of the church of Saint-Sulpice) (Hugo 2001, 341). Also unaccountable were those buildings that ignored their local climatic context (Hugo 2001, 342). The Paris Exchange, Hugo's narrator sarcastically remarks, was "evidently constructed expressly for our cold and rainy skies," with its Eastern-inspired flat roof entirely unsuitable for winter snowfall (Hugo 2001, 342). This "Paris of … plaster" was "decadent" and "miserable," and no longer capable of "being true and modern" or an authentic "expression of society" (Hugo 2001, 340, 464).

Historian of the book Elizabeth Eisenstein (1979, xvi) usefully nuances Hugo's memorable but shrill observation that "this will kill that." She argues that the printing press was *an* agent of change, but could not be *the* agent of change. As a consequence, the printed book did not simply kill off all that went before it, or dominate all that was around it. Throughout this period in Europe there were diverse interactions "between old messages and new medium, cultural context and technological innovation, handwork and brain work, craftsmen and scholars, preachers and press agents." Yet commentators, scholars, and writers of every stripe have been drawn to Hugo's successionist account of the triumph of one communicative media over another.[1] Some have used the example to comment on the nature of architecture, others to anticipate the innovations in communication following the book. It is useful to look at two such uses of this architectural death in more detail, for they rehearse the options we have with respect to generating a new terminal literacy.

Lewis Mumford, for example, writing some hundred years after Hugo, offered a quite literal interpretation of Hugo's view that the book killed architecture. Reflecting nostalgically on the close relationship between the craftsman and the vernacular architectures of colonial North America, Mumford lamented the architectural turn to a formulaic classical "language." This was an expertise learned, he argued, through printed books. Those technical books killed architecture, in his view, because they replaced an organic and socially connected traditional architecture with styles: "the Five Orders became as unchallengeable as the eighty-one rules of Latin syntax" (Mumford 1931, 42). As Mumford put it, book-transmitted and book-learned design expertise meant that "the master mason who knew his stone and his workmen and his tools and the tradition of his art gave way to the architect who knew his Palladio and his Vignola and his Vitruvius" (Mumford 1931, 41). Communication theorist Marshall McLuhan, in his book *The Gutenberg Galaxy* (1962), revisited Hugo's famous idea in order to take it in an entirely different direction. McLuhan positioned the invention of the printing press, and the collateral damage it wrought on other media, as just the beginning of an ongoing revolution in communication technology and media. The printed book, he predicted, would eventually also be killed off, giving way to visual, electronically mediated and less linear forms of communication. Most of us are familiar with McLuhan's analogy that in the wake of this next communications revolution the globe will become a village. But McLuhan also suggested that the world would, under the press of innovations in hypermedia, virtual and visual communications, become like a "Manhattan disco." In McLuhan's view it was the Manhattan disco (and all it stood for) that would kill the book.

In both these accounts, the architecture/book dyad is understood as a fight to the end. Umberto Eco (1996), chiming with Eisenstein, offers us a more pluralist option. One medium of communication and creativity, he suggests, will never simply supplant, erase, or otherwise "kill off" another. Eco is enthusiastic about the nonlinearity of hypertext, nonsequential writing, and reader-controlled links, and relishes the co-presence, jostling and interplay of multiple media: architecture, books, the web, are all welcome. But Eco does argue that a thickly pluralist and multiply mediated milieu demands that we give renewed attention to what literacy means and requires. Literacy must be loosened from its etymological roots in texts and reading, and be understood as a more fluid mastery of many media.[2] This is a literacy for a world comprised of multiple and co-present forms of cultural production: some dominant, some residual, and others still emergent, to borrow Raymond Williams's famous tripartite formulation (1989).

Like Eco, we want to read this famous literary instance of architectural death less fatally. It is without doubt a captivating trope of one way in which buildings are deprived of their symbolic power and architecture, more generally, meets its end. But what could architecture possibly take from the withered remains it seems to leave us with? Eco's alternative reading offers a template for moving forward, and not only because in his version architecture can live on. Eco draws our attention to the contemporary need to expand our notion of literacy. We, too, argue for this. Not a literacy with respect to reading architecture as one among many communicative media (although that it important enough); rather, a literacy that attends to the ways in which buildings die—the causes, the conditions, the circumstances—and the effects for architecture.

DROSS

Recent explorations of wasting conditions from an architectural perspective dwell often in the zone of typology. One example is Alan Berger's account of *Drosscape* (2006). Berger's methodology for discerning drosscapes is a variant of the kind of morphological analysis so central to landscape architecture. He flew over the changing and fast-growing edges of the cities of North America and photographed their "disturbing" landscape conditions (2006, 13). Berger's *Drosscape* audits the horizontalization of urbanism in North America, otherwise known as sprawl. Berger dubs this sprawl "drosscape" for two interrelated reasons. First, drosscape is a "negative effect" of "unplanned, uncontrolled, or market-driven development" (2006, 21). More precisely, Berger argues that this sprawl is a by-product of "life's expansionist waste-making tendencies" (2006, 24). Second, drosscape betrays signs of wasting within it, by which he means evidence of unproductive or underproductive use.

> It may be vacant strips alongside roadways, seas of parking lots, unused land, warehouse districts, a seeming endless stretch of setbacks and perimeters.... Seen at the local scale, e.g. driving or walking through ... the landscape of the horizontal city may appear diminished and wasteful. (Berger 2006, 26)

Drosscape mixes productively used land with underused and more open land in a chaotic and fragmented way, producing what Berger describes as "the in-between landscapes" (2006, 28). "Waste landscape is," he concludes, "an indicator of healthy urban growth" (2006, 36). It is land that is an "inevitable result of growth," but "liminal" in the sense that it is in transition, eludes classification, and is "awaiting a societal desire to inscribe [it] with value and status" (2006, 29). Liminality, anthropologist Victor Turner notes, using a resonant material metaphor, is a kind of death, wherein the ritual subject has been detached from society, and temporarily appears as "clay or dust, mere matter" prior to a stage of "reaggregation" (Turner 1969, 103). Berger suggests that these liminal spaces support various kinds of productivity and value. For example, they can host a range of correspondingly liminal social activities. As such these spaces, even while they remain "detached" from mainstream systems of value, are available to be appropriated by subgroups. A good deal of Berger's own effort in auditing and reflecting on these spaces was to "delineate and reclaim" their potential.

This altogether optimistic reading of drosscape is possible because Berger sees these spaces as both a necessary by-product of the capitalist urban growth machine and a potential asset for those marginalized by that machine. Contaminated land can be rehabilitated and reclaimed, leftover strips of land can be reprogrammed for additional activities, vacant lots and derelict buildings can be "adaptively reused." As he concludes, future urban growth "depends on salvaging and re-imagining the collective body of in-between landscapes" (2006, 39). In his drosscape manifesto Berger emphasizes the "productive integration and reuse of waste landscapes throughout the urban world" (Berger 2006, 236). Drosscaping as a practice comes, he argues, in the wake of the failure of the "big four": architecture, planning, urban design, and landscape architecture. It is a scavenger strategy. "Drosscaping, as a verb," Berger clarifies, "is the placement upon the landscape of new social programs that transform waste (real or perceived) into more productive urbanized landscapes" (2006, 237). He uses the existence of these accidental spaces as an opportunity to reinvigorate urban design: "drosscape provides an avenue for rethinking the role of the designer in the urban world." This is envisaged as a move away from heroic master planning toward a more modest, incremental, and collaborative process, wherein "designers work ... in the margins rather than at the center" (2006, 241).

Berger's project, as he acknowledges, runs alongside Lars Lerup's rethinking of the metropolis in the 1990s. Drawing inspiration from Italian philosopher Massimo Cacciari's meditation on the "metropolitan negative," Lerup subdivides the city into two types of land: stim and dross. Stim characterizes the places, buildings, and programs that are developed and designed for human use (are stimulating). Dross refers to the landscapes that are the wasteful residue of the urban fulcrum, its worthless dregs: "the ignored, undervalued, unfortunate economic residues of the metropolitan machine" (Lerup 2000, 93). Drawing an analogy with the urban landscapes sought out and made famous in the work of artist Robert Smithson, Lerup sees the city as full of "holes": fissures, vacated spaces, and untouched land. In these abandoned or yet-to-be-used lands, nature wins out against economy. The city is, he says, predominantly a result of motion and temporality, "constantly being carved out in front of one and abandoned behind" (2000, 86). This state of temporal "deformation" marks not simply the emergence of a new urban condition but a crisis for architectural creativity. This is, Lerup argues, the definitive end to modernism: "the Corbusian promenade and the Corbusian subject as the gentleman puppet on the architect's string" (2000, 86). Lerup seeks to move beyond a binary classification of stim and dross, and proposes the hybrid concept of "stimdross." This is not a spatially distributed categorization of used land and unused land, but a temporally defined categorization that registers the ways in which cityscapes move in and out of eventfulness. By reconceptualizing the city across the boundary between used land (stim) and unused land (dross), architecture can "recover from this holey plane some of the many potential futures" (2000, 99). This reclassification of the urban is, he argues, necessary because "our customary ways of describing, managing and designing are outmoded" (2000, 85). In this sense his waste discourse, like Berger's, comes in the wake of a perceived crisis-cum-opportunity for architectural creativity.

RUST

It is a binarized urban landscape that operates again as the basis for Antoine Picon's consideration of architectural negatives, conducted by way of two figures, the ruin and rust. Flying into Manhattan, he ponders the crystal magic of Manhattan's skyscrapers, against which stands the visual "purgatory" comprising "cranes, immense bridges spanning platforms lined with containers, refineries and factories between which are creeping swamps, everything in poor condition and rusted out, as though irreparably polluted" (Picon 2000, 65). Picon is puzzled by how disconcerted this vision makes him feel, and his essay is an inquiry into his own architectural unsettlement. For Picon such landscapes are irretrievably linked to the pragmatics of technology. Yet they also seem to offer an uncanny kind of picturesque: "where abandoned warehouses and rusty carcasses replace Poussinesque ruin." These are spaces "thoroughly devoted to utility," but in the context of a now technologized city saturated with commodified "aesthetic intention" (advertising, designed image and ambience) from which a contextual and contrasting nature has been expelled, they are "curiously invested with a more heightened possibility … poetic value more intense than other, heavily policed and regulated parts of the city."[3] They are "fodder for dreams," as is so clearly evident in the ways in which artists, from Robert Smithson on, have encountered, interpreted, and represented such spaces. But these landscape also cause anxiety. They are potentially limitless in character, extending as far as the eye can see. And at the same time they are stifling, delivering through that extensiveness "the impression of imprisonment and the feeling of death" (2000, 71).

The contemporary city, according to Picon, sees a "face-off" between two types of place, both of which are invested with strong emotional force. One is the shopping center, the other the garbage dump, and it is "between these two poles that entire sections of the contemporary urban experience are organized. Buy and throw away: this elementary cycle marks the rhythm of the days and weeks" (Picon 2000, 75). And finally, in the technologized city there is wear: "Metal oxidizes, plastic yellows and cracks." The technological city of utility and function goes hand in hand with obsolescence. In the traditional landscape, where nature played a part, there was a dignified death to "human works" such as architecture, as they "surrendered themselves progressively to nature in the form of the ruin." But in the technologized city, objects either disappear all in one go, as if by magic, or are relegated to obsolescence, "a bit like the living dead." Picon laments: "We have gone from ruin to rust, from trace to waste."

For Picon this debasement has happened because technological land-scapes are not produced with their "destination" in mind. Picon returns to Auguste Perret's critique of early-twentieth-century technology to illustrate this anxiety. Perret argued that art (as opposed to technology) builds a rapport "between the object and its end." That is why the Parthenon "sings eternally" as a ruin, whereas technology merely becomes "scrap metal" (cited in Picon 2000, 77). The ruin restores "man to nature", but rust "confines him in the middle of his productions as if within a prison, a prison all the more terrible since he is its builder" (Picon 2000, 79). This is why we fear rust.

Picon entreats us to enter into a more positive, although not necessarily easy, relationship with the character of these technological landscapes. He even imagines that there may be a recalibration of subjectivity in relation to such land-scapes, akin to the reorderings of subject and landscape that came in the wake of the Renaissance invention of perspective. This new order would be post-perspectival, and take sustenance from the scalar potential available in new technologies of visualization (the satellite view, the microscopic rendition). Picon suggests, then, that it is the *textural*, as opposed to the sculptural and the architectonic, that remains for architecture to investigate and cultivate.

Picon's suggestive thesis promises a new proximity between architecture and wasting conditions. In essence it is about how architecture might more comfortably live within the prison house of technological landscapes that have no end in that they are extensive and obdurate. Yet the strategy proposed by Picon is less one of dwelling closely with technological waste, than using new media to revisualize technological landscapes. His approach to waste is to turn it into texture, and in so doing reclaim it for architectural creativity.

39

SUBTRACTION

A more emphatically deconstructive thread relevant to terminal literacy has been offered by architect Keller Easterling, who has begun to think about the discipline of architecture through the concept of subtraction. Easterling points to the ways in which subtraction (demolition and removal) are a necessary part of architecture, but notes that traditionally the architectural response has been to resist (preservation) or to answer with "the construction of their own magnificent idea … a restorative or corrective plan" (Easterling 2003, 93). Demolition is often seen as architecture's enemy, and nowhere more so than by those architects who see it as their responsibility to preserve architecture's heritage. The preservation movement was forged around resisting demolitions of buildings considered to be of significance to the history of architectural creativity itself. In this sense, demolition could quite literally be an attack on the discipline's archive. The historical specificity of early preservation efforts later broadened to include a wider body of architecture, whose significance was derived contextually, from social or townscape relevance. A contextual way of thinking about conservation can alter the way architects relate to demolition. For example, the early-twentieth-century Italian architect Gustavo Giovannoni viewed the city as an organism. He directed his design vision to what he called the "real city," as opposed to the ideal visions of many of his avant-garde contemporaries. His solution for accommodating change in the city was not comprehensive demolition and reconstruction, for this would not respect the city's existing texture. Instead he proposed "building reduction" (*diradamento edilizio*), comprising the cautious demolition of existing buildings and the polite introduction of new ones (Menghini 2002). As we show later, the extension of conservation thinking to whole areas of the city has extended such models of design by erasure, wherein buildings deemed "inappropriate" or "ill-fitting" are removed in the interests of creating (or reinstating) a certain kind of townscape. This is subtraction in the service of an essentialist value. But it is also true that buildings do end, and with relative frequency, and often quite spectacularly. Neil Harris's cultural history of building lives documents how the end of a building is an occasion for reflection and ceremony, such that these final moments "absorb large amounts of our emotional and intellectual capital" (1999, 115). Building deaths speak to us of the expectations, attachments, and investments that architecture generates.

In this context of resistance and attachment, Easterling offers a more abstractly formed and speculative meditation on the fact of buildings coming down. She suggests that architecture is on the brink of another approach to being with the many "species" of subtraction, be it demolition, willful damage, natural disaster, or decay. She refutes architectural subtraction as proof of architectural failure, because it is a sign of an "architecture without permanence and therefore without worth." Rather, she entreats architecture to embrace subtraction as "a productive technique" and "an operative practice," "both a tool and a new territory" (Easterling 2003, 90). This offers a model for a more patient and nuanced cohabitation with conditions of wasting, a model that might offer novel possibilities for architectural expression and ethics. Easterling reminds us that subtraction is an insistent and necessary condition of architectural materialization. We may be a long way from institutionalized "special studies in subtraction" for architects, but we live in times where the fact of demolition, as with other subtractive forces, presses upon the profession and its buildings with new intensity.

Within late-twentieth-century architecture, it was British architect Cedric Price who was most famously at ease with the idea of architecture as subtraction. Building deaths held no fear for Price. He worked tirelessly for an "expendable architecture," and was outspoken in his disdain for the "three-dimensional disciplining" of a built architecture motivated by ambitions (and pretensions) of permanency. Architecture, for Price, was not about the "soul-destroying static fixes" of convention, but about mobility, flexibility, adaption (Price 1966, 433). Price designed for "inbuilt flexibility" and "planned obsolescence," and refused to entertain a goal of durability. For Price, good architectural design included the "time factor" (Heron 2007, 56). He was against what he called "slow architecture," the architecture of permanence and durability, which in his view always comes "too late." Few architects have dared to match Price's commitment to letting go of the architectural artifact. For Price, the conventional architectural answer often did not comprise designing a building. Sometimes it entailed removing buildings (such as his Lung for Manhattan) or simply offering up flexible space systems, an "anti-building" and, preferably, an "auto-destructive" one at that (Heron 2007, 57). He aspired to indeterminacy, transience, obsolescence, and demolition. He regretted that there was not a concrete made that would "eat itself after 15 years" (Mullin 2007, 97).[4] He was furious when his aviary at the London Zoo was listed by English Heritage, and loathed all such architectural systems of listing. And he was a proud member of the Federation of Demolition Contractors, which honored him with a telegram from its president on the occasion of a posthumous memorial celebration at London's Architectural Association.

EVENT

Buildings have multitudinous, ongoing and incremental endings. We act against these incremental endings by way of building maintenance. Thanks to maintenance and repair work, what is a vital scene of disassembling and reassembling is manifest as a stable architectural object. Steven Groák (1992, 105) has argued that it is meaningless to speak of a building's "lifetime" and, we may assume, "death."

> Foundations may survive for a thousand years, while the roof structure may be replaced after a thousand months. The sanitary fittings in the bathroom could last a thousand weeks, the external paintwork a thousand days, and the light bulbs a thousand hours. (Groák 1992, 105)

The significance of Groák for our project is how his approach to buildings activated "time in building affairs" (1990, 15). His thinking releases architecture from the accreted binary of a designed future or a preserved past. While he considers it "well-meaning" to conceive of buildings as "unchanging, stable, permanent, invariant," this is a misconception. In reality, he asserts, "buildings have to be understood in terms of several different time scales over which they change, in terms of moving images and ideas in flux" (1990, 15). Groák's interpretation of buildings resonates with a wider trend of thinking about architecture beyond and against its obdurate form. This is to foreground the eventfulness of architecture.

Aldo Rossi supports this line of thinking by considering the varying use value and age value of buildings, and how they contribute to a delicate "permanence" of built environments. In the opening pages of his book *A Scientific Autobiography* (1981), Rossi reflects on a story that Max Planck tells in the opening to his own "scientific autobiography." Planck recounts a story apparently told him by his schoolmaster, "about a mason who with great effort heaved a block of stone up on the roof of a house. The mason was struck by the fact that expended energy does not get lost; it remains stored for many years, never diminished, latent in the block of stone, until one day it happens that the block slides off the roof and falls on the head of a passerby, killing him" (Rossi 1981, 1). Rossi admits that it seems rather strange to open an autobiography with an anecdote concerning death. "But," he continues, "it is a death that is in some sense a continuation of energy." The principle of continuity of energy, its inauguration, its conservation, and its expenditure (planned or not) is central to the work of any artistic or technical enterprise. This principle is especially significant for architecture. "[I]f one fails to take note of this, it is not possible to comprehend any building, either from a technical point of view or from a compositional one. In the use of every material there must be an anticipation of the construction of a place and its transformation" (Rossi 1981, 1). For Rossi, energy, materiality, and change merge with a wider sense of temporality in architecture: "The double meaning of the Italian word *tempo*, which signifies both atmosphere and chronology, is a principle that presides over every construction; this is the double meaning of energy that I now see clearly in architecture, as well as in other technics or arts" (Rossi 1981, 2).

Also notable in this context is the work of Bernard Tschumi who, in a series of exhibitions, projects, and publications from the late 1970s, developed a distinctive interest in the architecture of events. Tschumi, railing against the heightened symbolism and ornamentation of the dominant postmodern architectural styles of the time, argued that architecture "cannot be dissociated from the events that happen in it." Through the concept of the event Tschumi initiated a renewed interest in architectural program. This was not merely a reinstitution of the old modernist dogma of function, but a rethinking of the hybridity, amorphousness, and sheer unpredictability of activities that were variously framed, supported, housed, or qualified by architecture. In his book *Manhattan Transcripts* (1981), which accompanied an exhibition of the same name, Tschumi offered a series of definitions of event. "Event," he states, is "an incident, an occurrence.... Events can encompass particular uses, singular functions or isolated activities. They include moments of passion, acts of love and the instant of death" (1981, xxi). In experimenting with and thinking through program and event spaces, Tschumi developed a range of notational experiments that sought to record the movement of singular and collective bodies in order to understand the relationship between scripted and unscripted events in space. Drawing on related representational conventions such as choreography and musical notation, Tschumi sought to open architecture to the unpredictability and improvisational possibilities that scripted events always contain. In doing so he emphasized the play between architectural program, the force of the unanticipated anti-program, and the importance of improvisational re-programming. Tschumi's postcard series "Advertisements for Architecture" (1976–1977) encapsulated his thinking in potent ways. Each postcard carried a key image, a punchy headline, and a short explanatory text. One, featuring an image of Le Corbusier's customarily pristine Villa Savoye in a state of disrepair—peeling paint, flaking plaster, and concrete blocks exposed—carried the headline: "The most architectural thing about this building is that state of decay in which it is." Highlighting the mutability of archi-tectural form in time, Tschumi urged architecture to embrace the possibility that it "negates itself" and "the form that society expects of it." Another postcard in the series featured the silhouette of a person falling from an elevated window, apparently pushed out of it. The headline reads: "To really appreciate architec-ture, you may even need to commit a murder." The imminent death captured in the image is a radical instance of anti-programming. Architecture, from this perspective, is defined less by the materiality of its built form, and more by its interaction—in this case as "witness" of and collaborator in a murder—with the event world that unfolds in and around it.

43

Tschumi's thinking on architecture and event represents an important exposure of architecture to more complex attitudes to time. That this happens through tropes of decay, negation, and death is no (mere) accident. As with Rossi's unfortunate passerby, killed by a falling block of stone, it is Tschumi's broaching of death and decay, his terminal literacy, which productively loosens architecture's twin investment in the values of natalism and obduracy.

WASTING

One of the most explicit engagements with architecture's negative is Kevin Lynch's oft-overlooked *Wasting Away* (1990). Lynch is well known among architects, but mostly for his influential earlier volume *The Image of the City* (1960), which offered a psychogeographical analysis of the postwar North American city. That book attempted to sketch out a new way of seeing the built environment in and through human perception and cognition. In *Wasting Away* he offers a sustained account of how society creates waste, manages waste, and variously lives poorly or well with it. His ambition in this wide-ranging and thought-provoking account is to offer a brief for living with waste well. Rather than lamenting the decay of buildings, or ascribing judgments of junk upon architectures that are considered under-designed or poorly designed, this volume offers a set of rules for living alongside the "tragic and marvelous" process of wasting (Lynch 1990, 166). Lynch's book is attuned to the multiple scales of wasting in which buildings are embedded. He is as attentive to the daily cycles of use and disposal that happen in buildings as he is to the periodic acts of abandonment and obsolescence that leave buildings, architectural edifices, and whole built environments unvalued and in ruins. Lynch not only offers a set of culturally and historically varied observations on wasting conditions and the built environment, he also sets out the basic positive guidelines for decay. These include planned obsolescence such that buildings could be designed to "decline gracefully" or be "easily replaced." For example, Lynch suggests that "in addition to asking that an architect show exactly how a building will look when it is occupied, he might be asked to show it remodeled for some other use, or as it will look in decay," or asked "for demolition plans for new buildings." Indeed, Lynch goes so far as to suggest that architectural designs should include plans for how buildings will be disposed of, including an estimation of the resulting costs and benefits. As we have seen from the various examples above, few architectural commentators have so frankly acknowledged the fact that buildings must die.

JUNK

It is nearly half a century since Peter Blake, architect, journalist, and socialist, fulminated against what he dubbed the "deliberate destruction" of the American landscape in his book *God's Own Junkyard* (1964). An avid supporter of modernism both as a style and as a political project, Blake decried the way in which American landscapes were being colonized by commercially driven building, including the visual noise generated by signage and the deregulated free-for-all of commercial development. He wrote against what he thought to be a nonarchitectural built environment of clutter, although the many photographs supporting his argument carry with them a certain enchantment which Blake himself could not repress. It is a dislike that Robert Venturi, Denise Scott Brown, and Steven Izenour only a few years later turned on its head. Venturi, Scott Brown, Izenour, and student collaborators at Yale University audited the Las Vegas strip and appropriated this very "junk" into a new proposition for an expressive, post-modern architecture. What one architectural critic saw as junk with respect to the clean lines and public good embodied in avant-garde modernist principles, others redeemed and incorporated into the logics of a newly expressive, communicative and playful postmodern architecture. Such are architecture's indecisive feelings for the inert. What one considers junk, another takes as inspiration. What one considers proof of the death of architecture, the other draws upon to breathe new life into the profession.

Rem Koolhaas's 2002 essay "Junkspace" reactivates the concept of junk architecture and takes this contradictory ambivalence to its commercial extreme. The essay has a schizophrenic mood: Jameson notes that it exhibits revulsion and euphoria in equal measure (2003, 73). The essay concerns "the residue mankind leaves on the planet," and specifically what "remains after modernization ... runs its course or ... what coagulates while modernization is in progress" (Koolhaas 2002, 176). This "fallout" is what Koolhaas calls "junkspace." This is not the residue of the production of architecture (for example, the waste that design and construction might generate). Nor is it the waste that architecture, once manifest, might produce (for example, the pollution in the form of light, heat, or greenhouse gases). This is the "architecture" that results not from comprehensive design or planning but from assembled building components whose organization is dictated by air-conditioning and circulation technologies. It is "ugly," "unstable," "inscrutable," and has a "fundamental incoherence" (2002, 188).

The paradigmatic example of this type of non-architecture is the airport—and one cannot help recalling the travel graphs reproduced in the opening pages of *S, M, L, XL* (Koolhaas and Mau 1995, xiii) that document the number of air miles traveled by Koolhaas and his office annually, such that the airport becomes, for him, the world (a synecdoche not exclusive to Koolhaas). But junkspace also includes, as Jameson (2003) notes, the full array of generic sites of consumption and spectacle. These are the spaces that are forever being expanded, refurbished, and upgraded. They give rise to exit routes that are too narrow, passages that go nowhere, circulation systems that do not flow, spatial orderings that either discard or, worse still, mimic hierarchy and composition, aesthetic schemes that are irrational brands ("High Tech, Taiwanese Gothic; Nigerian Sixties, Norwegian Chalet").

It is easy to see how junkspace operates against architecture's inherited conventions of "order," "coordination," "distinction," "hierarchy," "pattern," "permanence, axialities, relationships, and proportion" (Koolhaas 2002, 178). But ironically, junkspace also stands, in Koolhaas's view, as a mutation of some of architecture's more progressive tendencies. As he notes, it was architecture that delivered the idea of a megastructure that could be colonized and recolonized with ever-mutating, impermanent subsystems. It was also architecture that challenged the aspiration to comprehensive design with an embrace of collage, and fragmentary approaches to spatial organization. But junkspace is "subsystem only, without superstructure," containing "orphaned particles in search of a framework or pattern" (2002, 178), held together by verbs that are "unthinkable in architectural history": "clamp, stick, fold, dump, glue, shoot, double, fuse" (2002, 176). These processes and techniques coalesce into larger "mutant regimes of organization and coexistence that leave architecture behind" (2002, 178). Because junkspace "sheds architectures like a reptile sheds skins," and "is reborn every Monday morning" (2002, 178), architectural skills tend to be redundant. The perpetual transformation of junkspace in the name of "upgrading" and "continuous conversion" makes a mockery of the idea of the determinate plan, for example. Only the loosest and most suggestive of diagrams, or "radar screens," can serve to guide the shape and unpredictable temporalities of junkspace. In junkspace, Koolhaas implies, architects find themselves not leading but alongside assorted art consultants, interior designers, wayfinding specialists, graphic designers, security advisors, finance executives, marketing managers, advertising creatives, and space branders.

While junkspace may seem to architects to be "an aberration," it is, Koolhaas asserts, "the essence, the main thing" (2002, 175). Once incubated within the vast interior territories of airports, malls, hotels, and shopping centers, it now "can easily engulf a whole city" (2002, 186). It threatens to become "the new architecture" (2002, 183). As Koolhaas notes in a parenthetical aside addressed directly to architects: "You thought that you could ignore Junkspace, visit it surreptitiously, treat it with condescending contempt or enjoy it vicariously … because you could not understand it, you've thrown away the keys…. But now your own architecture is infected, has become equally smooth, all-inclusive, continuous, warped, busy, atrium-ridden" (2002, 182). The metastasizing of junkspace could guarantee that "[a]ll architects may unwittingly be working on the same building" (2002, 176).

The threat of junkspace is that without the input of overarching architectural design and planning, it merely "offers entropy." There is much to say about the notion of entropy with respect to architecture, and we return to this theme at various points in this book. For the time being, we might usefully reflect on what Koolhaas means when he says that this non-architecture is entropic. He is, likely enough, using the term in its more popular sense: declining into disorder. More technically, this term derives from the theory of thermodynamics and refers to the amount of energy in a closed system that is not converted into work. In this sense entropy is not simply disorder, but also always a condition of squandering (be it energy or effort) that accompanies the trajectory through time of any working system. Koolhaas's complaint, then, is that junkspace generates entropy too quickly—in fact, almost instantly. As he writes, junkspace is "reborn every Monday morning" (2002, 178). Its "promiscuous," "expansive," "parasitic" logic "conquers place" (2002, 184), and turns architecture "into a time-lapse sequence" to reveal a "permanent evolution" (2002, 182). Koolhaas portrays junkspace as a voracious, monstrous, malformed organism that "has to swallow more and more program to survive" (2002, 184), while exhibiting symptoms of "arrested development" and often "spawning stillbirths" (2002, 176).

What does this monstrous condition say to architecture's long-standing natalism? It is clear that junkspace is no mere memento mori, no subtle whisper that "buildings must die." Rather, it brazenly declares that buildings die all the time, and architecture dies with them. It is a death, furthermore, that perverts architecture's own midwife fantasies. Architecture's natalist drives, in Koolhaas's analysis, are possessed by aberrant motivating forces put to work in ever tighter cycles of value and redundancy, entropy and premature death. Junkspace is not merely a disciplinary matter, but heralds a wider planetary ecological threat. It will be, Koolhaas warns, "our tomb." "The combined pollution of all Third World cars, motorbikes, trucks, buses, sweatshops pales into insignificance compared to the heat generated by Junkspace," he specifies (2002, 183). Fredric Jameson, in a flattering account of Koolhaas's essay, remarks that these self-replicating, self-perpetuating typologies offer a "new language of space." He finds these spaces "rather exhilarating," although he admits they may well "condemn" architecture "to extinction" (2003, 73).

The outlines of a terminal literacy for architecture that we have sketched here offer the basis for the investigations to follow. They suggest looking awry at architecture, and using architectural wastings and endings to rethink what architecture's project might better be. In the pages that follow we seek to elaborate the important markers established by these thinkers. We do so in order to offer a revised brief for how architecture should be in the world—not simply as a world-making art, or merely as an arbiter of what is junk or dross, but also as a profession invested in the necessity and potentials of its own unmaking. In the next chapter we offer some theoretical tools that we think are essential to architecture's ability to live with its own inevitable wasting. These tools derive from a wider body of thinking about waste and garbage conditions, the making and unmaking of value, and death and dying. They are, in essence, the basis of a revaluation of architecture.

4

TOWARD A GENERAL ECONOMY OF ARCHITECTURE

[T]he Life of Spirit is not the life that shrinks from death and keeps
itself untouched by devastation, but rather the life that endures
it and maintains itself in it. It wins its truth only when, in utter dismem-
berment, it finds itself. This tarrying with the negative is the magical
power that converts it into being.

G. W. F. HEGEL (1977, 19)

What tools of thinking might enable architecture to knowingly coexist with the inevitability of deterioration and destruction? How might we reconstruct the creative economy of architecture such that it is shaped, not by simplistic metaphors of life, but by an ethic that recognizes its inevitable horizon of deterioration and death? This chapter traces relevant strands of social theory and philosophy that offer a roadmap for navigating the implications for architecture of conditions of building deterioration, wasting, and death. We draw concepts and key vocabularies from a range of sources relevant to a critical appraisal of architecture's natalist self-image, as well as its practices of design and creativity, and fantasies of permanence. The chapter necessarily extends our discussion of the concepts of architectural value (mattering) and form (matter) in chapter 3, for these twin concepts are important reference points for architecture as a creative discipline.

We begin our meditation on the first of these concepts, architectural value, by examining how the work of architecture (design, conception, and craft) and its created output (the building) are inextricably linked to the concept of utility. We inquire into the principles that frame architecture as something creative, useful, and valuable. We wonder why the principles of creativity and usefulness have had sustained critical reflection in architecture, while the question of value is framed in relatively conventional ways.[1] We look more closely at the concept of value in architecture by studying its flip side: deterioration, waste, and destruction. This inverted perspective helps to expose some of the central contradictions within received principles of architecture's creative worth. Such a vantage point allows us to better grasp, for instance, how architecture embodies what Barbara Herrnstein Smith (1988, 125) referred to as a "double discourse of value." Architecture sustains itself, on the one hand, within a sanctified and aestheticized cultural sphere of value (understood as inspiration, creation, taste, test of time, intrinsic and transcendental value) and, on the other, within an economic sphere of value (calculation, references, costs, benefits, prices, and utility). The contradiction of this double discourse comes into sharp focus in capitalism's logic of creative destruction. As we shall see, the viability of architectural creativity has depended in part on its incorporation into this self-perpetuating logic. We end this meditation on architectural value by drawing on Bataille's suggestive concept of "general economy," with its emphasis on unproductive excess, death and decay.

In thinking about the second of these concepts, form, we wish to draw attention to the ways in which processes of deterioration, waste, and death are necessarily confrontational, heralding various states of deformation. We usually think of deformation as meaning disfigurement or defacement—a notion which implies there was once something properly and fully formed that has, through some deviant agency, been altered for the worse. But we would propose that it is possible to think about deformation in less woeful (and judgmental) terms—to separate out deformation from devaluation and degradation. The final part of this chapter touches upon some theoretical concepts that appear to fatally challenge form and stability, but which really open the way toward a more dynamic and emergent understanding of architecture's project. In this final section we traverse a number of related thinkers who reorder even seemingly obdurate formations like architecture as fluid and contingent events. In this section we push the idea of a general economy of architecture to its very limits, entering into the realm of nonlinearity, open systems, relational ontologies, and the vitality of matter.

Rarely do the theorists and philosophers we draw upon speak centrally about architecture. At times they might use an architectural example, or speak through architectural metaphors. When that is the case it is useful, and we have taken advantage. But for the most part we are reading askance, picking across an epistemological ground where architecture features incidentally or as an elaborative aside. Furthermore, we draw on theory that for many years has stood at the sideline of, and even challenged, the project of development or progress in which architecture has played its part. Our starting point is the Enlightenment. It was then that architecture was harnessed to a specific notion of creating value. Architectural theorists like Anthony Vidler have usefully provided counterintuitive readings of architecture in the Age of Reason. But we wish to return to some of the central Enlightenment assumptions around how architecture functioned in the world as a way of accessing foundational thinking around the relationship between architecture and value, and by extension nonvalue or waste.

ARCHITECTURE AGAINST WASTE

The garbage philosopher John Scanlan argues that while the Enlightenment is commonly regarded as the Age of Reason, it could be usefully viewed otherwise—as an age of "rejecting waste." If the march of progress defines the Enlightenment, then the perspective of waste draws our attention to what lies in progress's wake. If reason takes the shape of a "sound building" or "good design," then what is the character of the "dead ends and back alleys" that lie behind these structures? None of the certainty of the Age of Reason could be projected, Scanlan argues, "without the creation of the rubble and excess of unnecessary parts" (2005, 63). It is a point that resonates, of course, with Walter Benjamin's figure of the Angel of History: being blown reluctantly toward progress to which his back is turned, helplessly surveying the destruction trailing in his wake.

The Enlightenment project, according to Scanlan (2005, 63), relied upon "removing some of the rubbish that lies on the way to knowledge." It was "a clear-out and clean-up of the lumber house of the human mind" which was "condemned as dark, dilapidated and dangerous ... unfit for habitation" (Porter 1990, 53). These metaphors of sound building and good design, of house and habitation, express architecture's role in the Enlightenment project of expunging waste and wasting. Architecture is implicated centrally in the distancing of order from disorder, of life from death, and of purity from danger. The Enlightenment emphasis on what Scanlan (2005, 60) refers to as a "cosmetics of order" complemented architecture and its ambition to realize itself as orderly form—built or idealized—that leaves behind any of the mess of designing and building, and denies future states of decay.[2] Such ordering was itself "a kind of alienation from the life and death of matter" (2005, 116). In the new order of the Age of Reason it mattered how light (and its optical sister, transparency) were accommodated and arranged. Michel Foucault has noted that light was emerging as a valued quality, as elaborated in his famous interview on space and power/knowledge, "[a] fear haunted the latter half of the eighteenth century: the fear of darkened spaces, of the pall of gloom which prevents the full visibility of things, men and truths." All aspects of scholarly, artistic, and political effort were directed to "break up the patches of darkness," to "eliminate the shadowy areas of society," and to "demolish the unlit chambers where arbitrary political acts, monarchical caprice, religious superstition, tyrannical and priestly plots, epidemics and the illusions of ignorance were fomented" (Foucault 1980, 153). The architectural management of light and transparency entered, among other things, into novel technologies of power, the most famous of which was Jeremy Bentham's Panopticon.

Architecture in the Age of Reason functioned as evidence of rationality, symbolically and materially. Along with cartography and surveying, it operated as a "partitioning art" (Serres 1995, 53) serving moral and economic imperatives to "enclose" the earth and dominate nature. In Old and Middle English the term "waste" referred to land not suited to human habitation. Waste, so defined, implicated nature generally, but more particularly those places and things that were "outside of an economy of human values," because they either could not be or had not yet been used for the benefit of humankind. Waste thought of in this sense reminds us of the very specific role architecture has played, and continues to play, in transforming wasteland. The seventeenth-century Lockean notion held that land "left wholly to nature, that hath no improvement" was waste (Locke [1690] 2002, 19). Furthermore, given that rational thought emerged in accord with Protestant Christianity, it was understood to be a human responsibility to God, that "wise Architect," to appropriate such waste land and improve it through human labor. As Locke ([1689] 1996, 97) put it: "[God] having endued man with those faculties of knowing … having given him reason, hands and materials, he should build him bridges, or houses." Waste, in this vision of productivity, is a category that is placed over common resources as a precursive gesture to legitimate enclosure and privatization, processes in which architecture has played a central territorial and symbolic role.

The material expression of this philosophical tendency often took the form of vast, ambitious architectural and infrastructural projects: the draining of swamps, the opening up of new land for agricultural production, the construction of new irrigation canals, rationally laid out town plans supported by infrastructures for improved transportation and sanitation.[3]

Architecture, then, has played its part as a technique for, and expression of, the appropriation of wasteland. It has both facilitated, and operated as a materialization of, the "proper" use of God-given natural resources and human ability. We can see clearly architecture's significance in this respect through a negative example: the British appropriation of the territories that came to be called Australia. Although the original inhabitants of this continent built various kinds of temporary and permanent structures, none of them aligned with what the European settlers saw to be "architecture" or "settlement." This in turn acted as proof that such land was unimproved wasteland (*terra nullius*) and available for appropriation. Architecture in this model of property rights is not simply something that comes after property, but operates in the name of enclosure as proof of rights sanctioned by Godly contract. Architecture's presence proves creative productivity and the refashioning of an indeterminate nature toward purpose. An absence of architecture is proof of idleness, itself a sign of squandering. The European Enlightenment consolidated the link between reason, value, and order. Architectural design functioned to order, to give form to the formless, to bring utility to the seemingly useless and value to the worthless. Indeed, in the Age of Reason architecture, with its mix of utility, beauty, and permanence, operated as the cosmetic of territorial order *par excellence*.

The link between ordering arts and the production of value is deeply embedded in modern thought and practice. For example, a twentieth-century variant was articulated by Thorstein Veblen who, in his 1898 essay "Why Is Economics

Not an Evolutionary Science?," commented specifically on the transformative power of all the "industrial arts" to turn waste into "land."

> [A]ll land values and land productivity, including the "original and indestruc-tible powers of the soil," are a function of the "state of the industrial art." It is only within the given technological situation, the current scheme of ways and means, that any parcel of land has such productive powers as it has. It is, in other words, only because, insofar, and in such a manner, as men have earned to make use of it. This is what brings it into the category of "land," economically speaking. (Veblen 1990, 337–338)

The "industrial art" of architecture is both an art of *creating* shelter and a tech-nology of partition, enclosure, and appropriation. Other philosophers of the twentieth century closely scrutinized this intellectual legacy, worrying away at its irrationalities and darkened corners. We have noted Foucault's diagnosis of the dark side of "architectures of light." Martin Heidegger, too, reflected on this kind of contradiction. In his meditation on space (*Raum*) he notes that its root, *räumen*, means the act of making room in a constructive and productive sense. It also denotes a shadow meaning, that of clearing, removing obstacles, or evacuating.[4] Architecture, then, is both a creative art and a powerful technology of enclosure and improvement that consolidates and expresses other registers of value. As powerful as its role has been in the production of value, that role means it is always vulnerable to the vagaries of valuation, and certainly so within the frame of capitalism.

CREATIVE DESTRUCTION

As we saw in chapter 2, Zygmunt Bauman (1992) lamented the nineteenth-century medicalization of death and its inauguration of a modern, Western repression of death in life. In his history of the political economy of death, Jean Baudrillard reminds us that this modern conception of death came into being alongside the "appearances of processes of accumulation" (1993, 145). For Baudrillard, the separation of death *from* life, and the repression of death *in* life, is unavoid-ably linked to accumulation or the spirit of capitalism. Under such conditions society is invested in the irreversibility of quantitative growth: what Baudrillard describes as an "aesthetic vertigo of productivity" (1993, 186) accompanied by "spiraling hoarding" (1993, 147). Time is, he argues, absorbed into value, and the ultimate challenge to value—death—is denied. The calculations of exchange value and the assessments of value equivalences rely on a repression of the endings that time delivers. As Baudrillard puts it: "Our whole culture is just one huge effort to dissociate life and death, to ward off the ambivalence of death in the interests of life as value, and time as the general equivalent" (1993, 147). Nowhere are the contradictions of this effort more blatantly revealed than in capitalism's logic of creative destruction.

Under capitalism, architecture's productive attributes—as creative expression and material form—are at the same time commodities. Architecture's creative and material value is, to use Marx's words, "resolved into" exchange value and subsumed into a market as "price." David Harvey, for example, sees the "built environment" as "a reservoir of fixed and immobile capital assets to be used in all phases of commodity production and in final consumption" (Harvey 1975, 120). When architecture enters into the artless category of "built environment," and is subsumed by the explanatory framework of political economy, then architects are stripped of any higher moral or artistic motivations, and become merely wage laborers. Emplaced within capitalism, and rendered by the restricted framing of its systems of value, architecture's creative worth is, ironically, both desanctified and given sustenance. It is *in* the market and *for* the market, and always subject to the vicissitudes of that market, unless another competing value (perhaps historic or aesthetic value) offers some salvation. Market valuation estranges architects from the product of their labor, as it does for all workers. Their building-commodity travels on into the world without them, at best carrying the brand value of their name, although, as we see later in this book, not even that can guard against the power of the market's vagaries. In large part, under capitalism it is the vicissitudes of competition and the fluctuations of the market, rather than any presence or absence of intrinsic value, that will determine the fate of buildings.[5]

While this may well be bad news for an individual building, it is entirely good news for the business of architectural creativity. Architects are one of that special class of intellectual or creator who are, Marshall Berman noted, "beneficiaries of … the demand for perpetual innovation" (Berman 1982, 117). This demand not only expands the market for their products and skills, it also often plays its part in stimulating "creative audacity and imagination" (Berman 1982, 118). Architectural creativity comes to depend on the market not only for its realization but also for its moral sustenance, even though the market is an ambiguous and unreliable source in this respect. As we have suggested, architecture's investment in a simplistic metaphor of life, and its commitment to the progenitive purpose of design, can blunt an appreciation of this wider economic truth. It is as fantastic as it is utopian to imagine that architecture might position itself outside of this Faustian tragedy in which honorable creative visions, while determined to transform waste into value, are haunted by the specters of want and need.

Architecture in capitalist contexts is foundationally bound to destruction. Furthermore, capitalism's need to expand and create new markets (be it by territorial expansion, investing in change, or forcing obsolescence) is generative of architecture. Berman, drawing on Marx's concept of "all that is solid melts into air," masterfully captures this contradictory dynamic:

> The bourgeois claim to be the "Party of Order" [and the] ... immense amounts of money and energy put into building, and the self-consciously monumental character of so much of this building ... testify to the sincerity and seriousness of this claim. And yet, the truth of the matter ... is that everything that bourgeois society builds is built to be torn down ... all these are made to be broken tomorrow, smashed or shredded or pulverized or dissolved, so they can be recycled or replaced next week, and the whole process can go on again and again, hopefully forever, in ever more profitable forms. (Berman 1982, 99)

As Berman concludes, architecture's apparent material solidity "actually count[s] for nothing and carr[ies] no weight at all." Monuments "are blown away like frail reeds." Even the most beautiful and impressive buildings—Egyptian pyramids, Roman aqueducts, or Gothic cathedrals—are closer in their social function to fragile "tents and encampments" (Berman 1982, 99). Architecture is pulled into what David Harvey dubbed capitalism's "perpetual perishing," wherein "capital builds a physical landscape appropriate to its own condition at a particular moment in time, only to have to destroy it, usually in the course of a crisis, at a subsequent point in time" (Harvey 1975, 124). Baudrillard suggests that this cycle of consumption and destruction is a kind of "mirror logic" that entails a "perpetual calculated suicide of mass objects" (1998, 46–47). For Harvey, as we shall see below, accepting that perpetual perishing is central to capitalism is an important first step in shaping a rigorous ecological attitude to, among other things, architecture.

The political economist would have us see the cyclical logic of creative destruction as belonging to an acquisitive and expansionist capitalism. The economist Joseph Schumpeter, to whom the phrase "creative destruction" is often misattributed,[6] elaborated this logic through a consideration of technology. Industrial and technological mutation, he argued, "revolutionizes the economic structure from within, incessantly destroying the old one, incessantly creating a new one" (Schumpeter 1975, 83). The dialectic between technological destruction and creation that Schumpeter describes has explicit implications for built environments and how they accommodate, inhibit, or enable economic activities over time. For example, if the use or function of a vicinity changes, its buildings may become unusable or unneeded. At other times, building technologies themselves become outdated or obsolete with respect to contemporary tastes or standards.

Michael Thompson's (1979) book *Rubbish Theory: The Creation and Destruction of Value* is an oft-cited source for the contemporary revival of interest in value and waste. It is less often mentioned that two of Thompson's key empirical cases were architectural: housing in North London, and an English country mansion named "The Grange." His meditation on these cases reminds us that,

55

relative to other fabricated things, architecture is usually designed and built to last. Many of the regulations and rules that guide architectural design and construction deliver a stability that other objects do not enjoy or require. We expect architecture to last, and we invest creative energy, material, labor, law, money, and emotion in architecture on the assumption that it will. This is translated into economic measures of value. Even relatively modest buildings such as houses are considered in economic systems to have relatively high and stable value because of their durability.

Houses, like most buildings, cannot be regarded as durable in any unqualified sense. Without maintenance and investment they will decay, and may eventually disappear. Indeed, as Steven Groák (1992) notes, buildings are only ever sustained as coherent and permanent artifacts because of the incessant microrenewals—a mending here, a replacement there—that their inhabitants or proprietors perform on them. In economics it is well understood that buildings have a life span. But that life was conventionally assumed to flow in one direction: toward reduced value and, eventually, no value. As Thompson suggests, a conventional view of the nature of housing "would be that, when new, a house had a certain expected life-span and a certain, quite high, value. As time went by the expected life-span would decrease, and so would its economic value. When it reached its allotted span its value would be virtually zero, it would be demolished, and the process would start again" (Thompson 1979, 35). Thompson is at pains to note that the economist often mistakenly interprets that life cycle to be a consequence of some intrinsic quality of architecture. This view mistakenly assumes that the "lastingness of bricks and mortar, tiles and plaster, timber and glass" in a building and "its career (its gradual physical and social decline) [are] the natural outcome of fair wear and tear, of continual use and the ravages of the weather." While the physical stability of a building might on occasions be "slightly modified" by a "fall in public esteem … deriving from the effects of obsolescence and the vagaries of fashion," in the view of the economist, architecture's "physical properties" determine its value as a consumer durable (Thompson 1979, 36).

Thompson shows how the value of objects is socially produced, contingent, and malleable. Object value can mutate from that of a durable to that of rubbish, and back again, sometimes regardless of material quality or integrity. The first of the two architectural cases he uses to make his point is a now-familiar story: the gentrification of inner-city housing. For Thompson, the all-too-evident cycles of devaluation and revaluation of North London housing in the 1970s offered a "ready-made laboratory" for the study of socially produced value (Thompson 1979, 35).[7]

56

Gentrification with respect to housing entails a process whereby working-class areas (originally often inner-city areas) deemed to be valueless "slums," worthy only of demolition, undergo revaluation and rejuvenation by others who judge those areas, and their building stock, to have potential value. The precondition for gentrification is the decline in an area's value because of disinvestment. That disinvestment might be a consequence of the deteriorated physical state of the building stock, the inadequacy of the supporting urban infrastructure, the stigmatized image of the neighborhood, or the outmoded style of building stock that it contains. The buildings in such areas of disinvestment pass into the category of waste or rubbish. They are, in effect, in place but out of time. In the second stage of gentrification, that very same architectural "rubbish" is seen by others as potentially valuable in economic and cultural terms. Buildings that are in place once again, thanks to changing circumstances, perceptions, or both, reenter time. The potential value (what in economic terms is called the rent gap) is realized by the investment of economic and cultural capital. Instead of demolition or modernization, the architectural object is lovingly restored, redecorated, and refurbished, sometimes with little more than the sweat and cultural equity of the gentrifier. The story of gentrification is so familiar to us now, and so fully absorbed into accounts of contemporary urban change, that it is hard to recapture how buildings so usefully served Thompson's then quite novel argument.[8] Thompson's architectural examples very effectively illustrated his wider argument about the socially and economically contingent value of things. They did so because buildings offer an evident irony: they are obdurate things that seem value-durable, yet they can switch from one value category to another and back again. If this can happen for the seemingly inflexible built object, then it is surely the case for all kinds of other artifacts. By looking at buildings, Thompson could convincingly argue that object value was not intrinsically related to material qualities, not even to claimed durability.

Thompson's second architectural example was The Grange, a country house in Hampshire, England, that in 1804 was renovated into the style of a Greek temple by the architect and antiquary William Wilkins. The Grange was a useful example for Thompson because it generated conflicting cultural valuations that were passionately articulated in the late 1960s, when its owner served a notice of the intention to demolish. One commentator regarded The Grange as "a sadly misused durable," whose architectural qualities were "breath-taking," "irreplaceable," and "the epitome of Neo-Classicism" (Inskip cited in Thompson 1979, 96–97). Another saw it as "a transient" that had overstayed its welcome; a "phoney," an "eyesore," and "a multi-legged prehistoric monster" (Toone cited in Thompson 1979, 96–97). As Thompson so succinctly concludes: "One man's rubbish can be another man's desirable object." Thompson's meditation on architectural value recalibrates an economic logic of valuation by way of the cultural sphere of taste. His is part of a broader scholarship that has attended to the mutable and divergent logics of cultural valuations of the built environment. As Thompson (1979, 102) notes, speaking against the systems thinking of equilibrium economics, the malleable value that the architectural object enjoys is "neither arbitrary, nor natural, nor homeostatic," it is fully social. Architecture's relative durability does not exempt it from the principle of mutable value, but it does ensure that architecture generally "circulates"—via processes of reinvestment, restoration, and revaluation—more slowly through its ebb and flow. As a consequence, buildings are regularly out of time—unused, unloved, unappreciated, devalued—but still very much in place (Hommels 2008). As we shall see in chapter 6, on obsolescence, it is one thing for a building to be deemed waste, and quite another for it to be materially broken up as waste. Unlike other waste objects, which can be managed or rendered invisible by being pushed into a garbage bin, stored in the attic, compacted in a landfill, or biodegraded, buildings often, resolutely and publicly, stay in view and in place regardless of their economic and public evaluations.

Thompson's work, as with much subsequent scholarship on gentrification, drew into view the role of taste in pushing and pulling architecture into and out of value. This is possible because architecture as a commodity is subject to what Thorstein Veblen described as "conspicuous consumption." Conspicuous consumption is the term Veblen used to explain the utilization of human resources not for need but for pecuniary display and competition. Because such consumption is excess to need, Veblen also saw it as a kind of squandering or, as he put it, "conspicuous *waste*." He detected in the logics of conspicuous consumption practices that were not rational in terms of current economic models. In explicating conspicuous consumption, Veblen specifically notes how it manifests in and through architecture and its "selective adaptation of designs." In his typically opaque style, Veblen deems unnecessary architectural ornament to be "ugly waste":

> It would be extremely difficult to find a modern civilized residence or public building which can claim anything better than relative inoffensiveness in the eyes of anyone who will dissociate the elements of beauty from those of honorific waste. The endless variety of fronts presented by the better class of tenements and apartment houses in our cities is an endless variety of architectural distress and of suggestions of expensive discomfort. Considered as objects of beauty, the dead walls of the sides and backs of these structures, left untouched by the hands of the artist, are commonly the best feature of the building. (Veblen [1899] 1965, 93)

58

Veblen reveals his own modernist predilections here, and in so doing echoes Le Corbusier's view that "trash is always abundantly decorated" ([1925] 2008, 179). The presence and absence of architectural ornament in the "better class of tenements and apartment houses" serves Veblen well. It allows him to distinguish between a consumption driven by human need and one accredited by canons of fashion, taste, and style. The latter, Veblen argues, leads only to excess, and "hold[s] the consumer [including the architectural consumer] up to a standard of expensiveness and wastefulness" (Veblen 1965, 70). For Veblen, the very capacity for such excessive consumption is the sign of superproductivity. Writing almost a century later, Manuel De Landa (2006, 98) makes a similar point in his assemblage analysis of buildings, noting that when slow-paced, conservative tradition was replaced with fashion as an architectural force, buildings became increasingly mutable and impermanent.

The phrase "creative destruction" is nowadays routinely linked to Schumpeter's analysis of capitalism's cyclical logics of development and progress. Recent scholarship, however, has suggested that the term entered into European thought of the time by way of an altogether more rounded value system. Schumpeter was notorious for not attributing sources, and it has even been said that his theory was merely a translation for a North American audience of ideas already circulating in continental economic theory. One such source was the German economist and sociologist Werner Sombart. Sombart was influenced by the Nietzschean idea that creation was inseparable from destruction, as articulated in Nietzsche's *Thus Spoke Zarathustra*. And that variant of the idea of creative destruction is understood, in turn, to have derived from the Hindu model of three supreme godheads—Brahma the creator, Vishnu the preserver, and Shiva the destroyer—a model of being in the world which opens to, rather than withdraws from, the cycle of life and death.[9] By drawing attention to this we are not suggesting yet another orientalist pathway of redemption for architecture. We are not offering up Hinduism as an alternative, essentialized cultural model of world-making. But we are suggesting that another logic of value, a different ordering of life and death, may already be inside the modern, Western concept of creative destruction. Might contemporary architecture redeem something of this forgotten meaning? What virtualities, cyclabilities, and deformations might architecture embrace in doing so?

AN ECONOMY OF DILAPIDATION

Pairing production and consumption is only one way to theorize the economy of wasting. David Harvey gestures toward this with his sense that "permanences— no matter how solid they may seem—" (and here we are drawn immediately to the permanence that is claimed by built architecture) "are not eternal but always subject to time as 'perpetual perishing.' They are contingent on processes of creation, sustenance and dissolution" (Harvey 1996, 261). Although the theories of value we have encountered thus far remind us of its vagaries (and what this might mean for architecture), they are all contained within a rather narrow conceptualization of economy. We must push further into the interplay between form (matter) and value (mattering) to equip architecture with a sacrificial sensibility suited to our times. We are guided on this path by the thinking of Georges Bataille.

Bataille was once dubbed, by an enraged André Breton, the "excremental philosopher" for his obsession with degradation and decay, and his interest in the reciprocity of life and death (Kendell 2007, 81). Breton was right. Bataille, by his own admission, sought to develop a "scatology" or "science of filth." In this sense, Bataille might just be what an architecture of the negative needs. Architecture has had its flirtations with Bataille's thinking already, and the news did not appear to be good. It certainly lowered the tone. Denis Hollier (1989) titled his account of the writings of Bataille *Against Architecture*. Among other things, Hollier returned to Bataille's explicit statements on architecture which appeared in the Critical Dictionary and were later published as a series of entries in *Documents* across 1929 and 1930.[10] Bataille, as Hollier (1989, ix) notes, wrote against architecture, which he saw as expressing and embodying a masterful authority, "orders and interdictions," ideal states, and powers of subjection. The form and formalisms of architecture aspire to durability; they presume to "cast time to the outside," and to oppose "all disturbing elements." Architecture's principle is that of "repetition": it is "the ideal and immobilizing harmony, guaranteeing that motifs, whose essence is the canceling of time, will last" (Bataille cited in Hollier 1989, 46). For Bataille it is the prison that is the Ur-form of this authoritarian architecture. Bataille thoroughly challenges the anthropomorphic, natalist, and utilitarian fantasies that give architecture unity of purpose, as well as form. He does this by way of his radical rethink of the nature of economy, which is of course necessarily a rethink of the theory of value.

60 Bataille's *Accursed Share* argued against an understanding of economy as necessarily cumulative and productive: "I am of those who destine men," he said, "to things other than the incessant growth of production." Bataille sought to challenge the Western civilizational fantasy that "the entirety of the world and of human experience can be made useful" (Kendell, 2007, 96). He did this by focusing on consumption. Bataille distinguished two kinds of consumption: one in which resources are consumed to meet basic needs (which he positioned as essentially part of the production process), and another in which resources are squandered. He pushed the idea of economy toward what he called the "sacred horror" of productivity's other: loss, sacrifice, expenditure, waste, death. He

positioned expenditure as the "motivating and terminal goal" of productive activity (Smith 1988, 139). His rereading of economy by way of this theory of *dépense* put "restrictive economy" accounts, with all their emphasis on productive activity, into play with the inevitable expenditures associated with "living matter in general." This Bataille dubbed "general economy" or "energy economy" (Bataille 1988, 12). The energy central to Bataille's rethinking of economy was not evident within standard economic concepts such as *Homo economicus*, utility, accumulation, or conservation, nor even something like Veblen's wastefulness of conspicuous consumption. Bataille understood that the "wealth" of the world (which for him was energy) could be used for growth, accumulation, and productive consumption, but he also insisted that it was radiated, absorbed, and lost without profit, in glorious and catastrophic incidences of unproductive expenditure. As he put it: "We cannot ignore or forget that the ground we live on is little other than a field of multiple destructions" (Bataille 1988, 23). Such destructions—death among them—Bataille saw as the "ultimate luxury," for they bore no return.

We might imagine that architecture, because of its creative aspirations and aesthetic attributes, is already other to, or more than, productivity in the narrow sense. Architecture's product cannot be reduced to utility, and garners its selfhood from balancing necessary purpose with a complementary artistic supplement (Hollier 1989, 31). Certainly, Bataille's perspective chimes with older debates on a modern system of the arts (as we saw in chapter 2) and places "architectural construction" among the arts that had real expenditures (labor, materials, and so on) as well as "symbolic expenditures" (Bataille 1985, 120). But for the most part the debates about the luxurious excesses of architecture's symbolic expenditures (such as ornament) compared to its utility are conducted inside the frame of architecture's agreed productive worth, as we saw with Veblen's meditation on value. Architecture's symbolic luxuries, although variably received, are generally delivered in a manner that is supplementary to utility and serves the expression of order. In a recent reading of Bataille through architecture, Elizabeth Grosz proposes that architecture should escape from its "straitjacket" by attending to "its own excesses, its bestial monstrosity, its alliances with forces, affects, energies, experiments, rather than with ordinances, rules, function or form." She understands, as Bataille did, that architecture is "far more than measured, calculated economy" (Grosz 2001, 154–155).[11]

The complex relationship between nonutilitarian architectural add-ons and utility is well demonstrated by the Gothic style, and certainly architect's expert on the Gothic, Ruskin, was attuned to the peculiar link between ornamental excesses and utility. Jessica Maynard (2005) has pointed out the synergies between Ruskin's account of the Gothic style and Bataille's notion of expenditure.

The Gothic for Ruskin, as he stated in *The Stones of Venice*, was "a magnificent enthusiasm, which feels as if it could never do enough to reach the fullness of its ideal: an unselfishness of sacrifice, which would rather cast fruitless labor before the altar than stand idle in the market" (cited in Maynard 2005, 139). It was an architectural style, as Ruskin noted in *Bible of Amiens*, that served "the purpose of enclosing or producing no manner of profitable work whatsoever" (cited in Maynard 2005, 138). Furthermore, Maynard's reading of Ruskin (by way of Bataille) captures the imperfection and incompleteness of the Gothic architectural project, which in Ruskin's view was endlessly in the making: a busy-ness captured by the term "fretwork," which evokes not only filigree, but also the worry and wearing away that can defer a project from completion.

Bataille's general economy of architecture speaks to aesthetic flourishes not simply because they are in excess to utility—luxurious—but because they capture logics of incompleteness and wasting. Bataille offers us a way of thinking about architecture not simply as purified ideal expressions, but as expressions connected to their base matter. He orients architecture toward "a movement of dilapidation" (Bataille 1988, 38). This is why he discussed at length the pyramids of the Aztecs, and the flamboyant ceremonies of human sacrifice that were staged upon them. These monuments were designed not to hide or replace death but to showcase an economy the center of which was the display of sacrifice. For Bataille, this display was anti-productive and anti-reproductive. And this is why he was fascinated by the excesses of human expenditure needed to construct sumptuary monuments like pyramids: "The worker who labors at the construction of a pyramid destroys [the surplus resources it has at its disposal] uselessly: From the standpoint of profit the pyramid is a monumental mistake; one might just as well dig an enormous hole, then refill and pack the ground … the pyramids … have the advantage of consuming without return—without a profit—the resources that they use" (Bataille 1988, 119). The pyramid, from Bataille's perspective on value, is "pure and simple dissipation" (Bataille 1988, 25). We might contrast this interpretation of the relationship between waste and pyramid to that of Le Corbusier. When walking through the slagheaps of Flanders, Le Corbusier is reported to have experienced a sublime moment, and dreamt that he was among the Pyramids of Giza. As Jeremy Till notes, in this dream "two states of matter, slagheap and eternal pyramid, are kept apart by only the most fragile defenses—an appeal to the notion of intent"; the pyramids are designed to be architecture, the slagheaps appear as if they were architecture (Till 2009, 69). It is Le Corbusier's formalistic architectural vision that sees the shape of the slagheap against a twilight sky as equivalent to a pyramid. But for Bataille it is their *very intent* that enters pyramids into the category of waste, as surely as the slagheap.

This is why, for Bataille, the demolition of buildings often serves a productive role in explicating his theory of general economy—be it American Northwest native peoples deliberately squandering resources by burning down their own houses (Bataille 1988, 76); the collapse of a factory chimney that marked the "stinking earth" of industry and acted as an "oracle of all that is most violent" (Bataille et al. 1995, 51), or the collapsing wall of a prison designed to teach philosophers about the "loutish, scallywag and non-continuous behavior of space" (Bataille et al. 1995, 75). It is not surprising that Bataille has been branded as the thinker who is against architecture. But he was only against an architecture that stood for or assumed a certain calculative logic and presumption of permanence. In elaborating the reverse logics of expenditure, Bataille famously drew on the "primitive economic institution" of the potlatch, derived via Marcel Mauss, wherein social status is acquired through the giving away and squandering of property. This example reminds us that Bataille may well be tarrying with loss and expenditure, but he is still invested in understanding how they operate productively. Bataille may also offer ways for architecture to reconstitute itself in relation to the nonproductive expenditure that necessarily accompanies its purifying idealizations, formalisms, and formations. By taking our vision away from architecture as the solid output of creativity, acquisition, utility, and conservation, he reconnects architecture to its base materialism. Only then might we think about an architecture that understands its necessary and inevitable squanderings, be they good or bad, productive or unproductive. As Bataille noted, the "squandering of energy … enters into consideration only once it has entered into the order of things" (Bataille 1988, 193). Bataille offers a vision that helps to disturb the value of architecture because it tarries with architecture's ends: not only the matter of *to what end* (purpose and utility) but also the questions of *when to end* (nihilism).

DEFORMATION

Edward Hollis begins his book *The Secret Lives of Buildings* (2009) with reference to a painting by the émigré artist Thomas Cole (who founded the Hudson River School), *The Architect's Dream*. A well-known image for architects and art historians, it shows a view of an array of differently lit buildings in varying architectural styles: Egyptian, Moorish, Gothic, Grecian. The buildings of ancient Greece and Egypt are washed in light, identifying them as instances of architectural perfection. Other, "rude" styles, notably the Gothic, are set in shadow, symbolizing their lesser architectural worth according to Cole. It is hard to know if this set piece is an architect's dream or a nightmare. For Cole, the slow march of architecture away from the ancients is nightmarish, as his color coding indicates. From another point of view, however, this composition of the co-presence of architectural styles may well illustrate an architectural dream come true: all buildings from all ages standing for all time. This is the dream of durability. Hollis (2009, 6) goes on to note how this dream "haunts" most classic works on architecture wherein great buildings are "described as if the last piece of scaffolding has just been taken away … as if history had never happened." This is a variant on natalist architecture—architecture that is forever young. As he says, we expect great architecture to be "timeless," and so designated as having a right to permanence or, at the very least, the right to reiteration.

Architectural history, Hollis observes, is written around the monuments that were built to last, as opposed to the housing that has been lost. There is, he argues, an assumption that for architecture to remain beautiful it must not change; buildings must aspire to be durable: "All architects hope that the buildings they have designed will memorialize their genius, and so they dare to hope that their building will last forever, unaltered" (Hollis 2009, 7). But in truth this is not so: buildings decay, their parts get used in other buildings, some of their bits become souvenirs, others get inappropriately restored, buildings burn and get buried. The architectural dream is really a "nightmare" comprising "a noisy, dirty entrepôt of multitudinous architectures in the process of constant change" (Hollis 2009, 8). Hollis's own book is about the rich and strange "lives that buildings lead," what he refers to as their "secret lives." These stories of lives led, Hollis argues, have been either overlooked or willfully ignored (Hollis 2009, 9). Architects design architecture to be durable, but that is always a relative attribute. Given a long enough time frame or a violent enough context, even the most durable buildings will disappear. Durability is not an intrinsic attribute of architecture, it is an attribute of how the social world approaches architecture.

Architecturally speaking, staying around for a long time—approaching permanence—is possible only if malleability and relationality are admitted. Long-standing buildings often outlive their original use, the original intentions of their maker, the original aesthetics that determined their form, and the technologies of their making. When they do so, in Hollis's anthropomorphic language, "they are free to do as they will." "[T]hey suffer numberless subtractions, additions, divisions and multiplications," resulting in, among other things, form and function "having little to do with one another." This protean secret life of buildings, Hollis argues, undermines the "confident dicta of architectural theory" (2009, 9). Hollis is making a case for what he calls the "biography" of a building. His is both a "history of the alteration of buildings and a manifesto for the same" (2009, 10). As Hollis notes, it is "shapeshifting" and "incremental change" that have constituted the "paradoxical mechanism" (2009, 14) of architectural durability. It is a similar observation about building reuse that led the sociologist Michael Guggenheim (2009) to invert one of Latour's central ideas, and dub renovated and reprogrammed buildings "mutable immobiles."

David Harvey offers a useful way of moving forward here. He thinks of place formation, in which architecture clearly plays its part, as a process of carving out "permanences" from the flow of processes creating spaces. But he also admits that these "permanences," no matter how solid they may seem, are not eternal: "they are always subject to time as 'perpetual perishing' … contingent on the processes that create, sustain and dissolve them" (Harvey 1996, 261). We have already seen how Harvey attributes some of this perpetual perishing to the creative destruction of capitalism, but he also acknowledges a more diverse array of agents: physical, social, cultural, and biological, as well as economic. For Harvey, "permanences" are but moments in the "overall spatio-temporal dynamics of ecological processes" (Harvey 1996, 294). Here Harvey's sense of a perpetually mutable built environment intersects with a range of other thinkers who operate with a newly ecological sensibility.[12] Connecting this ecological sensibility to architecture effects two important transformations. First, it further challenges the organismic assumptions that lay within the biographical and natalist fantasies of architecture. For example, De Landa (2006) has shown that organismic thinking is part of a wider tradition of social theory that overemphasizes coherent totalities, or what he calls "relations of interiority." Thought about in architectural terms, this would consist of seeing the building as a coherent whole, to be understood as a relatively autonomous and essential thing (an idea held very succinctly in the architectural idea of "the completed building"). De Landa replaces this with a Deleuzean-inspired sensibility of "relations of exteriority." Architecture, so understood, is an expressive and materialized assemblage, part of a wider relational field and, like other matter, enjoys morphogenetic capacities. Second, the ecological sensibility challenges architecture's temporal assumptions and aspirations. Architecture as assemblage is always part of matter-energy flow, such that our perception of it as durable and permanent is possible only if this flow is denied or actively worked against. This kind of temporality also places architecture into a more horizontal positioning with respect to the earth, part of what Serres (1995) calls the "natural contract." Biographical time is replaced with evolutionary time (Bennett 2010, 11).

Such a boundless architecture must understand that destruction is not simply of the short term and building of the long term (Serres 1995, 30). "Death" is in life, or—to put it in terms more aligned to the project of this book—it is part of the vitality of architecture. Deleuze offers us a useful way of thinking about such radical temporality and extensiveness through his concept of the event. This is quite different to an event thought of as a distinct happening, such as "a man has been run over," or even perhaps, to recall Tschumi's event architecture, a person being pushed through a window. When Deleuze answers the question "what is an event?" he calls upon us to comprehend a far more ubiquitous, less human-centered sense of eventfulness.

In contrast to the dramatic event of a man being run over, Deleuze offers an example of the Great Pyramid. The pyramid is a useful example, for it is routinely used to stand for architecture at its most permanent and powerful. For example, as an aside in his "junkspace" essay, Koolhaas himself observes that modern-day architecture no longer "leave[s] pyramids." The Great Pyramid can signify what Deleuze means by event because it demonstrates two things. First, it is a seemingly eternal object that remains the same over the succession of moments: thousands of years, "a period of one hour, thirty minutes, five minutes" (1992, 86). Secondly, it shows also "the passage of Nature or a flux: it is constantly gaining and losing molecules" (1992, 90). This image of the pyramid helps Deleuze to explain something about the eventfulness of the world: a seemingly permanent and "eternal object," like the Great Pyramid, realizes that permanence in a condition of flux.

Social theorist Jane Bennett extends this kind of thinking in relation to matter and materials of all kinds by way of her concept of vital materialism. For Bennett, things we apprehend as stable objects (such as buildings) are merely "matter in variation" or matter in movement: what she elsewhere refers to as matter as emergent gathering. She puts it like this:

> The stones, tables, technologies, words, and edibles that confront us as fixed are mobile, internally heterogeneous materials whose rate of speed and pace of change are slow compared to the duration and velocity of the human bodies participating and perceiving them. (Bennett 2010, 57–58)

For Deleuze, the event is ubiquitous and has specific implications for thinking about formed things—or, as he and Guattari called them, "expressive units": bodies, buildings, cities, and so on.[13] To think of an expressive unit such as a building as a coherent and stable form is merely a false abstraction from the real eventful flux of being. All such representable states of affairs are, as Deleuze puts it, "impure events."

A variant of the Deleuzean event has been proposed by Latourean scholars, working through the frame of science and technology studies. Latour offers a usefully empirical way of thinking about large technological systems like buildings, as well as the practices of their design and making. He sees such systems as comprising human and nonhuman elements in heterogeneous and contingent associations that propagate "*transformations*." For Latour, large technological systems of any kind are like "a never-ending building-site in some great metropolis," where there is "no overall architect … no design" and no stability. In an explicit statement on building technologies, Latour, working with Yaneva (2008), conceives of a building as a "moving project." For them, architecture is not only designed relationally but, once built, continuously re-forms in relation to the passage of time, as well as the planned and unplanned renovations wrought by the human and nonhuman agents it coexists with. Seen in this way, a building is flow, not form; it is creative, not merely a creation.

DECAY

Biologically speaking, decay follows death. It is the gradual disintegration of the detritus of a dead organism, and has many agents. Enzymes begin the work of decomposition: the dead organism, quite literally, begins to digest itself. In circumstances where the detritus is exposed, such as an animal carcass in the wild, resident enzymes are joined by scavengers—vultures, hyenas, flies, maggots, roundworms—which set to work on the soft remains of skin and flesh. Then come the grubs, snails, slugs, beetles and ants, as well as bacteria, fungi, algae, and other microorganisms. Each feeds on the detritus and breaks it down further, eventually disintegrating even bones. If we think relationally, decay is an important ecological service. En masse, microorganisms function as "source, sink and regulator of the transformations of energy and nutrients in soil" (Murphy et al. 2007, 37), releasing and recycling nutrient elements such as nitrogen, sulfur, and phosphorus into the soil, while also immobilizing significant quantities of carbon. Biological and ecological concepts of decay are full of activity, exchange, acquisition, and redistribution. Decay is as life-giving as it is life-taking.

Compare this with the chilling stillness encapsulated in models of decay delivered by the physics of entropy. In physics decay is linked to equilibrium, wherein matter reaches a state in which there are no longer any exchanges with the environment. As the physicist Erwin Schrödinger famously put it:

> When a system that is not alive is isolated or placed in a uniform environment, all motion usually comes to a standstill very soon as a result of various kinds of friction.... After that the whole system fades away into a dead, inert lump of matter. A permanent state is reached, in which no observable events occur. The physicist calls this the state of thermodynamical equilibrium, or of "maximum entropy." (Schrödinger 1967, 69)

In physics, decay is not a consequence of death but its harbinger. Decay here refers to the dissipation of energy and the arrival of entropy within the system of motion. Think, for example, of the amplitude of an oscillating mechanical or electromagnetic wave, which, without the input of energy, will suffer gradual diminution, finally arriving at a still point. This is decay as a condition of expenditure and dissipation: the decrease in the radioactivity of a substance, or the smoothing of the geomorphology of the earth's surface. Corrosion, for example, is a form of electrochemical decay in which certain base metals—including iron, tin, nickel, aluminum, lead, zinc, copper—and their alloys gradually disintegrate when exposed for prolonged periods to moisture and air.

Decay as a logic of loss features in other sciences too. Psychologist Edward Thorndike (1921) proposed a "decay theory" of memory to account for the gradual fading of a memory over time. Cybernetics pioneer Norbert Wiener posited decay as an aspect of entropy that disorganizes meaningful forms and patterns in transmission, thereby degrading their information value (1950, 21). In a more functional vein, decay can refer to a general deterioration of an economic or political system that inhibits its capacity to fulfill its intended purpose. Concepts of social decay, with their roots in nineteenth-century theories of moral and even cosmic decline, and aesthetic decadence, were activated both progressively and conservatively in social and political discourses throughout the twentieth century (Ritter 1986, 101). Decay, in this sense, is a part of life, albeit negatively as an index of disintegration or spentness.

In architecture, as in these other fields, decay could well be both a herald of death and evidence that death, functionally speaking, has already occurred. Unsurprisingly, architecture's natalist imaginary, and its partial investment in the organic metaphor of life, has colored its engagement with the phenomenon of decay.

PATINA/DIRT

For architecture, the stakes around the matter of decay are neatly captured in the distinction between patina and dirt. One person's dirt is another's patina. Le Corbusier bluntly disdained patina as a careless accumulation of dirt. Viewing a painting by Tintoretto in a European art museum was, he complained, like contemplating a "pool of tobacco juice" (1947, 128). The purist version of his architectural modernism privileged the values of formal clarity, light, and hygiene. On his first trip to America in 1935, Le Corbusier was captivated by the energy embodied in New York's burgeoning urban fabric. He compared New York to what he imagined the cathedral towns of medieval Europe would have looked like "when cathedrals were white because they were new."[1] The "whiteness" of these medieval cathedrals—which he read as "orderly," "fresh," "geometric," "courageous," and "tall"!—was so blinding that it eclipsed the existing built fabric "blackened by soot and eaten away by wear-and-tear." Such newness, Le Corbusier claimed, turned our eyes "away from dead things" (1947, 4).[2]

Le Corbusier saw in the architecture of prewar New York "cathedrals of our own time" (1947, 4). While the medieval cathedral manifested an ancient religious tradition, the skyscraper equivalents looked only toward a future of the perpetually new. The city "is like a house-moving," he observed, "all the furniture in confusion, scattered about, unkempt"; but the skyscraper heralded a city in which "order will come" (1947, 45). His enthusiasm for New York was enhanced, evidently, by his ability to ignore the dust and dirt that must have swirled around the building sites of that nascent city. He also projected forward into a forever-new future state, where buildings never got dirty. "Cleanliness is a national virtue in America," he generalized. "No filth, no dust." In America, he enthused, people "wash their shirts, paint their houses, clean the glass in their windows." This America contrasted to a culture-bound old Europe, where the "ethic" was to "cultivate dust and filth," and "preserve the cracks in the walls, the patina." Le Corbusier abhorred this "taste for patina" (1947, 46).

Le Corbusier's attitude was utterly distinct from that of the art historian Alois Riegl, writing some 30 years earlier. For Riegl, such surface stuff was not dirt but patina, a much-valued attribute of significant buildings and artistic objects. Riegl distinguished between various types of value. One of these was "historical value," which accrues by virtue of a monument's significance with respect to a specific historical moment to which it is linked and bears witness. All buildings, one way or another, have this attribute, but some buildings also have a little more. They have what Riegl dubbed "age value" (*Alterswert*), which accrues over time and is made visible by the presence of, among other things, patina. Age value, according to Riegl, has an advantage over historical value. The latter can be comprehended only by those who have precise knowledge about the monument's place in the sweep of historical events—an academic apprehension, if you like. Age value, on the other hand, is self-evident and available to "educated and uneducated" alike. It is, as Riegl claimed, "valid for everyone without exception" ([1903] 1996, 74).

Riegl was writing at the beginning of the twentieth century, and his concept of age value offers an alternative to Le Corbusier's modernist sensibility. It rests, as the term implies, on an understanding of the *contribution* of decay. Like Bataille's general economy, this economy of the aging monument understands dissipation to be productive. It also knowingly reorders the authority of creativity, away from the human hand and back toward the "lawful" forces of nature:

> **From the hand of man we expect complete works as symbols of necessary and lawful production; from nature working over time, on the other hand, we expect the dissolution of completeness as a symbol of an equally necessary and lawful decay. (Riegl [1903] 1996, 73)**

Riegl's "[m]odern man" does not create architecture against nature but freely gives it over to nature's "purely natural cycle of growth and decay." As Riegl expressed it: "The reign of nature, including those destructive and disintegrative elements considered part of the constant renewal of life, is granted equal standing with the creative rule of man" ([1903] 1996), 73). Here the natalist authority is replaced with a sense of architecture in time. Giving over to time and to aging is to align with "nature's lawful activity of disintegration," and submit to the "reign of natural law."

As has been well documented, Riegl's views had implications for the ethic and practice of art conservation. His evaluative frame rejected a restoration aesthetic, advocating instead a conservation approach that would "at most, prevent … premature demise." Natural decay of a monument must not be interfered with, and a conserved monument "may suffer neither addition nor subtraction; neither a restoration of what was disintegrated by the forces of nature in the course of time, nor the removal of whatever nature added to the monument during the same period of time, disfiguring its original discrete form" ([1903] 1996, 74). Yet for all of his interest in demise, Riegl also understood that there needed to be limits set on the "reign of natural law." Architecture was a beneficiary of those limits: "A bare, shapeless pile of stones will not," Riegl concluded, "provide the viewer with a sense of age value." Riegl admitted decomposition but at the same time defended form. For a monument to acquire "age value" it must both express "a trace of living growth" and retain "a distinct trace of the original form" ([1903] 1996, 74).

Within the professional fields of contemporary architectural and art conservation, patina and its causes are well defined. Patina refers to "the sum of material and textural changes that occur in the surface zone of all materials, especially in objects of physical cultural heritage." Such changes are "caused by aging, material decay and environmental impact, including the biological environment" (Krumbein 2003, 2). Corrosive forms of decay, such as oxidation, are distinguished from biodeterioration, the process whereby building materials are colonized and eroded by living organisms.[3] Many of the leading conservation agencies—such as the International Council on Monuments and Sites (ICOMOS), and the International Committee for Documentation and Conservation of Buildings, Sites and Neighbourhoods of the Modern Movement (DOCOMOMO)—have developed exhaustive inventories of building materials and their susceptibility to different kinds of decay, and their propensity for patination.

Despite the clarity of such definitions and the substantial catalog of precedents amassed for the professional purposes of architectural conservation, discerning between dirt and patina remains a vexed matter. For example, conservation architect and former president of the International Training Committee of ICOMOS Jukka Jokilehto is quite clear that patina "should not be confused with dirt." On the other hand, he acknowledges that such discernment might be problematic because what comprises patina as opposed to dirt is "not so much a problem of chemistry, but one of critical judgment" (Jokilehto 2002, 239). As art conservator and chemist Rutherford Gettens notes, there have been long-running debates—in archaeology, material culture studies, and art history—on patina. Significant moments in the early history of this debate are Filippo Baldinucci's definition of patina in his dictionary of art of 1681, which in turn drew on Pliny's discussion of the patination of classical bronzes in the first century CE. Pliny's distinction between *aerugo nobilis* (noble patina) and *virus aerugo* (vile or virulent patina) remains relevant for conservation discourse today. For Gettens, noble patina is chemically stable and enhances the "attractiveness" of the artifact, whereas virulent patina is corrosive and so degrades the artifact visually and physically. But the question of what enhances and what degrades age value is still open to judgment.

Historical geographer David Lowenthal offers a further refinement to the adjudication of an object's age value. He suggests that it is calculated in relation to other types of value, particularly use value and aesthetic value: "Whether decay ornaments or blemishes often depends on whether it affects something made for utility or for ornament." Generally speaking, we regard functional artifacts as less attractive as they age, "but hope that most art objects will remain perennially fresh." The case of architecture contradicts this general rule, however. With architecture, as opposed to paintings, "[p]atina improves" (Lowenthal 1985, 163). Lowenthal documents how the position that Riegl formulated on patina was active in the architectural romanticism of late-nineteenth-century Europe. William Morris, for example, argued that "the natural weathering of the surface of a building is beautiful, and its loss disastrous" (cited in Lowenthal 1985, 164). Similarly, in John Ruskin's view, signs of age on a building changed everything. Any "fine" building could be "improved up to a certain period by all its signs of age," and even an "ugly" building could be "made an agreeable object" by marks of antiquity (cited in Lowenthal 1985, 164).

Modernist ideology, despite its intellectual debt to certain principles of the arts and crafts movement—such as a fitness for purpose, tectonic materialism, and valorization of an aesthetics of simplicity (Mallgrave 2005, 170)—was antithetical to such thinking. As we have said, Le Corbusier saw in prewar New York the possibility of a modern city without patina and signs of age. Glass, steel, and concrete were supposed to substantiate this "machine-age" vision, and guarantee the appearance of perpetual newness. But the crisp lines, pure forms, and clean surfaces that these materials delivered to modernist architecture soon began to smudge, deform, and peel. They could not sustain the newness architecture promised. As this new type of aging came into view, so too was the issue of adjudicating age value inevitably reactivated. The modernist architectural commitment to experimenting with novel building materials and construction techniques complicated in new ways the old issue of proper aging and the acquisition of age value in buildings.[4] Of the complement of modernist building materials, it was concrete that came to be regarded as "symbolic of the age" (Banham 1999, 27). As the twentieth century wore on, the critique of concrete as an architectural material intensified. First its capacity to carry age value came under question. Kevin Lynch, reading the reports on weathering and deterioration studies conducted by the UK's Building Research Station in Garston (just north of London) in the 1970s, reflected: "Brickwork mellows with age, unless it should effloresce. Timbers darken or silver, and become eloquent of grain. But concrete cracks and discolors in meaningless forms" (1990, 87–88).

Later in the twentieth century, the architecture that Reyner Banham regarded as embodying the "false aesthetics" of the white-rendered concrete of purism gave way to concrete in various "raw" states. This was a use of concrete in architecture that sought to express "structural and material truth," presenting an unadorned concrete or *béton brut* (Banham 1999, 27).[5] But concrete in this form had problems of its own. As Lowenthal observed, raw concrete "becomes even more ugly every passing year, looking greasy if smooth, squalid if rough" (1985, 163). The building science studies that Lynch drew upon were part of a wider effort to understand and overcome the perceived aesthetic deficits of concrete. Adrian Forty's cultural history of concrete documents the substantial effort architects have invested in addressing this aspect of concrete's performance. Design responses particularly common in the decades up to the 1970s included treating concrete with assorted vertical, diagonal or hatched, and often bush-hammered ribs, grooves, and channels. Such surface treatments sought to shed soot, dirt, and dust so that concrete could retain its look of raw materiality (Forty 2013).[6]

As Forty notes, "the surface of concrete is not a reliable indicator of its internal condition" (2013, 58). Concrete is effective as a structural material only when its compressive strength is reinforced with the tensile strength of steel. Steel-reinforced concrete is structurally effective only if the steel is sealed within the concrete and not exposed to moisture and air, and only if the chemical and mineralogical composition of the cement is appropriately balanced (Honeyborne 1971, 1). If the steel is exposed, either through faulty construction or through cracks that appear in the concrete over time, then it will inevitably rust. The steel will begin to both weaken and expand. This ruptures the concrete casing, causing its external surface to crack and eventually spall. Crucially, this form of decay may not register on the external surface until it is quite advanced. In this sense spalling is usually a symptom of a much deeper problem. Such surreptitious decay from within is, among concrete professionals, colloquially likened to "cancer" or a "time bomb." Concrete in the "purely natural cycle of growth and decay" resolutely resists incorporation into ideas of age value, and refuses to offer a legible surface effect.

There is, then, a fine line between dirt and patina that signals bifurcating destinies of subtraction or addition, depreciation or appreciation. The contour of that line is determined by contingent admixtures of the style of architecture, its material attributes, the nature of the surface stuff, and prevailing taste cultures. An architectural aesthetic that looks back to the past and values age, as in certain romanticisms and in the restoration, preservation, and conservation movements, is both drawn to surface stuff, and wary of it. Patina, as an expression of age, is highly valued, and conservation practice long ago negotiated a careful path between zealous restorations that strip away patina and approaches that stabilize, not only the original architecture, but also its accreted surface stuff. In this approach to an architecture of decay, the conservator-architect intervenes to stabilize an effect that came after the event of design, but comes to be valued as an addition to the integrity of the original object. Indeed, much of the effort of the conservator-architect is, in conjunction with other experts, a policing role wherein the responsibility is to discern when accreted surface stuff becomes unwelcome because it is hostile to the original architectural object.

A TASTE FOR RUST AND BIORECEPTIVITY

The ongoing work by conservator-architects in discerning and policing the fine line between patina and dirt is rarely comparable to the generative work of designer-architects. Relatively little design energy is expended by the latter on that line, nor on the wider dilemma of decay and age value that it stands for. Indeed, architects are often popularly portrayed as considering such mundane matters as building decay irrelevant to the elevated work of creative experimentation. Some clients are famously long-suffering under the apparent indifference their architects show toward destructive agents of decay such as weather. A case in point is Emilie Savoye who, together with her husband Pierre, was client for one of Le Corbusier's best-known buildings, the Villa Savoye. So persistent were the leaks that bedeviled that building's famous flat roof that, even six years after it had been completed (in 1936), she was moved to complain to her architect: "It's raining in the hall, it's raining on the ramp and the wall of the garage is absolutely soaked. What's more, it's still raining in my bathroom, which floods in bad weather, as the water comes in through the skylight" (cited in Sbriglio 1999, 146–147). While Le Corbusier responded pragmatically by working with his contractors to patch the leaks, he also sought to get his client to better accept this problem, pointing out that her home also enjoyed international critical acclaim in part because of that very same roof. The Villa Savoye stands as an important architectural experiment in technological, functional, and formal terms. Yet that experiment was staked on the weather-tightness of the building.[7] The gamble between innovation and practical functioning is one often taken by architects. Pushing this boundary was even celebrated as a disciplinary badge of honor by another of the most notable architects of the twentieth century, Frank Lloyd Wright. He is said to have quipped that "[i]f the roof doesn't leak, the architect hasn't been creative enough" (cited in Brand 1995, 58).[8]

It is tempting to see these episodes as affirming the popular cliché that the purview of design creativity is simply too lofty to consider such mundane matters as building performance with respect to something like decay. In fact, the daily work of most architects is heavily determined by such material and climatological contingencies. Architects are obliged by training and law to take decay, especially weather-induced decay, seriously. Typically, they engage with decay to resist it in the name of preserving the integrity of the built design. This resistance is realized through design detailing of the building's fabric. The external surfaces of a building (roofs, walls, floors) are composed of various materials (stone, glass, thatch, steel, timber), and combined in various ways (bound, tied, nailed, glued, stapled). In colder climates they are, functionally speaking, designed in concert to produce an "envelope" which sheds rain, manages sunlight, heat, cold and wind, and excludes dust, dirt, odors and pollution. The effectiveness of the overall building envelope usually relies on a complex array of sub-elements, such as overhangs, parapets, copings, drip molds, sills, plinths, damp-proof membranes, flashings, gaskets, reveals, insulation strips, gargoyles, gutters and downpipes. The marshaling of these sub-elements into proper sequences represents a substantial investment of design energy, and is central to a building's ability to resist the threats of weather-induced decay.[9]

Kevin Lynch, as we have seen, was fascinated by the scientific research conducted at Britain's Building Research Station on weather-induced decay of buildings. Through their experiments they were able to develop an extensive catalog of weather-induced changes. These included "counter-shading," which is created by dirt drifting down and being deposited on upward-facing surfaces of a building, the more self-explanatory "rain-streaking," and the ghostly phenomenon of permanent shadowing left by long-term differences in light exposure, such as "shuttermarks."

The Building Research Station's catalog of weather-induced changes, published in two short reports in the early 1960s (BRS1964a; 1964b), for the most part regarded them as defects: changes that detracted from the building and contributed to the building's defection from its planned-for performance. But the reports also noted intriguing aesthetic effects that resulted from the

Here, the white streaks seen own from the ends of window and out prominently against ork and in some situations ond a slightly comical look e. In Fig. 6 b, a throat under returned at the ends to meet ace, thus largely nullifying of the projection. Figure 6 e uilding in which this type of unt has been largely avoided the wooden window frames recess of the wall face, with shing at the sills extending in. into the brickwork on

7

Terracotta

Many buildings executed in smooth-textured brick and terracotta show little evidence of the defects already mentioned in this Digest, especially where careful detailing has been followed by regular maintenance, as in the building illustrated in Fig. 7a. Where glazed materials cannot be kept clean, appearance depends largely on the effects of fortuitous washing of dirt deposited from the atmosphere by rain, as in Fig. 7b, where the ground

storey is faced with dark green glazed terracotta, and the upper storeys with cream coloured blocks.

Timber

The natural resistance to decay of timbers such as teak and western red cedar, for which it is often assumed that little or no maintenance is required, have led to their increasing use in external claddings. However, the weathering of such untreated timbers, at least in an urban environment, frequently results in unsightliness. The western red cedar panels on the building shown in Fig. 8, for example, had remained untreated for 5 years. Annual application of a linseed oil/paraffin wax mixture containing a fungicide is the minimum necessary to preserve appearance.

Metals

Some metals, e.g. copper, oxidize attractively upon exposure, whereas others such as aluminium alloys may become unsightly. Aluminium used externally requires anodic treatment, followed by periodic washing, to maintain appearance. Where the aluminium has not been anodized, more frequent washing is necessary, depending upon the extent of atmospheric pollution.

8

9

12, 13

10

11

Where this has not been done, as in Fig. 9, a spoiled appearance is likely. In this illustration dirt particles have caused disfigurement by pitting.

Cast stone

The appearance of cast stone can be just as marred by streaking and staining as can the natural material. Figure 10 is typical of the shabby appearance of cast stone affected in this way, though here it is relatively free from the crazing which sometimes occurs with cast stone. Water has dripped

over the surface from a ledge, the flashing being inadequate to throw it clear of the stone.

Concrete

Precast concrete cladding, like cast stone, may provide an economic alternative to natural stone; it also gives considerable scope in design. It is not, unfortunately, always free from visual defects. Crazing and cracking in concrete introduces the further risk that water may penetrate to the reinforcement, cause corrosion and lead to eventual disintegration.

77

5.1 Double-page spread from the Building Research Station's report on weather-induced changes (BRS1964b).

DECAY

"accidental," "unintentional," even "comical" "exaggerations" that weather had wrought on building materials (BRS 1964b, 1–4). Similarly, the BRS's report on the "control" of lichens, molds, and similar growths does not simply suggest removal. It also offers advice on how certain lichens and molds could be encouraged to grow for their "mellow and pleasing" effects (Farrar 1972, 1). Lynch's meditation on architecture in time shared such an aesthetic. He saw in the grainy Building Research Station photographs of weather-induced defects a range of architectural possibilities. He urged architects not to resist or expunge such weathering, and recommended that "materials be chosen for their qualities in old age," and "surfaces detailed so that the marks of time make them more expressive and diverse" (Lynch 1990, 88).

EXPERIMENTING WITH WEATHERING

A small number of architectural practices have experimented more intensively than is the professional norm on the materials that constitute a building's envelope. Their work shows how architecture can reach beyond the conventional view of decay to broach its ambiguous promise. Their projects offer important clues to a reordered relationship between design, building, and decay.

Some of that experimentation has been made possible because of new materials, such as the embracing of the process of electrochemical decay allowed by Cor-Ten, or "weathering," steel. Cor-Ten is an unfinished alloy of carbon/ manganese steel containing small portions of silicon, phosphorus, chromium, copper, and nickel. This particular amalgam sacrifices the surface, but only the surface, of the steel to oxidation when it is exposed to air and moisture. After a certain period, usually around one year, the rusted surface stabilizes and forms a "self-passivating" patina, or armor, that protects the steel against further corrosion and deeper forms of rusting.

Cor-Ten steel had been developed for industrial applications as a low-maintenance alternative to galvanized and painted steel. It was first deployed in architecture by Eero Saarinen in his design for the John Deere plant in Moline, Illinois, in 1958 (Smith, 1971). The adoption of this controlled decay material for the headquarters of a high-profile farm machinery company, whose reputation was built on innovation and, no doubt, against the image of rusted farm machinery, was considered radical. It is no surprise that this proposed architectural application of Cor-Ten steel took much persuasion on the part of Saarinen and his project team. John Deere employees were being asked to live with the obvious effects of decay on the surface of the steel: that early stage of rapid oxidation, as well as the contamination and staining of other adjacent surfaces that occurred through water-borne runoff from the rusting steel during its year-long stabilization phase. Whether these employees saw their virulently oxidizing surroundings as

78

disturbing or "velvety," as Rem Koolhaas later put it, is not known. What is known is that the architects validated their radical choice of material by appealing to the company's rural heritage, location, and clientele, and, more abstractly, to the idea of "nature" itself. The proper character for the headquarters of a company such as John Deere should not, as Saarinen put it, "be a slick, precise, glittering glass and spindly metal building but a building which is bold and direct, using metal in a strong and basic way" (Saarinen cited in Martin 2006, 73). Cor-Ten delivered this character, producing, as project architect John Dinkeloo observed, an aesthetic effect that "only nature can give" (cited in Martin 2006, 73).

5.2 John Deere and Company Administrative Headquarters, construction mockup with Cor-Ten steel (April 28, 1960). Architect, Eero Saarinen (Manuscripts & Archives, Yale University).

Saarinen and his team not only had to win over their clients, but also to convince their suppliers, the US Steel Corporation, to mill a special batch to their more exacting architectural specifications. To support their case to client and manufacturer alike, the architects conducted detailed and elaborate two-year in-situ weathering experiments, and constructed a full-scale two-story mockup of a section of the building in Cor-Ten steel. This allowed the architects and contractors to understand how the surfaces would perform with varying degrees of moisture—humidity, puddling, inundation—and gave them the opportunity to experiment with new techniques of welding required in an architectural application of the material. The success of these experiments led to the specification of Cor-Ten steel to all exterior elements of the seven-story John Deere complex.[10] The aesthetic and technical success of the building launched Cor-Ten as a commercially viable material in architecture. US Steel promoted it vigorously (Smith 1971, 212). The precedent that the building established, combined with US Steel's marketing nous, spawned a "taste for rust" in architectural culture more generally (Lowenthal 1985, 165). It is a taste that can be seen expressed around the world today, both in prominent projects (Herzog and De Meuron's Caixa Forum in Madrid, and OMA's Guggenheim Hermitage Museum in Las Vegas) and lesser-known ones (Sports Centre by Barbosa and Guimarães in Portugal, and a Tokyo art gallery and office block by Kensuke Watanabe).

DEERE & COMPANY
ADMINISTRATIVE CENTER

5.3 John Deere and Company
Administrative Center
as featured on a corporate
brochure cover (c.1966)
(Manuscripts & Archives,
Yale University).

Another significant moment in this minor history of architectural receptivity to decay is Carlo Scarpa's Banca Popolare building in Verona (1974–1981). Its significance in this context rests on one tiny construction detail. Part of the front façade of the bank is composed of two layers. A series of circular openings are cut into the outer masonry layer, while square wooden-framed windows are located on the second layer behind. This elegant double-layered façade softens the light in the interior spaces, offers visual depth to the Piazza Nogara, which the building addresses, and, in the words of Kenneth Frampton, establishes an "oriental interplay" (1995, 329) between inside and out. Scarpa's sketches for the space between the two layers also show that he intended it to be planted with foliage that would overspill the windowsill and hang into the square. Being open to the rain, the interstitial space had to be drained. Scarpa manages this by inserting a drain from the floor of the space and running a downpipe behind the façade, terminating it in a delicate gargoyle on the face of the building further down. He lines the downpipe with two vertical fluted reddish limestone marble strips. This simultaneously hides and symbolically traces the position of the downpipe and the water it channels. It also anticipates the rainwater that will wash the façade and streak from the lower lip of the oculus.

A number of commentators have reflected sensitively on this detail in Scarpa's work. Mostafavi and Leatherbarrow, fascinated by the inventive handling of rainwater on this project, suggest that Scarpa intentionally provides "the means through which stains would appear" (1993, 103). This seemingly minor architectural detail prompts them to ask far-reaching questions: must "[d]irt, filth, grime stains" be regarded as "aesthetic deformities" that should be eliminated? They urge us to recognize dirt not as an aberrant other to a building's inviolable form, but as a constituent part of its material fabric. Subsequently, Kenneth Frampton noted of this same detail that it not only accommodates the weathering of the façade but also anticipates "the inevitable transformation of the building over time" (1995, 329). And Marco Frascari, in a more poetical vein, suggested that through this detail the "ugly effect" of the rainwater staining becomes "a discreet decoration born under the sign of wonder" (1999, 15).

Today the façade of Scarpa's Banca Popolare carries more mundane signs of weathering. Most of these—such as the discoloration under projected windows, the streaks on their glass surfaces, and even blackening around those very circular openings that we discussed above—fit within the British Research Station's definition of "unintentional." A number of architectural projects in the 1990s continued with such experimentation in weathering and decay. Two of Herzog and De Meuron's early projects, the Ricola Europe storage and production plant and the studio for artist Rémy Zaugg (1995) (both in Mulhouse, France), offer further examples. Both projects are relatively conventional in plan, section,

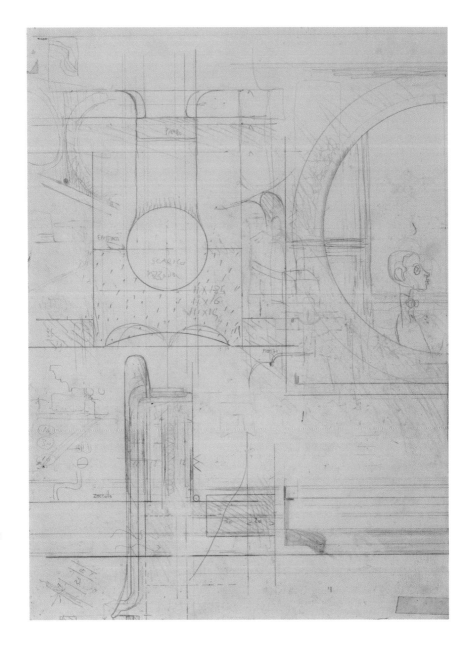

5.4 Banca Popolare, Verona. Sketch and construction details of the circular windows of the Piazza Nogara façade. Architect, Carlo Scarpa (Centro Archivi, Fondazione Maxxi).

5.5 Banca Popolare, Verona. Façade to Piazza Nogara. Architect, Carlo Scarpa (Klaus Bergheimer).

CHAPTER 5

and material composition. Their novelty rests on the fact that they stage their own decay. Rainwater, algae, lichens, and molds are encouraged to attach to, grow on, and stain the black concrete walls of these buildings. In this work, "one can feel immediately that intense alchemical pleasure of following the path of one liquid dissolving into another or filtering through a sponge, a rain dripping down a wall" (Zaera-Polo 2005, 181).

Gigon and Guyer's renovation and extension of the gallery housing the Oskar Reinhart Collection in Winterthur, Switzerland (1998), takes pleasure in similar effects. The relatively simple volumes of the building are constructed of precast concrete panels and arranged around an existing villa (built in 1915, extended in 1924). The concrete panels contain a mix of pulverized limestone and copper, both materials that feature in the original villa. Rainwater is channeled from the roof directly onto the concrete façade. As it makes its way down the façade, the rainwater interacts with the copper ions in the concrete, and encourages patination of the surface. As Annette Gigon notes, the handling of the façade in this way was part of a design strategy that sought to complement without literally imitating the existing building. As with Saarinen's design at Moline, much experimentation was required in exposing the building fabric to the effects of decay.

> We were trying to match the new part of the building to the existing historic villa (1915) and its gallery extension (1924) in terms of material rather than form and detail. We wanted a concrete façade and at the same time a patina that formed quickly, as occurs with metals, particularly copper. So we started by adding finely powdered copper to the concrete. But we didn't get the change to the green coloring we were looking for until we used a concrete mixture that also had limestone added. (cited in Gigon and Hodgson 2007, 39)

As in Saarinen's project, the architectural experimentation at the Oskar Reinhart gallery was guided by a sense that the fabric, through its exposure to a certain kind of decay, helped to emplace the building in its biotope. Gigon notes that the particular concrete mixture they developed for this project was "a kind of alchemistic approximation to this difficult *genius loci*" (cited in Gigon and Hodgson 2007, 39).

Forty (2013) suggests that these projects, and others like them from the 1990s, represent a break with the mid-century worry about staining concrete, and actively engage with its aesthetic possibilities. For Jeffrey Kipnis, projects such as these embody a "cosmetic" aesthetic attitude.[11] Architectural cosmetics, he suggests, can be distinguished from more conventional architectural ornament that is attached, like jewelry, to the "body" of the building. Cosmetics, by contrast, interact directly with the building "skin." In so doing, architectural cosmetics, by analogy to "blush or shadow or highlight," generate a more diffuse atmosphere (1997, 25). This creative innovation is founded on an embrace of conditions, such as rust or lichen or mold, that the profession has historically regarded as nuisances and sought to repress. It does not reside in the application of paint, cladding systems, or other decorative motifs to the building fabric. Rather, it stems from a recognition of the bioreceptivity of certain building materials: their "roughness, porosity, moisture and … chemical composition," as well as their susceptibility to colonization by microorganisms (Guillitte 1995, 216). Creativity in this materialist, cosmetic and bioreceptive mode engages closely and critically with orthodox architectural obligations to detail, assemble, and weatherproof the building envelope. It reconfigures what is normally meant by architecture's creative capacities. It does so through a conscious staging of particular electrochemical, mineralogical, and biological processes inherent in decay. The architecture emerging from such creative experimentation establishes a complex dialogue—articulating, dramatizing—with the singular biotope within which it is located.

FROM COSMETICS TO HYPERPATINA

The projects we have discussed so far have all attempted, in one way or another, to displace conventional understandings of decay as an aesthetic deformity or material threat to the integrity of realized architecture. Cor-Ten steel, like modernist *béton brut*, offered the possibility that a building might express its materiality in a direct, unadorned, and self-evident way. Cor-Ten, as we have seen, goes further by securing longevity through the self-passivated decay of its own surface. The rainwater grooves in the façade of Scarpa's Banca Popolare complicate the modernist privileging of formal legibility by elevating the status of dirt as ornamental effect and registering the passage of time. The late-twentieth-century work of Herzog and De Meuron, Gigon and Guyer, and others, extends this theme by mingling a taste for rust with sensitivity to the bioreceptivity of certain materials.

Semiotically speaking, the patinated and cosmetic surfaces of these buildings tend toward the indexical. The surface marks, stains, blemishes, streaks, and growths result from the configuration of the building envelope and its interaction with its own biotope in a particular place and time. The configuration of stains on Herzog and De Meuron's Ricola Europe building, for example, will be quite different in 20 years. It would also be very different if the project had been built in the tropics, where higher temperatures and humidity levels ensure that airborne pollution sticks and bonds more aggressively to building surfaces. If Gigon and Guyer were to build their Winterthur gallery anew in the subtropical desert environment of Phoenix, Arizona—to consider a further example—they might be tempted to substitute a local material like scoria for limestone in the aggregate of their concrete panels. This new concrete surface would, in turn, interact differently with Arizona rainwater. Rainwater is rarely pure. Its proximity to oceans, industry, and cities alters its composition, as it always absorbs gases and particles—nitrogen and sulfur, dust, pollen, bacteria—from the local atmosphere. Once it hits the roof, rainwater is further altered by the roof's material composition (concrete, terracotta, slate, thatch, asphalt, galvanized iron), the kind of detritus that accumulates on it (such as bird droppings, composted leaves), and things that grow there (weeds, lichen, moss). By the time the rainwater dribbles onto the concrete panels of our imaginary Gigon and Guyer Arizona gallery, a unique chemical interaction is guaranteed and a distinctive aesthetic effect will unfold.

The variable surface marks of architectural cosmetics embody, more technically, a motivated relationship between signifier and signified. The aesthetic effect that results is distinct from a symbolic semiotic, such as the guttae, egg and dart patterns, dentils, and other applied ornamentation of the classical system. In the symbolic semiotic register, signifier and signified are arbitrarily related. So the relationship between them, and the meaning that follows, is produced through social and cultural convention. This is precisely the process we discussed in chapter 1, whereby the tropes of decay and death come to be embedded in classical ornamental systems. The appreciation and celebration of patina and cosmetics as an alternate kind of architectural aesthetic are conventional too, of course. This is evident in the elaborate design experiments that Saarinen, Gigon and Guyer, and other proponents of a patinated architecture conducted to secure legitimacy—from clients, material manufacturers and suppliers, building users, and members of the public—for their aesthetic. The agreement they secured through these experiments rested, in substantial part, on an appeal to everyday concepts like nature, *genius loci*, or site specificity. These concepts, in turn, are underpinned by an indexical logic. Exposing the building fabric to a certain kind of decay allows the building to register the local biotope through time. The ugly "sign of wonder" that Frascari discerned in the fluted marble strips of Scarpa's Banca Popolare façade signifies the passage of rainwater across it. More mundane and unintended signs of weathering subsequently overwhelmed this elegant gesture. These, along with the stains, streaks, and marks that other architects cultivated, comprise a distinctively indexical architectural aesthetics of decay that registers a naturalized biotope as sense of place.

The projects we have discussed to date register relatively benign and uncomplicated biotopes—rural America, small-town Italy, suburban France and Switzerland. The aesthetic effects that have resulted from the interaction of building envelopes and their respective biotopes, while displacing normative modernist values, remain consistent with the long-standing appreciation for patina that we find threaded through romantic traditions in architectural history.

The project for a museum by French practice R&Sie(n) sited in downtown Bangkok—and dubbed "Dustyrelief" for reasons that will become clear below—takes our interest in a biotically responsive surface to an entirely different level. In this project, R&Sie(n) complicate our discussion of architectural decay in their unflinching engagement with the polluted and profoundly unnatural environment of one of the world's megacities. They connect with a city that has also had a turbulent economic history, and in so doing touch on themes of obsolescence and disinvestment (see chapter 6). R&Sie(n) remain concerned with matters of locality, and what Andreas Ruby has described as the "garbage condition" and "pollution as genius-loci indicator" that informs their architecture (2004, 68). Their work in general, and on the Bangkok museum in particular, breaks with the naturalized sense of good taste that lingers around the aesthetics of architectural patina and cosmetics of controlled deterioration encountered thus far in this chapter.

One of the primary design motivations for R&Sie(n)'s Bangkok museum is the highly polluted biotope of that city. The project operates within a similar indexical register to the cosmetic architectures we have thus far encountered. Yet its more aggressive engagement with a radically degraded, culturally modified, "spoiled" or "corrupted" architecture-biotope pushes at the boundaries of our thinking about design, decay, wasting, and death (Roche et al. 2005; see also Gissen 2009b, 22). The architects for the project, François Roche and Stéphanie Lavaux with Jean Navarro and Pascal Bertholio, suggest that their starting point was the dusty textures, luminosity, and gray palette—the "local color" (Ruby 2004, 68)—of Bangkok's polluted atmosphere. As Roche states: "The pollution cloud, CO_2 residue" of that city "filters and standardizes the light with only gray spectral frequencies." This gave rise to a rich aesthetic vocabulary for the architectural team: "luminous, vaporous, pheromonal, hideous, shaded, transpiring, cottony, rugged, dirty, hazy, suffocating, hairy" (Roche and Lavaux 2004, 137).

Bangkok's atmosphere long ago stopped being understood as natural in any obvious way. It contains a high proportion of particulate matter, which is primarily attributed to the combustion of fossil fuels in the city's heavily trafficked streets. Particulate matter, as the name suggests, comprises small particles of solids and liquids, and can include ash, carbon soot, mineral salts and magnetic oxides, heavy metals such as lead, and other organic compounds. For over 20 years, and certainly since Bangkok's modernization started to be registered through the replacement of bicycles with motorbikes and cars, this kind of airborne pollution has been consistently measured at significantly higher levels than in comparable Western European or North American cities. This has had serious and well-documented consequences for public health in that city (Vichit-Vadakan et al. 2008, 1180).

5.6 View of Bangkok skyline toward Chao Phraya river, Thaksin Station in the middle ground and the incomplete Sathorn Unique Tower in the foreground left (2010) (Stéphane Plapied).

The morphology of modern Bangkok is, of course, economically determined. This city, and many others—Kuala Lumpur, Jakarta, Seoul, Singapore, Tokyo—in the Southeast and East Asian region, were subject to a severe economic crisis beginning with the collapse in value of the Thai national currency, the baht, in July 1997. By 1998 over 1,000 businesses were closing each month in Bangkok, and the national economy contracted by 10 percent. An estimated 2–3 million people lost their jobs, many of whom returned to the rural towns and villages of their origin, leaving Bangkok depopulated. The city fabric itself was transformed. Overnight, the construction of office blocks, condominiums, shopping malls, and the Bangkok Elevated Road and Train System (BERTS) stopped (Wilson 2003, 213). The BERTS project was abandoned in 1998 with some 1,000 concrete pilings already installed, bequeathing an instant "stonehenge"—as it was dubbed—that has more recently begun to collapse.[12] Even more dramatic were some 300 speculative office blocks that were left incomplete. In the years that followed the economic crisis the city's skyline was dominated by "ghost towers" (Barta 2007) that, to Roche's eyes, formed a "cadaver scape," where "death was part of the situation." Bangkok was left "as a new landscape, like a forest with trees falling down producing the new nitrogen for the rebirth of the next generation." This "very sweaty and warm situation" presented a wholly "new condition for urban planning" (Roche 2012).

90

5.7 Newspaper report of collapse of abandoned infrastructure for the elevated "Hopewell" train system in Bangkok (February 2012) (*Bangkok Post*).

The R&Sie(n) team proposed an architecture that engages directly with this overdetermined condition. Their museum proposal is shaped by two distinctive geometries which are most clearly visible in section. The first is a Euclidean geometry that organizes a stacked series of white exhibition volumes. These volumes, connected by a more labyrinthine system of circulation corridors, stairs and escalators, are intended to provide exhibition spaces that conform to the curatorial norms of the globalized art system. The second is a topological geometry. The weight of this alternate logic is carried by the building's external cladding, which takes the form of a metallic chain-link "textile" draped over the primary volumes of the complex. This external geometry stands in sharp contrast to the white exhibition volumes and circulation spaces within. The cladding is distinctive too, in its materiality and the way it is intended to function with respect to the surrounding atmosphere. The metallic cladding is designed to be electrically charged so as to attract magnetic particulate matter out of the polluted atmosphere of the city. Over time, as this material magnetically attaches to the chain-link textile, and as other particulate matter accretes to it, the external cladding of the museum thickens, hardens, and becomes more opaque. The study models for the project suggest that, in the advanced states of this process, the museum will appear as an amorphous fuzz. The exterior of the museum feeds off Bangkok's polluted atmosphere to produce a topography of dirt, a literal "dusty relief." It is a design proposal for what its architects call a "negative spectacle" (Roche 2012). Certain interstitial spaces within the complex promise a more direct encounter with this accreting surface of dirt. In cafés, shops, and circulation spaces the black dirt of the external cladding is visible from the interior, and so infiltrates the antiseptic white surfaces for the display of art.

The Bangkok museum proposal has a predecessor in an R&Sie(n) project titled "Transfer" (1993). This more modest project takes the form of two tree houses suspended among a grove of beech trees and conifers in the Compiègne forest, northern France (Roche and Lavaux 2004, 94). Roche's concern in this project was investigating the potential "porosity" of architecture to its immediate environment, and the ways in which there might be "conflict between the strength of the growing of the trees and the fragility of the architecture." Likening this struggle to that captured in the entanglement of architecture, roots and branches at Angkor Wat, Roche's tree-house project sought to show architecture's variable capacities to "resist the potential of destruction from the growing of the trees." The tree-house project was an attempt to appreciate nature's resistance to domestication, its "monstrous" and "barbarian" character, and its capacity to exact a kind of "revenge" on architectural systems. It proposed a "transactional" architecture in which nature and culture were "porous to each other" (Roche 2012).

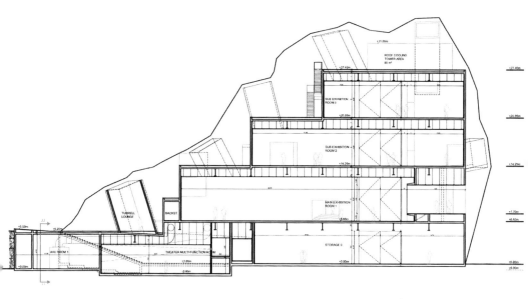

5.8 Bangkok museum project. Longitudinal
section. Architect, R&Sie(n) (François Roche).

5.9 Bangkok museum project. Study model
showing magnetized cladding system.
Architect, R&Sie(n) (François Roche).

DECAY

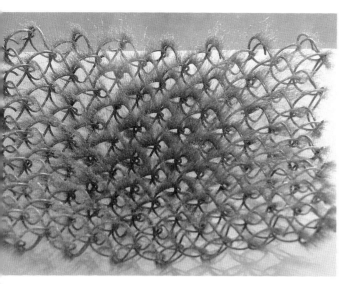

94

This interest in an unfolding transaction between nature and architecture informed the approach R&Sie(n) took to the Bangkok museum. While the tree-house project staged a struggle between architecture and a relatively pure nature, in Bangkok it was architecture set in relation to an "impure" environmental atmosphere. The design for the Bangkok museum resisted the idea of a static, "strong," or "petrified" architecture with a fixed formal character. Instead, as Roche notes, it prioritized openness to the ambiguities of the environment:

> The Dustyrelief museum is the perfect example of this ambiguity, as a building that is collecting the dirtiness of Bangkok's biotope…. The aesthetic protocol that is the genesis for the building transforms this preliminary chemical condition … by collecting "urban failure" as a substance, as a materiality. (cited in Elfassy and Roche 2010)

This is not a stabilized or durable architecture, it is an architecture that seeks to "reveal the situation … here and now." Nor is it simply an "eco-smart-bio-green," moralistic alibi for architecture, as Roche puts it. Rather, it is a "building-as-machine that is able to aggregate, fix, and recycle the filth, while simultaneously extracting from this process the aesthetic protocol of its appearance" (cited in Elfassy and Roche 2010).

Roche's team are, explicitly speaking, back to Le Corbusier's "white" cathedrals of Manhattan in their engagement with Bangkok: "And how to do architecture in this situation? It is certainly not to adopt a kind of *Cathédrale Blanche*," retorts Roche. The black fuzz of the Bangkok museum stands as a deliberate perversion of Le Corbusier's vision of cathedrals of white. Roche is not interested in an "architecture of full light" which, he insists, is part of architecture's propensity for "dreaming of eternity." As he notes, even the recently sparkling architecture of Abu Dhabi is now "encrusted with sand" (Roche 2012). Roche and his team cultivate an architecture that is knowingly situated and ongoingly responds to its situation.

The Bangkok museum aspires to create a negative spectacle that "carries a degree of the palpitation of life and death, a palpitation between existence and non-existence" (Roche 2012). This hyperpatinated architectural vision is as troubling as it is suggestive. Roche's complex and nuanced approach is not that of the shrill "architect as creator." Rather, it is marked by a kind of openness, an architectural co-constitution where the end architecture is "designed" as much by the site as by the architect. This complex, elusive, and undecidable architecture has implications not simply for buildings materially manifest, but also for the very idea of architectural creativity.

96

ARCHITECTURE "NOT-QUITE BEING"

An architecture that accretes and co-constitutes itself through its interaction with atmospheric pollution has been given further impetus recently. Innovations around protocell technologies in the fields of synthetic biology, chemistry, and material science have attracted considerable architectural interest. Protocells are minimal, artificial versions of cells that have the capacity to self-organize, regenerate, and evolve. They have core chemical functions that characterize simple forms of life: "a *metabolism* that extracts usable energy and resources from the environment, *genes* that chemically realize informational control of living functionalities, and a *container* that keeps them all together" (Hanczyc 2009, xv). Because protocells have the potential to be chemically "programmed" to interact with their real-world environments—responding to stimuli, consuming matter or energy, navigating through and adapting to them, producing new cellular configurations—scientists talk of creating "synthetic living systems" (Hanczyc 2011, 31).

This capacity for interaction with real-world environments means that protocells could be put to very practical use, such as generating a new class of smart materials that are "more responsive, intimate, tactile" (Cronin 2011, 36). Protocells in some applications may even be used to halt decay. Applied to rotting wooden pilings, for example, they can accelerate chemical petrification processes and so halt, even reverse, the process of decay (Hanczyc 2011, 31). Protocell technologies offer the possibility that buildings might also selectively extract and sequester harmful greenhouse gases, such as carbon dioxide. Architect Rachel Armstrong argues that protocells carried in building coatings such as paint could be programmed to "consume" carbon dioxide, convert it into calcium carbonate (limestone), and in so doing produce a hard, protective shell for the exterior of the building (Armstrong 2012, loc. 316). This technology also promises buildings that might be "self-healing," whereby cracks and fissures in the building fabric are sealed—"healed"—over organically.[13] Protocell technologies could be programmed to change their mechanical properties "to modulate the environment (temperature, luminosity, humidity)," "generate power," "and even compete with other building 'organisms' for material, information and resources." Such systems would constitute "a type of living technology where biology and nanotechnology would be fused together" (Cronin 2011, 36).

The promise of protocell technology typically exaggerates and amplifies architecture's natalism. It does so often through precisely the tropes—creativity, birth, life, healing—that came to be associated with architecture in the Renaissance (see chapter 2). As chemist Leroy Cronin enthuses: "No longer would the imagination of the architect be static; it would evolve in such a way that the encoding of the structure would shift his or her role from architect to creator" (Cronin 2011, 43). Armstrong agrees, proposing that architects move beyond an "architecture made of inert materials" to one "that grows itself" (Armstrong 2012). She unambiguously proclaims the liminal protocell state to be the basis of a "living" architecture. As she elaborates, with Neil Spiller, "protocell architecture" draws on the capacity of protocells to "avoid entropy and the decay toward equilibrium, in other words, death." Protocell architecture, in their view, builds on alternative synthetic biology to promise "a new living system that has been 'midwifed' into existence by human design and technological innovation" (Spiller and Armstrong 2011, 21).

While protocells have some of the properties of living systems, they are not usually considered "fully alive." Protocells could be usefully regarded, in the words of Laurie Zoloth, as "not-quite being" (Zoloth 2009). While architectural interest in protocells tends to emphasize the generative and life-giving properties of the technology, scientific and philosophical discourse tends to articulate the inherent ambiguity of not-quite being, the dangers of biologizing patterns of cellular interaction, and the implicit threats that protocell technologies pose. Discussion on protocells and their design, when shorn of the buoying powers of architectural natalism, becomes more tentative, uncertain, and cautious. For example, protocell technologies carry uncertain environmental and health risks. Since protocells proliferate, self-replicate, and evolve in new and unpredictable ways, they have the potential to elude safeguards and systems of control, no matter how well designed. They may even start "competing with existing life forms." As Bedau and Parks soberly note, "[m]uch of the positive potential of protocells stems from their ability to self-replicate and evolve, and the very same power raises the specter of life run amok" (2009, 9). So protocell technologies raise complex ethical issues. Through them new, hybridized life forms are being created, and as with other such contemporary instances of the engineering of life, worries arise. As George Khushuf argues, "ethical reflection must be incorporated up front, as a vital part of the research itself" (2009, 224). Others have even raised the question of intellectual property with respect to the products of protocell constructions (Lentzos et al. 2012, 138). Here we glimpse a mortal contradiction within protocell architecture: who (or what) in the end is the architect; who (or what) designs and creates this architecture?

A protocell installation by architect Philip Beesley and engineer Rob Gorbet—shown in various venues, including the Laboratorio Arte Alameda in Mexico City, and the Canadian Pavilion at the Venice Architecture Biennale (2010)—offers some insight into this new kind of architecture in which autonomous cellular creativity augments the hand of the design architect. The "Hylozoic

Ground" installation was composed of an interactive geotextile designed to gradually accumulate the "stray organic matter" generated by passing human traffic suspended in the surrounding air. The geotextile consisted of a structural matrix of Perspex supporting hundreds of "pores," "peristaltic" mechanisms, and assorted light and movement sensors. It was complemented by a "wet system" of primitive "glands," designed to stimulate simple chemical exchanges that produced protocells specifically coded to collect traces of carbon dioxide from the surrounding atmosphere. This, and various other forms of detritus, coalesced into a viscous substance on the geotextile, and generated a kind of "synthetic earth" or "hybrid soil" (Beesley 2010, 20). The soil, in turn, was intended to give rise to a new condition capable of supporting new forms of organic life. The installation was no unambiguous affirmation of life. Rather, in Beesley's words, it exuded a sense of "quiet death" (2010, 25) and promoted an engagement with the deathliness of life, a sense of "abject fertility" (2010, 13).

5.13 Hylozoic soil: Alameda Field, Philip Beesley, Mexico City, 2010. Detail of a glandular mechanism (Pierre Charron, ©PBAI).

This project is related in spirit, technique, and method to Beesley's earlier experiments in biodegradable geotextiles, such as "Endothelium" (with Haley Issacs, 2008) and "Haystack Veil" (with Warren Seelig, 1997). Both projects worked with geotextiles designed to erode in situ in order to produce hybrid organic systems, often as a means of remediating existing degraded landscapes. The "Haystack Veil" consisted of a network of cut saplings and twigs knitted together and propped some 40 centimeters above the forest floor site in Deer Isle, Maine. The structure was designed to rot back into its site over time, so mingling with mosses and lichens and adding nutrients to the soil. Beesley describes the earth as a "thickened blanket" (Manaugh 2010, 45), which, as we saw at the opening of this chapter, results from the long and complicated process of decay in which enzymes and scavengers—vultures, flies, maggots, roundworms, grubs, snails, slugs, beetles and ants, as well as bacteria, fungi, algae, and other microorganisms—operate en masse to enrich and invest the earth with nutrients.

Despite a certain wariness regarding the "scalability" and industrial applicability of these laboratory- and studio-linked experiments in synthetic biology (Baldwin et al. 2012), the possibility of sequestering CO_2 emissions into the fabric of the building resonates with the idea that R&Sie(n) explored in Bangkok, and with the experimental tradition in architecture that reaches back to Eero Saarinen's use of Cor-Ten for the John Deere World Headquarters building in Moline, Iowa. Together these various experiments in deforming and reforming offer suggestive frameworks for thinking about and practicing architectural creativity. Each in different ways actively threads the project through the material conditions, economic contingencies, or environmental circumstances of the work. These experiments, often revealing perversely formed relationships between the building and wasted and polluted biotopes, broach a distributed agency of design delivered to architecture through processes of decay.

6

OBSOLESCENCE

An obsolete building is in place but out of time. Obsolescence arises when an artifact or technology loses value, sometimes through physical deterioration but often as a consequence of newer or better alternatives becoming available. In many areas of product design, obsolescence is knowingly incorporated into the design vision through something called planned obsolescence. In architecture this has only rarely been the case, although there are some notable exceptions that we touch upon in this chapter. The temporality of architectural obsolescence is quite varied. It can happen incrementally, detail by detail: a room whose assigned use is forgotten, a window whose insulating capabilities no longer meet new standards, or an ornamental schema whose time has passed. But it can also happen suddenly and emphatically, as when a purpose-built building is left abandoned when intended occupants never materialize, or move on soon after they arrive. The market, technology, taste and fashion all play their part in the making of obsolescence. They do so through architecture's shadow identity as real estate.

Architectural historian Daniel Abramson (2009, 163) has argued that, architecturally speaking, we are living in an "age of obsolescence." Susan Strasser (1999) would agree. Her social history of trash blames obsolescence on fashion, which constantly and rapidly reorders consumer wants. Gilles Lipovetsky, in *The Empire of Fashion* (1994, 20), calls it the "reign of the ephemeral." Architecture has had a vexed relationship to fashion, and its upbeat temporality. Fashion, often read as surface ornament, was the enemy of architecture's slower cycles of value formation and its foundations in utility and purpose. While prominent architects have engaged actively with the issue of ornament, it has generally remained a stigmatized disciplinary question. Nineteenth-century architect and writer Gottfried Semper, for example, advocated an architecture of "dressing." He developed a compelling account of the emergence of architecture as a social and tectonic art through the very ornamental and atmospheric effects of

103

building materials and how they were combined. As a consequence he insisted that architectural ornament and creativity should emerge from its material basis, and not be subject to the vagaries of fashion, which he regarded pejoratively (McLeod 1994). The architects of the modern movement also had a contradictory relationship to fashion. On the one hand they were in the vanguard of rapid stylistic change, yet they contrasted their interest in architectural purity—in part expressed in the white and non-ornamented surfaces of their forms—to the stylistic vagaries of fashion-led changes in taste. As Mark Wigley (1994, 152) notes, modern architecture was "explicitly launched against fashion."

Architecture may well imagine itself as resisting the vagaries of fashion by accessing a design truth that might rest upon tectonic and material fidelity, precision of utilitarian fit, or formal decorum. But it is not so robust once built and living out its second life as real estate; real-estate architecture is subject to cycles of investment and disinvestment, the churn of creative destruction. Sometimes its cycles are slow, but at other times they are shockingly quick. Even buildings can be subject to the kind of fast-paced obsolescence we nowadays normally associate with electrical products or fashion. In fact, architecture, unlike many other products, can suffer a painful variant: an instant or premature obsolescence that leaves behind incomplete architectural carcasses. The popular media report routinely on these deferred architectures, not least because their incompleteness is so evident. China, media reports suggest, is full of them. There, rapid marketization and the intense pressure from central government on provincial authorities to meet GDP targets have fueled the rise in megascale infrastructural development. Land-holding provincial governments are drawn to the revenue opportunities of leasing land use rights to commercial developers, and in many provinces such arrangements account for more than half of the overall income. In 2009, fixed-asset investment accounted for more than 90 percent of China's overall growth, and residential and commercial real-estate investment made up nearly a quarter of that (Powell 2010). As architect Neville Mars and coauthor Adrian Hornsby (2008) note, China is a society "under construction." In many cases such construction has proceeded ahead of demand. The result is large, near-complete, but almost entirely empty developments. It is a modern-day equivalent to building pyramids, more about creating wealth and expressing political and fiscal autonomy than providing for accurately assessed need. While many of China's poorly housed may aspire to the type of homes, neighborhoods, and lifestyles promised by such developments, most are financially out of reach. Such megadevelopments therefore depend on a state-supported creation of demand. This might include granting urban residency (*hukou*) to rural migrant homebuyers, abolishing *danwei* welfare housing to create demand, or providing low-interest mortgages. It might also include "massive and systematic" demolition of old housing. So prevalent is demolition in China that there is a populist term, *chaiqian jungji*, meaning the "economy of demolition and relocation" (Hsing 2010, 108–109).

In Beijing, for example, the *Chai* (拆) symbol (meaning destruction or antiquated things or ideas that should be destroyed) adorns building after building (Zhao and Bell 2005). The symbol is used by demolition firms to indicate which properties are to be pulled down, but as anthropologist Adam Yuet Chau (2008) has shown, it has a stigmatizing and unsettling effect on the houses and people around, a herald of a fate to come. It has also entered into popular culture through the widely circulated photographic work of Wang Jinsong entitled *One Hundred Signs of the Demolition* (1999).

Newspapers and current affairs programs outside China have delighted in reporting on the as yet unoccupied developments generated by China's state-sanctioned building boom.[1] Dongguan's New South China Mall, the Inner Mongolian urban development of Kangbashi near Ordos City, Henen Province's Zhengzhou New Area, and Songjiang District's Thames Town, all have notoriety as instant "ghost towns." Their empty streets, shops, escalators, and apartments, and their unmaintained infrastructures, are marveled at with an ambivalent wonder. From the perspective of a recession-hit West, the squandering of resource and effort they express is at once unthinkable and enviable. But are these really ghost towns in the usual sense of the term? A ghost town, conventionally speaking, is a town that was once inhabited but, for some reason, is no more. It is a town that has *become* obsolete as a town because of change of use and people vacating it. The emptiness of these megadevelopments follows a different sequence and temporality. These are not examples of the instantly obsolete so much as developments suspended in speculation.

Economically turbulent and aspirational Asia has many such "ghost architectures." Sometimes they are completed buildings that await occupation, sometimes they are quite literally interrupted architectures, creating what Heynen et al. (2006, 1) referred to as a "social and physical wasteland" of "unfinished skyscrapers." The Asian financial crisis of 1997 was the culprit in many cases. The years preceding the crisis had generated an economic "bubble" of growth dependent upon urban real-estate development and consumer culture (Wilson 2003, 203). As we saw in chapter 5, in Bangkok, where the financial crisis was first felt, some 300 speculatively built office blocks were left incomplete. These "ghost towers" (Barta 2007) formed what architect François Roche dubbed an urban "cadaver scape" (2012). One such ghost tower was the 49-story Sathorn Unique.

Sathorn Unique was designed by the Bangkok-based firm Rangsan and Pansit Architecture as an elegant private residential address in the postmodern mode. It is essentially a slab block, stepped at one end and capped by an enormous glazed dome. The ornamental system is eclectic, including ionic columns, giant cornices, Roman arches, pediments and loggias. Hundreds of balustraded balconies protrude from the façade to give the whole building the effect of a giant piece of upholstered urban furniture. Construction was abruptly stopped in 1998, before the building was complete. Today Sathorn Unique's ruinous concrete shell speaks of a now out-of-date style. On the upper levels rusting steel reinforcement rods jut out into thin air, and the central dome remains uncompleted. Unfinished and unused, it has been colonized by trees and vines, rodents and other unofficial users. Garbage has accumulated in the grounds. Two escalators installed to link ground and first floors have never been used. And "the smell of urine is overpowering," reports journalist Patrick Barta (2007).

In the West, large buildings that stay in the urban landscape but do so without use are often called "white elephants," a name that captures well the fact that they are large and imposing things of ambiguous value and not easily disposed of.[2] The idea of the "white elephant" has its roots in an "old Siam" tradition of the royal acquisition and giving of white elephants (Tobler 2007). In Southeast Asia, the white elephant holds considerable value because of its rarity, and was often associated with, and owned by, royalty. These rare animals were not required to work or go to war, and were expected to be adorned with gifts, cleaned and fed, fussed over and made available for public veneration. As a useless but costly possession the white elephant displayed to all the wealth of its royal owner. On occasions a royal might even decide to gift a white elephant, knowing that its costly uselessness would bring financial ruin to the recipient. White elephants, including those of the architectural kind, are not simply big and ugly. Their deferred or abandoned utility speaks of economic excess, wastage, and squandering.

Conditions of near-completeness or incompleteness are common within precarious economies such as those of Southeast Asia, where building traditions have always included those that proceed incrementally, and often informally. Yet there is something about the scale of Sathorn Unique that gathers attention and cannot be ignored. Certainly one neighbor reported that he worried about the wind blowing off a jagged piece of wood with rusted nails hanging from the tower overhead. "Sooner or later, a wind storm will set that relic free," he commented (cited in Barta 2007). Few are still associated with the building on a daily basis. A pack of wild dogs is reported to roam the first floor, but nonetheless artists engage with it,[3] and bloggers boast about access:

107

6.1 Perspectival rendering of Sathorn Unique
Tower, Bangkok. The 49-story Sathorn
Unique was designed by Bangkok-based
firm Rangsan and Pansit Architecture,
and proposed a high-profile downtown
development comprising 659 residential
and 54 retail units (Rangan and Pansit
Architecture).

OBSOLESCENCE

6.2 Construction of Sathorn Unique was suspended in 1998 as a result of the Asian financial crisis. Today it sits as a towering ruin, accessed by the occasional squatter or keen urban explorer, and guarded, it is blogged, by ghosts and a pack of wild dogs (Florian Blümm).

6.3 Abandoned escalators on the ground floor at Sathorn Unique Tower, Bangkok (Stéphane Plapied).

6.4 Sathorn Unique Tower, 2008 (Jonathan Burr).

OBSOLESCENCE

After a tip off from some of the locals, a small climb got me into the lobby area. Inside, a man had set up a shrine, and was providing offerings to his God. Children who were playing around the outer area of the building had clearly been warned of the dangers inside. Although they were smiling, they were clearly fearful of the building, perhaps due to the ghost stories and other tales of fear their elders had instilled in them. For good reason too—this is a particularly dangerous site, with plenty of opportunities to take a 40+ level fall through one of the many unsealed shafts that exist, often in total darkness.... I realized this abandoned building was not to be taken lightly. (Snaffler 2011)

At least one local agrees. A modest, impromptu shrine occupies the formal space designed to accommodate what would have been a far more elaborate house spirit shrine. The incense ensures the house spirit will not be angered by the worshipper traipsing through, and keeps at bay any malevolent ghosts. The image of the king, considered auspicious, attaches his prestige to this fallen building.

Architectures of instant obsolescence occupy an in-between status with respect to their meaning. They are both an unrealized aspiration and, as emplaced white elephants, "architectural outcasts" (van der Hoorn 2009, 44). They also tell us a great deal about the vulnerability of architecture to the unpredictabilities of the globalized development and real-estate markets of which they are a product.

6.5 An impromptu house shrine has been established in the part of the building formally designated for a shrine (Boris Hamilton).

IN PLACE, OUT OF TIME

These cases of spectacular, instant obsolescence capture the popular imagination and feed a fascination with, perhaps even a horror of, uncompleted mega-architectures and all the squandering of hopes, materials, money, and labor they represent. These cases, however, share little with the longer-duration, often more mundane processes of obsolescence with which architecture is commonly associated. What these spectacular, fast-track instances do share with the wider story of architectural obsolescence is the fact of architecture's obduracy. Unlike a piece of clothing that goes out of fashion, or an electrical appliance that gets surpassed by a new model, buildings cannot be put away in a cupboard, easily binned, or taken to the charity shop. Obsolete architectures remain tenaciously present in the place they began, and because of that it is very hard to exercise the kind of amnesia, or "economy of ignorance," with respect to them as we do with more transient objects in our lives (Scanlan 2005, 129). Specified, as they usually are, in a given place and for a particular use, buildings that are out of time lack the plasticity enjoyed by more minor objects. In simple terms, it is expensive to adjust, modify, or retrofit buildings so that they may enter back into the cycle of value.

Obduracy-in-obsolescence is the peculiar condition of architecture. When buildings fall out of time, they often stay in place. Buildings may well be suspended in this valueless present for lengthy periods. On occasion they will be rediscovered, revalued, and perhaps even regenerated. But at other times they eventually meet the more adamant fate of demolition. And, when a building falls out of time incrementally and quietly, those who conduct their everyday lives in its vicinity are obliged to tolerate it.

The story of building obsolescence is inevitably one of political economy. Architectural design plays but a small part in whether a building's duration is stretched or shortened. The cycles of capital investment and disinvestment that operate as primary forces in the fate of buildings are uneven. Friedrich Engels knew this when he reported upon the housing conditions of the English working classes. His account of the Manchester of 1844 reminds us that even within a general context of economic growth, as was the case in early industrializing England, architecture and its users benefited in haphazard ways. Speaking of the relatively recently built worker housing in Ancoats, then a district on the edge of Manchester, Engels could not contain his dismay at the fact that it was obviously not built with longevity in mind. The outside walls looked sturdy enough, but they were often merely one, or even just one half, brick thick. Inner walls were "as thin as it [was] possible to make them." The housing contractors were building cottages on land with limited leasehold tenure, and as a consequence made "no unnecessary expenditures upon them … [and landlords] spen[t] little

6.6 Ancoats, Manchester. The backs of houses
showing the fraying thin brick skin, 1899
(Manchester Local Image Collection).

or nothing in repairs." Some streets even stood empty, with the cottages "falling rapidly into ruin and uninhabitableness" (Engels [1892] 1987, 96). Engels concludes, with incredulity:

> It is calculated in general that working-men's cottages last only forty years on the average. This sounds strangely enough when one sees the beautiful, massive walls of newly built ones, which seem to give promise of lasting a couple of centuries; but the fact remains that the niggardliness of the original expenditure, the neglect of all repairs, the frequent periods of emptiness, the constant change of inhabitants, and the destruction carried on by the dwellers during the final ten years ... who do not hesitate to use the wooden portions for firewood—all this, taken together, accomplishes the complete ruin of the cottages by the end of forty years. Hence it comes that Ancoats, built chiefly since the sudden growth of manufacture ... contains a vast number of ruinous houses, most of them being, in fact, in the last stages of inhabitableness. I will not dwell upon the amount of capital thus wasted. (Engels [1892] 1987, 96)

Engels encountered in Ancoats the variable temporal horizon of city building, a presumed point of obsolescence expressed in miserly design but grounded in economy.

Architectural obduracy may suit the predilections of political interests wishing to make statements of permanence and power, but its fixity does not suit so well capital's need to be value in motion. The accumulation process experiences, as urban planner Rachel Weber puts it, "uncomfortable friction when capital ... is trapped in steel beams and concrete" (2002, 520). Capital demands liquidity of an architecture that is solid matter. Real estate—or spatialized capital, as we might think of it—is different to other kinds of investments and assets. Among other things, because it is immobile it has its value in part set by location. A building necessarily enjoys (or suffers) the exclusive and therefore scarce attribute of location. It also has its value set by the nature of the "improvement" it offers to the land it is on. Sometimes this relates to the quality of architecture, but more often it is merely an accounting of a building's serviceability with respect to a specific use, and its condition with respect to appraisals of depreciation.

113

Capital flows through architecture (as investment, as real estate, as asset) in a dynamic and erratic fashion. As Weber notes: "At various points in its circulation, the built environment is junked, abandoned, destroyed, selectively reconstructed" (2002, 520–521). Sometimes this happens quickly, resulting in rapid churn. At other times it happens slowly and, in the wait, whole tracts of cities can be laid to waste, left abandoned or in a prolonged state of dormancy. As we outlined in chapter 3, this is what Schumpeter and others have understood as capitalism's power of creative destruction.

In most modern cities the state, through planning mechanisms, intervenes in such processes. For example, it guards against the kind of cynical miserliness that Engels witnessed by establishing building regulations and standards. But the state may equally serve the need of capital to liquidate architecture. One such example has been well documented by Daniel Abramson, who for some years now has been on the trail of obsolescence. Focusing mainly on the US context, Abramson charts how the term "obsolescence" came into use with respect to the built environment in the early twentieth century. Buildings were subject to evaluative criteria that determined they had reached, if not the end of their material life, then certainly the end of their "commercial life." New calculative technologies such as Reginald Pelham Bolton's (1911) principle of "financial decay" tabulated the variable rates by which buildings lost or held their value and utility (cited in Abramson 2009, 161). By the 1920s the National Association of Building Owners and Managers, at the invitation of the federal government, had submitted plausible building life spans, based on a series of "autopsies" it had conducted of demolished buildings in 1920s and 1930s Chicago (Abramson 2010, 159). And by the mid-twentieth century the US real-estate pricing and tax codes both benefited and relied upon standardized tabulations of expected building life spans and building depreciation rates. As Abramson notes, these kinds of calculations set in stone the idea that "a building's value was representable in time and money, inexorably declining and rendering demolition inevitable" (2010, 160). In these conditions architectural aspirations for permanence barely had a chance. In the postwar era, as inner-city areas declined and city-dwellers fled to the suburbs, whole neighborhoods were subject to zoning designations that assumed they had outlived their usefulness. Abramson documents, for example, the 1951 zoning of an entire inner-city area of Boston as "An Obsolete Neighborhood."[4]

Variants of this kind of thinking manifested in a range of postwar and postindustrial planning designations. Many of these designations came under the heading of "blight." Planning historian Bob Beauregard refers to blight as "structural obsolescence." In *Voices of Decline* he charts the diverse discourses of decline that sentenced entire tracts of North American cities to demolition. Urban decline was not only accepted, it was seen as inevitable. Specialist magazines of the time, such as *Survey Graphic* (1940), calculated the "life and death curve of an American city" (cited in Beauregard 1993, 85). The problem facing city builders of this time was the tendency for capital to "leap over and build on new land rather than to replace buildings which have become obsolete" (Colean 1953, cited in Beauregard 1993, 137). And of course, decline was intensified by mortgage and insurance policies that "redlined" entire neighborhoods, thereby denying them access to capital that might support new economic activity and material improvements. As New York newspaperman and housing activist Henry M. Propper noted:

"old buildings and entire sections of our great cities cannot be sold for junk or towed out to sea and dumped. The city must face its obsolete districts as long as they exist" (cited in Beauregard 1993, 62). The language of change used with respect to such areas was one of "renewal" or "redevelopment," and the precondition that licensed such intervention was blight: the evaluation that the built fabric that existed was no longer fit for purpose, that it was obsolete.

What constituted an area's eligibility for redevelopment was linked to a range of "blighting factors." The built environment comprised one of these factors: the age of the buildings, but also their structural condition, as well as their suitability with respect to contemporary standards of space, ventilation, and light. But other variables would also be drawn upon to determine the temporal worthiness of a neighborhood: mortality and disease rates, income, and even in some instances racial composition. Using the example of Boston, Abramson (2012) has shown how a public health standard, the Appraisal Method for Measuring Quality of Housing, deployed a range of criteria by which it could be adjudicated if an area merely needed minor improvements or to be torn down. Here we see the beginnings of a state-endorsed and produced "language of destruction" through which blight became the primary justification for capitalism's cycles of creative destruction (Weber 2002, 526).

We might imagine that such processes belong in mid-twentieth-century urban planning, but Rachel Weber has shown how state-supported obsolescence is still partner to urban transformations in North American cities. Her focus is on tax increment financing districts (TIFs), which create a special taxing jurisdiction around blighted or run-down areas, thereby making them attractive for redevelopment investors. In such systems the state's future property tax revenues are earmarked to fund the up-front costs of redevelopment (including demolition of existing buildings). Similarly, local state authorities can often acquire properties designated as TOADS (tax-delinquent, obsolete, abandoned, or derelict sites). They are then usually demolished by the state, allowing the land they are on to reenter the market at a higher value. Through the melting away of "obsolete" buildings, local authorities are able to attract distant investors with empty, deterritorialized spaces—property free of buildings. In effect, the state operates to resolve a contradiction between architecture's obduracy and capitalism's demand for liquidity and flow. The state translates inherently ambiguous concepts like blight and obsolescence into a certainty of valuelessness, to be capitalized upon. Such activities "suppress rental income and exchange values" associated with a building, and the restricted flow of investment leads to further deterioration and ultimately to demolition. As Weber notes, "it is … when the building becomes so structurally deteriorated as to be uninhabitable and abandoned, that utility and exchange value move in concert" (Weber 2002, 523).

FACING OBSOLESCENCE

Thus far this story of architectural obsolescence locates agency beyond the hand of the architect, placing it in the invisible and, in terms of design, belated hands of politics and the economy. Yet, as Abramson notes, architects did not merely resist or wish away these threatening forces. A small number of avant-garde architects actively faced the likelihood that their architecture might have trouble surviving in the new age of obsolescence. They did so through the logic of flexibility. For example, designs that embraced the notion of the open-plan factory shed aimed for "universal internal adaptability" as opposed to "obsolescence's degradations" (Abramson 2010, 162). Abramson refers to one notable example, Renzo Piano and Richard Rogers's Centre Pompidou. Because all mechanical services were located on the exterior of the building, the interior was open to reprogramming and reuse—what Piano called "transformability": "We have a book of rules for the client. There is a five-year transformability. Then there is a one-year transformability. And a one-week transformability." But while the architects relished their own cleverness in accommodating change through designing a flexible interior, they did not fully give their building over to the fate of obsolescence. Indeed, flexibility was a defense against just that fate. "Beaubourg isn't built for 20 years, but for 300, 400, 500 years," claimed Renzo Piano (cited in Silver 1997, 180).

Jean Baudrillard (1994) denounced the misplaced and contradictory architecture of the Beaubourg. The building's flexibility and transparency incensed him. It spoke not of a politics of open and responsive change or social potential, but of what he saw as a hypermarket of mass-cultural consumption. In his wrath, he did not spare the building. He called it a "carcass of flux," "an incinerator," and "a machine for making emptiness," a "space of deterrence" (1994, 61–62). While the architects saw the building as creative and creating, Baudrillard saw it as dead architecture. He was not convinced by the building's claims: "As for the material of the works, of objects, of books and the so-called polyvalent interior space," he skeptically commented, "these no longer circulate at all." He joked about the consequences of open plan on the workers: "Seated in their corner, which is precisely not one, they exhaust themselves secreting an artificial solitude, remaking their 'bubble'" (1994, 62). All this wrath just because Baudrillard decried the populist and open cultural work the building contributed to. His ire led him to speculate on—or, more accurately, hope for—the building's end. Setting fire to it is useless, he lamented, for "Beaubourg cannot even burn, everything is foreseen. Fire, explosion, destruction are no longer an imaginary alternative to this type of building" (1994, 69). Might it, he wondered, bend under the strain of mass consumption (it was said to bend if the number of people in it exceeded 30,000)? As Silver's (1997) "biography" of the Beaubourg notes, the building's popularity was producing problems. These included the souveniring of detachable elements such as chairs, ashtrays, and coat hangers. "Beaubourg," Baudrillard notes, "could have or should have disappeared the day after the inauguration, dismantled and kidnapped by the crowd ... each person taking away a fetishized bolt of this culture itself fetishized" (1994, 69). This implosive violence of mass appeal—what Baudrillard called the social "involution" of inertia—was, ironically, his only hope for seeing an end to the Beaubourg and all that it stands for.

Other architects have given themselves over more explicitly to the idea of programmed obsolescence. We have already met one of them in an earlier chapter of this book: the British architect Cedric Price. Price, as we noted, was less interested in securing the permanence of buildings, and openly advocated an ethic of building demolition. He worked tirelessly for an "expendable architecture," and was outspoken in his disdain for the "three-dimensional disciplining" of a built architecture with ambitions (and pretensions) of permanence—what he called "slow architecture." For Price the architectural answer was often not a building at all, more a flexible space system or an "anti-building."

Price thought that good architecture should always include the "time factor" (2003, 56). This is wonderfully illustrated by his Potteries Thinkbelt project (1965–1968), which was a proposition to transform industrial wastelands in Staffordshire, England, into an innovative science and technology teaching institution. It was not a building or set of buildings to be located within a conventional university campus, but a program for regional regeneration that integrated three existing settlements. The proposal had to grapple with the fact that much of the land was, due to previous use, unstable. It also sought to take advantage of the residual, but underused, rail and road infrastructures. The design was also underwritten by a commitment to break down the walls between universities and the working classes, offering a subregional plan for industry and learning that was porous and integrated. The proposal had both temporal and spatial flexibility. For example, the so-called "transfer areas" were transport links between the three key settlement nodes in the proposal, as well as places where container-style teaching units could be lifted on and off trains and moved about depending on the needs of the institution.

The Thinkbelt proposal included an elaborate Life Span and Use Cycle Chart. The chart laid out with crisp precision the various components of the scheme, and then further specified these components in terms of "elements" defined by temporality ("temporary structure" and "static structure"), function ("information store units," "accommodation towers," "living spaces," "general teaching zone"), and typology ("inflatable structures," "fold-out decks," "living units"). The diagram captured intensities of use as well as variable "life span" estimates. In Price's scheme it was only infrastructure (roads, rails, etc.) that was given the

117

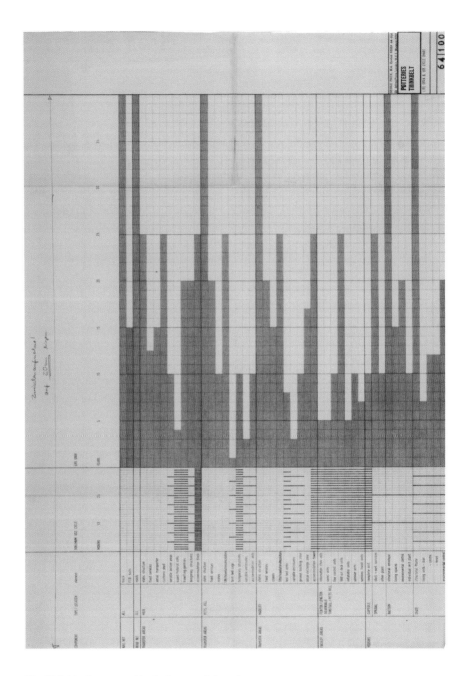

118

6.7 The Thinkbelt proposal includes an elaborate
Life Span and Use Cycle Chart (Collection
Centre Canadien d'Architecture/Canadian
Centre for Architecture, Montréal).

benefit of a long life (40+ years). "Static structures" were to enjoy only 25 years. Many elements, such as the inflatable units, were destined for short time spans ranging from three to ten years. Here the sacrificial certainty of Price's vision was plainly laid out.

BRACING FOR CHANGE

Throughout the twentieth century, more ordinary variants of such avant-garde ideas of architectural flexibility circulated. The structural autonomy offered by steel-frame construction using the H-beam or I-beam fed this imagination. Abramson cites the example of one Charles F. Abbott who, in a 1930 essay on obsolescence, exempted steel entirely from the process. "It is not steel that becomes obsolescent," Abbott argued, "but the design of the interior and exterior equipment." He goes on to declare that "steel is the most flexible material possible for an age of obsolescence" (cited in Abramson 2012, 164).[5]

In Britain similar claims were being made, albeit in a more contentious context. This is revealed in the story of Britain's only steel-framed residential high-rise constructed in the postwar project of welfare housing provision. The Red Road housing estate in Glasgow was designed by local architect Sam Bunton, and completed in 1966. Bunton was an enthusiast of the steel-frame skyscraper, and visited New York and Chicago—cities with the longest history of this kind of construction, and most advanced examples—to learn more. The Red Road Estate comprised six 31-story point blocks and two 26-to-28-story slab blocks. Its innovative and, some later claimed, experimental construction consisted of a steel frame, supporting 5-inch in-situ-laid concrete floors, and asbestos-cement insulation board and fully compressed asbestos cement sheeting for the outer cladding (Sam Bunton and Associates 1966). The decision to use steel was driven in part by the small size of the site, and the demands of the local housing authority to push densities up to some 212 persons per acre, significantly more ambitious than the London County Council's maximum of 136 (Horsey 1982, 177). But also in the mix of this turn to steel was local industrial restructuring, which had impacted negatively on shipbuilding and the related steel manufacturing industries. The local steel industry was "jostling to enter the housing market" (Glendinning and Muthesius 1994, 232). In architect Sam Bunton it found a great advocate. In numerous letters to the local paper, where there was an animated and ongoing debate about the relative merits of steel-frame versus steel-reinforced concrete construction, Bunton spoke earnestly on behalf of structural steel. One part of his argument was the need to utilize the "the spare capacity and skills of the shipyards," which at that time were working to only one-third of their capacity (Bunton 1963a). Certainly, around the time construction began on Red Road, the steel industry was keen to self-promote.

The British Iron and Steel Federation placed an advertisement about the merits of steel in building construction in the *Glasgow Herald* (March 11, 1963). The North-east Coast and Scottish Heavy Steel Makers joined forces with another advertisement asserting that "steel is right … [f]or better housing," and stressing its "speed," "economy," and "versatility." Versatility was a feature that Bunton also mobilized in favor of his increasingly over-cost scheme.[6] In one of a number of letters written in defense of his choice to use structural steel and cladding, as opposed to steel-reinforced concrete, he explained its desirability in terms of usual cycles and costs of obsolescence. Speaking negatively of steel reinforced concrete, Bunton observed:

> reinforced concrete, whether poured or precast, inevitably means the heaviest monumental buildings which one could possibly devise. Indeed, after 100 years of use I would forecast that it will take as long to demolish them as it takes to build them!

In contrast, a steel-framed Red Road would mean that:

> 10 years from now it will be a simple matter to remove the external and internal walls and reveal the steel structure in its naked form once more, ready to undergo transformation. For example, on the assumption that families in the next century will require more living space, the area which presently contains six families per landing can be replanned to accommodate, say, four families per landing. Architects would then reclothe the frames with external walls, windows, internal partitions and finishings using the exciting materials and methods stemming from one hundred years of progress. (Bunton 1963b)

Such claims about the versatility of steel-frame constructions were not always realized. In the case of Red Road this was most definitely the case, as we discuss in what follows. Indeed, the very materials used to clad Red Road eventually militated against flexibility, as did a shrinking welfare state and a popular disaffection with high-rise housing. Rather than serve as a frame for endless cycles of regeneration, Red Road became stuck in time.

120

BUILDING FOR TIME

Architectural propositions of flexibility have offered the profession a modest agency with respect to cycles of creative destruction and the logics of obsolescence that accompany it. For the most part, however, such propositions have remained in the realm of the experimental and the unbuilt. This is exemplified by the schemes of Britain's Archigram and Japan's Metabolism Group, whose designs for changeability and replaceability were only rarely realized. One that was realized—albeit, as we shall see, without ever exploiting its changeability— was Kisho Kurokawa's Nagakin Capsule Tower, Tokyo, a residential apartment block competed in 1972. The design for the building included so-called "timeless" internal circulation cores that accommodated 140 prefabricated concrete capsules that could be plugged in. The plan was that when these capsules became too worn, or out of step with living requirements, they could be unplugged and replaced with more up-to-date versions. Flexibility and responsiveness were the foundations of this architecture. Some 40 years after it was built, not one capsule has been replaced. Normal schedules of building repair and maintenance rarely extend to such a comprehensive vision of upgrading. Without such upgrading, the residents have now deemed their homes obsolete (Solomon 2007). In 2007 they voted for the scheme to be demolished, worried about its ability to withstand earthquakes, its layers of asbestos, and its generally dilapidated condition. Rem Koolhaas and Hans Ulrich Obrist, commenting on the fate of the building, noted that its vulnerability was intensified by the architect's enthusiasm for novel materials which, subjected to the forces of time, have meant that it "is as fragile as the sum of his materials' half-life" (Koolhaas and Obrist 2011). As the *New York Times'* architecture critic Nicolai Ouroussoff reported after a visit to the building:

> Corridors smelled of mildew. Some tenants had taped plastic bags to their door frames to catch leaks, and many of them were bulging with gray water. At one point a tenant took me up to a bridge that connected the two towers, where I could see chunks of concrete breaking off from the corner of one of the capsules. (Ouroussoff 2009)

Kurokawa's Capsule Tower remains standing only because "financial malaise" has meant the residents are as yet unable to find a developer to take on the task of demolishing the building and redeveloping the site. It would seem that returning to the architect's planned program of a capsule-by-capsule upgrade simply does not offer enough flexibility (or make enough financial sense) for these aspirational and building-weary residents.

There are other architectures that willingly live with time limits, most notably those designed to be temporary, such as exposition architectures, or architectures conceived with the ambition to be "time-specific." From the nineteenth century on, expositions or trade and produce fairs generated a number of impressive and innovative architectural interpretations of the temporary building. Working within this tradition, and designing for mainstream sites as well as specialist exposition events, is the Korean group Mass Studies, founded by Minsuk Cho. They see their work as being part of, and a response to, a wider Asian convention of the "logic of replacement," where there is little hesitation around demolishing buildings that no longer serve their purpose. One of their own early building refit projects met with just such a fate, being demolished a mere two years after completion. This kind of "forced temporality" is the backdrop to one continuing strand of their work. Although the studio creates buildings that are

6.8 Diagram showing life expectancy of typical building materials and of the Nagakin Capsule Tower (Kisho Kurokawa), completed in 1972 and now showing signs of deterioration (Koolhaas and Obrist 2011).

concrete block

foundations

CONCRETE BUILDINGS 175 years

poured footings

Construction Materials Lifespan in Years

Material	Years
fluorescent tube	3
computers and copiers	7
furniture and fixtures	13
dishwashers and microwave ovens	13
freezers and refrigerators	14
carpet	16
kitchen units	18
vinyl floor covering	18
air conditioning fan	18
exhaust fans, counter tops, HVACs	25
KHRUSHCHEVKA "DISPOSABLE" (сносимые серии) 25 years — low-cost, five-storied apartment building introduced in the USSR in the 1960s	25
suspended ceilings	25
radiators	27
hydraulic passenger elevator	31
dismountable steel / aluminium partitioning	31
steel profiled sheet cladding (external walls)	37
plasterboard walls	37
PVC sanitary fittings and soil vent pipes	44
PVC windows	45
PLATTENBAU BUILDINGS 45 years — prefabricated construction method typical of East Germany introduced in the 1960s	46
aluminum windows	46
toilets	47
cast iron sanitary fittings and soil vent pipes	51
PANELAK 60-years — prefabricated, prestressed concrete panel building in the Czech Republic and elsewhere in the former Soviet bloc	60
KHRUSHCHEVKA "PERMANENT" (несносимые серии) 60 years — low-cost, brick or concrete block apartment building introduced in the USSR from the 1960s to the 1980s	60
cable	73
profiled steel and reinforced concrete floor	74
precast concrete floor slab	82
plattenbau panels: concrete precast panels	82
CONCRETE FRAME BUILDINGS 75 to 100 years — (Modern) construction method, eg. Candilis 1968-1968. Bobigny HLM, Paris	75-100
STEEL FRAME BUILDINGS 75 to 100years	75-100
fair-faced brickwork	92
timber pitched roof	92
TIMBER FRAME BUILDINGS 100 years	100
chimney	125
BUILDINGS 125 years	125
brick and stone walls	133
stucco	133
	165
	170
	175
	175

designed to last for a long time, "if not forever," they also sustain an interest in pop-up architecture (Cho/Mass Studies 2010, 202). Their temporary architectures are expressions of duration: of design, of construction, of built form, of recyclability. They design in such a way that "the material strength and durability of the construction are a direct function of the anticipated duration of the activity it is supposed to host" (2010, 203). For example, the short-life "ring dome" was constructed entirely out of hula hoops. They think of this as an interdependence of space and duration, a "time-specific architecture."

TABLE 6.1

Minsuk Cho/Mass Studies summary analysis of their own time-specific architecture (Minsuk Cho/Mass Studies 2010, 213).

	RING DOME	AIR FOREST	EXPOPAVILION
Design duration	2 months	5 months	7 months
Construction duration	2 days	3 days	10 months
Building duration	26 days	7 days	6 months
Size	61m2	673m2	7683m2
Material reuse	Hula hoops	PVC/nylon Pneumatic structure	Art panels, 90% Recyclable

For the mainstream of the profession, an interest in flexibility within durability is the challenge. For example, Nicholas Grimshaw's Herman Miller Factory, Chippenham, England (1976), set a precedent in industrial design by installing a cladding system of panels that were completely demountable. The panels and glazing could be interchanged by unskilled labor, allowing the staff to alter the building as needed. This approach was further developed in his later Igus Factory in Cologne, Germany. Not surprisingly, Grimshaw's work has formed the basis of a wider movement in architecture interested in adaptability. Stewart Brand's *How Buildings Learn* (1995, 12) gave specific expression to this idea, in effect offering a long elaboration of DEGW's Frank Duffy's now well-known statement: "there isn't any such thing as a building. A building properly conceived is several layers of longevity of built components." Brand captures this idea in his now well-known diagram of the "shearing layers of change" in a building.

The technical challenge encapsulated in Brand's notion of shearing layers, and the ethos of an architecture moving with time, has in the early twenty-first century become the focus of a multidisciplinary (engineering and architectural) research group in Loughborough, England. The Adaptable Futures team concerns itself precisely with the project of "extending the life of the built environment," and does so with a justification grounded in sustainability concerns.[7] The group is dedicated to thinking about how to design *for* time. It is invested precisely in the creative moment, pondering how architects might *pre*configure the buildings they design to accommodate the changing uses demanded of them, and so maximize their value "through life" (Schmidt et al. 2010, 1). Adaptable design is built around a suite of qualities or, more aptly, abilities: adjustability, flexibility, movability, refitability, convertibility, scalability. The Adaptable Futures group set their approach to design against what they see as ineffective architectural conventions. "Designers," they argue, "tend to ignore these temporal aspects, focusing on an aesthetic fixation and functional performance, freezing out time in pursuit of a static idealized object of perfection." Elsewhere they note that architecture's traditional tools for representing designs—drawings and "design calculations"—are not up to the job of designing flexible architecture (Schmidt et al. 2010, 1).

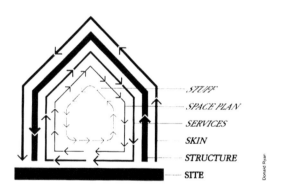

SHEARING LAYERS OF CHANGE. Because of the different rates of change of its components, a building is always tearing itself apart.

6.9 Stewart Brand's diagram of shearing layers of change. "Because of the different rates of change of its components, a building is always tearing itself apart" (Brand 1994, 13).

A key focus of the group is precisely the kind of interface points in a building where components of different life spans might, in Brand's words, "tear" against each other. The group sees such entanglements as having two solutions. One is to minimize the occurrence of such points; the other is to develop what they call "technologies of decomposing." For example, the team has developed and is trialing a Design Structure Matrix (DSM) that they hope might be applied as a diagnostic tool to any design, and at any stage in the design process. A DSM model evaluates how well a proposed design will be able to respond to change, detecting dependency relationships between layers or elements that might limit future flexibility (Schmidt et al. 2011). They are in effect developing a tool to support the kinds of ideas encapsulated in John Habraken's and his Stichting Architecten Research's (SAR) Open Building philosophy. Habraken advocates that buildings be separated into two autonomous parts: the permanent skeleton ("support") and the changeable fit-out level ("infill") (1972).[8] Habraken's proposal developed against the lack of personal expression afforded by modern mass-housing delivery, but through the work of Stephen Kendall and others has come to be a core strategy in sustainable approaches to design. As Kendall (1999, 1) put it:

> This perspective of a building stock with planned stability and capacity to change is fully complementary with the pressing issues of environmental ethics, cradle-to-grave embodied energy, recycling, use of non-toxic materials and other vital issues in the worldwide sustainability agenda.

Open Building design produces artifacts that are never finished and that open out to the design potentials of future users and building managers. This is anything but an architectural death wish. Such approaches look to extend the longevity of architecture through the logics of adaptability and flexibility. They at once acknowledge the force of obsolescence, and operate as a resistance to it. A building that changes over time is also an architecture that can stand in time.

LIVING WITH OBSOLESCENCE

It is a stereotypical understanding of Japanese architecture, embodied in the shrine complex at Ise Jingu, that buildings stay in place through change. The central buildings of the complex are meticulously disassembled and rebuilt in twenty-year cycles according to precise protocols and patterns (see Shinbunsha, Tange, and Kawazoe 1965). Many Shinto shrines in Japan date from the seventh century, and over thirty, according to architectural scholar Cassandra Adams (1998), continue to be maintained in the traditional manner. Their temporal resilience depends on their being regularly subject to reconstruction cycles (Coaldrake 1996, 38). These cycles vary in length from two to sixty years, though twenty-five is typical. The range of reconstruction work is diverse: from simple painting and roof repairs to the disassembly and reassembly of an entire build-ing (Adams 1998, 49). The cultural principles embodied in Shinto reconstruction cycles suggest that Japan is content with a building stock that is rapidly turned over.[9] In fact Japanese professionals in the fields of construction and facilities management worry about "short-buildings-life syndrome," a negative condition deemed to account for wastage of resources. For example, in Japan the average number of years before a house is demolished is around 30, which is signifi-cantly shorter than the United States at 55 years and the UK at 77 years.[10] There is a suggestion that this short-life syndrome is a reflection of different levels of investment in maintenance. In Japan, for example, the proportion of total investment in building work allocated to maintenance and renovation is a mere 25 percent. In Western Europe, including Britain, it is about 50 percent (Eguchi et al. 2011, 74). Surprisingly, the pace of building loss in Japan is more rapid when it comes to steel structures—mainly commercial and industrial buildings. Researchers estimate that in less than 30 years over 50 percent of steel-framed buildings will have been demolished, with their average life being just 30 years, compared to the 40 years that a reinforced-concrete building might expect—although it is important to note that steel is theoretically far more amenable to being reused than reinforced concrete. In Japan it is accepted that the "design life" of a new building (the expected life span) is likely to be longer than its actual life.

Such figures are confirming and confounding when thought of in relation to architect Sam Bunton's ambitious vision for the Glasgow's Red Road high-rise housing estate introduced earlier in this chapter. Bunton claimed that the steel frames of the slab and tower blocks of Red Road would endure well over 100 years, capable of being reclad, refitted, and upgraded almost in perpetuity. But on Sunday, June 10, 2012, the first of the blocks was demolished by the local demolition company, SafeDem. It had stood for 46 years.

When the Glasgow Housing Association (GHA) announced that Red Road was no longer viable, it placed this decision within a wider adjudication about Glasgow's postwar multistory housing stock. Such estates cost a great deal to modernize, the GHA argued; their maintenance costs were high, they had documented social problems, and they were not suitable for all family types. They were also very unpopular, even among the most disadvantaged of hous-ing clients, for housing preferences were firmly with the bungalow and semi-detached typology. There was very low demand for them and the rents were relatively high compared to other types of social housing. And of course, in a housing system where state-based housing authorities had for over 30 years been moving toward public-private partnership housing provision, or simply selling off public housing through right-to-buy schemes, such unlettable and undesirable housing was nothing but a burden. The GHA's decision sits, of course, within a wider history of controversy around residential high-rises, and specifically those designed and built within public housing provision systems. Red Road, as with many other estates like it, had played its part as evidence of how this type of housing would not work. The rash of post-occupancy social science that came in the wake of such high-rise housing documented its social pathologies and diagnosed its architectural ills.[11] As housing historian Patrick Dunleavy has observed, "[h]igh-flat building was the most extreme and conspicuous form of mass housing provision [and] … has since become one of the most widely proclaimed … 'failures' of public policy in this field" (1981, 3). As a stigmatized and residualized type, high-rise housing belonged to another age.

Demolishing a building takes a long time. Some seven years passed between the date when the Glasgow Housing Association announced that Red Road was no longer viable and the demolition of the first of its eight towers. During that time residents were slowly relocated as their tenancies came up for renewal, or alternative options became available. Other, short-term, emergency tenants moved in and rattled about in an increasingly empty estate. The concierge team kept manning the CCTV desk of the entrance station and continued their routine block checks, catching the lift to the top of the building and methodically walking down the stairs, checking for things that might be awry. They would pick up a needle here, remove some abandoned furniture there, but for the most part there was nothing urgent or substantial to be done: the building was, after all, coming down (Strebel 2011).

Deciding to demolish a building can also take a long time. With a high-rise housing development like Red Road the official decision came slowly, even though from the outset it faced detractors who thought such novel (dense and tall) housing typologies were wrong-headed. The final decision to demolish is not made in isolation. A decision that appears to be the end of the story must also be stitched into a new story of redevelopment or regeneration. Finding the capital for realizing such new stories—including for the expensive prerequisite processes of user relocation and building demolition—is time-consuming and, in an era of neoliberal private-public partnerships, market-dependent. In the meantime, such estates continue to be used: lovingly called home by some, resentfully tolerated by others, complained about bitterly by those whose coffers they drain even as they fall further out of value.

Red Road had all the usual problems of high-rise, state-sponsored housing. It also had some of its very own that were related to what the Glasgow Housing Association, in a letter announcing a public consultation about the fate of Red Road, called its "non-traditional" construction. Its blocks were, as the GHA explained, "built using a steel frame which required the widespread use of

6.10 213–183–153 Petershill Drive,
slab block of the Red Road
high-rise housing estate, Glasgow.
Disassembly begins with
stripping the cladding of the
steel-framed structure, 2012
(Derelict Glasgow) (Chris Leslie).

6.11 Detail of the exposed steel frame
and secondary structure of 213–
183–153 Petershill Drive slab
block, 2012 (Derelict Glasgow)
(Chris Leslie).

6.12 Demolition of 213–183–153
Petershill Drive, 2012
(Chris Leslie).

asbestos to ensure adequate protection from fire" (GHA 2004). Residents and workers at Red Road knew about the asbestos. They were living with it, and the local authority was helping them manage that fact. The asbestos posed no immediate health risks, but it nonetheless in various ways shaped how the estate was *in time*. First, it deterred most residents from leaving their mark or making their apartments their own. On moving in, all residents were warned about the presence of asbestos. One resident recalled with horror an incident where a fellow tenant had tried to alter the inner layout of their apartment: "You been in a two bedroom? Well you see the archway ... somebody tried to take that away. Well I mean that's asbestos.... But I mean, [they] should never have touched it" (Red Road resident interview 5, 2005). Rather than radically changing their flats, most residents had to be content with furnishing it "round about," a technique wallpaper was especially well suited to. The housing authorities, on their part, also had to keep an eye on how residents lived with asbestos:

> Well there was not really that much you could change because of the asbestos, see that was there. We did not know at the beginning. But they [the Housing Authority] used to come up and check if it were broken. They would come and they would take it away. You know how kids can maybe pick at things. And they told you if you put any pictures up to cover the nails with paint. (Red Road resident interview 5, 2005)

The presence of asbestos meant that comprehensive maintenance and upgrading programs were so costly and logistically challenging that the GHA was deterred from implementing them. Residents learned to live not only with asbestos but with the more general deterioration of the blocks. Another resident spoke passionately about the complexity of making a home in such an unhomely environment at a public meeting to discuss the fate of Red Road:

> I live 29 up in the 123 block ... I had an inspector out from Allied Construction and he told me that the blocks were not structurally sound. There is structural damage my house suffers from. I mean you see the cracks in the walls opening and closing with winds, the high winds. What I was told was, "don't paint the walls put up wallpaper and hide it." And they came out with boxes of Polyfilla! (Resident, Red Road Meeting, 2005)

This may have sounded like a complaint about Red Road, but as this resident went on to clarify:

> Well I think you [the meeting organizer] have taken what I have said the wrong way, that I hate these flats. I love my flat. Don't get me wrong. I do. I adore my flat. I have spent a fortune doing that flat up, and all on contract. But at the same time, I can't afford to decorate every year because these walls are opening up. (Resident, Red Road Meeting, 2005)

Red Road estate had undergone a major upgrade in the 1980s: new lifts were installed, stair access routes were altered, and a manned concierge security service with supporting CCTV was introduced. This upgrade, however, had to overlook a weakness that became increasingly obvious: the windows. Yet another resident articulated the problem:

> See that up there [pointing to the window area], that's all asbestos up there. Up there next to the blinds, that ceiling, aye. They no took it away yet. See, we always wanted [new] windeas [windows]. The draft that comes through them windeas, now, they're up, how long did I say we have been here? Forty years. We haven't had a new windea, understand what I mean? (Red Road resident interview 2, 2005)

When they were installed in 1966, the prefabricated, steel-framed windows of Red Road were yet another component of this housing vision that supported the flagging local steel industry. Their novel tilt-and-turn mechanism ensured that residents could, with relative ease and safety, open and clean both sides of their windows, regardless of the height of their flat. Yet almost 50 years on, these very same windows were part of the story of how Red Road was moving out of time even as it was staying in place. Encased as they were in an asbestos-ridden building, the cost and logistics of replacement were beyond sensible calculation. Without upgrading of its windows Red Road was increasingly out of step with revisions to energy and thermal comfort standards for housing, laid out in the 2002 Scottish Executive's Sustainable Scotland statement and reiterated in the Scottish Housing Quality Standard. This Standard required all properties to be free from serious disrepair, energy-efficient, healthy, safe, and secure. It also required that social landlords produce housing-quality delivery plans that outlined a program of action ensuring that these standards were met by 2015. The final blow for Red Road came in the form of new, formalized *living standards*: that is, a revision of thinking about minimum standards for residential livability. These standards set down specific goals for housing technologies such as windows, which required them to be double-glazed, with low-emissivity glass and energy-efficient frames. The introduction of these new standards meant that the Red Road housing estate was increasingly understood as a "failure" not only by residents who lived there, but also by those who managed it.

Ironically for Red Road, and for its now deceased architect Sam Bunton, it was asbestos—a material that was to play a relatively minor and largely replaceable role with respect to the development's structural steel—that became the vital material of its demise. Asbestos cement manufacture, another of the local Clydeside industries that Red Road's construction supported, became a controversial and, for many, lethal local industry. Within Scotland—and especially its industrialized Clydeside, of which Glasgow is a part—asbestos hazard is a recognized heath risk, and a potent and politicized issue. Mesothelioma rates in Scotland are almost a third higher than for other parts of the UK, and in Clydeside almost 50 percent higher (Gorman et al. 2004, 184). This has resulted in intensive union activism and civil society campaigning on behalf of sufferers and their families. It has also meant a heightened sensitivity among state agencies with respect to asbestos. Red Road was safe to live in with its type and kind of asbestos; there was no direct risk to residents. But in the Scottish context the asbestos content of the building created sensitivities around, as well as genuine obstacles to, the longer-term viability of Red Road. Especially at the demolition stage, the presence of asbestos shaped the approach and sequencing used by SafeDem. The demolition entailed an extensive asbestos removal program. The first phase entailed determining exactly where in the building the asbestos was. It was found in both the internal and external walls. Then a set of experimental floors was cleared of all asbestos materials according to strict industry codes of practice. This included sealing off each flat, smoke-testing the seals, and then proceeding to remove the asbestos flat by flat. During and after removal there was monitoring by an independent analyst and the National Health Service to certify "air clearance." As the SafeDem website reported: "You may not see much happening on the site but the asbestos removal works will continue for several months" (SafeDem 2012). Indeed, the meticulous stripping out of the Red Road steel carcass took over a year. It was only then that the building was blown down.

High-rise estates of this kind exist in many cities, and several of them, like Red Road, have come down or will come down. The Red Road story may not be peculiar among them, but with all its original aspirations for responsiveness and adaptability it is exemplary for the insight it gives into the unpredictable lived experience of architecture in time, the often slow slide into obsolescence, and the often uneven experiences of such conditions. The story of Red Road's demise reminds us that obsolescence is not simply a state that appears from nowhere as a categorical fact. It is a value judgment, and the conditions that give rise to such judgments may well be lived with for many years before the resources and will to designate those conditions as obsolete materialize. Across the life of Red Road its residents and managers cohabited with obsolescences of many kinds. They were in a relationship with a housing technology that traveled an extraordinary arc from being the tallest, and one of the most structurally novel, high-rise developments of its kind in Europe in 1966 to being a ruinous reminder of a vision that was imprecisely realized. Over the course of that arc some aspects of the estate remained in place and in time, and were even upgraded; others fell increasingly behind the times. Other materials, like asbestos, went from being bit players in the estate's structural story to operating as vital but lethal attributes in the building's categorization as "unviable," and so obsolete.

7

DISASTER

We commonly describe, and legally define, "natural" disasters as acts of God. It is not hard to understand why. The Old Testament is stocked with vivid demonstrations of God's destructive power, as these famous passages from the book of Isaiah show:

> For the windows of heaven are opened, and the foundations of the earth tremble. The earth is utterly broken, the earth is split apart, the earth is violently shaken. The earth staggers like a drunken man; it sways like a hut; its transgression lies heavy upon it, and it falls, and will not rise again.

> O Lord, you are my God; I will exalt you; I will praise your name, for you have done wonderful things, plans formed of old, faithful and sure. For you have made the city a heap, the fortified city a ruin; the foreigners' palace is a city no more; it will never be rebuilt. (Isaiah 24:18–20, 25:1–3; English Standard Version)

These passages from the so-called "Isaiah Apocalypse" are one part of a set of prophecies in which the prophet warns of the destruction God will visit upon the earth to avenge the human violation of His law. The shaking, splitting, and breaking of the earth demonstrate God's violence in grand abstraction. Similarly, the opening of "the windows of heaven" is a recognizable metaphor for all-engulfing and indiscriminate floods (Sweeney 1996, 319). But the fully indiscriminate force of this Godly wrath, its power in relation to humankind's vulnerability, is perfectly captured by Isaiah's reference to more ordinary, earthly things: the staggering of a drunken man or the swaying of a fragile shack in the fields.[1] Isaiah sets these delicate images of vulnerability against the emphatic consequences of God's destruction: the trembling of foundations, the crumbing and collapse of grand buildings, even whole cities, which are made "a heap," "a ruin," "no more," "never [to] be rebuilt." Just as architecture served Enlightenment thinking as an expression of man's covenant with God to create utility out of wild and waste land, the wrathful breaking of that same architecture is a reminder of who is the ultimate "wise Architect."

Acts of God, in this Old Testament sense, have a clear theological rationale. They avenge human violation of God's law and the pollution of the earth. They also carry a sense of human liability and responsibility and are avoidable, we are promised, if we obey His law. The phrase "act of God" has a peculiar persistence even within largely secular, contemporary legal discourse, where it is generally deployed to differentiate events for which humans are responsible from those over which they have no control. In the not quite secular language of law, an act of God is "[a]n event due to natural causes (storms, earthquakes, floods, etc.) so exceptionally severe that no one could reasonably be expected to anticipate or guard against it" (Law and Martin 2009, 12). It typically applies only "to those events in nature which are so extraordinary that history of climatic variations and other conditions in a particular locality affords no reasonable warning to them" (*Words and Phrases*, 272). In contemporary legal usage, the mysterious agency of God is largely understood to stand for the natural agencies of geology or climate. Within laws of contract and tort relevant to natural disaster the term operates, nonetheless, as a marker determining the boundary between human and nonhuman responsibilities.

Terms like "natural hazard" foreground the physical power of nature above not only divine forces but also human agency. This is given clear expression in certain genres of popular science which actively work to naturalize disaster. Popular book series such as *Nature on the Rampage* (Heinemann) and *Forces of Nature* (National Geographic), or film series such as *Nature Unleashed*, focus on different "natural forces"—fire, earthquake, flood, drought, and avalanche—in turn. Some "hard" scientific research also follows this naturalizing pattern by identifying singular natural hazards and attributing to them, often by implication, full responsibility for disasters. These discourses, in different ways, install a monolithic and simplified natural agency and in many respects are no more accurate than acounts that refer to the wrath of God. In both explanatory frameworks the question of human responsibility remains out of the picture.

136   Distinguishing between human and nonhuman responsibility in the complex aftereffects of natural disasters is difficult to do, and it is surprising how often the wrath of God is genuinely invoked. The sheer volume of legal precedents for the use of the phrase "act of God" (numbering over 50 entries in *Words and Phrases*), and the subtle and context-specific variations in meaning that accrue each time it is applied, confirm this. There are, it seems, as many "acts of God" as there are variations in climate or geography. Take the extreme case of Hurricane Katrina (Steinberg 2006, xi). The religious right was quick to capitalize on the coincidence (by a matter of two days) of the annual New Orleans Gay Mardi Gras, "Southern Decadence 2005," and the landing of Hurricane Katrina in that city. Referring to Katrina, Michael Marcavage blogged that "this act of God

destroyed a wicked city" (2005). By contrast, historian Ted Steinberg notes that "more secular types took to conjuring up sinister explanations" for the disaster, with "the Russian KGB and Japanese gangsters," by turns, being blamed for "play[ing] God with the weather using cloud-seeding technology to orchestrate" it (2006, xi). President George W. Bush, in his attempt to negotiate the political consequences of the disaster aftermath, pronounced in a commemorative service at the National Cathedral in Washington, DC, some two weeks after the hurricane had subsided, that the federal government would "take responsibility" for mistakes in the management of the disaster relief efforts. But, referring to the "humbling," "arbitrary," "vast and indifferent might" of the hurricane, he declared the event itself and the suffering that followed in its wake to be a reminder "that God's purposes are sometimes impossible to know here on earth" (cited in Stout 2005). Bush, of course, was widely criticized for hiding his own government's record of slow response and neglect of flood mitigation infrastructures behind that of a greater Authority.[2] He faced a broad-based critique whose accord rested on an understanding that the relation between human and nonhuman agency in the disaster was more entangled than Bush was prepared to admit.

Barry Turner's book *Man Made Disaster* (1978) offered an early articulation of this alternative model of the so-called natural disaster, and investigated in detail the ways in which human decision-making played an important, often determining, role in the formation of such disasters. He argued that disasters were neither chance occurrences of nature nor the acts of a vengeful God, nor even related to the failure of particular technologies in themselves. "It is better," he argued, to approach "disaster as a 'socio-technical' problem, with social, organizational and technical processes interacting to produce the phenomena to be studied" (Turner 1978, 3). Disasters, in his view, resulted from the failure of systems in which social and technical agencies interact. Turner's systems approach allowed him to pinpoint the seed of a natural disaster long before its full and catastrophic consequences were manifest. Small, seemingly insignificant operational cultures or managerial decisions could be "incubated" for years before erupting with disruptive, dangerous, and seemingly arbitrary force (Turner 1978, 72). As subsequent scholars in the field have noted, drawing a definitive line between human and nonhuman agency is "a very partial and inadequate way of understanding the disasters that are associated with (triggered by) natural hazards" (Wisner et al. 2004, 6). Rather, it is important to appreciate the "system vulnerability" (Turner 1978, xx) and what others have called the "landscape of vulnerability" for particular natural hazards (Hilhorst and Bankoff 2004, 1). As disaster sociologist Kai Erikson notes: "if one were to draw a map of places in which disasters are most likely to strike, we would also be sketching at least an approximate map of places in which the vulnerable are most likely to be gathered" (1976, 1). The concept of vulnerability is useful, because it helps to articulate the variable landscape of co-dependencies between natural and cultural factors in disaster situations. As much as secular society has de-deified acts of God, it has been the work of sociologists and risk analysts that has ultimately denaturalized them.

This has specific implications for understanding architecture in the context of disasters. Built architecture is often both a victim of disasters and, if inappropriately designed or poorly assembled, a contributing agent to a disaster's negative impact. For example, rapid urbanization in cities of the Global South sees ever greater numbers living in poorly serviced and informally constructed settlements. These populations are highly vulnerable when they are exposed to natural hazards such as earthquakes, fire, floods, and tsunami (Pelling 2003, 21). This vulnerability will not increase the incidence of a natural disaster, but it certainly escalates the risk such disasters pose, as evidenced in recent events in Manila, Banda Aceh, and Port au Prince.

We can gain an insight into architecture's vulnerability in the context of natural disaster from building science. Groák suggests that all buildings necessarily interact with exogenous environmental and contextual conditions. Building performance is then about how a building relates to these externalities, which he thinks about in terms of siting and flows. Buildings must inevitably be sited in a biotopic geography—climate, topography, geology, flora and fauna—which in turn provides what Groák refers to as a "system of reservoirs with which those of the building interact" (1992, 36). A building's performance should be interpreted in terms of "flows, filters and reservoirs of matter, energy and information." This pertains both to normal circumstances but also, significantly, to any extreme circumstance generated by a natural disaster. Groák proposes an analytical framework for determining a building's performance capacity "based on the description of fundamental flows of energy and matter— and the ways these distend, hurtle, pause, wait, accelerate" (1992, 38). Natural hazards create architectural disasters when "catastrophic flows … exceed the local site/regional reservoir capacities and lead to monstrous transfers of energy and matter" (1992, 37). Shigeru Ban, whose work we will discuss below, puts it in rather more simple terms: "It is rare for people to die from the earth shaking beneath them. People die because they are crushed underneath collapsing buildings" (cited in Miyake 2009, 22). When the flows of energy and matter through and around a building are too great, too fast, too intense, then the building is not merely a victim, it joins with nature to become a perpetrator of disaster.

The contemporary era of climate change and mass media generates a virtual stream of natural disasters. Those who have been subject to earthquake, fire, flood or tsunami know just how Janus-faced architecture can be in the unpredictable and intensified flows of energy associated with such disasters: one minute a shelter and refuge, the next minute a weapon. And, thanks to mass media, even those spared such direct experiences watch in horror, as many of us did with the 2011 Tohoku or Great East Japan earthquake and tsunami, as buildings of various kinds switched from looking as frail as paper to being a tormenting projectile, and back again. In what follows we look more closely at the intersection of disaster and architecture. We examine a range of historical and contemporary responses that have evolved in and through the "routine" of disaster. We focus on the interface between cultures of building, architecture, and geology. Taking the biblical texts we began with rather literally, we do so by way of a series of examples relating to houses of God.

CHRISTCHURCH EARTHQUAKES

The earthquake that struck the New Zealand city of Christchurch at 12:51 p.m. on Tuesday, February 22, 2011 wrought devastation across the city. Measuring 6.3 on the Richter scale, its effects were intensified by the fact that the ground upon which Christchurch stands was subject to extensive liquefaction. Buildings that may have withstood the tremors generated by the 6.3 earthquake had foundations that could not withstand the forces of flow and subsidence set off by the earthquake (Tonkins and Taylor 2011). Large swathes of the city's fabric, particularly its center and eastern suburbs, were destroyed. 185 people were killed, and many more were injured.

It was not an isolated event. A severe earthquake (measuring 7.1) had preceded it on September 4, 2010. Two aftershocks (measuring 5.7 and 6.3) followed it on June 13, 2011. Indeed, the complete seismological record for the area shows that since September 2010 Christchurch and the surrounding Canterbury region had been subject to over 10,000 earthquakes and tremors, although most of them were weak or slight, measuring only between 2 and 3 on the Richter scale. When the epicenters and magnitudes of these earthquakes are mapped and animated digitally, what is revealed is a constant seismic peppering of the city and its hinterland. Such disturbance is a routine fact of life in this part of the world.[3]

Of course this kind of seismic record also illustrates, with stark clarity, the scale, speed, and intensity of the earthquake that struck on February 22, 2011. Architecturally speaking, the losses were heavy. Some 100,000 homes, over 3,000 business premises, schools, community buildings, and museums were damaged in one way or another. In the Central Business District some 50 percent of the buildings were severely damaged. Emergency legislation was passed in the form of the Canterbury Earthquake Recovery Act 2011, establishing the Canterbury Earthquake Recovery Authority (CERA), whose task it was to determine which structures were safe and reparable and which were beyond repair and needed to be demolished. CERA established guidelines for demolition, warning that demolition was a complicated process needing building consents, archaeological and heritage assessments, debris waste management plans, and salvage rights protocols. Significantly, CERA also enacted an emergency zoning system for Christchurch, which sought to handle both the immediate issues of making the built environment safe and serviced, and longer-term questions of reconstruction. In a matter of weeks an entirely new map of the city emerged. The four-category emergency rezoning of Christchurch established a gradation for directing the distribution of effort. The zoning system not only assessed the extent of damage to existing buildings, it also sought to assess "the nature of the land that sits underneath communities" such that longer-term decisions could be made about the suitability of a particular area for reconstruction. In the period following the immediate response and rescue stage, the Red Zone was the focus of much of the reconstruction effort. In this zone most buildings and supporting infrastructure were so badly damaged that they required rebuilding. This was also the area that was at high risk of further damage from low levels of shaking (e.g., aftershocks), and the area that posed most risk to the public in terms of building collapse. Access to the Red Zone was controlled for some time after the earthquake—so much so that in response to public curiosity CERA hosted open-access visits that allowed the people of Christchurch to see for themselves the damage to the center of their city. One building in the Red Zone that the residents of Christchurch were very keen to see up close was their iconic Christchurch Cathedral.

Of all the buildings lost or damaged, it was the fate of the Gothic revival Anglican cathedral in the center of the city that encapsulated the enormity of the disaster for both the city and the nation. From the time of its consecration in 1881 the cathedral had come to stand for Christchurch; it was an icon of the city. In the earthquake the cathedral's famous spire collapsed, part of its roof caved in, many of its buttresses cracked, and its structural integrity was compromised—by most accounts—beyond repair. In the immediate aftermath of the earthquake, just some three hours after the event, the then-dean of the cathedral, Peter Beck, insisted that "the partial destruction of the iconic building in today's massive earthquake is unimportant in light of the great human cost the disaster will incur" (NZPA 2011). But in the weeks and months that followed, as the human and infrastructural losses mounted, the material damage to the cathedral, and what this meant for its future, came to bear a nation's grief and shock. The images of this icon in ruins readily absorbed the collective significance of the disaster within the city, both in New Zealand and across the world.

7.1 Christchurch Cathedral, New Zealand,
minutes after the earthquake on
February 22, 2011. Photographer Keith
Lynch, still shaking from the shock,
captures the moment on his camera phone
(Keith Lynch).

7.2 Christchurch Cathedral following the
February 2011 earthquake (James
Braithwaite, Fairfax Press).

DISASTER

The damage to the cathedral was quickly assessed to be irreparable. Warwick Issacs, in his capacity as General Manager (Demolition) of the Canterbury Earthquake Recovery Authority (CERA), wrote to the cathedral's property trustees. The letter began with the matter-of-fact heading: "Demolition of your building at 100 Cathedral Square: Christchurch Cathedral." It spelt out the fate that city engineers and insurance assessors had scripted for the building.

The purpose of this letter is to:

- Advise you that I have determined that your building is dangerous in terms of the Canterbury Earthquake Recovery Act 2011 (CER Act) ... ; and

- Give you notice in accordance with Section 38(4) of the CER Act that your building is to be demolished to the extent necessary to remove the hazards. (Issacs 2011)

Accepting the assessment, the bishop of Christchurch, Victoria Matthews, deconsecrated the cathedral on November 9, 2011, in readiness for what seemed the inevitable. In deconsecrating the ground the bishop had readily ceded to an assessment that was performed under the exceptional authority bestowed upon CERA by the state of emergency. But the bishop's acceptance of this determination did not reflect the views of others. The decision to demolish the remains of the cathedral triggered a long debate on whether the building could or should be restored. It is a controversy that has gripped the nation, drawn attention from commentators worldwide, and to which we return in more detail below.

As its name suggests, Christchurch is a city of churches. This is not surprising, given that it was planned as an Anglican settlement. Not all of the city's churches suffered as the cathedral did on the fateful day of the earthquake. Less than half a mile away, St. Michael and All Angels church (c. 1869) survived relatively unscathed. St. Michael's is a substantial public building in its own right, being the first church in this central region of New Zealand. Its history has been closely intertwined with that of the cathedral. For example, when the cathedral was under construction it was St. Michael's that served as the city's "pro-cathedral"—a parish church temporarily serving as a cathedral. For a brief moment, it was even mooted that Christchurch Cathedral be built on the site of St. Michael's, although ultimately its eventual central city site was settled upon (Press 1864, 2). The two churches also share an architectural lineage that goes beyond their similar Gothic revival style. The architect for St. Michael's, William Crisp, was apprentice to Robert Speechly. It was Speechly who was appointed in 1864 by George Gilbert Scott, architect of Christchurch Cathedral, to oversee its construction.[4]

What accounted for the distinctive fortunes of these two otherwise closely related churches in the earthquake? Some local commentators speculated that it was a theological outcome: that God had spared one but not the other. Did the cathedral suffer because prostitutes worked in nearby Latimer Square? Was its demise proof of the power of New Zealand's self-proclaimed Wizard, who daily stood outside the cathedral's front door offering his alternate theology to anyone who would listen? Could it have been because the cathedral had opened its doors to secular festivals such as the annual laying of fresh flowers in its aisle on the occasion of Christchurch's annual garden festival? Cathedral dean Peter Beck refuted the theological conspirators. Reflecting a now modern Anglicanism that accepts science alongside God, he verified that the Christchurch disaster "was not an act of God" but just "the Earth doing what it does" (cited in Matthews 2011). Such are the vagaries of religiosity in the explanation of natural disasters. In the Christchurch disaster a man of God stands for secular scientific explanation, while in the Katrina disaster a man of politics (President Bush) freely invokes an act of God. Both explanations are, as we have argued, insufficient in and of themselves. As we shall see, the very different fortunes of this pair of churches are far more than a matter of singular causal accounts, scientific or theological. As we have suggested, explaining the scope and reach of "natural" disasters is also a matter of politics, economics, and sociotechnical attributes.

STONE AND WOOD CHURCHES

On June 5, 1869, when St. Michael's was commissioned, it was not long after Christchurch had experienced what is estimated to have been a magnitude 5.7 earthquake. The stone church of St. John's, nearby in Latimer Square, suffered badly in the June earthquake (Daily Southern Cross 1869, 3). The parish committee responsible for commissioning the building and funding its construction proceeded cautiously in their deliberations, mindful not only of the fate of St. John's but also of the tough economic climate. Churchwarden R. J. S. Harman reported to the local press that they and the parishioners "had considered two things—what the church should be built of, wood or stone; and what should be its size." The decision on what the church should be built of was explicitly shaped by the recent earthquake experience: "Owing to the late severe shocks of earthquake, the vestry came to the conclusion that it would be useless to attempt building any part of stone. Therefore it was decided that wood should be the material" (Star 1869, 2). In this decision we see into one early instance of what came to be a national preference in building materials: wood over stone or masonry. Whereas in non-earthquake areas stone is routinely regarded as a more durable building material, here in Christchurch it is the wooden building that stands for longer. The St. Michael's decision, however, was not simply about a hoped-for relative durability. It was also a pragmatic fund-raising decision, which was attuned to the skepticism around using stone for building in this earthquake-

143

prone context. As the Churchwarden noted, it was "also felt that they could not canvass for subscriptions with success *unless* they decided in favor of wood" (Star 1869, 2; emphasis added). As the subscription notice in the local newspaper at the time prominently proclaimed, the proposed "re-building [of] the Parish Church, the temporary Cathedral, the Mother Church of Canterbury" would be "a wooden church on stone foundations" (Jacobs, Harman, and Ainger 1870, 1). Parishioner J. E. Graham noted enthusiastically that the project "would be a great advancement in church architecture" (Star 1869, 2).

St. Michael's was completed in May 1872 and, as planned, was largely wooden. Matai, a native New Zealand species of black pine, was used as the primary structural and cladding material. Columns supporting the arches in the nave were carved from single matai trunks, while huge and intricately carved tie beams supported a corrugated-iron roof. The church was primarily clad with matai weatherboard tongue-and-groove paneling. William Crisp modestly described it as a building "of wood, on stone foundations, with open timber roof of good pitch, and with ample projection at eaves and gable" (Press 1870, 2). Recently, with around 150 years' hindsight, New Zealand's Historic Places Trust could afford to be more expansive. They describe St. Michael's as "a prime example of the Gothic style superbly translated into timber." Crisp's design, they note, drew upon "the style of French Gothic architecture of the fourteenth century, which had been revived in Britain by Victorian architects." The Trust, while also noting the stylistic debts to "George Frederick Bodley's church of St. Michael and All Angels in Brighton, Sussex (1859–1861)," emphasizes the fact that "these influences translated into the vernacular material of New Zealand wood" (Historic Places Trust 2012).

As we have said, the wooden structure of the church rested on stone foundations. As is often the case with civic or religious buildings, there was a symbolic laying of the foundation stone. The event was auspiciously set for the Sunday after the feast of St. Michael and All Angels. The stone was installed to the words of Hymn 295, "[t]his stone to Thee in faith we lay." Crisp, as the church's architect, placed a hermetically sealed glass vase containing a commemorative inscription and copies of contemporary press reports into a cavity in the stone. He then handed a ceremonial trowel to the bishop, who proceeded to spread the mortar ready to receive the stone that was carefully lowered into place. The stone was then struck with a mallet and solemnized with a prayer. During the singing of hymns, led by the combined choirs of neighboring churches, a collection was made in aid of the building fund. The churchwardens "laid upon the stone the offerings of the people," then Sunday school children were allowed to approach the stone and deposit upon it "the several sums they had collected" (Press 1870, 2). In St. Michael's, timber and stone are harmoniously in order.

Timber is instated as the primary building material because it is understood to guarantee for St. Michael's the ability to stand through the damaging effects of an earthquake. In this New Zealand context it was already understood that, architecturally speaking, timber was more durable than stone.

This material order did not, however, find its way into the plans for the development of Christchurch's first cathedral. As the fledgling Anglican settler colony's only cathedral, it carried a heavy burden with respect to collective civic aspirations. The heavier this burden, the more intense the controversy over what building materials should be used, and their capacity to deliver and express the durability desired. As we have said, the building was designed by George Gilbert Scott, whose substantial career output—including 39 cathedrals and 476 churches—saw him regarded, after Pugin, as the architect "most representative" of the Gothic revival (Clark [1928] 1964, 159). It was designed quite literally sight (and site) unseen, for Scott never visited New Zealand. Two locally based architects, first Robert Speechly (to 1873) and subsequently Benjamin Mountfort (from 1873), were appointed as supervising architects. Despite the recent collapse of a stone church and the decision to build St. Michael's in timber, Scott's brief was to produce the design for a stone cathedral. His original design returned, however, with a proposition for a hybrid timber-and-stone structure reinforced with iron. His proposed use of timber was regarded as novel and innovative. In developing the framing he drew inspiration, in part, from medieval barns and other utilitarian buildings in England, which he considered the "humbler remains of our traditional architecture" (cited in Lochhead 1999, 135). In Scott's proposal the timber formed "an internal skeleton" and was "cased in a stone shell." Architectural historian Ian Lochhead was later to claim that the scheme "combined the permanence and dignity of stone with the lighter weight and flexibility of timber" (Lochhead 1999, 134). Scott was aware that Christchurch was earthquake-prone and, with his timber frame proposal, hoped to offer something that was more earthquake-resistant. Both Scott and his supervising architect, Mountfort, understood that it was the timber frame and not the stone casing that carried the building's primary structural load. In an earthquake the timber would have greater capacity than the brittle stone to flex, and accommodate the seismic forces. The scheme sought, therefore, to reconcile both the fears regarding the ability of the building to withstand earthquakes and the aspirations for expressed permanence in stone.

Scott's original hybrid timber-stone scheme met with mixed responses. Mountfort, understanding the experimental space they were in, was worried that the combination of materials might not resolve the earthquake risk at all: "From the different weights of the two materials, wood & stone, I would anticipate a different quality and kind of vibration when they are set in motion by the earth's wave, and one coming to rest before the other and broadside on to it, the result will be a bad fracture of the stone or a crushing of the wood" (cited in Lochhead 1999, 142). James FitzGerald, Canterbury's Emigration Agent in London and an influential figure in the commissioning of the cathedral, was more enthusiastic. He wrote to Bishop Harper, the first bishop of Christchurch and chair of the commissioning group, pointing out that "[f]or the money you will not get a better design than this for a plan." Anticipating resistance to the proposed oak frame, he appealed to the growing common sense about how stone behaves in earthquakes compared to wood: "A large oak framing would be very handsome and it would be so strong that in an earthquake it would stand if the walls were shaken" (cited in Lochhead 1999, 129). There was also the not so trivial matter of timber availability in New Zealand. Scott proposed to prefabricate the timber frame from oak in England and have it shipped to New Zealand in parts. The bishop was still unconvinced and immediately disapproved of the timber frame proposal, insisting that stone be the primary structural material.

A public debate on the substitution of wood for stone ensued. Honorary Secretary to the Cathedral Commission Henry Jacobs noted in a letter to the editor of the local newspaper, the *Press*, that the proposal for timber framing was inappropriate given the difficulty in accessing suitable timber locally and the expense of shipping prefabricated frames from England. He reported that Scott had been sent a suggestion "to build the piers [of the nave] of stone, together with some information as to the facilities of obtaining stone" (Jacobs 1863, 4). Scott himself acknowledged the difficulty of sourcing the timber, and proposed "an alternative plan made for a *stone* arcade and clerestory" (cited in Lochhead 1999, 139). There is some suggestion that Scott dragged his heels in submitting the stone alternative in the hope that his original wood-framed design would prevail (Lochhead 1999, 139).

Others with interests in the cathedral expressed "grave doubt as to the wisdom of this alteration" from wood to stone (Press 1865, 3). One well-informed set of parishioners with a notable architectural sensibility penned a letter to the local newspaper justifying their views in detail. To use stone, they argued, was to ignore the fact of Christchurch's susceptibility to earthquakes.

> First, because it is idle to ignore the fact that the whole of these islands have been at one time or another visited by dangerous earthquakes. Not long ago we heard an old New Zealand settler, a gentleman well acquainted with geological science, lamenting, after a visit to Christchurch, at the lofty rubble stone walls he saw built there, all of which he felt sure would some day be shaken down. (Press 1865, 3)

In their view the insistence on stone was simply a misplaced convention with respect to church architecture, and particularly so in the case of a "modern" New World church:

146

we always regret the introduction of large stone columns into any modern church, where they obstruct light and sound, and are totally incongruous with the requirements of a modern service. It is simply a superstition in architecture. (Press 1865, 3)

Other correspondents made equally ardent and articulate pleas in favor of wood. Some of these cases were on the basis of economy: "It ought to be of wood, not stone. A wooden building would not cost more than one-fifth the price of a stone building of equal architectural decoration." The matter of cost was not easily settled with respect to this planned major work. That is because it was unclear if the project would be proceeding with the benefit of the completion of a railway to the stone quarries at Heathcote Valley to the South of the city. As stone supporters argued, the completion of the railway would reduce the cost of building in stone "to at least one-half of the present … some say even to one-third" (Press 1863, 1).

The relative merits of stone versus wood with respect to the quality of durability plagued this controversy. It was the assumed superior durability of stone, as both a structural and an expressive fact, which underscored the bishop's insistence on that material. He and his Cathedral Commission felt that stone was the only material that could meet the planned "magnitude" of the cathedral project, which was to provide a large-scale and permanent place of worship (Press 1865, 3). In the minds of the Cathedral Commission, the longevity of a building's material should be closely calibrated to the building's useful life. The cathedral, being a building with a long projected life, should be constructed of stone, they concluded.[5] In a letter to the *Press*, the bishop and his Commission condescendingly conceded that some smaller churches might be suitably built in wood, but that this was simply not appropriate for a cathedral. This group of stone supporters recognized the "sad folly of building *small* stone churches," judging that using durable material for such buildings was "useless and wasteful," and ignored the fact that lesser religious buildings might "become useless long before the more perishable materials have decayed" (Press 1865, 3). Naturally, such misplaced aspirations—the likelihood of future obsolescence—could not possibly apply to the cathedral dreamt of by these visionaries.

Which material type bestowed durability on a building was, however, at the very heart of this controversy. Those advocating wood argued, as we saw above, that its flexibility would ensure the cathedral would survive earthquakes. Others in the controversy clung to stone as the more durable material. Others again felt that durability was an entirely misplaced aspiration in this New World context.

Stone has little advantage over wood, except in its durability, and durability is not wanted in a country where nothing can be possibly built now which will not be swept away as worthless in twenty or thirty years. (Press 1862, 1)

It is clear that this Christchurch resident, unlike the bishop, had already accepted that buildings in his earthquake-prone home might have to operate through a different temporality to those of Old World Britain.

Mountfort could see no structural or architectural reason for substituting timber for stone. "There were no special structural reasons for the abandonment of the wood," he reflected. But as the detailed design work proceeded, he recognized that "the general feeling was so averse to the idea of a Cathedral being built in any other material than stone, that the wood was abandoned and the stone interior substituted" (cited in Lochhead 1999, 143). The construction of the cathedral went ahead, according to Bishop Harper's original wishes, in stone.

Incompatibility between too tall, rigid, stone buildings and the seismically active context was manifest even before the cathedral was complete. As the site was being prepared for the construction, two significant earthquakes struck. The seismic activity left Mountfort with reservations about the change from wood to stone. Writing to the cathedral's prime architect, Scott, he confessed: "I should not feel comfortable as to the possible consequences of any movement in the [stone] substructure" (cited in Lochhead 1999, 142). Scott responded in 1874 with a design that was even more radical in its use of wood than the original 1863 proposal. Again it was rejected. To settle the matter once and for all, a third "neutral" voice, that of Christchurch-based architect W. B. Armson, was called upon to adjudicate. Armson, whose neutrality is in doubt because of his ongoing role as a consultant to the Anglican Church, found in favor of stone (Lochhead 1999, 143).

Despite Mountfort's variously expressed worries about replacing timber with stone, he ultimately oversaw the construction of a stone edifice. Indeed, following Scott's death in 1878, Mountfort was responsible for key variations that suggest that he gave in entirely to the local pressure for stone. Most significant of these was his redesign of the spire. At the request of a donor, one Robert Heaton Rhodes, Mountfort replaced Scott's timber-framed spire with a "stone spire with massive pyramidal pinnacles at its base" (Lochhead 1999, 144). The new spire was taller, heavier, and more brittle in structure. It was completed by May 1881, and the cathedral was consecrated in November of that year. The spire quickly became the most recognizable landmark of Christchurch. As a visitor from Auckland observed in 1881, "The lofty and graceful spire is the first object which [the visitor] sees when approaching Christchurch by train from the port, and the last which he loses sight of many miles out to sea" (cited in Lochhead 1999, 147).

Within a month of the cathedral's consecration, Christchurch was struck by a strong earthquake. While no serious damage was inflicted on the cathedral, some of the stonework at the top of its spire was displaced and fractured. The spire was repaired and its stone cladding was reinforced with iron (Lochhead 1999, 147). A further earthquake struck the city in 1888. An eyewitness reported that its seismic force caused a number of the stones to "shoot out" of the spire structure. The spire then "swayed for a second or two, having a peculiarly weird effect in the kind of half-light which prevailed, and then ... when the violence of the shock was over, down toppled the whole of the topmost portion" (Press 1901, 5).

The steeple of Christchurch Cathedral may well have been a city landmark that spoke to the triumphant success of this Anglican New World settlement, but it was also serving as an omen of a fate yet to come. After the 1888 quake, Mountfort proposed a lighter, hollow structure, topped by a counterbalanced cross "to allow of swaying." This time stone cladding was rejected and brick was used, on the advice of the Irish-born architect and engineer James Thomas Waters. Waters had extensive experience in working in earthquake-prone Japan, where he had been appointed as one of the so-called *yatoi*—"hired foreigners"— brought in by the Meiji government to assist with their modernization project.[6] His Japanese work experience lasted around 13 years (1864–1877) and focused mainly on the reconstruction of the Ginza quarter of Tokyo, whose timber houses had been lost in the famous fire of 1872. Waters's reconstruction replaced the city's traditional wood construction with the fireproof material of brick and added a modern, Western-style look to the city (Cybriwsky 2011, 80, 265). The *Press* reported excitedly on his experience in Japan, "where earthquakes are frequent," and his advice carried weight because of it. Unsurprisingly, given his extensive experience of working with brick in Japan, Waters "brought forward the suggestion ... that the renewal should be in fire[ed] brick" (Press 1901, 5).[7] As it turns out, Waters's experience with brick was in the name of modernization more than earthquake resilience. In the Great Kanto Earthquake of 1923, most of the buildings in Ginza bricktown were destroyed (Cybriwsky 2011, 80). But hindsight was not available to those worrying away at solving the problem of the cathedral's spire. His suggestion to rebuild in brick was accepted.

The innovation provided no guarantees for the steeple, and no answer to the question of whether the cathedral had been built with the best materials for an earthquake-prone area. In 1901 Christchurch was hit by another earthquake, and again the spire suffered damage: the *Press* report on the event reminds us of how damage to the spire was becoming routine:

> Saturday's earthquake and its effect on the spire of the Cathedral at once recalled to the minds of all who could remember it the even more disastrous shock, as far as Christchurch was concerned, of September 1st, 1888.... The spire had already been injured by the eathquake [sic] of December 5th, 1881, which brought down a large mass of stone from the point where the tapering stone work is crowned by the cap supporting the finial stone. (Press 1901, 5)

7.3 Photograph of crowd outside Christchurch Cathedral with earthquake damage to spire, September 1, 1888 (Anonymous, Alexander Turnbull Library).

The material used to construct the spire was again in public debate. It was, the *Press* reflected, understood that "solid masonry" and the "bolting through" of the spire was the problem in the earlier earthquakes, a problem that the application of brick was supposed to remedy. The *Press* correspondent concluded that this latest incident of earthquake "re-opens the question as to whether that re-building was satisfactory, or whether the old suggestion of a wooden spire will at length have to be adopted" (Press 1901, 5). Church governors were also reflecting back on their original decisions, and following the 1901 earthquake the brick spire of the cathedral was replaced by a timber and copper-clad structure (Press 1901, 5). Ian Lochhead has argued that the copper-clad spire exists "as a conspicuous record of the cathedral's vulnerability to seismic events" (Lochhead 1999, 147). It also shrouds a history of controversy, at the center of which stands the question of which materials would generate a more permanent edifice in this earthquake-prone New World setting.

The repeated incidents of spire collapse at the cathedral stand in sharp contrast to the relatively incident-free history of the cathedral's near neighbor, the timber-built St. Michael's. On the occasion of the devastating 2011 earthquake, this difference was starkly articulated. St. Michael's survived relatively unscathed. The cathedral was, as we have seen, all but destroyed. With the cathedral inoperable, there was no choice but to hold the service to commemorate those who had died in the disaster at St. Michael's. For the people of Christchurch the debate was over: the proof of what that nation had come to learn over decades of building was all around them. It was a timber church that held their grief and bore their hopes for recovery. Timber was the more durable material. The cathedral stood in ruins because it had insisted on a durability that did not belong in this place.

The evidence was repeated throughout Christchurch, as the quake damage postmortem revealed. Other timber churches like St. Michael's had emerged from the quake virtually unscathed. The timber sections of public buildings, such as the Provincial Council Buildings, "suffered little damage," and "that which occurred was largely the result of falling masonry" (Lochhead 2012, 6). Hybrid timber-structured and stone-clad churches—"descendants of Scott's unbuilt cathedral design" (Lochhead 2012, 8)—also fared well. Engineering assessments of the city's building stock also showed that low-rise timber structures performed well and in many instances provided "vital support" to unreinforced masonry elements (Hare 2012, 7). Assessment of other types of engineered timber structures—industrial buildings, schools, water tanks, swimming pools, housing, community buildings, and bridges—also concluded that they behaved "remarkably well" in the Canterbury earthquakes (Buchanan, Carradine, and Jordan 2011, 401).

As the early parishioners of St. Michael's instinctively sensed, as Scott and Mountfort understood, and as has been confirmed by many of New Zealand's building scientists subsequently, timber structures perform well in earthquakes. They do so because they are intrinsically lighter and are composed of a large number of smaller elements, so have the ability to distribute load along multiple paths (Deam 1997, 3). As Lochhead concludes, "one of the lessons learned [from the 2011 earthquakes] is that our colonial timber Gothic buildings are very resilient." The reservations which both Gilbert Scott and Benjamin Mountfort expressed over the building of Christ Church Cathedral using conventional load-bearing masonry construction "have been vindicated." Ironically, "the damage that has occurred to Scott's Cathedral can only serve to enhance his reputation rather than detract from it" (Lochhead 2012, 8).

Of course, material composition alone cannot determine the fortunes of one building over another in the context of a natural disaster. Many reinforced masonry buildings do survive earthquakes, such as the Palace Hotel and US Mint buildings in the San Francisco earthquake of 1906 (Tobriner 2006, 166). The fire that followed in the aftermath of that earthquake also consumed many of the timber buildings that had survived. The fate of a building in an earthquake does not rest on one "magic" element, be it a building material, structural system, construction practice, or geological fortune (Tobriner 2006, 167). That said, building materials matter, not simply because of any intrinsic quality but because they "behave" in extensive socio-technical-ecological relations. The story of Christchurch's religious buildings reminds us that the qualities of individual building materials with respect to the forces and flows of natural hazards are recalibrated by the architectural techniques that combine them in and through design. Their qualities are also called upon to carry and express wider cultural and economic values, such as the aspirations of a settler colony to create a permanent edifice. It is this more complex socio-technical-ecological rationality that determines how a building functions in the face of a natural hazard.

152   This relational lens brings into focus not just the power of the earthquake, nor merely the relative merits of specific building materials, but the relationship between these constituent parts and other features. The architectural outcomes of an earthquake are the result of transactions between the seismic activity below the earth and the architectural decisions taken on its surface. In the instance of Christchurch we see how foundational deliberations—literally and figuratively—shaped the fortunes of a building that was built for durability but with materials that militated against that very quality. It reminds us, too, of the importance of architectural experimentation as embodied in Scott's original structural design for the cathedral, which involved a load-bearing timber structure with a stone—or URM/unreinforced masonry—casing. It was precisely such

structural design that was assessed by engineers to have performed so well in the 2011 earthquake. The cathedral in Christchurch not only enshrined the hopes and aspirations of a fledgling settlement, it also enshrined the dogmatism of Old World Anglicanism, against the mood of experiment and innovation that the New World context and all its challenges presented. That willfulness was embedded in stone which, in the context of local seismicity, turned against that mood and incubated the disaster that finally befell the cathedral. It was, in short, an accident waiting to happen. Stone expressed, but also ultimately foreshortened, the cathedral's own vanity of durability

The designs for both Christchurch Cathedral and St. Michael's involved, in effect, the transportation of stylistic and structural protocols of a European-derived Gothic architecture into New World contexts. The controversy was in part generated by whether this transportation of style would extend to the materials used. Was this a transportation of a style (stone to stone), or was it a translation (stone to timber)?

This controversy around the appropriate material for Gothic architecture was already present in Europe. Gothic architecture, as art historian Otto von Simson argues, was innovative and distinctive for its recognizable structural features, such as "the cross-ribbed vault, the pointed arch, or the flying buttresses." It was the way these structural features shaped appearance through the use of light which best articulated the "new relationship between function and form" found in Gothic architecture (Simson 1956, 3–4). Whereas older Romanesque architecture had functioned merely as "a scaffold for the display of great murals or mosaics," in Gothic architecture "ornamentation is entirely subordinated to the pattern produced by the structural members, the vault ribs and supporting shafts." The whole Gothic "aesthetic system" is determined by these (Simson 1956, 5). The stone medium lay at the heart of the Gothic aesthetic system, integral to realizing the unique relationship between structure and appearance.[8]

Championing the Gothic revival in the early nineteenth century in his book *The True Principles of Pointed or Christian Architecture*, Augustus Pugin appraises the conventional preference for stone. As he notes, Gothic architecture was conceived in, and realized through, stone. Wood was used only as a "last resort," and then "as a case of absolute necessity" (Pugin 1853, 31). In Pugin's view this commitment to stone meant that wood was misunderstood and marginalized as a building material. As a consequence, many modest wooden buildings were "mutilated or utterly destroyed" without consideration of the "cost of their demolition." "But, alas!" he lamented, "[h]ow many equally fine roofs have been demolished and burnt by the brutal ignorance of parish functionaries!—how many have been daubed over by the remorseless whitewash!—how many painted in vile imitation of marble!" (Pugin 1853, 32). The design principles Pugin promoted in the name of Gothic revival were already modernist in sensibility, developing a feeling for the "honest" expression of materials, including wood. Pugin recognized, for example, that wood is "founded on quite opposite principles to those of stone." "The strength of wood-work is attained by bracing the various pieces together on geometrical principles," as was evident in the ancient roofs of churches and domestic buildings. He adds: "the construction of these, so far from being concealed, is turned into ornament." As he concludes, "this essential portion of a building becomes its greatest beauty" (Pugin 1853, 30).

CARDBOARD CHURCHES

On Monday, April 16, 2012, just over one year after the earthquake commemoration service at St. Michael's, the bishop of Christchurch, Victoria Matthews, accompanied by Richard Gray from the newly formed Transitional Cathedral Group, jointly announced their intention to work with architect Shigeru Ban on a new "Transitional Cathedral." The project was proposed for Christchurch's Latimer Square, where the stone Gothic revival church of St. John's once stood. It was, as noted above, the damage suffered by this church in 1869 that convinced the parishioners of nearby St. Michael's to forsake stone for wood. Ban's temporary structure is in every way different to the philosophy of building a stone edifice that was foundational to both St. John's and its mother church, the cathedral. Its purpose is not to offer a permanent edifice to God, but to "serve as a place for community worship and gathering until a new permanent cathedral is built" (Christchurch Cathedral 2012). It is expected to last ten years. Despite fundraisers facing budget increases (due, among other things, to stringent safety regulations), building consent for the cardboard cathedral was granted in July 2012. Work began on the foundations on the 24th of that month, and a week-long festival celebrating the completion of the cathedral was held in August 2013.

154
The idea for a temporary cathedral was broached following the February 2011 earthquake by members of the Christchurch Anglican diocese. After seeing post-disaster projects by Shigeru Ban in Japan, Italy, and Rwanda, they approached the architect asking him to consider designing for Christchurch. The brief reflected the diverse space requirements of a modern cathedral, extending beyond simply the cathedral itself. It called for a 700-seat cathedral space, but also a suite of ancillary facilities for concerts, exhibitions, and civic and community events, as well as a set of smaller spaces to accommodate a café, shop, meeting rooms, and offices. Ban responded enthusiastically. For anyone who knows his work, it will come as no surprise that he proposed cardboard tubes for the primary structure of the cathedral. He further suggested that the ancillary buildings be composed of linked shipping containers located alongside the cathedral.

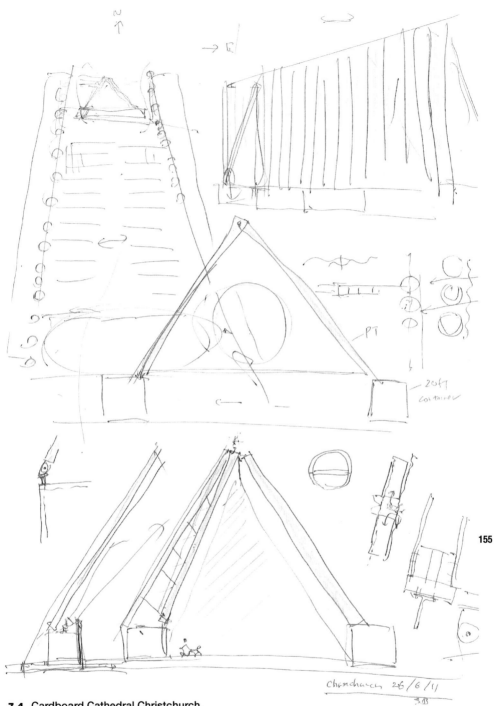

7.4 Cardboard Cathedral Christchurch,
sketch, 2011 (Shigeru Ban).

DISASTER

The building complex would also incorporate structural timber and steel where needed, and would rest on concrete foundations. For all of this complexity, it was the idea of a cathedral constructed of cardboard that captured the public imagination. The contradiction of cardboard, that most humble, ephemeral, and usually disposable of materials, serving as the structure of a grand, albeit temporary, religious edifice proved irresistible for commentators. The project launch was reported internationally, with almost all headlines celebrating the cardboard. On that occasion Dean Peter Beck reflected that Anglicanism had traveled a long way from the didactic visions of the cathedral's founders. For him, Ban's cardboard cathedral "has a really nice feel about it. It's almost tent-like, and I like the idea of pitching our tent in the center of the city" (cited in ONE News 2011).

The official media release for the design focused on both the structural and symbolic dimensions of paper and cardboard as materials for the new building. Structurally speaking, paper was lauded, for although it "may appear to be a fragile material … it is also able to bear substantial pressure." Symbolically, this quality of strength in fragility was likened to the people of Christchurch themselves: "the same could be said of the people who have suffered from the Christchurch earthquakes" (Christchurch Catheral 2012, 2). Ban's status as a Japanese architect also mattered, just as Thomas Waters's Japanese connections had mattered all those years ago as the cathedral governors sought to resolve the problem of the unsteady spire. Increasingly New Zealanders see their country as part of a shared community of earthquake-vulnerable places located along the Pacific's ring of fire. Engaging Ban would, the proponents of the project argued, "build links with Japan" (Christchurch Catheral 2012, 3).

Compelling evidence for Ban's suitability to the Christchurch project was offered by his design for Takatori Kyokai Church, in Kobe, Japan. Following the earthquake that destroyed so much of Kobe in 1995, Ban designed what he dubbed the "paper-tube church." The church it was to replace had primarily served Vietnamese refugees, and while it survived the seismic activity, it burned down in a fire started in the earthquake's immediate aftermath. Ban's new church was intended to offer the congregation a temporary place to worship and gather. It needed to be simple, cheap, and capable of being assembled quickly by volunteer labor. His design consisted of 58 lightweight cardboard tubes—each 5 meters in height, 330 millimeters in diameter, and 15 millimeters thick—which operated as columns supporting a tent-like, Teflon-coated fabric roof. The cardboard columns, arranged in an oval, also defined the main gathering space in the center of the church. A rectangular volume clad with translucent plastic panels enclosed these columns. An overhanging roof was later added to the front of the church. As designed, the church building measured just 168 square meters. It was complete and fully functioning just nine months after the disaster (Ban 1999, 44).[9]

7.5 Cardboard Cathedral Christchurch,
model, 2011 (Shigeru Ban).

DISASTER

Intended to be a temporary building, the paper-tube church remained on site until 2005, some ten years after its completion. By this time, the Takatori congregation had expanded and could no longer be accommodated in Ban's modestly sized building. By the time of the last service in 2005 the church had achieved some notoriety. Simply pulling it down and binning the cardboard was considered inappropriate, despite this being precisely what Ban had anticipated. Instead, those associated with the church began to consider alternative scenarios of reuse. Entertaining the concept of such afterlives was made possible by the fact that the cardboard structure, although designed to be ephemeral and temporary, had retained its integrity.

Around the time that Ban's paper church was being decommissioned and its afterlife (or not) contemplated, a ceremony commemorating the tenth anniversary of the Kobe earthquake was held. It was attended by Liao Chia-Chan, then chairman of the New Homeland Foundation, a Taiwanese charity focused on regional development in that country. Liao heard of the fate of the Takatori church at the ceremony, and began exploring the possibility of relocating the building to Puli, a city in Nantou County in the Taomi region of Taiwan. That area, too, had suffered a substantial earthquake, albeit some years before, in 1999. In 2005 it was still recovering economically. Much of the recovery effort was centered around capitalizing on the tourist potential of this area. Liao thought the paper-tube church would serve as a focus for this effort, as a community center and tourist draw. It could also serve as shrine to the 1999 earthquake. Further to this, and in a predictable development frame, the relocation of the church had the potential to operate as an "exchange platform" between Japan and Taiwan on matters of earthquake recovery. Ban's structure was disassembled, transported to, then re-erected on its new site in the township of Puli. A further membrane of steel and polycarbonate was added to the original structure by the design of local architect Jay W. Chiu to aid waterproofing. The new structure opened to the public in Puli on May 25, 2008. As David Chen reported, "over 1000 people participated in lifting cardboard tubes and witnessed [its] rebirth." Along the way, Ban's paper church was renamed the "Paper Dome" (Chen 2009a, 16).

The cardboard structure and the ethos of ephemerality associated with it suited the post-earthquake development trajectory of Puli (with a population of 12,000), which focused on ecotourism and was directed toward forming what Taiwan dubs the Taomi Ecological Community. The recycling of the building, its modest materials, and its history that links it to the Kobe earthquake are all celebrated in the area's official ecotourism branding. As Chen noted:

> the new locale adds a new significance to the Paper Dome.... When the quake struck, Taomi had lost more than half of its buildings and was already on the verge of economic collapse as one of Puli's poorest villages. After the

7.6 Disassembly of Takatori church, Kobe, 2005 (Meel-Ya Chen, Newhomeland Foundation, Taiwan).

7.7 Loading cardboard columns of former Takatori church, Kobe, to container for shipping to Taiwan, 2005 (Meei-Ya Chen, Newhomeland Foundation, Taiwan).

DISASTER

7.8 Remaining foundations at Takatori church site, September 2005 (Marcus Trimble).

7.9 Blessing foundations of new site for Paper Dome (the former Takatori church), with cardboard columns stacked in the background, 2005. Puli, Nantou district, Taiwan (Meei-Ya Chen, Newhomeland Foundation, Taiwan).

7.10 Ceremonial raising of cardboard column, 2005. Puli, Nantou district, Taiwan (Meei-Ya Chen, Newhomeland Foundation, Taiwan.

7.11 New Paper Dome building located on its site in Puli, Nantou district, Taiwan, 2012 (Nan-wei Wu and Liang-ping Yen).

7.12 Inauguration of the Paper Dome commemorating the "921" (September 21, 1999) earthquake in Taiwan in 1999. Shigeru Ban and parish priest preside.

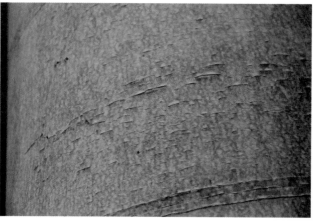

7.13 Water-stained columns at the
Paper Dome building, 2012
(Nan-wei Wu and Liang-ping Yen).

7.14 Cracking surface of the card-
board column at the Paper
Dome building, 2012 (Nan-wei
Wu and Liang-ping Yen).

quake, it was reborn as an eco-tourism destination and now offers a successful example of post-disaster recovery based on environmental conservation. (Chen 2009a, 16)

Tourist numbers climbed in the years after the construction of the "dome," which also prompted a revival in paper-related crafts (Chen 2009a, 16).

The shifting of the building had its own modifying effects on its cardboard structure. The higher humidity in Taiwan caused the cardboard columns to swell, and so deflect from their stone foundations (Chen cited in Wu and Yen 2012). The columns were also exposed to rain during the move from Kobe. This has left a number of curious stains and streaks; curious, because the marks seem to defy gravity by traveling horizontally around the columns. The stronger sunlight in Taiwan also causes concern for the durability of the cardboard. These material fragilities had an unexpected rejuvenating effect on the local paper-making cottage industry. Some of the more vulnerable columns are repaired and supplemented by paper made in local factories. This is a matter of material necessity, cultural promotion, and "regional brand development" (Chen cited in Wu and Yen 2012). Deputy Director of the Paper Dome Meei-Ya Chen said: "We hope these kind of traditional cultural factories can be seen again. The traditional cultural factories are not only tradition, but also a new face. We hope the new cultural creative brand can be seen here" (cited in Wu and Yen 2012).

There was some discussion among the Paper Dome community on whether to paint over the stains on the other columns. It was decided to leave them as they were. Chen reflects: "we thought [painting the columns] would damage their original appearance." In addition, it was felt that as the "water stains mean a memory, a story," they are worth keeping. These water stains "are the most original memories and performance" of the building.

> Basically, I love [the Paper Dome] very much. It is very beautiful, especially during the night. I love to contemplate in the church at night. In my opinion, the Paper Dome in Taiwan helps us to think about the meaning and function we expect to have. Because we went through the rebuilding process after the 921 earthquake, we hope that friends, both domestic and international, could help in finding answers to the rebuilding process after earthquakes here. The Paper Dome could become a place of passing experience. (cited in Wu and Yen 2012)

Ban's paper church was never meant to have an afterlife. It was designed to serve a temporary purpose, and to be replaced when a permanent church was rebuilt. The temporary nature of the church is often linked specifically to the paper materials used by Ban. But for Ban, *paperness* has no necessary or exclusive relationship to the temporary nature of the building: "It is not that it is made out of paper that it is temporary; the church can stay [put] like that" (cited in Quinejure 2006).

163

Certainly, as Ban admits, building in paper is relatively cheap and his tubes are light and easy to assemble, allowing a building to go up without the resources needed for a more permanent structure. But the people he built for did not see the paperness of the building as part of its temporariness. As an experienced builder, Ban notes, "[p]eople felt that I had made no difference between temporary and permanent. That's just how this kind of architecture works." Ban is interested in paper as what he calls a "weak material," widely used in traditional Japanese architecture in the form of soji screens. But he also stresses that it is really "log cabins and Greek architecture" that motivate his tectonic. "According to me there is no real difference between temporary and permanent houses, or between refugee shelters and on-order houses. The quality must remain the same" (cited in Quinejure 2006).

At the same time, Ban is interested in weak materials and understands that they can operate more effectively in seismic situations. As he puts it, "Resistance to earthquakes is my main concern" (cited in Quinejure 2006). On his use of paper and cardboard in architecture, Ban notes that it is not a consequence of some inherent "ecological consciousness," but that "I simply dislike wasting materials. If we could find more than two uses for one material, resource, labor and cost efficiency would be improved." The first time he used paper tubes in an architectural context, for example, was when he adapted the leftover materials following an exhibition of Emilio Ambasz's work in 1985. "It seemed a shame to waste. They were turned into ceiling panels, partitions, and display stands, marking the beginning of paper architecture" (Ban 1999, 49).

RUIN

It is impossible to speak about architecture's endings without addressing the ruin. Yet to do so now seems rather redundant. So much has already been said about ruins, and fascination with them continues to find new expression in experiential and representational realms. As Rose Macaulay noted in *Pleasure of Ruins*, we have through the ages "meditated before ruins, rhapsodized before them, mourned pleasurably over" them. Our motivations in doing so are diverse and contradictory: "aesthetic pleasure in its present appearance ... morbid pleasure in decay ... righteous pleasure in retribution ... mystical pleasure in the destruction of all things mortal and the eternity of God ... egoistic satisfaction in surviving ... masochistic joy in a common destruction" (Macaulay 1953, xv–xvi). In the context of modernity the ruin, and states of ruination, have a particular hold. We have already talked extensively about capitalism's logics of creative destruction and the destructive wake of modernizing visions of various kinds. Walter Benjamin's reflection on Klee's Angel of History is so often cast into the air in contemporary commentary on ruination that his wings must surely be tattered and torn. If he is still looking back with despair across a ruined landscape as the winds of progress drive him forward, then he may well be fluttering there by a feather. He may also be wondering which way is back and which way is forward. As for ruins, Benjamin knew only too well that there was more to them than a past architecture lingering in the present. The cult that formed around ruins was for Benjamin a product of modernity's obsession with the passing of time projected onto the demise of things (Huyssen 2006, 11). In his formulation of a "Baroque cult of the ruin," Benjamin ([1928] 1998) suggested that the ruin stands as a register both of the passing of time and of resistance to time's destructive forces. Moreover, certain aesthetics incorporate in their creative essence the expressed fragility of anticipated ruination, as in the case of the baroque. Derrida noted just this point in relation to architecture when he observed that the baroque was precisely the realization that "[i]n the past, great architectural inventions constituted their essential destructibility, even their fragility, as a resistance to destruction or as a monumentalization of the ruin itself" (Derrida 1990, 11).

In what follows we chart old and new fascinations with ruins. We do so in a context where architecture itself has declared that the "age of the authentic ruin is over" (Huyssen 2006, 20). We are concerned with what ruins mean (and don't mean) for architecture's creative journey. In part the chapter treads familiar ground for those who know ruins and the scholarship on them. But it also seeks to push architectural thinking about ruins in new directions. Central to our task here is to interrogate what it is that the ruin stands for or offers to those who encounter it and enthuse about it. For example, during the eighteenth century ancient Roman ruins were valued as empirical evidence of a lost golden classical age. This then gave way to a more impressionistic appreciation of ruins and their capacity, even as contrived reproductions, to stimulate subjective emotions such as melancholy (Hunt 1992, 128). In late modern social sciences of high-rise housing, ruinous conditions stood for social and architectural dysfunction—the absence of proper infrastructures for modern living. In the covert building explorations of contemporary ruin enthusiasts, we might ponder what excesses (of sanitized, commodified, and programmed space) feed their yearning for spaces that are dilapidated, illegal, and unscripted. In each of these instances, the ruin's positivity depends on what it does not have—completeness, full form, order. In this sense the ruin is rarely received merely in and of itself, for itself. It usually carries with it that which it is not—an absence, a loss, a hope, an ideal. But there are contexts and settings where ruinous conditions operate through a different logic. This is the realm of the informal. Informal architectures are not the *once was* that has degenerated into the evidence for another (lost) way of being. They are the ready-to-hand products of what is possible in this moment and under these circumstances. They are by many standards (those of health authorities, planners, perhaps even their aspirational creators) insufficient architectures. Without professional designers they are not, some would say, architecture at all. Because of these very features, informal architectures offer us ways to see other processes of design and improvisation, alternative logics of value and valuation, and distinctive temporalities of duration and decay. They take our interests away from ruins *per se*, and toward the shifting and circumstantial nature of ruination. In what follows we wish to view architectural ruins through a mobile and uncertain lens of value. We are not simply suggesting that because value is relative, ruins mean different things to different people at different times, or are valued differently over time, although that is true and we do address it. We turn our attention not to the value of the stabilized ruin artifact, but to the very question of what alternative values lay in ruination as a process.

168

RUINOUS CREATIVITY

It is rare to talk about the ruin in functional terms. In *The Aesthetics of Ruins* ([1970] 2004), for example, Robert Ginsberg notes that the ruin is in essence a building that has undergone a loss of function, at least with respect to its previous use. Architecturally speaking, the ruin has conventionally sat within the realm of aesthetics, and what Dylan Trigg (2006) has called "the absence of reason." Much of the irrationality of ruination is about the return of nature, and not merely in the form of some polite patination or a few roosting pigeons. Nature's return, as a central feature of ruination, was highlighted by Georg Simmel. For Simmel, the ruin exhibits a unique balance between "mechanical, inert matter which passively resists pressure" (inert architecture) and what he called "informing spirituality" or "natural forces," which "push upward." The "shift" that architecture experiences under conditions of ruination is a "cosmic tragedy," for it marks "nature's revenge" (1959, 259). It reminds the creative onlooker that "nature has a never completely extinguished, rightful claim to his work." This chastening realization places human creative agency back in line with the general economy of the cosmos.

Part of what dictates the not-so-fine line between obsolescence and ruin is that the building that manages to enter the category of ruin somehow withstands, or avoids, or has yet to meet, the fate of demolition. But another part is based on what is accumulated in this state of being spared. A lengthy past allows a building to accumulate loss: brokenness, bentness, excrescence, staining. All of these seemingly negative attributes—these so-called "injuries of time," as John Ruskin (1857, 165) put it—are precisely what lovers of ruination deem positive and valuable. Ruskin noted the special attraction of what he called "the lower picturesque," which comprised an appreciation not only of the "ruin" but of more general conditions of "disorder." Some who came across such scenes were filled with "regret," seeing them not as pleasurable to the senses, but as evidence of expiration, abandonment, and impoverishment. The lover of the lower picturesque, by contrast, viewed both ruin and disorder with equal "delight":

> He alone delights in both; it matters not of what. Fallen cottage—desolate villa—deserted village—blasted heath—mouldering castle—to him, so that they do but show jagged angles of stone and timber, all are sights equally joyful. Poverty, and darkness, and guilt, bring in their several contributions to his treasury of pleasant thoughts. The shattered window, opening into black and ghastly rents of wall, the foul rag or straw wisp stopping them, the dangerous roof, decrepit floor and stair, ragged misery or wasting age of the inhabitants,—all these conduce, each in due measure, to the fulness of his satisfaction. (Ruskin 1857, 9)

Ruskin questioned the motives of those who joyously reveled in impaired buildings, himself included (Macarthur 2007, 97). He wondered if he and his type were "heartless," succumbing to the organic upholstery of ruination and allowing it to cover over the cruelties and violations—poverty, natural disaster, war, famine—from which it came. Yet he concluded that the lower picturesque is important precisely because it registers these more unsettling signs of an "accumulation of loss" alongside the picturesque "injuries of time." This sensitivity for both disorder and ruins "ought to be cultivated," Ruskin proposed, so that it might support a more critical and knowing attitude toward the violations, aesthetic and otherwise, of modernization.

Writing as she did about the ruins of a war-torn Britain, Macaulay (1953, 453) saw newly created ruins as "stark and bare, vegetationless and creatureless." These war-damaged buildings were not yet ruins proper, for they still "smel[t] of fire and mortality." Not so the ruin of the picturesque, which "enshrined ruins as consummate exemplars of the irregular, the accidental and the natural." These proper ruins had evidence of time passing. They were buildings that stood against time and in time. This temporality has drawn the ruin into a field of aesthetic and philosophical reflection the likes of which most other architectures rarely enjoy.

The ruin is poised between wholeness and complete dissolution. Stabilized so, it has fed the imagination and practice of architecture for centuries. For example, J. B. Jackson (1980, 102) argued, in his classic essay "The Necessity of Ruins," that "ruins provide the incentive for restoration," and serve as the motor of authentic history. But they are not only a mechanism for looking back. They carry us forward too. Nowhere is this more evident than in the late-eighteenth- and early-nineteenth-century architectural fascination with the ruins of ancient Rome. As Frank Salmon (2000) has shown, almost every European architect of note in that period went to study in Rome. In Britain, he observes, fashionable eighteenth-century architects subscribed to a "cult of the ruin." This interest in ruins cohered around the circle of architects associated with Robert Adam, and carried on to the early nineteenth century through the likes of John Soane. A visit to Rome was considered central to any ambitious architect's career plans.[1] The purpose of their visit was the study of ruins, or antiquities:

> When they got to Rome, the students saw the ruins first and foremost as pieces of buildings, to be physically pored over, perhaps imaginatively restored and certainly made use of in various ways in new buildings. (Salmon 2000, 19)

Such ruins must have reminded their eager architect-scholars of the immortality of architecture, whispering: "Buildings must die." Yet they also operated as inspiration for ongoing architectural agency. They were both *memento mori* and a source for creativity. These architect-scholars recognized the value of the ruins they encountered *as ruins* that generated creative effects. Hegel observed just such a dialectical creative dynamic in his *Philosophy of History* ([1837] 1956, 72–73):

> The sight of the ruins of some ancient sovereignty directly leads us to con-template the thought of change in its negative aspect. What traveler among the ruins of Carthage, Palmyra, Persepolis, or Rome has not been stimulated to reflections on the transience of kingdoms and men, and to sadness at the thought of a vigorous and rich life now departed.... But the next consider-ation which allies itself with that of change is that change, while it imports dissolution, involves at the same time the rise of a new life—that while death is the issue of life, life is also the issue of death.

It is often assumed that such professional encounters with ruins were in the vein of sublime contemplations, unleashing, as Lowenthal reports, a "thousand ideas" and an "awful astonishment" (1985, 173). Yet Salmon's detailed accounting of such study tours reminds us that they could also be very pragmatic, includ-ing surveys and careful recordings of the ruins. Archaeologist-architects such as James Stuart, Nicholas Revett, and Julien-David Le Roy were the first to study the classical ruins systematically. Their work reinvigorated an interest in the core values of architectural classicism, which had become unmoored from the timeworn authority of Vitruvius by speculative histories of the "origins" of architecture. The techniques of observation, survey, and reconstruction that these early scholars pioneered allowed ruins to nourish modern, eighteenth- and nineteenth-century, architectural design by reauthorizing the ancient principles of classicism.

By the 1840s, the classical turn fed by these study tours was being chal-lenged by the revival of medieval Gothic architecture. Augustus Pugin cham-pioned the Gothic revival in Britain, and was one of the movement's most articulate advocates. While Pugin explicitly discouraged visiting ancient classical ruins, he was highly attentive to the remains of Gothic structures in Northern Europe, and saw them as source material for an alternative, modern Gothic architecture. Medieval precedents, many of them ruinous themselves, fed the Gothic revival. Architects continued to tour and measure and sketch and reimag-ine through these Gothic originals. The ruin, in short, unites the two dominant, and seemingly antithetical, architectural approaches to the past through a shared "archaeological literalism" (Salmon 2000, 227). While the ruin appears to stand at the end of architecture, it has operated as an inspirational source for suc-cessive waves of architectural creativity. Both traditions used observations of ruins as a first step for nourishing architectural revivals of the day.

One of the most famous images of the mid-nineteenth century is Joseph Gandy's rendering of his colleague Sir John Soane's newly completed Bank of

8.1 Arch of Titus, Rome. View from the
west side toward the Forum. Etching
from G. L. Taylor and E. Cresy,
*The Architectural Antiquities of
Rome* (Royal Academy of Arts,
London, 1821).

England in ruins. Much has been said about the ways in which this image reso-nates with the cult of the ruin evident at that time. The painting was first shown at the Royal Academy in 1832, and was displayed along with words from *The Tempest*: "The cloud-capt towers, the gorgeous palaces, / The solemn temples, the great globe itself, / Yea, all which it inherit, shall dissolve" (Sir John Soane's Museum 1999). Daniel Abramson reads the painting as allegorical, equating the Bank with "the venerated ruins of antiquity" as opposed to being merely a commercial institution (1999, 219). In showing Soane's Bank of England in ruins, Gandy acknowledges both its right to stand in time and the likelihood that it will succumb to time. Yet through this admixture he is able to communicate another, more eternal force. Depicting the Bank of England as a ruin is a statement of its value: this is a building good enough to join those predecessor ruins which offer so much ongoing inspiration to architects. This is a building good enough to be archived in the library of ruins. Such a depiction proceeds with the understanding that a ruined building stands, as the Roman ruins did for Gandy and Soane, not as the humble endpoint for an architecture seemingly embarrassed about its own vanity, but as evidence of an enduring worth. In this image there is as much hope for architecture's ongoing creative agency and durability as there is for it to succumb to nature's return.

173

8.2 "Presentation drawing of the Bank of England in ruins"/ "Aerial sectional view of the Bank of England from the south-east," J. M. Gandy (1830) (The Trustees of Sir John Soane's Museum).

CREATING RUINS

Ruins are finely calibrated artifacts of the struggle between architectural agency and nature's agency. That this is the case was given perverse expression in Albert Speer's "theory of ruin value." Julia Hell has documented the Nazi interest in Roman ruins, and the way in which the classicism they represented was taken up into its "imperial gaze." The plan to (re)build Berlin in neoclassical style was made with future ruination explicitly in mind. As Hell notes, Hitler thought that if the great Berlin (and Empire) he was creating ever met the fate of Rome, it must have buildings that could rise to the occasion of being ruins that represented how great Berlin (and its aspired-to Empire) once was. Hitler's architects were directed to build for "eternity." It was in this context that Albert Speer famously developed what he, by his own admission, "pretentiously" dubbed a "theory of ruin value." As Hell notes, Speer's theory was generated after witnessing the demolition of buildings to make way for his vast grandstand structure and Zeppelin Field at the Nazi Party rally grounds at Nuremberg. Speer looked upon the rubble and decided that modern buildings would make "dreary ruins," for they were "poorly suited to form that 'bridge of tradition' to future generations." Instead, Speer wanted to produce an architecture that even in a state of decay "after hundreds or (such were our reckonings) thousands of years would more or less resemble Roman models" (Speer 1970, 56). He proposed the use of resilient materials (such as granite) as opposed to "all such elements of modern construction as steel girders and reinforced concrete, which are subject to weathering" (Speer 1970, 528).[2] He also adopted stylistic and structural features that adhered to "principles of statics" such that even if a roof or a ceiling had disappeared from the building, the walls could still "withstand the impact of the wind" (see also Scobie 1990, 93–95). Only by designing according to the "law of ruins" could a building of the Third Reich "transmit [its] time and spirit to posterity."[3]

The attention that this fragmentary and barely realized architectural vision receives nowadays has been the subject of explicit comment from Hans-Ernst Mittig. He has argued (1993, 21) that there is no trace of the theory of ruin value in National Socialist archives. He goes so far as to suggest that the theory may not have existed until 1969, when Speer first published his memoirs. Mittig speculates whether the attention given to this variant of "ruin theory" is a fact of history or itself an artifact of the contemporary fascination with ruins. What is certain is the ironic aftereffect of Speer's "theory," which valued gentle and slow destructive agency over time just when the violent destructions of war lay immanent.

In modern times, the creative inspiration architects derive from ruins has many contexts. We might, for example, think about what ruins mean from the

174

other end of a war, when destruction has had its way, when future visions are chastened, and when those involved confront the thought "never again." Such a perspective is evident in the practice of architect Arata Isozaki, for whom ruins and ruination have been a preoccupation. Very early in his career Isozaki reflected upon the war ruination of Hiroshima in a photomontage project, *Hiroshima Ruined Again in the Future*, for the Electric Labyrinth exhibition of 1968. Of course, since Isozaki is Japanese, it was not only war ruins that impacted on his experience. Earthquakes, too, shaped his thinking on architecture and ruins. Later, working with collaborators, he developed an installation that comprised rubble from the Kobe earthquake surrounded with images by photographer Ryuju Miyamoto which attempted to grasp the scene in the immediate aftermath. In his book *Japan-ness in Architecture*, Isozaki reflects openly on his interest in "the scenery of ruins" and the ways in which they have operated as "a source of imagination." In his work they do so through a perverse logic. They are not romantic traces of a world past, but signs of the future of architecture and the city. "Professing faith in ruins was equal to planning the future," he commented (2006, 99). Furthermore, Isozaki's thinking was not oriented around picturesque ruins stabilized by nature's return. In his writings, ruins merge with other more violent and deformed states, such as rubble, and processes, such as violent destruction and demolition. His project does not offer a romantic lingering in which the play of time, duration, and ephemerality might be enjoyed, but a glimpse of a terrifying, unformed raw materiality. Reflecting back on Tokyo, and on Hiroshima damaged by war, he observed: "The scene there was more than ruins. It was next to nothing" (2007a, 856).

Isozaki confronts head-on the fact of rubble as anti-architecture:

rubble is the bare materiality of things. It is the bankruptcy of that mode of being signified by architecture, or urban design, or even mere décor. What is dramatically revealed here is the materiality, the thingness, that had been hidden all along. This is the last stage before disappearance. (Isozaki 2006, 100)

For Isozaki the term "bankruptcy" encapsulates why architecture must bother with destruction. Architectural bankruptcy (ruination) arises from the twinned logic of indifferent (or, more accurately, impotent) planning and the artless developer-driven churn characteristic of modern cities. In two essays, written some four decades apart, Isozaki reflects on the image of a future city that he saw to be destined for ruins.[4]

In the first of these essays, written in 1962, Isozaki stages an encounter between himself and a colleague called "S," who owns a company called "City Demolition Industry, Inc." (2007a). S used to be a killer, and in this job he was artful and careful. He became disillusioned with his original career because his

8.3 "Re-ruined Hiroshima," Arata Isozaki
(1968) (MoMA).

177

RUIN

work was being overtaken by a new scale of everyday and indifferent killing over which he had no control—road fatalities. These threatened the very principles by which S worked, and "nullified" his profession. Of course, the road accident was but a symptom of the real culprit or "ravager," which was the city itself. This was "the killer of all killers," for it effected its fatalities anonymously and without a sense of responsibility or professional standards. And it was the city, specifically a Tokyo in ruins, that was the target for S's new demolition business: "Tokyo … was like a building whose foundations had decayed, walls collapsing and water pipes getting thinner, structures barely standing, braced by numerous struts and supported by a jungle of props and buttresses, patches and stains from the leaks in the roof" (Isozaki 2007a, 854). This is not some passive ruin which one contemplates, but an enemy ruin, a "gigantic monster … that must be destroyed as soon as possible."

In the first essay, Isozaki lays out the fictional prospectus of "City Demolition Industry, Inc." Its aims include "the complete destruction of large cities which have been repeatedly engaged in vicious mass murder." The company intends to effect this clearance by any possible means, including "human power, dynamite, atomic and hydrogen bombs." Alongside this, the company plans to deliver other kinds of havoc (abolishing house numbers, poisoning water, disturbing communications networks). Although destruction and disruption are the main thrust of the company's prospectus, it also contains seeds of an alternate and utopian vision. The prospectus also talks about making way for "a civilization in which elegant, pleasant, and humanistic murder can be carried out easily," and calls for the return of "legal city planning provisions" and "proposals for Utopia city planning in the future."

There are enough clues in this essay to tell us that "S" is really an alter ego for Isozaki himself. "I am a kind of schizophrenic, divided," he notes in a recent reflection on the essay (cited in Koolhaas and Obrist 2011, 49). "S" represents the "creative work" of mundane but potent forces of urban transformation, as opposed to the design architect. Isozaki is envious of S, for he feels that S's vision of destruction will be more easily realized than his own concrete hopes. "I make concrete proposals, concrete countermeasures, and improvements on them. I am made to feel ever more keenly the impossibility of putting my proposals into practice," he laments.

Some forty years later, Isozaki restages an encounter with S in the second essay (2007b). His first observation is that the project of "City Demolition Industry, Inc." is now almost completely in place: "today's cities have become precisely what S's company prescribed." In fact, Isozaki considers the ideas of the company old hat and dated: what "a dinosaur of an architect would cook up." So fully realized is S's vision, Isozaki suggests that his company be renamed "Urban

Self-Destruction Enterprise." Physical and functional destruction is proceeding indiscriminately, thanks to land sharks and the Kobe earthquake. Even Isozaki's own home office succumbed, being prematurely deemed obsolete and then demolished. Utopian visions are simply destructive, as is evident in the generic design of mass public housing, which merely produces "broken boxes that are in ruins" (2007b, 862).

These strange essays place ruins and ruination at the center of Isozaki's architectural creativity. As Jameson writes:

> for Isozaki ruins also express the same stark and simple forms as they emerge from chaos; ruins are also elemental building blocks—the architect scarcely knows whether he is constructing a building or the ruins of a building. (Jameson 2007, 849)

We glimpse in Isozaki the kind of "ruinous refinement" for which Bataille's general economy reaches (1999, 86). The recursive sensibilities of Isozaki's architecture are striking and derive, by his own admission, from ancient Japanese space-time concepts. These are encapsulated in the concept *ma*, which he used as the basis for a 1978 exhibition in Paris. Isozaki presents *ma* as a gap or interstitial space—a "productive *emptiness*," he calls it (2006, 100). States of ruin, which are expressed through the Japanese term *kare kajikeru* (dried and emaciated), exist in the space of the interstice *ma*. For Isozaki, the ruin is not merely an authoritative source material for an enlivened expressive language of architecture. The ruin, as *ma*, challenges many of the binary oppositions between the formed and the deformed in architecture.

THE NEW IN RUINS

Over time, many have walked through ruins with purposeful agendas in mind. Certainly the sociologist William L. Yancey did so in the late 1960s, when he entered a housing estate that had been standing for not much longer than ten years: Minoru Yamasaki's Pruitt-Igoe. Yancey described a ruined place:

> Walking into the project, one is struck by the mosaic of glass that covers what were grassy areas and playgrounds. The barren dirt, or mud when it rains, is constantly tracked into the apartments. Windows, particularly those on the lower floors, are broken out ... cover[ed] ... with plywood. Streets and parking lots are littered with trash, bottles, and tin cans. Derelict cars provide an attractive source of entertainment for children. Fences around "tot-lots" are torn; swings, sliding boards, and merry-go-rounds are noticeably unpainted, rusted, and broken.... Within the buildings themselves, the neglect is more apparent. Entering the buildings via one of the three stairwells, one is struck by the stale air and the stench of urine, trash, and garbage on the floors. The elevators are used as public rest rooms, as well as a means of transportation.... Many are without handrails and are in need of painting; all have the

reputation of breaking down between floors.... On the fourth, seventh, and tenth floors are open galleries or halls, the only level public space within the building, one side of which is lined with broken windows and steel grating.... Open garbage is often found on the floor next to the incinerator. The laundry rooms, located off the gallery, are sometimes used as lavatories. Residents and officials were observed urinating in them. (Yancey 1974, 75)

Macaulay (1953, 453) would call this a "new ruin" and, because of this, might not classify it as a real ruin at all. Some would say this is mere architectural trash. There is certainly none of the inspirational weight or evocative charm we have encountered with earlier ruins. We do not put those more revered and stabilized ruins alongside these other states of ruination in order to better understand the nature of the ruin *per se*. Rather, we want to push further our inquiry into how ruination nourishes architectural creativity. The detection of ruination in high-rise housing, we suggest, operated as a variant of the architectural encounter with more ancient ruins, functioning again to generate architectural creativity.

8.4 Pruitt-Igoe windows, still from the film *The Pruitt-Igoe Myth*.

The kind of high-rise development that Yancey encountered in Pruitt-Igoe was a derivative of avant-garde concepts for multistory, high-rise living advocated in the early twentieth century by architects such as Gropius and Le Corbusier. Under the pressure of housing shortages of various kinds, and fueled by a new belief in the social power of technological innovation and design science, such models for modern living entered into state-based mass housing schemes in the middle of the twentieth century. Many of these manifested as distant cousins of the avant-garde prototypes, reshaped into a middling modernism by budgets and bureaucratic efficiencies. For public authorities facing severe housing shortages or intolerable housing standards, such high-rise schemes offered a "technological shortcut to social change" (Dunleavy 1981, 100). It has become commonplace for critics of this housing typology to refer to the high-rise flats built at this time as "experiments" in building technology and even, as Hanley (2006, 105) puts it, "experimenting with lives."

The promise of such schemes was short-lived. The high-rise housing typology was, from the outset, surrounded by debate. Social science scrutiny, conducted in the form of post-occupancy surveys, delivered to this experimental housing typology and the debate it generated a set of social scientific facts that sought to test if it was working and, if not, why not. During this period a number of powerful quasi-scientific urban design theories emerged, including George Kelling's "broken window theory" and Oscar Newman's notion of "defensible space." In the case of broken window theory, a condition of architectural ruination was elevated to an indicator of social dysfunction. As Wilson and Kelling (1982) put it, "one unrepaired window is a signal that no one cares [and] such an area is vulnerable to criminal invasion." Other scholars, like geographer Alice Coleman (1985), who modeled her methods on those of Oscar Newman, used indicators of ruination (graffiti, building vandalism, excrement) to measure what she dubbed "design disadvantagement."[5] These social sciences, and the theories of design they propagated, became powerful discursive tools in the turn away from high-rise housing within state-managed housing systems. They played a part in the ending of modernism's dream of designing the architectural foundations for mass housing provision as effectively as the wrecker's ball. Sites of high-rise ruination, such as these, operated as evidentiary fields much like the ruins of antiquity had before them. But what they revealed was not a lost state of perfection but an experiment deemed to have gone wrong. They revealed the "bad" ruin, one that needed to be fixed or, as we famously see in the case of Pruitt-Igoe, eradicated by demolition.

Many such high-rises have now been demolished. For example, Liverpool, like many cities in Britain, had met its postwar housing needs primarily through the high-rise typology. But during the 1990s, the Liverpool Housing Action Trust

(HAT) was mandated to develop and regenerate the city's housing stock. Of the 67 high-rise housing blocks that came into the Trust's hands at the start of the process, 54 were demolished and 13 refurbished. As part of that redevelopment process, Liverpool Housing Action Trust adopted a Percent for Art policy, with the view that art practices would play a part in ensuring that communities understood and coped with the change they were experiencing. Two outcomes of that mandate were the *Up in the Air* and *Further Up in the Air* projects. These were initiated by local artists, but realized using HAT's funding and property. Some ten artists were given the opportunity to occupy, for six weeks, four empty flats as accommodation and a further seven as studios in the Kenley Close tower block in Sheil Park. This, by the artists' own admission, was an "opportunistic" project which took advantage of a high-rise space poised between use and demolition. It is one minor instance of the way in which art practices are pulled into the gravitational field of dilapidated buildings. The most evident (and well-documented) of these is Gordon Matta-Clark's destructive engagements with about-to-be-demolished buildings.[6] His art practices include the breaking up and breaking through of buildings already poised on the brink of valuelessness. Matta-Clark's art retrieves architecture from its consignment to waste, revaluing and rebuilding it as art through a logic of dismantling. This kind of creativity comes in the perverse affordance offered by a building that is transiting from use to waste. Such dispensable "new" ruins afford further expressive ruinations in the name of art. The art of ruins is quite distinct from the kind of aesthetic unity that was understood to develop in the ancient ruin over time and through nature: that more Kantian notion that Ginsberg ([1970] 2004) refers to as "matter build[ing] its own unities among ruins." In ruin art the artist actively harvests the vitality of decaying matter, sometimes indulging in its slow-time distress, other times blasting it apart with artistic agency.

NEW RUINOLOGIES

182

We write at a time when there is an intensified and renewed awareness of the ruin and states of ruination. The eighteenth-century fascination with the ruin was closely linked to the emerging field of aesthetics, and its interest in sensory perception, the cultivation of human imagination and understanding, and the development of an appreciation for nature. Now everyone wants to get dirty with ruins. Whole subcultures of urban explorers are developing an alternative aesthetics based on direct engagement with decaying urban and quasi-urban terrains, with their own specialist subdivisions such as the bunkerologist, the place hacker, and the psychogeographer.[7] Unlike their eighteenth- and nineteenth-century predecessors, urban explorers are not simply contemplating the ruin at a distance as an architectural artifact within a picturesque landscape composition, or using it as a template for the architectures they create. These new ruinologists do not care for ruins sanctioned by good taste or compositional principles. They seek out the unloved and unremarked, the forgotten and derelict buildings. They break into, trespass, explore, photograph, video and sound record. They report on buildings' atmospheres and specters, their dangers and challenges, their atrophies and inertias, on blogs, in the occasional exhibition, and in books. There is a great deal of terrain to be explored. This largely (although not exclusively) Western enthusiasm is well met, as Tim Edensor (2005a, 4) notes, by the many ruins that nowadays litter postindustrial landscapes.

A new genre of visual culture has emerged alongside urban exploration — what Joann Greco dubs "ruin porn," over which "architecture buffs drool."

> A wheelchair sits center stage, its orange vinyl back echoed by a round tabletop that leans against a wall, painted in a familiar shade of institutional green. A mattress, flattened and grimy, lies tossed onto a floor that's littered with fallen plaster. In the foreground, an overturned metal trashcan speaks volumes. A mirror reflects the whole sad scene. It's romantic, it's nostalgic, it's wistful, it's provocative. It's about time, nature, mortality, disinvestment. Pursuing and photographing the old is an addictive hobby. Dozens of blogs and online galleries share strategies for entry [to abandoned buildings], and showcase ever-bulging collections of moss-covered factory floors and lathe-exposed school buildings. (Greco 2012)

The headquarters of ruin porn seems to be Detroit, itself the premier city for speculation about a wider urban condition of shrinkage that has started to be grouped under the term "eschatopolis."[8] Powerful and anachronistic images of Detroit's ruinous "landmarks" are depicted in large-format books such as Moore's *Detroit Disassembled* (2010) and Marchand and Meffre's *The Ruins of Detroit* (2010). In this vein, photographer Sean Doerr worked with author Dan Austin in the making of *Lost Detroit* (2010), a book that relishes the stories behind the city's "majestic ruins." These Detroit offerings are but a subset of a wider apocalyptic urbanism. We might think here of the wave of science fiction documentaries such as National Geographic's *Aftermath: Population Zero* (2008) and the History Channel's *Life after People* (2008), which use digital visualization tools to show the crumpled and overgrown future state of well-known architectural landmarks. A number of commentators have begun to ask whether it is not time to reposition ruin porn within a more complex understanding of processes of ruination. Their ponderings resonate with similar admonishments expressed in the nineteenth century with respect to renderings of poverty and slum districts: Ruskin's "lower picturesque" and what Herman Melville reproved as "povertiresque" (cited in Lowenthal 1985, 166).

183

One of the unsettling aftereffects of the new ruinology is its contradictory disinterested interest in states of decay and atrophy. As Garrett (2011b) notes, although a diverse community, urban explorers are joined by a desire "to locate and explore disordered, marginal, interstitial and infrastructural space through recreational trespass." The productive purpose of such venturing is obscure and open to debate. Some say it is merely another form of extreme leisure. Others claim it is a kind of community activism grounded in the sense of empowerment that comes from transgressing forbidden urban infrastructures. Yet others suggest it has social value, because it reveals and rediscovers forgotten or ignored buildings. As Canadian explorer Michael Cook blogs: "our cities are more productive, more democratic, more sustainable, and more secure when we are collectively aware of and understand the infrastructure that serves us, whether in our buildings, on our streets, or under our feet" (cited in Garrett 2011b). Rather than these modern industrial ruins representing formless decline, he sees them as a (underused) reservoir of possibility. Tim Edensor is engaged in a similar rescue mission when he writes of his long fascination with industrial ruins: "I am interested in re-evaluating industrial ruins in order to critique the negative connotations with which they are associated in official and common sense thought." This is no mere personal indulgence. Edensor sees industrial ruins as "exemplary spaces." He reports upon them in the hope that they can "be used to critique ways in which urban space is produced and reproduced." For Edensor (2005a, 17), industrial ruins are "deliciously disordered" sites that critique the "highly regulated," "disciplinary," "aestheticized" spaces demanded by commercial and bureaucratic regimes. In contrast to such spaces, industrial ruins have different affordances and regulatory regimes. As such they "open up the possibilities for regulated urban bodies to escape their shackles in expressive pursuits and sensual experience." They offer space for the illicit, the illegal, the adventurous, the curious, the innovative, and the expressive. Such interstitial or "loose" spaces, and the kind of unprogrammed creativity they engendered, have recently become the focus of architectural consideration (Franck and Stevens 2007; Baum and Christiaanse 2013). Like Edensor, Franck and Stevens see such spaces as offering an alternative aesthetics and politics.

184

Such potentialities were certainly evident in Berlin after the fall of the Berlin Wall.[9] Many derelict and unused spaces in East Berlin served as squats or were acquired via temporary leases. In these spaces clubs were run that spawned an entire subculture of alternative use. Anja Schwanhäußer (2010), for example, has shown how an aesthetic praxis based around ruination was cultivated in and through improvisational subcultural use of abandoned buildings in 1970s and 1980s Berlin. This "second city" of squatting operated with alternative architectural (and other) values. For example, the spaces squatted had been "removed from the circulation of capitalist valorization" through abandonment, and so were available to become "open spaces for experimentation" (Proll et al. 2010, 11, cited in Göbel 2012, 122). Helmut Hartmut Böhme, in talking about the aesthetics of ruins, refers to this as *De-Architekturierung* (de-architecturing), wherein the functional or representative meaning of an intact structure is set aside. In the case of Berlin, the users valued the ruinous states of these buildings for the unique atmospheres they generated, as well as the flexibility they afforded for their creative endeavors.[10] Recent work by Hanna Göbel (2012) has shown how architectural cultural entrepreneurs in Berlin are now reshaping the contemporary built environment of the city through a ruin aesthetic acquired and honed by way of these earlier subcultural experiences.[11]

RUINOUS INFORMALITY

Squatting and ruination have quite different meanings and implications in the context of the Global South. There, squatting is not associated with the occupation of and engagement with the "deliciously disordered" aesthetics of unused infrastructure. More usually it is associated with a "lifestyle" (an evident misnomer in this context) characterized by the complete absence or substandard provision of formal infrastructure. The term is often used interchangeably with informal settlement or shantytown. Although there are important distinctions between these categories, all refer in one way or another to unplanned settlements.[12] Often located on the edge of, or marginal sites within, cities, such settlements are the result of an architecture without architects or planners. They are built by and serve the urban poor, who are themselves often migrants who come to the city with little more than the determination to find their fortune and help those they leave behind through remittances. Such settlements come into being because housing provision does not meet the demand produced by such urban immigration. In Global South contexts there may not be the capacity or the will on the part of relevant state authorities to provide suitable housing, while the private sector sees little market potential in this impoverished and often mobile population. Informal housing is an affordable option because it is often developed incrementally, is often cheaper because it is on land without infrastructural services (such as sewerage or roads), and because it is often initiated on land over which there is no formal ownership or leasing arrangement. There is a wide variety of housing "types" within informal settlements, and what is built depends on taste, the materials and technical skills available, the economic means of the householder, the security of their tenure, and how the state responds (or not) to their presence.

In explanations of contemporary urbanism, a lot often rides on such informal settlements.[13] In *Planet of Slums* (2006), Mike Davis argues that they mark

185

more than anything that "watershed in human history" wherein the number of urban residents now outnumbers the rural. Some 95 percent of humanity's "final buildout," as he calls it, will happen in and through such settlements. In a similarly flamboyant manner, Peter Hall and Ulrich Pfeiffer (2000), in their overview of urbanization in the twenty-first century, spoke of "informal hypergrowth." If this is the case, we might well ponder why it is that the ruinous conditions of the Global North and its past are dominant in shaping how architecture thinks and acts. What of these other conditions of informality and dilapidation? Do they have anything to say to professional architecture's creative sense of itself? How has architecture addressed these conditions of informality?

Davis is largely pessimistic about what such informal settlements mean: for quality of life, for equality, for politics, for the planet. Others cannot but see them as a problem and a challenge (United Nations 2003). Yet others suggest more optimistically, perhaps romantically, that they speak of the agency, endurance, and resourcefulness of those they house.[14] In her (2005) meditation on urban informality, Ananya Roy posits that they might offer a broader epistemological basis for planning more generally. She argues this on three fronts: the desirability of planning modalities producing the "unplannable"; how planners might use informality to mitigate vulnerabilities among the poor; and how informality requires recognition of different models of rights and authorization. Roy and AlSayyad (2004), for example, argue that informality is best thought of not as a housing typology (or an economic sector) but as a mode of city building.

Colin McFarlane (2008) notes that informal settlements have long attracted the attention of those seeking to intervene in and resolve the "problem" of developing cities. Sometimes such interventions are in the name of the rights and well-being of those who are housed in such settlements; at other times they are attempts to intervene in and wrest back control of those parts of the city considered "lost" to illegitimate or undervalued uses. Architecture plays its part in such processes, and has often done so with the endorsement and sponsorship of international aid agencies, national and municipal states, and nongovernmental organizations. The wider disciplinary effects of such efforts are, however, often contained within subdisciplinary backwaters, bounded by categories such as "self-help housing," "development," or "sustainable architecture." These schemes carry with them an always complicated politics that floats between paternalism and empowerment. But they also carry relevant models of engaging with informality from which mainstream architecture might learn. They speak of architectures that are designed with incremental modalities to the fore, in which building processes depend on complex ecologies of recycling, reuse, and reprogramming, and creative agencies are distributed and deployed in temporally unpredictable ways.

In the final part of this chapter, we wish to draw upon the often sidelined repertoire of architectural responses to informal settlements. Here we might think of John Habraken's support-and-infill principle, John Turner's notion of autonomous housing, Balkrishna Doshi's community housing project at Aranya in India, and, more recently, the work of Elemental in the town of Iquique, Chile (Aravena and Iacobelli 2012).

Engagements with informal housing offer alternative models with respect to the autonomy of architecture's creative agency, as well as its authority with respect to form and program. John Habraken has depicted this as a debate between the "provider paradigm" and the "support paradigm" (1972). In a provider paradigm, professional architectural agency is strong in conventional design terms. The architect designs housing and so determines, along with other relevant professionals, the technical dimensions of a settlement, including the housing, the planning, and the infrastructural services like sanitation. Often these interventions are well connected to systems of mass production and centrally provided, regulated and maintained services. Settlement security is, then, provided largely through agents external to those housed. The support paradigm, in contrast, has a differently distributed agency. In this paradigm the architect, working with other service professionals, delivers basic infrastructure that enables the agency of settlers to create and maintain their own built environments. Architectural creative agency is in this instance given over to a temporally elongated collaboration with the informal settler/s who incrementally (and variably) design and build their homes and neighborhoods as their resources, energy, and creativity allow. Such collaborations not only blur the line between architectural and nonarchitectural agency in design, they also unsettle the divide between the social and the infrastructural. Abdoumaliq Simone suggests that the infrastructure of cities of the Global South cannot be thought of merely as technical systems, "objects and spaces." In infrastructurally impoverished cities, "persons and practices" serve as the "platform" that provides for and reproduces everyday life. They do so with endless creativity, "precisely because the outcomes of residents' reciprocal efforts are radically open, flexible, and provisional" (Simone 2004, 408). Returning to the matter central to this chapter, such incremental architectures usually imply that the ruinous, the salvaged, and the recycled are co-present, and mingle with the newly designed. This complicates the received definitions of the ruin in architectural and cultural history, which position it variously as material manifestation of loss, as a delicate yet obdurate record of the "injuries of time," or even as scholarly evidence of a golden age in the case of antiquarian empiricism. This other "ruination" is anticipated and designed for. It is a ruination of in-progress aspirations—it is more incompleteness than loss, and so heads in a different direction to the usual ruin.

187

This kind of "ruin" and "disorder" shifts the way we might understand the capacity of ruination to nourish future architectural creativities.

One of the most extensive, ambitious, and interesting of such incremental architectures is the PREVI (Proyecto Experimental de Vivienda, or Experimental Housing Project) initiative in Lima, Peru. It was one of the first engagements by mainstream architects with the contemporary phenomenon of rapid urbanization and informality (Mateo 2012).[15] The project was initiated in 1965 by the Peruvian government, supported by the UN, and organized by British architect Peter Land. The proposal sought to develop a strategy to better accommodate the residents of the informal settlements rapidly developing in Peru. At Land's suggestion an international competition was held, and a selection of diverse architects—such as Aldo van Eyck, James Stirling, Fumihiko Maki, Charles Correa, Christopher Alexander, Oskar Hansen—were invited to take part. Launched in 1969, the built project was partially realized in stages from 1972 onward.

The book ¡El Tiempo Construye! Time Builds! (García-Huidobro, Torres Torriti, and Tugas 2008) documents the history of adaptations and adjustments residents have made to the fabric of the original PREVI settlement some 30 years on. This history, as housing scholar and activist John Turner notes in the "Preface" to the book, has allowed those interested in incremental housing—be they historians, civil society activists, government planners, or architects—to assess the aspirations the PREVI originators had for the project.

Initially, the jury for the PREVI competition identified three winners from the 26 invited participants. But then the commissioning team, led by Peter Land, changed tack. Rather than construct just one of the winning proposals, as had been intended, Land's team developed a master plan for the site—with regular plot sizes, standardized construction principles, and prescribed population densities—into which "samples" of all of the 26 invited projects were placed (see Kahatt 2011). Participating architects were each allocated 20 housing units to design within the new master plan. Of the 26 projects, 24 were constructed (Land 2008, 14–15).[16]

188

This change in direction met with a mixed reception. For some, the new approach, with its collage of architectural samples laid over Land's master plan, compromised the original designs, disconnecting the housing from any alternate, whole-site urban design visions. Others complained that the mosaic approach prevented the realization of certain economies of delivery based on industrialized systems of construction (Salas and Lucas 2012). As one of the participating architects, Frederick Cooper, reflected, collaging many different design proposals on a much smaller scale made it impossible to respond to what he regarded as the big question: mass housing provision (Cooper and Ramis 2012). The imposition of a single, new master plan meant that the development was more centralized in its delivery and governance. As Rodriguez (2012) notes, the changes relinquished "any chance of the project's autonomy," overly empowering the state as the main housing agent, as well as the architects. Nonetheless, today the settlement supports a large and diverse community, provides an environment that offers economic opportunities, stable shelter, and good infrastructure (plumbing, drainage, waste management services, and public transportation). The typological diversity of the settlement and the urban plan has supported the emergence of distinctive neighborhoods with strong identities.

In PREVI, much was at stake in the balance struck between the original architectural visions and the ongoing, resident-led development it facilitated. The participating architects approached this question differently, but each in some way had to rethink what it meant to "future-proof" their architectural designs. The PREVI housing was designed with a range of devices that sought to catalyze anticipated and desired forms of change. For example, the proposals had the ability to accommodate higher population densities, to engender mixing of uses, to encourage domestic economic initiatives, and to allow residents to "value-add" to their homes by altering and extending the built fabric to their own needs and preferences. All this opening up to future redesign required a new kind of future-proofing. The architects needed to anticipate and facilitate change. A design that imagined it was complete, or resisted change, had no place in PREVI. Furthermore, the designs often sought to guide or accommodate future change in ways that minimized negative effects. In the case of residents incrementally building onto the original design, architects designed ahead such that the follow-on additions might not compromise light and air quality in interior spaces, or result in the juxtaposition of incompatible uses, or create outright danger from fire, flood, or collapse. Aldo van Eyck, for example, positioned the kitchen centrally within the unit he designed, and included angled walls to ensure that natural ventilation and light would penetrate into the kitchen regardless of the future development of the dwelling. Others, like James Stirling, designed each dwelling unit around a central courtyard that was intended to accommodate stairs to encourage vertical growth.[17] For all of this, as architect Juan Pablo Corvalán notes, "none of the precautions and measures were enough" to accommodate the changes that emerged. Every one of the architect-designed units ended up "encrusted with geological layers: extra floors, pitched roofs, balconies, external staircases, faux-marble façades" (McGuirk 2011), such that today there is "an almost total blurring of the original intentions" (Corvalán 2007). Architectural design principles were overrun by user-initiated innovations: "none of the designs operated as imagined ... genius ideas were misused and architectural form disfigured" (Corvalán 2007).

But surely such "hybrid vigor," as Corvalán put it, meant that PREVI was a success? How is it that this is read as "disfigurement" and "misuse"? One answer may lie in the staggered and elongated time frames of many of these elaborations. The growth of the urban fabric at PREVI has not unfolded smoothly, or in coordinated increments. Spurts of building activity in one plot usually contrast with relative inactivity in another. The construction activity itself has been full of its own provisionalities, indicated by the distance between an aspiration to extend, add-on, or improve, and its full realization. PREVI today is littered with the telltale signs of such interrupted, incomplete, or improvised schemes: steel reinforcement rods protruding into the air, unplastered or un-painted walls, cladding composed of recycled materials, and rooms part built. Builders mix concrete in the street outside one house, while painters are at work on the façade next door, and rubble and building materials stand in piles, not knowing whether they are heading toward an end or a beginning (Palma 2011). The urban fabric of PREVI today supports all these multiple states—the vigorous and the provisional, the pristine and the prematurely aged, the thriving and the fal-low. It is perhaps this contradictory state that allows such vigorous creativity to be diagnosed as "disfigurement" against the original architectural visions, even while those visions anticipated change. Perhaps Corvalán's final adjudication on PREVI is more accurate, if ambivalent. He concludes that it is a "successful failure." Its mixing up of architectural approaches "was both a sacrilege, and [a] master move."

HOTEL OF SLEEPLESS NIGHTS

During a visit to the city of Jakarta in 2004, we came across a shack on the bank of a small stream near a brand-new housing estate on the fringes of the city. It was a ramshackle construction made from recycled materials that presumably had been gleaned from around the neighborhood. The construction had a casual sense of style about the way it had been assembled: a kind of "shack chic," you might say (Fraser 2003), that can probably also be found in the favelas of São Paulo, the townships of South Africa, and the barrios of Mexico City.

190

The distinctive thing about this shack was the image that appeared on one of the cladding panels. It spelt the words "Hotel Ora Molor." The sign looked vaguely familiar. The lettering had come from elsewhere—an advertising sign for Marlboro cigarettes, now cut up and reordered, and applied to the shack's exterior. The Neo Contact font was unmistakable. It and its partner cowboy were devised by the famous advertising creative Leo Burnett. They formed the visual anchors of one of the most successful advertising campaigns in modern history, one that transformed Marlboro from a brand that appealed to less than one quarter of one percent of the American market in the early 1950s, to the most popular in the world just 20 years later.

In their reconfigured and relocated form, these same letters now stand for the bricoleur's ingenuity, often romantically associated with informal settlements, and readily absorbed into the shack chic aesthetic. But this informally reconfigured global brand also carries with it another story, one that is pertinent for thinking about the ruin and the informal. The letters of the Marlboro sign were rearranged into Javanese, the language of many of the migrants who come from central and eastern Java to settle in Jakarta. It roughly translates into the phrase "Hotel of Sleepless Nights." It's a clever, self-knowing, and self-deprecating joke that speaks of the likely shortfalls of the improvised and pulled-together architecture to which it is attached. This "hotel," really a shack, offers minimal resistance to the monsoon rains and the tropical heat of the dry season. Being quite open to the elements, it has little capacity to keep the mosquitoes at bay during the night. To sleep in this ruin, to find a home within this type of informal architecture, could lead only to sleepless nights. It is here, in this humble aside, that we see the political and creative potential of thinking otherwise about the "new ruins" of informality. This innovated hotel sign turns the relationship between stark impoverishment and capitalism on its head with wry humor. We are drawn to its disorderly charms. We do not want to stand distant from the message communicated by its impoverished and substandard built circumstance, nor from the political potential of its parody. But nor do we want to fix this scene with an architectural solution of the old kind. We see in this improvised sign and its surrounds a new variant of Ruskin's so-called "lower picturesque." Ruskin saw a purpose in dwelling on such disorder, which was to cultivate an appreciation that might keep an overly ordered modernizing aesthetic at bay. The Hotel of Sleepless Nights, along with the "success failure" of informality more generally, might similarly offer mainstream, contemporary architecture another way of being with itself, its creative project and its built artifacts. This might be an architecture that willingly innovates in collaboration, designs for other nonarchitectural designers, and welcomes and accommodates "deformations" and "misuses," be they formal, programmatic, or other.   191

8.5 "Hotel Ora Molor / Hotel of Sleepless Nights," Jakarta (2004) (Stephen Cairns).

DEMOLITION

Architecture must be a heart-breaking art.... Paint a picture,
write a book, and you possess your creation forever,
even if it is no good. But design a building and you have it
for twenty years and then the wrecker takes charge of
the situation.
"WRECKER'S REMINISCENCES" (NEW YORKER 1931)

Death hangs about some buildings. This was the case with Toyo Ito's U-House in Najano-Honcho, Japan. The house was designed in 1975 for Ito's sister and her two daughters. They were in mourning, having just lost their husband and father to a long struggle with illness. The house was built on a plot of land next to where their parents lived, but was not designed to be a "normal" family home. It comprised a white U-shape with a roof that inclined toward an inner courtyard laid out with black soil. The curved concrete walls had no windows, but there were slot-like openings in the ceiling. The interior was one room/corridor that followed the U-shape of the house. The building was designed to be a portrait of this bereaved family, to reflect its emotional state. It was to provide "spiritual consolation." As Ito recollected, "This house was associated with a family which had just been confronted with death and withdrew from the world outside behind a concrete wall" (cited in Tsukada 1999, 80). The building was in the image of "an introverted family." Ito's bereaved sister (his client) acknowledged that the building reflected a "kind of darkness" within her. The dark soil served her wish to be near nature: not a pretty nature, but the nature of submergence. As the late critic Koji Taki noted: "this dark soil ... looked like the soil from the very beginning of time" (1999, 37). The building itself, set low into the landscape, was "like an underground labyrinth" (Ito cited in Tsukada 1999, 82). But there was also light. As Ito's sister reflected: "I did not long for a gentle soft light ... but a strong light with the vitality to dispel the darkness" (she had in mind the kind of light spots found in the otherwise dark paintings of Georges de la Tour). The architect provided for this with the openings in the ceiling, snow-white interior walls, and recessed lighting, which together made the building shine like a white ring in black darkness. This was a building that was "full of life that, at the same time, had the mystery of death concealed behind it" (Taki 1999, 45).

The uniqueness of the U-House as an interpretation of the domestic dwelling as well as the melancholic character of the commission gave it considerable

9.1 U-House, Toyo Ito & Associates.

195

DEMOLITION

notoriety. Yet on February 28, 1997, the U-house was demolished. The clients had spent some twenty years there, getting over the tragedy that gave rise to the commission. They had outgrown the house, and were leaving. Apparently it was their wish that the house be demolished. They had moved on but their home, which had "a hardly changeable unambiguous symbolic meaning," had not (Taki cited in Tsukada 1999, 85). The house, ordered by an inflexible formalism, was in a state of spiritual obsolescence. Its demolition occasioned wider reflection. The client was interviewed and academic papers were written, many of which took the opportunity to reflect retrospectively on Ito's career, as if the architect had died along with the demolished building. The U-House was at once a deeply personal and tragic commission, and a building which was, as Taki suggested, stylistically "far removed" from Ito's current work and his interests in, among other things, the "aesthetics of the ephemeral" and "short-lived transience" (1999, 35, 39). This was one of Ito's buildings, but did it stand for his architecture? The architect was there to see the demolition. According to reports he saw it as a significant event, and witnesses assumed it was traumatic: "It was demolished in a terrible way in front of his own eyes. Did an architect ever before watch the annihilation of a building that he had constructed?" (Ito cited in Tsukada 1999, 80). The answer to this question is yes. In fact, as this chapter will reflect, architects have routinely had to witness the demolition of their own buildings.

What does demolition mean for architecture's sense of itself and the fate of its creative output? Demolition annihilates architectural fantasies of permanence. It pulls down architectural creativity made manifest in built form. It erases the material referent of a building's circulating meaning. Thought of building-by-building, demolition must be understood as architecture's mortal enemy. Architect and critic Gerhard Auer even goes so far as to ask whether buildings (especially newly intelligent ones) should be given "human rights": "What is a demolition without the building's permission? Is this murder? Or indeed with its permission, is this euthanasia?" (Auer 1995, 30). A building's right to live on, to extend this anthropomorphism momentarily, is rarely in the hands of its architectural creator. It is embedded in a political economy of creative destruction, sutured to cycles of fashion and attachment, subject to forces of nature, and slowed down or hastened by regulatory frameworks. Demolition, while the end of one architectural story, is usually the necessary precursor to the beginning of another. Although this is not always admitted, the logic of creative destruction, of which demolition is a part, presents architecture with deep satisfactions. Practically speaking, it means that there is always a job to be done. More foundationally, demolition allows architecture to occupy relentlessly the ur-rationale of its creative drive, which is to turn "unimproved" land to productive use. Architectural demolitions inevitably have a sacrificial logic. They supply a *tabula rasa*, even in contexts that are fully occupied, giving architecture access to space such that it may literally rise again. Demolition is also an important tool in architecture's ability to replicate itself as a profession invested in creativity. As Keller Easterling (2003, 81) has noted, *tabula rasa* is the mode of subtraction most compatible with architectural desire. This is architecture's perverse secret: its professional stability, and its ability to reproduce itself, depend upon demolition, as both a material fact and a psychic desire. As architectural scholar Jeremy Till has noted, "construction and demolition are closer than most architects would dare admit" (2009, 68).

In recent years the history and business of building demolition has attracted both popular and scholarly interest. Helene Liss (2000), drawing heavily on the showcase of buildings demolished by the media-savvy North America-based Loizeaux Family of Controlled Demolition, Inc., has documented for an evidently curious popular readership what she calls the "art" of building demolition. In her opening pages she observes that the urge to demolish is as foundational as the urge to build. Liss sees demolition as a civilizing necessity that "allows the physical constructs of a developing society to evolve." In Jeff Byles's (2005) history of demolition, appropriately entitled *Rubble*, demolition is once again positioned as architecture's necessary opposite. His wide-ranging account of demolition technologies, the demolition industry, and demolished buildings and cityscapes, reminds us that built environments are always at the same time unbuilding environments, and that nowadays "erase-atecture" is as common as architecture.

That this is the case is nowhere more evident than in cities. Cities grow. Part of that growth is expansion onto green-field sites, which may never before have had their productive purpose refracted through architecture. But in the context of the modern industrial and postindustrial city, a good deal of urban growth is through processes known to us in terms such as "improvement," "modernization," "renovation," "renewal," or "redevelopment." We need only think of Haussmann's late-nineteenth-century renovation of Paris which, in the name of creating Paris anew, covered the city, for a time at least, with demolition sites. That erasure left a lasting legacy of melancholic reflection in literary and artistic impressions of the time. The remarkable photography of Charles Marville and Henri Le Secq, for example, inaugurated a genre of demolition photography that remains vital to the present. Their (and other) photographs did not simply capture manifest buildings, but architecture in the event of urban transformation. The buildings photographed were sometimes still standing, but were captured because they were soon to be no more. Others were already disaggregated rubble or collapsed walls, an architecture already unmade by the Paris soon to come (Rice 1999).

197

As Walter Benjamin (1999a, 97) has reflected, modernizing Paris left us with the "gloomy awareness that along with the great cities have evolved the means to raze them to the ground." Such processes are everywhere and ongoing in cities. We might also think of New World cities like New York. Max Page's comprehensive account of its cycles of "creative destruction" through the end of the nineteenth century and during the early twentieth century shows in graphic detail the place of demolition in the "restless renewal" of urbanization (Page 1999, 21). Manhattan Island was subject to intensive and repeated demolitions. So widespread and rapid was the pace of change that the editors of a 1927 edition of *Architecture* observed that the new buildings of New York "are scarcely occupied before they are torn down to make way for better ones." In this instance the human will to demolish in order to renew outstripped any natural processes of building decay: "The great steel frames of its structures," wrote the editors, "will never disintegrate from rust—they are scrapped before the rust can start" (cited in Page 1999, 5).[1] The state, through the authority of planning and welfare, can play an important role in these processes. In mid-twentieth-century Britain, for example, state-sponsored or endorsed slum clearance saw many cities demolish existing housing stock at a faster rate than it was being built. And in post-independence, land-constrained Singapore such state-coordinated erasures were the hallmark of modernization (Koolhaas and Mau 1995, 1035).

9.2 Breaking through Avenue de l'Opéra:
roadworks on the Butte des Moulins,
from Passage Molière, c. 1877, photographer
Charles Marville (1816–c. 1878) (Charles
Marville, Musée Carnavalet, Roger-Viollet).

9.3 Ruined town hall: the village hall, Paris
(IVe arrondissement), 1871. Photographer
Charles Marville (Charles Marville / BHVP
Bibliothèque historique de la Ville de Paris /
Roger-Viollet).

In this latter case compulsory acquisitions and demolitions meant that extensive parts of the city-state were cleared of shop houses and kampong settlements to produce the "razed plane" upon which a new nation could, quite literally, be built. Many cities like Singapore live in a condition of permanent instability, wherein growth, expansion, and renewal go hand in hand with the raw mechanics of destruction and displacement. Tokyo, for example, is best thought of as a new city, for most of its architecture has been constructed or reconstructed since the Second World War, and more than 30 percent of all its structures have been built since 1985. In Tokyo in the 1990s city builders were daily demolishing 12,339 square meters (132,644 square feet) of buildings, and newly constructing 62,861 square meters (675,755 square feet) (Tokyo Metropolitan Government 1994, 16).[2] Fast-expanding cities in China and India are today experiencing their own "great mega project era" (Zhang and Fang 2004), facilitated by "demolition drives" in which the rights of the precariously housed and insecurely tenured are often brutally set aside. For example, in China land and housing reform included the 1991 Demolition Regulation, which guaranteed local governments the authority and power to issue demolition permits without seeking residents' consent, and to enforce demolition in cases of disputes (Weinstein and Ren 2009).

In this chapter, we touch upon four instances of architecture and demolition. The first of these is fictional: the now clichéd caricature of architectural creativity embodied in Ayn Rand's *The Fountainhead*. The second is mythological: the way in which the demolition of Pruitt-Igoe has served architecture's sense of itself. The third sits on the border between the real and the imagined: an online self-help group for architects whose buildings are demolished in their own lifetime. And the final instance is a practical proposal for urban design by demolition. Our purpose is to occupy the complex ambivalence that exists in architecture's necessary relationship to processes of demolition.

ARCHITECTURAL SUICIDE

Let us begin on very familiar architectural ground: with Howard Roark, the arrogant and misunderstood architect at the center of Ayn Rand's 1943 novel (and later film) *The Fountainhead*. Rand's fiction uses the architectural figure of Roark to offer a defense of a creative egoism which is free of obligation and intent on pursuing the purity of artistic expression. Roark, for example, reflects at one point that he would sooner see one of his designs "blast[ed] out of existence" than be misunderstood or misused: "It would be a worthy ending ... so much better than to see it growing old and soot-stained, degraded by the family photographs, the dirty socks, the cocktail shakers and the grapefruit rinds of its inhabitants." As Roark puts it, he is not at all interested in "second-hand lives," in which creativity is compromised by utility or collective responsibility. This, he argues, is the mode of the "parasite" (Rand 1994, 712). The final reckoning of the creative merits of Rand's fictional architect happens in a courtroom scene. Roark has been brought before the judiciary because he has done something illegal: he has demolished a building without authorization. More than that, he has done something unthinkable: the building he has demolished was one he designed. The moral motor of *The Fountainhead* is Roark's uncompromising sense of himself as an architectural creative. This articulates itself as Roark's pure and rationally driven modernist style as opposed to a mimetic, collectively oriented, populist style. So precious is this quality to Roark that he is willing to do two apparently unthinkable things, both of which entail a form of architectural suicide. The first is to allow one of his designs to be built without his name being attached to it. The nihilistic paradox of *The Fountainhead* is that Roark's stridently modernist architectural design can be built only when, discredited as he is, he allows another, rival architect to propose the design as if it were his own. The second is to willfully destroy a building that he designed, but that has been improperly realized. Roark is so compromised by this mal-realization that he has no choice but to destroy his own bastardized building. In the first instance of nihilism, Roark's identity as the named architect is set aside in the interests of seeing his design realized. He trades immediate recognition for creative posterity; suppresses his creative authorship in order to see his art anonymously live. In the second instance of nihilism, the blowing down of the bastard building, an improperly realized expression of Roark's creative persona is sacrificed in the interests of preserving a higher, but now still unrealized, creative integrity.

Rand, at her Mills and Boon best, has us access the moment of demolition by way of Roark's lover, who has been sent by him to the building site to distract the night watchman. She watched as

> [t]he upper part of the Cortland building ... tilted and hung still while a broken streak of sky grew slowly across it. As if the sky were slicing the building in half.... Then there was no upper part, but only window frames and girders flying through the air, the building spreading over the sky, a long, thin, tongue of red, shooting from the center, another blow of a fist, and then another, a blinding flash and the glass panes of the skyscrapers across the river glittering like spangles. (Rand 1994, 644)

With the explosion his lover, who is sheltering in a trench, is thrust to the ground; her breasts, her mouth, are pressed to the earth, her thighs are pounded and her body twists "in a long convulsion." Rand concludes, in a barely required clarification: "It was like lying in Roark's bed." There could be no more explicit expression of how this instance of architectural self-annihilation is serving a wider natalist purpose of architectural reproduction.

9.4 Demolition sequence from
The Fountainhead, director
King Vidor, 1949 (Warner
Brothers).

Even in Rand's fictional world, the blowing up of a building must be accounted for. Roark is placed on trial. His persuasive defense resets what the jury adjudicates on. Rather than deliberating on Roark's responsibility for an act of criminal destruction, they find themselves considering this fact in relation to his right (the creative's right) to unfettered individual expression. Roark's defense, which of course channels Rand's philosophy, is worth pausing over, for it draws into view one—routinely caricatured—variant of architectural creativity. It opens with an account of the human value of the unsubmissive (selfish) creator whose goal is to realize a pure creative vision, irrespective of the needs of potential users or the obligation of collective benefit: "The creator served nothing and no one," Roark explains to the jury, except the "glory of mankind" (1994, 711). He is concerned not with "disease," the logic of the "parasite," but with "life" and autonomous creativity (1994, 713). Roark has to destroy his altered design because it is a "double monster. In form and in implication." The world of collective obligation or architectural duty is, he says, part of a modern "orgy of self-sacrifice." It is, Roark admits to the jury, "a world in which I cannot permit myself to live."

Roark's case is persuasive, and with little deliberation the jury acquit him. In so doing they tacitly confirm that the central crime to be played out in *The Fountainhead* is not the wanton destruction of a building, but interfering with an architect's autonomous creative purity. *The Fountainhead* uses an instance of architectural self-destruction as a means of affirming architecture's true purpose. In the destruction of his improperly realized building, Roark's pure artistic genius is recognized, juridically anointed and, in a truly architectural happy ending, rewarded by a skyscraper commission (from his lover's cuckolded husband) that allows him to design and build an uncompromised "monument" based on his own design. In Roark, Rand captures something of the perversion that is at the heart of our book: the necessary and paradoxical relationship between architecture-as-creativity and nihilism.

There is a deep contradiction between Rand's philosophical defense of architectural creative freedom, embodied in Roark, and her wider politically conservative commitment to laissez-faire capitalism (Burns 2009). As the history of built-environment development testifies, architecture is routinely subjected to cycles of disinvestment and states of obsolescence. With every opportunity for creative freedom comes a moment of necessary destruction. Roark's model of architectural creativity is a fleeting possibility in wider cycles of creative destruction, over which the architect has little or no control—a fact architecture sometimes resists in its own image of itself.

DEMOLITION AS SCAPEGOAT

Of course, contemporary architecture has a far more famous and real demolition than that of Rand's imagination: the 1972 implosion of one of the 33 eleven-story blocks in Minoru Yamasaki's modernist-derived Pruitt-Igoe housing scheme in St. Louis (completed 1956). The demolition of Pruitt-Igoe enters architecture as an event, which functions as a "truth spot" for social scientific, populist, and architectural accounts of modernism as a failure (Gieryn 2002). It also circulates as an image, specifically through the photograph by Lee Balterman of *Life* magazine. This paradigmatic demolition has played an important role in architecture's ongoing creative journey. We have already discussed in chapter 8 the ways in which Pruitt-Igoe, as with other similar housing schemes, suffered disinvestment and residualization, which resulted in it being seen as an unviable housing solution. Such histories of wasting and obsolescence set the scene for demolition which, despite its costs, is the final act of disinvestment. Demolitions of mass, high-rise housing schemes were commonplace in cities throughout Europe and North America in the latter half of the twentieth century. For state municipalities and housing authorities such schemes became a burden: costly to maintain, hard to let (and so poor revenue-earners), and difficult to privatize. The 1972 demolition of Pruitt-Igoe was but one early example of what has become a common step in contemporary urban renewal.

Pruitt-Igoe has come to stand for the violations of modernism, and these violations are in turn a problem for the creative persona of architecture. What does a productive and essentially benevolent profession do with such pathologies? How can a profession rid itself of what it considers to be bad history? It represses and erases. Yamasaki makes no mention of Pruitt-Igoe or other "just plain bad" buildings in his elegantly produced 1979 autobiography *A Life in Architecture*. We might imagine that Yamasaki disowned Pruitt-Igoe because of its fate, but in an early public discussion with a skeptical housing scholar he had already distanced himself from the high-rise as an appropriate typology for housing, noting that in designing the estate as he did he was working "within constraints" (Yamasaki 1952). Yamasaki's ambivalences and repressions speak to a wider critique, in which Pruitt-Igoe came to be an icon of failed modernism. We have already detailed the sociological critique of Pruitt-Igoe, which led to its categorization as housing out of place, or housing waste. That critique was matched within architecture, and began with James Bailey's 1965 piece "The Case History of a Failure," published in *Architectural Forum*. The linking of the 1972 "trial" demolition to the "failure" of modernist architecture was reported upon in a range of professional journals such as *Architectural Forum*, *AIA Journal*, *Architecture Plus*, and the *Architects' Journal*. The *Architects' Journal*, for example, called Pruitt-Igoe "the modern movement's most grandiloquent failure" (June 26, 1972, 180). That language of failure was repeated in the reports in *Life*, *Time*, the *Washington Post*, and the *National Observer* among others.

9.5 The second, widely televised
demolition of a Pruitt-Igoe
building that followed
the March 16 demolition
(April 1972) (U.S. Department
of Housing and Urban
Development).

These immediate responses consolidated the meaning of the Pruitt-Igoe demolition. Thus began an ongoing process of reiteration in which architects of various ilks drew upon Pruitt-Igoe as a rhetorical starting point for their re-visioning of architectural creativity. It was, of course, Charles Jencks who influentially used the demolition of Pruitt-Igoe to mark the death of modernism and the birth of postmodernism. In his 1977 volume *The Language of Postmodern Architecture*, Jencks announced: "Modern Architecture died in St. Louis, Missouri, on July 15, 1972 at 3:32 p.m." Preceding Jencks, and marking an intersection between the sociologies of high-rise living in Pruitt-Igoe and architectural design, was of course the work of Oscar Newman. He may have developed his theory of defensible space by cross-tabulating building design audits and police records of crime incidents in New York high-rise projects, but it was the iconic image of the demolition of Pruitt-Igoe that appeared on the dust jacket of his 1972 book, *Defensible Space*. Colin Rowe and Fred Koetter also used this iconic photograph in their introduction to *Collage City* (1978), which proposed a more contingent and distributed architectural creativity than was represented by modernism's total planning and design solutions. Similarly, C. Thomas Mitchell, in his (1992) book *Redefining Designing*, used Pruitt-Igoe as his starting point for a case for an new architectural creativity motivated not by formalist concerns but by user experience. That he used an image of "[t]he most publicized failure of award-winning architecture" over twenty years after the event was cause for pause, and he admitted that "[m]uch has been written about this project, perhaps too much." For all of this reiterative gesturing, very little has been said about architecture's obsessive return to this scene of destruction.

It is common in the instance of technological failure for an inquiry to follow, the point of which is to understand what happened and to apportion blame. The architectural attention to Pruitt-Igoe has for the most part been rhetorical rather than forensic. Questions may have been asked, but they have all led to one answer: that this was an architectural failure. Katherine Bristol calls this the Pruitt-Igoe myth. As Bristol (1991, 163) notes: "Anyone remotely familiar with the recent history of American architecture knows to associate Pruitt-Igoe with the failure of High Modernism, and with the inadequacy of efforts to provide livable environments for the poor." Bristol documents in detail how the architectural and populist discourse in the immediate aftermath of the demolition functioned to create that myth through a process of "mystification" in which there seems to be "a one-line explanation: The design was to blame."

Bristol belatedly does the work of trying to spare modernism, and Yamasaki, this blame by offering a wider analysis of the housing policy and financing that led Pruitt-Igoe to suffer underinvestment and become a sink for a racialized poor. She concludes that it was not "megalomaniac designs" that caused the failure and tragedy of Pruitt-Igoe. In fact, and contrary to architecture's own myth about this event, "the architects were essentially passive in their acceptance of the dominant practices of their society." As she noted: "The architects had no control over the project's isolated location, its excessive densities, the elimination of amenities, or the use of high-rise elevator buildings. Their task was limited to providing the form of the individual buildings and incorporating as much amenity as possible, given the restricted budget" (Bristol 1991, 169). So why has architecture been so content to blame itself for the Pruitt-Igoe failure? What purpose has this mystification served?

When a specific object or animal or person is asked by the collective to carry blame, as Pruitt-Igoe has been, then they are operating as a scapegoat. The figure of the scapegoat and its function in the social collective has received considerable attention from social psychologists, anthropologists, and philosophers. For example, in the social psychology of the 1940s, scapegoat theory was developed to explain prejudice. The theory focused on the ways in which a dominant group's experience of frustration in relation to processes over which they had no control (such as economic or political change) could result in the designation of a minority group as the cause of the problem.[3] More nuanced interpretations of scapegoating have been advanced by anthropologists, specifically the French anthropologist René Girard. Girard's thinking about the scapegoat emerged from his wider interest in the workings of religion as a way of dealing with the violence at the heart of the world. Humankind is, he argued, constituted by acquisitive mimesis (we always want what the other has/desires), and this throws us into conflictual rivalry, a rivalry in which we lose a sense of our original self. This foundational violation is managed in society by way of the scapegoat who, although innocent, is seen to be the cause of this violence, and a polluting force. Sacrifice of the innocent victim (often one with extreme qualities) negates the guilt of our violations, and restores order. As Girard puts it in his book *The Scapegoat*:

> the victims are chosen not for the crimes they are accused of but for the victim's signs that they bear for everything that suggests their guilt relationship with the crisis … the import of the operation is to lay the responsibility for the crisis on the victims and to exert an influence on it by destroying these victims or at least banishing them from the community they "pollute." (Girard 1986, 24)

Attaching itself to the demolition of Pruitt-Igoe may well have been the way a profession undergoing unprecedented internal rivalry and introspection could keep in check potentially fatal forces. As Mélanie van der Hoorn (2009, 51) notes, drawing on Hubert and Mauss, "architectural eradication often aims at goals comparable to those of a sacrifice: to get rid of an impure status or to reach a superior one." In scapegoating Pruitt-Igoe, a type of architectural creativity deemed to pose the risk of putting the entire architectural system in jeopardy was marked as being of negative value, and killed off. And through this sacrifice professional architectural order and authority was restored.

We might imagine that the demolition of a building is an emphatically deterritorializing act. We might even believe Charles Jencks, and feel that the demolition of Pruitt-Igoe delivered architecture from a mode of wrong-headed creativity. For Jencks, the demolition of Pruitt-Igoe marked the end of an era of modernist architecture in which the creator architect positioned him/herself as the design authority, and imposed comprehensive design solutions generated by rational principles. Although never really expressed in these terms, the assumption in postmodern critiques of modernism is that it was a despotic and imperial architecture: an architecture with too much power. And certainly, as we have seen, the social studies of lived high-rise modernisms offered ample evidence of an architecture of violation that in turn hosted other kinds of violence. But we have also seen that those architects who used Pruitt-Igoe to speak against modernism reiterated the idea of architecture as formative and, in so doing, could not quite let go of its despotic character. In place of a despotic modernism Jencks and others propose a more responsive, looser and more communicative postmodern architecture: invested in context, reflective of the past, embedded in conversation. There is in this critique of modernism a flight away from a certain kind of architecture toward another more relational variant. But to what extent was this really a challenge to architecture's creative will?

Deleuze and Guattari offer a resonant story of architectural destruction and flight when they outline their post-semiotic philosophy. In that project the notion of "deterritorialization" stands in opposition to that which is "territorial" and, among other things, semiotically despotic. Significantly, as they put it, "deterritorialization follows a line of active destruction or abolition" (1987, 135). Their discussion of deterritorialization usefully includes a reflection on an architectural demolition and can help us understand just what might (and might not) have been destroyed in the scapegoating of Pruitt-Igoe. In *A Thousand Plateaus*, Deleuze and Guattari address the subject of signifying systems through the example of Jerusalem's Holy Temple, which was destroyed twice over: the First Temple by the Babylonians (587 BCE); the Second Temple by the Romans (70 CE). Deleuze and Guattari argue that Jewish history is foundationally linked to these "renewed proceedings of destruction." These events, the second of which resulted in the commencement of the Jewish flight, generated the ambivalent semiotic of Jewish diasporic subjectivity. The destruction of the Temple forced the Jews into a deterritorialized nomadism, yet in this very state of flight they discovered new possibilities for being. By leaving behind their subjection to the violation of their temple, the Jews escaped the despotism of imperial signifying systems, and created the possibility of existing in terms of their own making. Although, as Deleuze and Guattari note, the diaspora retained its nostalgia for the rebuilding of a temple "that would finally be solid" (1987, 123), they were no longer victims of its violation. In fleeing, the Jewish diaspora became their own scapegoat, and indeed "a scapegoat laden with all the dangers threatening the [despotic and imperial] signifier."

Architecture's use of the demolition of Pruitt-Igoe offers a modern, secular inversion of this structure of scapegoating. In this contemporary architectural variant, modernism is positioned as despotic (violating and violent) and, because of that very quality, understood as "bad" design. The postmodernists sacrifice modernism through the figure of the Pruitt-Igoe demolition and the design "failure" they ask it to stand for. Herein lies a contradiction. Rather than explaining away the failure of Pruitt-Igoe in non-design terms (it was poor maintenance, it was miserly budgeting, it was changing tastes), architecture draws the failure to itself and consolidates it as a matter of poor design by its own hand. Once encased in a myth of their own making, a new breed of architects feel obliged to sacrifice modernism through the scapegoat of Pruitt-Igoe. By ridding architecture of bad design, this new generation of architects is able to purify and reauthorize their role in creative world-building.[4]

ARCHITECTURAL MELANCHOLIA

For architects invested in the professional myth of creativity and permanence, there may be no greater wound to their professional identity than witnessing a building of their own design being demolished. For a natalist profession this must feel like the truncation of the arch of destiny. This is certainly how the late Scottish-based architect Isi Metzstein experienced it, noting that it is "a bit like losing a baby."[5]

Isi Metzstein was a founding member of a loosely affiliated group of architects (and architectural enthusiasts) who have all had one or more of their buildings destroyed in their lifetime. Together they have established an online forum, called The Rubble Club, in which they are able to mark their lost or threatened buildings and express their views about this loss. Touted as an idea in the late 1990s, and then given articulation by way of a website a decade later, the motto of The Rubble Club is "Gone but not forgotten." The Club operates much like any self-help organization, offering a virtual space of recognition and support for architects afflicted with the "trauma" and "bereavement" of seeing one of their buildings demolished (BBC Online, 2009). Such trauma is a commonplace experience for the professional architect. As cultural historian Neil Harris notes, progress has meant that the "abbreviation of the lives of buildings" is coincident with "the extension of the human species" (Harris, 1999, 118). Whether the pace of building loss has increased, or the frequency of architects "outliving" their buildings has increased, is unclear. As Harris (1999, 125) notes, we assume that the "mortality rate" of buildings has increased, but there are few longitudinal (or even contemporaneous) databases upon which to make such generalizations. Certainly we know anecdotally and experientially that the new technologies and materials of the twentieth century hasten the onset of obsolescence as much as they offer new possibilities for architectural creativity. And, as we saw in our discussion of obsolescence (chapter 6), leasing and tax laws increasingly assume that a building will have only a limited number of years as economically viable, and so contribute to built environment churn. As The Rubble Club complained: "buildings struggle to limp through a mere 25 years." These are certainly not the first architects to be bothered by this. For example, in 1930 Graham Aldis made a case for office-building "modernization" as opposed to wholesale demolition and rebuilding—not on the basis of sentimental attachment or aesthetic merit, but because it made good economic sense (cited in Harris 1999, 126).

The founding assumption of The Rubble Club is that when an architect's building is demolished within his or her lifetime, an injustice or a moral wrong has occurred. Like all associations, the Club has rules of membership, and losing one of one's buildings is not the only prerequisite. The destroyed building's architect must be alive, and he or she must not have been party to their building's destruction. Moreover, the building must have been built with "the intention of permanence." If the design was intended to be temporary (to come down), then demolition is to be expected and, presumably, accepted. Finally, the building must be deliberately destroyed. It does not count if it is destroyed by accident.

What can we understand about the meaning of demolition for professional architecture from the membership criteria of The Rubble Club? Well, the first thing we might note is that Howard Roark would not have been allowed to join. In destroying his own building he transgressed the cardinal rule of membership, which is not to have "connived" in the destruction of one's own building. We might also note that if a building was designed to be temporary, then the architect could not suddenly decry the realization of that design destiny when it came down. And finally, the destruction has to be purposeful, not accidental: we could say, by human design as opposed to fortune's spite. For all of this specification, there is no Committee of Governors policing membership to The Rubble Club. As founder Isi Metzstein put it: "Self-knowledge makes you a member of the club, it's all a fantasy but not an entirely empty fantasy" (2008). But what exactly is the architectural fantasy at the heart of The Rubble Club?

In his account of the "lives" of architecture, Harris (1999, 134) argues that over the past century architectural deaths have been "invested with a new and elaborate set of rituals." The Rubble Club can be read as one such ritual process. Its emergence reflects the fact that under capitalism's creative destruction we are simultaneously "energetic" reshapers of our physical environment and "elegiac" re-presenters of the structures we are "reducing to rubble." That said, there is a whiff of tongue-in-cheek about The Rubble Club. Although the lost buildings of The Rubble Club appear to cast a long shadow over their architects, there is little evidence of actual emotional trauma among members. Indeed, at least some of the work done by The Rubble Club is to hold architecture in place virtually. For example, their website is used to draw attention to buildings slated for demolition, and so perhaps garner support for not demolishing. And for those buildings already gone the website offers virtual immortalization, wherein the now disappeared architecture lives on in photographs and anecdotal stories ranging from architects reminiscing about the building's design to enthusiasts commenting on their everyday attachments. By and large the structures registered through The Club fall outside of the protective armory of heritage, although many of them are recognized within the profession as worthy examples of recent architectural styles (brutalist buildings being well represented), and were in their day prize-winning designs. Buildings can be recognized by The Rubble Club regardless of any measure of aesthetic or architectural or heritage value, but all of them belong to architecture—they are the result of architectural design. If this website gives comfort to the injured architects and their buildings, then it is by way of a negative recognition in an archive of the disappeared.

For Rubble Club members the injury of building demolition is complex. It insults their creative or artistic ego. As Metzstein put it, "the careless knocking down of landmarks illustrates the fragility of [architects'] masterworks." Such "masterworks" were often designed, he argued, in advance of the tastes of the general public. Metzstein himself, for example, claimed that he designed "into the future," producing buildings that were meant to be "physically and metaphorically permanent and timeless" (Metzstein 2008). Demolition inflicts a double injury on an architect: not only has a "masterwork" gone, but also it has gone before enough time has elapsed for it to enter permanently the unassailable category of architectural art.

The loss of a child is tragic, and a period of mourning is an inevitable stage in the grieving process. That said, the emotional register of The Rubble Club is more one of melancholy than of mourning. It was Sigmund Freud who gave us the modern understanding of melancholia: as a psychic deviation in the normal process of mourning that follows the loss of a loved one. Freud described the way in which melancholia establishes itself in the human psyche in reaction to the loss of an external object or ideal (a loved person or an abstraction that has taken the place of a loved one, such as one's country). Although such a loss normally gives rise to mourning in the bereaved subject, in some instances there is a prolonged, even permanent, refusal to break the original attachment to the lost object or ideal. This resistance can be so intense that there is a "turning away from reality and a clinging to the object through the medium of a hallucinatory wishful psychosis" (Freud 1957, 244). With the melancholic the lost object or idea becomes internalized, drawn into the ego; within this inner world, the ego absorbs both the love and the rage felt toward the lost object/ideal. Freud describes the painful dejection, disinterest in the world, damage to self-regard, and delusional expectation of punishment that can afflict those suffering from melancholia. Metzstein certainly exhibited traits of the melancholic ego. He was, he admitted, "depressed" by contemporary architecture, and joked that he read newspapers only in order to "stay hostile" to the world (Metzstein 2008). In his original essay on mourning and melancholia, Freud concludes that the melancholic suffers so because he has not only lost an external object but experienced also a "loss in regard to his ego": as he puts it, "the shadow of the object [falls] upon the ego" (1957, 249).

Within the loose membership of The Rubble Club there is, however, another line of reasoning that gestures toward an entirely different logic of architectural violation. These members of The Rubble Club are just as invested in holding onto their buildings and the idea of architectural permanence as Metzstein was, but they defend the right of their buildings to live not on artistic but on environmental and economic grounds. As Rubble Club secretary John Glenday has argued, "demolition is usually the least environmentally friendly option" (cited in Anon. 2009, 6). What is lost by their calculation is not only the building itself, but the energy that has been expended in creation. Stephen Hodder, director of Hodder Associates, whose design-winning swimming pool (the Berners Pool in Grange-over-Sands, Cumbria, UK) was slated for demolition just a few years after completion, reflected: "What I mourned was how expendable all that energy was when so many people had given so much." [6] Here the damaged architectural ego is reconstituted as a virtuous but unheard professional with a grasp on the big picture of environmental sustainability.

DESIGN BY ERASURE

In her ethnography of "undesired architecture," Mélanie van der Hoorn (2009) charts the often contradictory attachments the public have to eyesore buildings. The eyesore is a building that has been rejected, a status that expresses a disassociation between the building and its host circumstances, be they economic, use-based, or aesthetic. Rejected buildings, van der Hoorn notes, are often considered to be "corrupt in themselves," in that they have dropped out of use and entered into states of decay, or may even have dropped out of use because they were damaged or contaminated. But they are also "corrupt" in the sense that they are viewed by many as reprehensible for the damage they do to their surroundings (2009, 2). While such buildings are often hated and subject to death wishes, if they are eventually demolished their erasure can engender mixed feelings. Furthermore, rejected buildings are not always subject to elimination; they are often lived with as eyesores, and can gain some meaning and status (desirability) even as they are understood as undesirable. This is because demolishing a building is hard and expensive. Although rejected buildings attract considerable energy with respect to the claims made about their undesirability, the sheer materiality of architecture means that this undesirability is not always realized as demolition.

The emotional economy of the Oxford Film and Television series *Demolition* (2005) accommodated little of this ambiguity. The program staged a fatal encounter between hostile public opinion around architectural "eyesores," as they were dubbed, and their architect culprits. Its tenor seemed more that of retribution than of resignation or reconciliation. As one nominating member of the public asserted to camera: "I do not mean to offend the architects, but they have offended me." The sentence for these architectural "mistakes" was perhaps the ultimate punishment: demolition. As *Demolition*'s compere admitted: "you might think an architect would run a mile from such an idea." Certainly, *Demolition* generated its share of critical architectural commentary. British architectural commentator Deyan Sudjic (2005) thought it "wretchedly ill-conceived" television, especially so in the wake of a recent history of unplanned building destruction such as the attack upon and collapse of the World Trade Center, and the Indian Ocean tsunami. But at the core of *Demolition* was powerful architectural endorsement. It was not as anti-architectural as it might first have seemed.

Demolition was the televisual realization of an idea that the then president of the RIBA had been touting to various government department reviews of built environment listing procedures and urban and regional planning policy (RIBA 2003a; 2003b). Under the leadership of George Ferguson, the RIBA presented to these government reviews a "specific new proposal" for a pilot study of a mechanism for Grade X-listing of buildings "perceived to be particularly detrimental to the appearance and character of conservation areas." Once on the Grade X "hit list," a building so designated would be eligible for "demolition/alteration grants." The proposal mirrors incentive schemes that have for many years underscored heritage listing, and which ensure owners of buildings with social, architectural, or townscape value get financial support (tax breaks, access to restoration grants and expertise) for building refurbishment and reuse. X-listing similarly would offer financial incentives to take a building down, or impose penalties for not taking a building down. As such, it sought to militate against a certain kind of blight by encouraging demolition.

Ferguson and his idea of X-listing were center stage in *Demolition*, offering it an intellectual anchor point and professional legitimation. *Demolition* might have looked like sensationalist reality TV, but the presence of the architectural profession reminded us that it was not. Despite this, the program creators could not resist their sensational gestures. Only seven minutes into the first episode, viewers witnessed the unthinkable: the president of the RIBA taking a sledge-hammer to Westgate House, Newcastle. Given that the demolition of a building like Westgate House takes months of unpicking that starts from the inside and works out, followed by an implosion that then requires more months of clean-up, this was but a gesture, albeit one with considerable force. After smashing through a glass panel, the hard-hatted, sweaty, and breathless Ferguson turned to camera and panted: "[i]t has a certain irony, an architect demolishing a building, but I think it's a blow for better architecture."

Ferguson's agenda of X-listing emerges out of a conservation-linked urbanism, directed at preserving and creating what he dubs "positive and appropriate regeneration." His target is not simply buildings that are out of character or out of scale with their surroundings, which are the obvious laments of conservation designers. Such buildings may be "universally hated" aesthetically, but if they are still enjoying viable use then they are not eligible for X-listing. Rather, Ferguson's target is the building that is suspended between use and disappearance. These are the buildings that are trapped in the temporal pause that speculative developers routinely impose upon the built environment. These are the buildings that emanate an aura of decay. This is the architecture of blight. To be X-listed a building must be "vile," "unviable," and "violating," to paraphrase Ferguson. Such buildings are designated architectural waste, matter out of place. They should be removed in order to create an aesthetically more coherent and livable townscape. As an idea, X-listing shares much with the time-sensitive urban design proclivities of Kevin Lynch, articulated in his book *What Time Is This Place?* The aesthetic aim of urban design, Lynch argued, "is to heighten contrast and complexity, to make visible the process of change. The achievement of the aim requires creative and skillful demolition, just as much as skillful new design" (1976, 57). As George Ferguson stressed, X-listing is "a creative proposal—as creative as the repair or removal of unsightly scars on historic buildings" (personal communication, November 25, 2010).[7]

Although *Demolition* delighted in documenting popular hatred for nominated buildings, and its title sequences featured blow-down after blow-down, very little of the program entailed witnessing or realizing demolition of the nominated

9.6 George Ferguson, then president of the RIBA, takes a sledgehammer to Westgate House, Newcastle, for the purposes of the TV series *Demolition* (2005).

structures. In fact, much of it was dedicated to using architectural expertise to explain how nominated structures might be retained or refurbished, and the program's insistent message was that this process of architectural destruction served the greater cause of creating better architectural design. This was not simply "subtraction as a space-making tool" (Easterling 2003, 81), which is the clearing of ground for new architecture. It was also at the same time subtraction as a place-making tool, wherein architecture deemed not to fit into a wider town-scape or urban design vision is removed in a delicate reconfiguration of urban morphology. It was an idea that Sudjic found inexcusable: "To suggest that dy-namite is the enlightened planner's best friend is to take us straight back to the mentality that produced so many of Britain's worst buildings in the first place," he commented in a response to the airing of the first episode of *Demolition*. Draw-ing on a sustainability argument, Sudjic pointed not toward unliked or unused architecture as "matter out of place," but in another direction. From his point of view, "[t]earing down buildings before their time is the ultimate in profligacy. Making buildings consumes precious resources and energy and we shouldn't just throw them away without a struggle to make them better" (Sudjic 2005).

We might imagine that the kind of editorial architecture proposed by X-listing belongs to the refining judgments of conservation architects interested in the reinstatement of lost or violated townscapes. But with the enlarging of architecture from the scale of the building to the scale of urban design, such editorial extractions are undertaken routinely, and not only in the name of con-servation. For example, in the Koolhaas and OMA proposal for an "extension" for La Défense in Paris (1991), Koolhaas noted with some disappointment that the area to be designed over was "full" of "undeniably inferior buildings ... [that were] an index of 20th-century architecture ... most ... in disrepair ... many ... extremely unpopular" (Koolhaas and Mau 1995, 1096). Faced not with a *tabula rasa* but with an urban district that was already occupied, Koolhaas's team asked themselves "a very poisonous question": "How many of these buildings deserve eternal life?" (1995, 1097, 1099). Their answer was: not many, for these buildings, according to them, were unlike any of the contexts worth preserving in Europe. They were made from "materials not intended to last forever," their programs were "merely articulations of a momentary financial legitimacy," and "they were not conceived with claims of permanence." Their site was full of "short-term architecture" (1995, 1099), and Koolhaas had no time for it. As a step in the process of redesigning the area, he "declare[d] every building in the entire zone that is older than 25 years worthless—null and void—or at least potentially removable." With this one-stroke revaluation of the existing archi-tecture, Koolhaas and his team were able to make way for their own creative intervention. Their program for attaining this opening was "inaction," which,

217

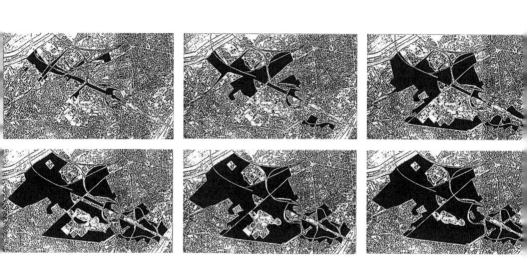

218

9.7 OMA's scheme Mission Grand Axe,
La Défense, Paris (1991) (OMA).

they argued, would lead to building redundancy that in turn they saw as space "liberating." As they hopefully speculate: "underneath the thinning crust of our civilization a hidden *tabula rasa* lies in waiting" (OMA 2012).

Of course, because this is OMA and Rem Koolhaas, none of it happens unknowingly or naively. It is a moment for pause and reflection. Koolhaas understands that a decision to design by erasure is made in the tight space of possibility left to architecture by two preceding events. One is the bad name given to demolition by earlier instances of architectural erasure: Haussmann's Paris; Le Corbusier's Plan Voisin. The other is the circumspection around demolition enforced by built environment preservationism. As OMA noted, "The idea of starting from scratch is now, in Europe, literally unthinkable; the dream / nightmare of the *tabula rasa* is dead—completely abandoned" (OMA 2012). They navigated their way through this precondition by devising a delayed program of "liberating" land. They proposed five-yearly cycles of incremental demolition, alongside the preservation of buildings of merit or sentimental value. By manipulation of the timing of erasure, OMA's proposed scheme "surreptitiously" sought to produce the *tabula rasa* necessary for their creative vision to be accepted and realized. In this sense, these proposed creative demolitions operated to re-create *tabula rasa*: to return land, albeit fleetingly, to the unique status of unproductive waste requiring the improving progression of architecture (Gamboni 1997, 215). Their scheme resonates with, but is less audacious than, the anti-architecture of Cedric Price's entry for the International Foundation for the Canadian Centre for Architecture's International Competition for the Design of Cities (1998–1999), which called for a proposal for a 12-block corridor of derelict rail yards between Pennsylvania Station and the Hudson River in New York City. Unlike the other finalists (the competition was won by Peter Eisenman), Price proposed not to build but to further empty the site in order to produce "A Lung for Midtown Manhattan." This was an explicit expression of a wider sympathy between Price and demolition that we have encountered elsewhere in this book. This is architecture by erasure.

219

ECOLOGICAL
HORIZONS

In 1972 the architect and designer Victor Papenek claimed that industrial design had "put murder on a mass production basis ... by creating a whole new species of permanent garbage to clutter up the landscape" (1972, ix). He was referring to the very same problem that, some decades later, vexed the chemist Michael Braungart and the architect William McDonough. Sharing a background in environmental activism, Braungart and McDonough joined together to write *Cradle to Cradle: Remaking the Way We Make Things*. First published in 2002, their book quickly became a bestseller. It is, all in one, a political call to arms, an environmental manifesto, and a handbook for sustainable design. The essence of their argument is captured in the book's title, which takes the well-worn adage "cradle to grave," a metonym for birth to death, and replaces grave with cradle. The title promises a virtuous circle of perpetual renewal, in which a terminal endpoint need never be encountered, where inertia is overcome and waste abolished. Our own approach could not appear to be more distinct, concerned as it is with the value of thinking about architectural graves of various kinds, and lingering as we do on themes of inertia and waste. We are traveling in similar directions, but we seem to be decidedly glummer than they are. In this final chapter we use Braungart and McDonough's idea to frame our concluding reflections upon why buildings must die and why, *contra* Woody Allen, architecture needs to be there when it happens.

221

CRADLES FOR GRAVES
Braungart and McDonough's book offers a solution to the environmental crisis by reconceptualizing design as "cradle-to-cradle design." This new concept is intended to reorient all aspects of the design and manufacturing process: from raw material extraction and processing, to the conception, design, and assembly of manufactured goods, to the lifetime performance of those goods, as well as their designed-for redeployment in as yet unforeseen future uses. Within the

framework of environmental interventions, their proposal was radical. It was no longer enough, they argued, for society to imagine that environmental degradation could be alleviated by being "less bad"—by consuming less or consuming differently, for example. Instead they proposed a radical reconfiguration of the logics of resource use, production, and consumption by introducing an extended idea of environmental stewardship realized through the very act of design itself.

It is useful in this case to dwell on the book's title, not least because it has become a widely used slogan, and even brands a certification scheme for sustainable manufacturing.[1] The title is, of course, a rewording of the saying "cradle to grave," which has been in popular circulation in English-speaking countries from the nineteenth century on. "Cradle to grave" is a term that succinctly expresses the span of a human life, but it also came to imply the quality of human lives and how they should be lived. For example, the term is used by one of the characters in Edward Bellamy's utopian science-fiction novel *Looking Backward* as a way of explaining a duty with respect to the lifelong care and nurture of citizens (Devine 2001, 2115). The term was also formally embedded in twentieth-century concepts of responsibility in welfarist politics, and in 1948 featured as one of the creeds in the UK's newly established National Health Service (Rivett 1998). From the late 1960s "cradle to grave" was used in more commercial contexts, both with respect to manufactured products and in relation to a new environmental ethic of care—for example, life-cycle assessments used in manufacturing to determine environmental impacts associated with a product over its useful life. Similarly, various tools of "industrial energy analysis" work to establish resource and environmental "profiles" and measure total energy use with respect to the manufacture (cradle) and afterlife (to grave) of products (Boustead and Hancock 1979; Horne, Grant, and Verghese 2009). So, in their reconceptualization to cradle-to-cradle design, Braungart and McDonough consciously play on and invert these established meanings of "cradle to grave."

In *Cradle to Cradle* the authors indicate something of their thinking in realigning the idea of cradle to grave. They took inspiration for the title from the well-known saying "The hand that rocks the cradle/Is the hand that rules the world" (Braungart and McDonough 2002, loc. 59). These lines, from a nineteenth-century American poem by William Ross Wallace, eulogize the role of motherhood and nurture in the shaping of worldly power and influence. Notably, the context for this honoring was American colonial settlement, in which the nurturing work of the homebound mother was depicted as her "mission here upon our natal sod." Braungart and McDonough redeploy this natalist mission for a world facing the challenge of environmental degradation, and therefore in need of a newly nurtured form of design and manufacture. In this sense the title reflects well the hypernatalism of their project.

As the subtitle to the book suggests, cradle-to-cradle design is intended to "remake the way we make things." Braungart and McDonough argue that cradle-to-grave design dominates modern manufacturing, and relies on unchallenged design assumptions associated with unrevised systems of production bequeathed by the Industrial Revolution. In such systems of production there is little concern for how and where the things produced will end up. They are waste-producing systems based "on a linear, one-way cradle-to-grave model. Resources are extracted, shaped into products, sold, and eventually disposed of in a 'grave' of some kind, usually a landfill or incinerator" (2002, loc. 371).

In contrast, cradle-to-cradle design relies on reconnecting (one might say reconciling) this waste-producing "technosphere" with the "biosphere." Braungart and McDonough think of the biosphere as a circular metabolism in which all matter is ultimately recovered as nutrients in one form or another. In this model there can be no waste, for in nature "waste equals food." "Nature," they insist, "operates according to a system of nutrients and metabolisms in which there is no such thing as waste" (2002, loc. 1153). The technosphere, by contrast, is typically structured as a linear system in which the material and productive inputs and waste outputs operate indifferently to each other.

Cradle-to-cradle design eradicates the category of waste by translating it into the material basis for new products and new creativity. The authors take a metabolist lens to the technosphere, understanding it as being comprised of "technical nutrients," materials or products with the capacity to be cycled back into the technosphere (or harmlessly into the biosphere) once their utility is spent (2002, loc. 1312).

This is a radical rethinking of the notion and practice of recycling. Recycling, although often well intentioned, is ultimately not enough for Braungart and McDonough. They see it—much like Robert Lilienfeld and William Rathje do in their book *Use Less Stuff*—as a mere "aspirin" for a "large collective hangover." Recycling, McDonough and Braungart argue, is more accurately described as "downcycling." The results are typically inferior because they take little notice of the specialized character—rare, expensive, toxic—of the materials that comprised the original product. These—often subtle—material characteristics are usually indifferently reconfigured or aggregated in recycled products, which can have unknown hazardous side-effects as a result. Instead, they argue, products should be designed for "upcycling." The concept and practice of upcycling is really the key to a system of design and manufacture that eliminates waste. As such, cradle-to-cradle design would consider not simply function and form, but also the chemical composition of materials—their "technical nutrient" composition—as the key to their ability to be upcycled into another function and form at a later date.

Cradle to Cradle aspires to be a practical book; it offers a series of case studies of designers and manufacturers who have switched to this recommended mode of operating. Given that one of the authors is an architect, some attention is paid to the design and manufacture of buildings. In Braungart and McDonough's view, an architecture that is locked into the undesirable cradle-to-grave model is exemplified by those designs that assume universal solutions, such as certain modernisms and the International Style, as well as contemporary generic architectures. In essence, buildings derived from a one-size-fits-all approach to design are singled out as especially problematic on the basis that they are "isolated from the particulars of place," its "material flows," and, importantly, its "natural energy flows." A cradle-to-cradle building should behave like a tree, they argue, and be connected to the flow of natural energies around it (sun, wind, water), so that it is able to, for example, change with the seasons, produce more energy than it consumes, and purify its own water.

A cradle-to-cradle architectural technosphere should also be adaptable, and to illustrate this, the authors turn to the loose-fit urbanism of downtown Manhattan. The scale of the volumes, the high ceilings and high windows, all contribute to the possibility of many cycles of use — "warehouses, showrooms, and workshops, then distribution centers, then artists' lofts, and, more recently, offices, galleries, and apartments" (Braungart and McDonough 2002, loc. 1748). In many respects this model does not speak well to Braungart and McDonough's core argument. This is an instance of building reuse and reprogramming, which is mostly a user recycling of relatively obdurate forms, rather than a radical rethink of architectural design principles. As sociologist Michael Guggenheim has observed (2011), the architectural imagination around change of use in buildings can at times be constrained by a vocabulary wedded to categorical states, like building form and type.[2] Yet McDonough and Braungart use the Manhattan model as a start point for urging architecture (as with all industrial design) to think about itself as if, and as in, a biological system. As they note, drawing on some observations by Stephen Jay Gould, biological systems are often organized loosely, and create "more stuff or information than is minimally needed to maintain an adaption." In short, biological systems have a "capacity for redundancy," and do so because the "extra" material "becomes available for constructing evolutionary novelties" while the basic functions are still being performed (cited in Braungart and McDonough 2002, loc. 2295). In such biomimetic architecture, innovation is designed in from the start. Capacities of redundancy, convertibility, and adaptability are planned for on the drawing board, such that the built end product can endlessly be redesigned in its material, ecological, and social realization. This is an architecture of perpetual beginnings.

224

DESIGN FOR DECONSTRUCTION

In the preface to the 2008 edition of *Cradle to Cradle*, Braungart invokes the popular view of King Canute's arrogance, narcissism, and folly when he sat on his throne at the seashore and tried to order back the tide. Braungart distances the cradle-to-cradle design project from that of Canute. Their quest is not to order back the rising technological tide that washes over the earth's environmental systems. Rather, Braungart asks that we start to ride the wave of technology in order to serve the biosphere better.[3] Yet Braungart and McDonough are themselves no less ambitious and, as many critics snipe, no less ineffectual than Canute. Cradle-to-cradle design aspires, as we have seen, to nothing less than the eradication of the concept of waste through a fundamental reshaping of the technosphere according to the metabolic principles of the biosphere.[4] The model that Braungart and McDonough advocate has been taken up by many chemists, designers, fabricators, and manufacturers. Yet there are also those who are wary of the cradle-to-cradle concept, skeptical of its biocentricity, and doubtful about its insistence that we can design, manufacture, and consume without waste.

One obvious consequence of cradle-to-cradle design is rethinking the endpoint of a building's life. In a cradle-to-cradle architectural design, the way a building ends should be a consideration on the drawing board. Designing a building would include designing its end. "Design for Deconstruction"—or DfD, as it is often known—is a pragmatic, industry approach to the cradle-to-cradle idea. We would note that "deconstruction" in this usage owes more to the construction industry than to continental philosophy—a not insignificant distinction to which we return below. The United States' National Institute of Building Sciences refers to deconstruction in their *Whole Building Design Guide*, where it is defined as the "systematic disassembly of a building generally in the reverse order of construction, in an economical and safe fashion for the purposes of preserving materials for their reuse" (Keeler and Burke 2009, 286). In the DfD approach, materials and assemblage systems are selected in readiness for the end of the building's life, so that they are better able to be upcycled, rather than laid waste or poorly recycled. The aspiration of design for deconstruction is to code the logic of unmaking into the building from the very earliest point of its making.

Design for deconstruction is not merely about how best to put the construction process in reverse at the end of a building's useful life. That is an area of expertise belonging to the demolitionist. Nor is this simply about salvage operations, whose core categories are reuse, reclaim, recycle, destroy, dump (Addis 2006, 16). DfD is about designing for a building to end well. This depends on understanding "how the elements in the building are distributed, accessed and connected at the planning stage before the building is built" (Bougdah

225

and Sharples 2010, 250). To achieve this ambition, researchers from various disciplines—architecture, building science, chemistry, garbology—have had to concentrate on the death of buildings more forensically than ever. This work has revealed new complexities within the process of unmaking buildings. While a number of general principles for DfD have been proposed, core difficulties remain around these processes of unmaking. For example, it is generally accepted that DfD is best attained if building elements are fewer and larger, if services are detached from structure by going around and not through, if the materials used for construction are not toxic, and if the number and types of connections are fewer and stronger, but reversible. DfD aims are facilitated by as-built visual documentation, as well as deconstruction plans. Also helpful are bar-coded building components to assist with recording building "layers" to aid the sequencing of deconstruction. But it is also agreed that the design of connections has been the single most difficult factor in DfD. This determines how easily elements can be separated, and what condition they will be in afterward. Most standard building connection systems or fixing technologies—screw fixing, bolt fixing, nail fixing, welding, mortar, resin bonding, adhesives, rivet fixing—rarely allow building components to be disconnected. Morgan and Stevenson suggest that of the three types of connection usually used in a building—direct (interlocking), indirect (linked by an interim component), and infilled (glued or welded)—it is only the indirect connection that is the most amenable to successful deconstruction (cited in Bougdah and Sharples 2010, 250).

During the latter part of the twentieth century, a quite different kind of deconstruction was the mark and mode of a small number of high profile, avant-garde architects. These architects produced architecture that was deconstructive in a formal sense: investigating given architectural orders and subverting, displacing, and reordering them according to looser and typically fragmenting formal protocols. This architecture remained firmly within the profession's insistent natalism, and for all of its deconstructive form expressed the place of the design architect in conceiving and producing the built. It was, as Jacques Derrida noted, a perfect expression of the profession's ability to repeatedly reenter the world "according to methods that are each time original." It took that philosopher of deconstruction to push the deconstructive claims of these architects to the kind of limits that interest us in this book. In a letter to Peter Eisenman, the well-known proponent of architectures of deconstruction, Derrida pondered: "What kind of deconstruction is this? What could bring the architecture of 'the period' … back to the ruin, to the experience of 'its own' ruin?" (Derrida 1990, 11). This question could be only partially answered by those architects who operated— and even those who denied operating—under the name of stylistic deconstruction. Yet those architects, designers, and fabricators who operate within the DfD

226

paradigm wrestle directly and materially with the intricacies of deterioration, demolition, and building termination. In so doing their design work more explicitly embraces philosophy's challenge for architecture to experience its own ruin.

THE SCALES OF RECYCLING

Researchers in the field of life-cycle analysis (LCA) necessarily focus on matters of waste and death. LCA is a process whereby the material and energy flows of a system are quantified and evaluated. Where a product "life" begins and ends seems self-evident: a natural resource is extracted, processed, incorporated into a designed product through manufacture, consumed, dumped. But the "life cycle" of products is often thought about variably, with distinctly determined components in differently calibrated temporalities and scales. Take as an example certain food systems, where the "cycle" goes from, say, soil-to-table or farm-to-fork, and then on again—through either the bin at the gate or the pipe in the bathroom (Morawicki 2012, 96). These endpoints are in a sense arbitrary. The life cycle of food may "end" at the moment it is eaten, but what of the waste it generates: is that not still part of the cycle?

For someone conducting an LCA, the reality that first comes into view is not some cosmologically calibrated cycle, but more localized and empirically traceable production-consumption-waste loops. It may well be that the difference between a cradle-to-cradle and cradle-to-grave approach is a matter of how the boundary of a "life cycle" is drawn. Empirical applications of LCA require important preliminary assessments of "parameter variability" and "system boundary," in other words the scale and reach of how components in the cycles under assessment will be tracked (Landis 2010, 432). In the application of LCA to large-scale, longer-term infrastructural assemblages like buildings, determining such boundaries is complex. For example, Scheuer et al. (2003) reported on the LCA of a projected 75-year-life-span building (the Sam Wyly Hall) on the University of Michigan campus. Their assessment attended to primary energy consumption, as well as demolition and other end-of-life burdens. They concluded that current formats for LCA were entirely too static for the dynamics associated with the relatively "long service life" of buildings. Within these relatively lengthy time frames, a building might support various uses and have quite different operating phase burdens. Furthermore, Scheuer et al. (2003, 1062) concluded, a major weakness of their own use of LCA was that it would have been impossible to conduct such a thorough assessment if the building they were examining had not already been built. In admitting this, they point to one of the key obstacles to the wider uptake of LCA in architecture and related professions. Saunders et al. (2013) conducted focus groups with architecture, engineering, and construction professionals about the use and relevance of LCA to their work. Many

227

participants agreed that it was a desirable technique, but also reported that the data collection and input to the models used for such assessments were too time-consuming and costly. Furthermore, clients were rarely willing to carry the burden of such additional costs. Their temporal horizon was far shorter (and certainly more immediately embedded in economics) than the long-term temporality of environmental benefit that LCAs serve.

Braungart and McDonough's cradle-to-cradle paradigm imagines as extensive a system boundary as possible, ensuring that a product's environmental impact is understood in relation to the raw materials extracted as well as its design, production, and consumption, and what happens after use. Their vagueness with respect to where such boundaries of assessment might be drawn is such that we are left to assume that their ultimate reference point is so extensive as to be planetary or cosmological. The more modest and empirically accountable framings of LCA approaches, if adequately resourced, allow the interplay of resource, production, and consumer behavior to be more thoroughly understood, and carefully stewarded. In the case of buildings, even if the entirety of a life cycle remains elusively complicated or expensive, such auditing and predictive modeling may well provide the basis for environmentally benign sub-cycles to be determined and adopted.

There are voices in the fields of waste management and environmental ecology that are more openly critical of the aspirations of cradle-to-cradle design. Chemist Friedrich Schmidt-Bleek—head of the Wuppertal Institute for Climate, Environment, and Energy—affirms what we call the latent Canutism of the cradle-to-cradle project. He notes that its goals are so ambitious as to be fanciful. The macro- and centralized planning, and the new logistical systems that would be required to underpin such an approach "without waste," are simply unfeasible. Consequently, cradle-to-cradle is a kind of wishful thinking that in turn supports a "hedonistic, self-centered and consumer-oriented society," where lifestyle choices are made without hesitation; it encourages "a clear conscience." As Marc Angélil and Cary Siress wryly observe, "consuming" under this kind of regime "means never having to say you're sorry" (2010, 256).

Schmidt-Bleek's own approach resists the biocentric trap evident in cradle-to-cradle design. He has no interest in developing design-manufacture-consumption systems that claim to mimic the biosphere. His interest is in developing suitable technical and regulatory interventions in systems of production and consumption in order to reduce ecological stress. Further than this, he even suggests that resource productivity and efficiency can increase alongside, and because of, such ecological goals. Central to Schmidt-Bleek's proposition is the vision of a "dematerialization" of the economy by a reduction in the total material flows in any given system of design, production, and consumption (Schmidt-

Bleek 1999; 2009). In order to support this vision, he has developed techniques for "estimating the ecological stress potential of goods and services from cradle to grave" (1999, 8). The key unit of measure here is his "material intensity per service" (MIPS). MIPS measures the material (energy) input for any service over its life span—"resource extraction, manufacturing, transport, packaging, operating, re-use, re-cycling, and re-manufacturing are accounted for, and so is the final waste disposal" (1999, 9). Importantly, Schmidt-Bleek insists on the place of the "grave" in his calculations.

Fólix Guattari ([1989] 2000, 66) has warned that natural equilibriums will require "vast programmes" to "regulate the relationship between oxygen, ozone and carbon dioxide in the Earth's atmosphere." Vast is certainly the scale at which the cradle-to-cradle project is most comfortable. Guattari also asserts that this big project cannot rely on mimicking the logic of nature. What is needed, he asserts, is a "machinic ecology." This is no essentialist assertion of the value of life, but a case for a more environmentally aware "mastery of the mechanosphere." Guattari and Schmidt-Bleek are, then, unlikely partners: the latter offers empirical support and practical realization for the former. In different ways they speak of the need to develop more refined predictive models that can track the swirling geometries of cycles, eddies, and interconnected trajectories that would constitute an environmentally responsible machinic ecology.

TOWARD AN ARCHITECTURAL COMMONS

The cradle-to-cradle thinking of Braungart and McDonough, and Schmidt-Bleek's cradle-to-grave accounting, offer differently conceptualized life-cycle "wholes" for designed and manufactured products (including architectural ones). The former imagines elements of the world brought together in specific times and places, for specific durations, as designed and manufactured products. Designed well, the elements of these products would, at the end of the life of one use, quickly and harmlessly reenter another part of the technosphere in another use, or harmlessly fold back into the biosphere. This is, as we have noted, a vision of design and manufacture in which there is nothing but endless beginnings. The vision operates on unaccountable scales. On the one hand, it is macro-expansionist in that it positions manufactured objects as assemblages or pause points in a much larger biospherical whole. On the other hand, this biomimetic vision depends upon a chemist's ability to enact a micro-reduction of the world of manufactured objects into "technical nutrients" ready for harmless reabsorption into the expanse of the biosphere. Manuel De Landa's (2006) concept of assembled wholes helps us to understand what is happening in such templates for ecological design and manufacture. For Braungart and McDonough, the only meaningful "whole" is a biosphere that is more cosmological and evolutionary than it is historical or materialist. For Schmidt-Bleek, in contrast, the meaningful scale of life-cycle wholes is set not only by the big and extensive scales of cosmology or evolution, but also by history. His measures of "ecological stress" are concerned with concrete emergent wholes—the assemblages of the inorganic, organic, and social that have come together in real geographies and temporalities to create specific matter with specific environmental effects.

Let us now take up this point of history and press it hard against the vision of cradle-to-cradle design. Let us do this by homing in on the key player in the cradle-to-cradle system: the "technological nutrient." Let us say it is a piece of quartz. That quartz is, for the time being, held in the form of concrete that about 150 years ago was slapped down between a couple of bricks in the wall of a Manhattan "loft." Remember: Braungart and McDonough argue that such loft spaces exemplify the kind of "capacity for redundancy" that allows for convertible use and innovation characteristic of a biological system. Placed as it is within a (commercial) architectural assemblage, it is not simply part of the sweep of architectural history; it is also a commodity with value. That value exists not so much in and of itself—who cares about that squish of cement between the bricks?—but as one of the many things holding together a Manhattan building.

Over the course of almost two centuries that building assemblage was made to service commerce, then languished as a low-value, underused location for all sorts of economic and social peripherals, then was culturally revalued as artist's loft space, then economically capitalized upon by the real-estate "loft living" sector (Zukin 1982). This technical nutrient is also a gentrification nutrient: it is an artifact in the institution of property. Indeed, as part of the technosphere, it has been held in place by this upvaluing commodity assemblage. Commodification plays an important role in the destiny of our "technical nutrient," including shaping the when and the where of how it might realize itself as a "nutrient" servicing the integrity of a vast ecological whole. Cradle-to-cradle design fixates on the moment of return. The located detour the quartz crystal is subject to as a part of a squish of cement, held in place by rising property values and conservation regulations, is a pause point or permanence with respect to its role in the ecological whole. The "cycles of use" or instances of "convertibility" are seen as mere way stations on the quartz crystal's greater journey toward its more extensively conceptualized destiny. In cradle-to-cradle thinking there is a collapse of the commonality assumed to be a feature of the biosphere, and the privatization and enclosure associated with commodification. Uncoupling this collapse may be more urgent than any technical system of building disassembly.

So, why not adopt cradle-to-cradle's cheery outlook? The optimistic ideals of cradle-to-cradle are, to adapt Žižek's words, embedded in a "utopia of a self-enclosed circle in which all waste, all useless remainder, is sublated: nothing gets lost, all trash is re-used" (2011, 35). Schmidt-Bleek's idea of acknowledging the "ecological rucksack" of things may weigh us down more, but at least we can rummage through it and see what is there.

This does not mean that architecture should not bother to lighten the ecological rucksack of its work, but it does acknowledge that such a project is incrementally achieved and may never be finally realized. So, in the meantime, how might architecture design, what idiom will it use, and what moral imagination will it draw on? What is clear is that architecture will design in what Bataille called "a field of multiple destructions" (1988, 23). Many of us have limited and unevenly distributed choices with respect to how we deal with this world crowded with junk, obsolescences, and end things. Some, whose lives are already precarious, will use such dross to build and design and make do. Others will do everything they can to forget it exists, and often employ architects to help them do so. Architecture can design either facing toward waste and death or looking away. It is our view that looking away is useless, and in this book we have tried to create the basis for a terminal idiom, such that death and waste can play their parts in architectural creativity. We are suggesting here a stance with respect to architectural deaths and endings that is counter to the usual understandings of the relationship between life, death, and creative action. Such endings, as we have shown, are often thought of in contradictory ways. They can be and often are construed as a counterforce to the profession-affirming creative act of architectural design. In this view, such destructions are a defeat of architectural effort, and a verdict quite literally of ruin, to paraphrase the philosopher of mortality John E. Seery (1996, 17). Alternatively, such endings can also, especially in cycles of creative destruction, be seen as providing new opportunities for design. The first of these relationships may carry the moral high ground, but both are premised upon setting death apart from and against architectural action. This is an architecture that creates only in the name of beginning. It is like Hannah Arendt's (1958, 246) natalist defiance of death. Although humans "must die," she argues, death has nothing to do with why they were born: humans were "not born in order to die but to begin." For Arendt, the "beginning something new" was political action. Here we substitute creative agency. But should architectural action be only in the name of a memorialization of life against death? We have tried in this book to gesture toward a less defensive relationship between architectural creative action and death, and in this last chapter we warn against the tempting option of doing away with death entirely through the cyclical fantasy of eternal renewal.

Žižek suggests that "the properly aesthetic attitude of a radical ecologist" is about "accepting waste … [of] discovering the aesthetic potential of waste, of decay, of the inertia of rotten material which serves no purpose" (2011, 35).[5]

This chimes with the aesthetics of the Viennese apartment development known as the Hundertwasser. Completed in 1985, it was the product of a conflictual cooperation between the Austrian artist Friedensreich Hundertwasser and architect Joseph Krawina. The Hundertwasser offers a model of architectural deterioration, which is enchanted with the decrepit states produced "when mold forms on a wall, when moss grows in the corner of the room and rounds off the geometric angle." We too are interested in microbes and fungi, and agree that "their moving into the house offers architectonic changes from which we have a great deal to learn." For Hundertwasser, what architecture must strive for is "uninhabitability and creative moldering" (cited in Harries 1998, 241–242). But for us, uninhabitable architecture really would result in dead buildings. We do not suggest that buildings should lie down and die in that sense. Nor do we suggest that architecture, as art has the freedom to do, abandons quality and invests in decrepitude, or emulates cast-off debris, "beneath the level of roadside junk," as a commentary upon showroom finishes (Drucker 2004, 588).

We began this book by admitting to the perversity of our thesis. We wanted to point out the deathly states of buildings, in their many forms and circumstances, in order to engender a feeling for the inert. Following processes of building decay, obsolescence, disaster, ruin, and demolition has opened out a rich idiom around which to build a terminal literacy. This idiom runs deeper than ruinous aesthetics. It extends out to questions of ecology, and is yoked to logics of capitalist creative destruction. It was not our intention to point to deteriorating, decrepit, and destroyed buildings and merely whisper gratuitously: "Buildings must die." We offer this investigation as an extended memento mori for architecture to help recalibrate its purpose. In short, this book about the death of buildings is composed in the name of architectural agency and its capacity to make worlds differently.

CHAPTER 10

NOTES

1 INTRODUCTION: A FEELING FOR THE INERT

1. Lacan develops his account of subjectivity through the development of visual systems. In the perspectival system, imaginary lines structure the relationship of the viewing subject in space. This, Lacan says, is a kind of "mapping of space" in which the subject is located. The vanishing point of the perspectival system is complemented by another point marked by the viewer. So two sets of imaginary lines form complementary cones—one reaching out to infinity, the other to the viewer's eye—that meet at the picture plane. Regardless of the representational media, this system presents a "point-by-point correspondence of two unities in space." Leonardo's perspectival studies build on the Vitruvian description of the correspondence of the human body in this space (Lacan 1981, 86).

2. The richly visual documentation of Detroit's demise continues to grow. Indicative accounts include Austin (2010), Moore and Levine (2010), and Marchand and Meffre (2011).

3. For readers interested in such war-related destructions and more general conditions of urban violence we would recommend Ashworth (1991), Lang (1997), Lambourne (2001), Linethal (2001), Davis (2002), Vanderbilt (2002), Schnieder and Susser (2003), Graham (2004a), Bevan (2006), and Weizman (2007, 2012). The specific case of the attack on the World Trade Center is discussed in Sorkin and Zukin (2002), Davis (2003), and Langewiesche (2003).

4. See, for example, studies on demolition including Liss (2000) and Byles (2006).

5. See, particularly, Buchli and Lucas (2001), Neville and Villeneuve (2002), Hawkins and Meucke (2003), and Campkin and Cox (2007).

6. For example, Arnheim (1971), Smithson (1979, 1996), Bois and Krauss (1997), and Knechtel (2007).

7. See specifically Edensor (2005a, 2005b, 2005c) and De Silvey (2006).

8. Resonant architectural commentaries include Mostafavi and Leatherbarrow (1993), Hill (2003), Easterling (2005), Stoner (2012), and Forty (2013). We have also found value in the temporal emphasis of Stewart Brand's (1995) *How Buildings Learn* and the more recent collection *Time-Based Architecture* (Leupen et al. 2005).

9. William Rathje was an archaeologist who understood the value of looking at the waste of the present. See Rathje and Murphy (1992) and Rathje (2001).

2 DESIGN, CREATIVITY, AND ARCHITECTURE'S NATALISM

1. Such language can be found extensively in architectural discourses, as is noted by Kipnis (1997), Colomina (2000), Forty (2004), and Ingraham (2006), among others. Anthropomorphic metaphors are also evident in the way philosophical and social theoretical discourses refer to architecture, as indicated in Lyotard (1991) and Deleuze (1992). As Ingraham (2006, 10) notes, architectural anthropomorphism can coexist alongside of architecture's "indifference to life."

2. See, as examples, Bloomer and Moore (1977), Jencks and Kropf (1997), Whyte (2003), and Bastéa (2004).

3. See George Hersey's (1999) wide-ranging review of the biological analogy in architecture in his book *The Monumental Impulse: Architecture's Biological Roots*.

4. Contemporary trends in biomorphic and biomimetic architecture are well accounted for in Feuerstein (2002) and Gruber (2011).

5. The various illnesses and infections of buildings are well accounted for by Walter Goldstein (2010) and Michelle Murphy (2006). Buildings can also be regarded as being "in pain" (Vidler 1990), or as "wounded" by deliberate acts of vandalism, terrorism, or war (Wigley 1995b; Linethal 2001; Bevan 2006; Graham 2004a; 2011).

6. An accessible philosophical account of the meaning of death for the living is offered in Shelly Kagan's *Death* (2012).

7. These abstract philosophical themes are glossed as "exploratory" and "transformational" creativity in more recent literature on the theory of creativity (Gaut 2009, 208; Boden 2004, 29). An "exploratory creativity" accepts and operates within a set of prescribed generative rules and conceptual space. This kind of creative practice is more generic. A "transformational creativity," by contrast, attempts to reach beyond the possibilities of a given conceptual space, and seeks to transform the very rules that give shape to that space. Both kinds of creative practice involve at least three separable components—an agent, a process, and a product. Analyses of creativity typically privilege one of these components over the others, be it the artist, poet, or architect agent; the process of painting, composition, or design; or the product of the painted work, the poem, or the building.

8. The architect interviewed was Sunand Prasad, former RIBA president.

9. If the practice of *disegno* makes an opening between the architect-as-conceiver and the tradesman-as-builder, then the emergence of the studio as an institutional space can be understood as a spatial manifestation of such an opening. Located away from the mess of the building site, the studio emerged as a space of intellectual and creative work. In the studio the conceptual, creative, and exploratory work of *disegno* could be carried out on the clean surfaces of the drawing board. The studio's emergence as the sanctioned space of architectural design was accompanied by that of other institutional practices (such as exhibitions and public lectures) and spaces (such as drawing libraries and architectural museums), and came to be associated with the modern figure of architect-as-conceiver (Hughes 1986, 52–53).

10. Accounts of this transformation can be found in Pevsner (1940), Barasch (1990), and in Carl Goldstein (1996); on the empiricist/rationalist split, see Herrmann (1962).

11. This is discussed in Vidler (1981, 105); see also Barasch (1990, 171).

12. As Kant notes in the third *Critique*, "the beauty of a building (such as a church, palace, armory, or summer-house) does presuppose the concept of a purpose that determines what the thing is [meant] to be, and hence a concept of its perfection, and so it is merely adherent beauty" (Kant [1790] 1987, 77).

13. See Anthony Vidler's (1981) essay, and Paul Oskar Kristeller's two essays (1951a, 1951b) on "The Modern System of the Arts" for an extended discussion of this period.

14. Le Corbusier's description of his own design process in the pamphlet *Textes et dessins pour Ronchamp* (1955) amplifies this idea. As Menin and Samuel report, he approached a design problem by resisting making sketches and instead storing the problem in his memory. "The human brain," he believed, "is made in such a way that it has a certain independence: it is a box into which one can pour in bulk the elements of a problem and let them float, simmer, ferment. Then one day, a spontaneous initiative of one's inner being takes shape, something clicks; you pick up a pencil, a stick of charcoal, some coloring pencils (color is the key to the process), and *give birth onto the paper: out comes the idea*" (Le Corbusier cited in Menin and Samuel 2003, 82). Indeed, architectural historian Jan Birksted goes so far as to suggest that Le Corbusier understood his own design process as an "immaculate conception" (Birksted 2007, 305). Le Corbusier subscribed to the Renaissance ideal of *disegno* in a very direct way. In his book *Creation Is a Patient Search* (1960), he describes the "liberating experience" of learning to paint, and how it reminded him of the transformation of architecture as craft to architecture as art. "As if," Edgar Kaufmann acerbically notes in his review of the book, "he had brought forth a new dogma full blown like Minerva from the head of Jove" (Kaufmann 1961, 290).

15. This phrase has been attributed to various people. Some attribute it to William Morris, others to the early promoter of the arts and crafts in Germany, Hermann Muthesius. Others say it was a modernist slogan: Walter Gropius apparently adopted it as his personal motto, and used it as a founding pedagogical principle when he taught at the Harvard Design School following World War II. Still others report that modernist architect Mies van der Rohe coined the phrase. In Italy it is usually attributed to postwar modernist architect Ernesto Rogers, or to product designer Massimo Vignelli.

16. Robbins (1990) notes that the Smithsons' interest in found conditions was in conversation with the British pop art scene of the 1950s.

17. See also Harris and Berke (1997).

18. The rejection of total design for "collage" urbanism is proposed by Rowe and Koetter (1978) and resonates forward to Koolhaas's (1995) generic urbanism and Rieniets, Sigler, and Christiaanse's "open city" design approach (2009). As Jencks (1977) shows, postmodernism delivered eclecticism, ad-hocism, and other contextualisms. The architectural turn to retrofitting and reuse is documented and accounted for in Dunham-Jones and Williamson (2011) and Baum and Christiaanse (2013).

19. Notable accounts of the profession's sense of itself have been produced by Saint (1985; 2007), Cuff (1991), Ray (2005), and Till (2009).

20. In this test subjects are required to isolate and identify geometric figures that are embedded in larger, more complex figures. The results showed a "remarkably high preference [among architects] for complex asymmetrical and dynamic figures, as opposed to simple and symmetrical ones" (Goldschmit 1999, 531).

21. *Filarete's Treatise on Architecture and the Ideal City of Sforzinda.* As Kruft informs us, "Antonio Averlino, who adopted the surname Filarete (Friend of Virtue), was born in Florence around 1400, where he trained as a goldsmith and bronze founder, possibly in the workshop of Ghiberti.... His treatise on architecture was probably written in the years 1461–64 ... in the narrative form of a dialogue, and describes in daily stages the planning and building of the fictitious town of Sforzinda. The work has with some justification been termed a 'diary novel'" (1994, 52).

22. Filarete is regarded as the less scholarly writer. He is, by his own admission, rather modest, saying of his own scholarship: "I am not too experienced in letters or in speaking" (cited in Mallgrave 2006, 37), and observing on a number of occasions that Alberti was better informed and skilled at writing. So while he reinforced many of the principal themes of Alberti's writing, there was a sense in which he also departed from them in more imaginative and unruly ways, being drawn away from the academic ground by his own prose and imagination. As Mallgrave points out, "For one thing, Filarete was not a humanist and did not have the intellectual command of classical sources so evident in Alberti's writings. Second, Filarete did not try to emulate the 10-book structure of Vitruvius.... His treatise rather takes the form of a dialogue, essentially a polemic, in which Filarete tries to convince the members of the Sforza family (the rulers of Milan between 1450 and 1535) of the superiority of 'ancient art' (classicism) over and above 'modern art' (the prevailing Gothic style)" (Mallgrave 2006, 36). Filarete affirms, with Alberti, that he is "very skilled in architecture and especially design which is the basis and means of every art done by hand" (Filarete cited in Mallgrave 2006, 37). Filarete's "coarse accent" and "erratic punctuation" (Mallgrave 2006, 113) have tended to mean that his work is taken less seriously than Alberti's, and it was not widely read at the time of writing. For Onians (1971), Filarete makes a significant contribution to architectural history through his emphasis on ancient Greek architectural culture, rather than the Roman that was Alberti's touchstone. In this respect he anticipates the later eighteenth-century neoclassicism in Europe.

23. Filarete famously recounts the story of the birth of architecture from Adam's upheld arms. God's Adam had the perfect proportions for his emphatically anthropometric architecture (Filarete 1965, 10 [book 1]). See Agrest (1988) on this theme.

24. Rykwert notes in a footnote (1981b f5, 495) that Vitruvius's wording—"*Ita ... generibus duobus ... tertium genus in operibus est procreatum*"—draws on the Latin *procreare*, meaning "beget," which was rarely used figuratively.

238

3 TERMINAL LITERACY: DROSS, RUST, AND OTHER ARCHITECTURAL JUNK

1. We cite necessarily Anthony Vidler's (1977, 1987) influential readings of Hugo within architectural theory. Émile Zola (1872), for example, inverted the sense of Hugo's phrase "this will kill that," applying it to the destructive effects of one coming (modern, iron and glass) architecture over another (old stone structures) in late-nineteenth-century Paris. Roland Barthes noted that Hugo's observation helps us to understand the city as a written text, and we users and inhabitants of the city as "readers" who "sample fragments" to assemble endlessly variable urban narratives (Barthes [1967] 1988, 199).

2. In this pluralist context, Eco remains skeptical of visual media, and in particular those "prefabricated images," which deliver "prefabricated definitions of the world" (Eco 1996). With visual communication strategies "it is easier to implement persuasive

strategies that reduce our critical power" (Eco 1996). As a consequence he still privileges the text, regarding it as supporting and encouraging critical capacities to critique and scrutinize those visual media.

3. Picon's "problem" with these technological landscapes is that they eschew the traditional ordering of nature to culture. In the "traditional landscape," by which Picon really means the landscapes designed in the European tradition, the "works of man" (which we can assume include architecture) stood in a knowing relationship to nature such that both cultural "work" and un/cultivated "nature" enhanced or even "completed" one another. Industrialization altered that relationship in that it gave rise to extended conditions of urbanization that appear to be "independent from the framework of nature."

4. Price would, no doubt, have enthused at Omer Haciomeroglu's 2013 design for the "ERO Concrete De-Construction Robot" that reportedly "eats concrete" and "literally erases buildings" (Alter 2013, 1). The robot uses high-pressure water to break down the concrete fabric of condemned buildings, leaving the reinforcement steel intact for subsequent reuse. The liquidized concrete and aggregate is also reusable, while the traditional dust and pollution associated with conventional demolition practices are substantially reduced.

4 TOWARD A GENERAL ECONOMY OF ARCHITECTURE

1. Exceptions here include the 2005 Royal Academy Forum entitled "Value: Culture and Commerce," led by Richard MacCormac and including Charles Jencks, Dickson Robinson, and Jean-Louis Cohen. For an edited version, see Melvin (2005).

2. Scanlan's (2005, 65) use of the phrase "cosmetic of order" activates the etymology of *kosmos*, meaning order and/or ornament.

3. Such large projects of transformation are well documented in Kaufmann (1955) and Picon (1992). An unconventional interpretation of architecture in this time is offered by Vidler (1987). On Locke, property and architecture, see also Ingraham's forthcoming book *Architecture's Claim: On Property*.

4. This is discussed fully in Krell (1995, 55–56), as well as in Mitchell (2010, 70–72).

5. This fate is well described by Marshall Berman in his *All That Is Solid Melts into Air* (1982, 117).

6. Revisionist scholarship on Schumpeter suggests that he may have drawn heavily on the untranslated German scholarship of Werner Sombart, the first to use this term (McKee 1991).

7. Thompson knew this "laboratory" well, as he lived in this part of London from 1966 to1971; he also worked there as a builder's laborer in order to fund the PhD research that was reported upon in *Rubbish Theory*. As Thompson himself notes, he stripped out fireplaces and other fixtures from houses that were considered "rubbish," and sold them on to the gentrifying "knockers-through," as he dubbed them.

8. The term "gentrification" was first coined by the British sociologist Ruth Glass who, in the 1960s, began to describe such processes in Kensington, London. See Glass (1964).

9. Reinert and Reinert (2006) argue that Hinduism was a religion that inspired Nietzsche's educator, Arthur Schopenhauer.

10. Georges Bataille and Michel Leiris make remarks on architectural fabricated forms in various entries in the Critical Dictionary Bataille edited, which was published in 1929 and 1930 in sections of the magazine *Documents*. Although architectural attention has naturally been drawn to the entries "Architecture" (Bataille) and "Skyscraper" (Leiris), themes pertinent to rethinking architecture are to be found in a number of the other essays by Bataille, such as "Factory Chimney," "Formless," "Dust," and "Space (questions of propriety)." See Bataille et al. (1995).

11. See Angélil and Siress (2010, 261–262) for a reading of Bataille's concept of general economy in terms of the wider discourse on recycling and sustainability.

12. For example, Guattari's ([1989] 2000) *The Three Ecologies* proposed a new "eco-subjectivity." Included in this is what Guattari refers to as a "machinic ecology" ([1989] 2000, 66) (see chapter 10 below).

13. Deleuze and Guattari offer an immanent and radical notion of being, encapsulated in their post-subjective concept of the "body without organs," a figure of life not bound in or by body and subjectivity. For them, the body without organs is "the model of death." It is the unformed, the deformed, the dispersed: "no mouth, no tongue, no teeth—to the point of self-mutilation, to the point of suicide" (Deleuze and Guattari 1983, 329).

5 DECAY

1. Charles Dickens was equally struck by the whiteness and sense of newness of the buildings of small-town colonial America during his visit in 1842. "Every little colony of houses has its church and school-house peeping from among the white roofs and shady trees; every house is the whitest of the white; every Venetian blind the greenest of green; every fine day's sky the bluest of blue…. There was the usual aspect of newness on every object, of course. All the buildings looked as if they had been built and painted that morning, and could be taken down on Monday with very little trouble" (Dickens 1842, 170).

2. Le Corbusier regarded the "white" cathedrals of medieval Europe as a pan-European architecture which stood, therefore, as a progenitor of a modern international style. "An international language reigned wherever the white race was, favoring the exchange of ideas and transfer of culture. An international style had spread from the West to the East and from the North to the South" (Le Corbusier 1947, 4).

3. These processes are discussed in detail in Salvadori and Charola (2011), Krumbein (2003), and Guillitte (1995).

4. The application of glass represented, as Benjamin notes, a kind of banishment of bourgeois identity-as-possession, but also stood for a material "impoverishment." "Objects made of glass have no 'aura.' Glass is, in general, the enemy of secrets" (Benjamin 1999c, 734). With glass (and steel), modernist architects "have created rooms in which it is hard to leave traces."

5. Other modern materials such as "glass-fibre decays more disagreeably than stonework." "[T]he aesthetics of metal decay" is a complex category itself; Lowenthal deems "rust on iron, tarnish on silver, white crusts on lead and tin" "odious." He insists that "only to copper and bronze does a time-induced oxidized surface add lustre of a 'noble' patina" (Lowenthal 1985, 163).

6. See also Gargiani and Rosellini (2011).

7. As we note in chapter 3, the riskiness of this experiment is something that Bernard Tschumi understood well when he chose an image of a ruined Villa Savoye for one of his "Advertisements for Architecture" (1976–1977) postcards, and claimed that its "state of decay" was its key architectural feature.

8. On weathering and leaks in architecture, see also Sully (2009), Hill (2012), and Mayer and Bhatia (2010).

9. It is important to note that other subarchitectural technologies—toilets, sinks, plugs—are dedicated to managing the expulsion of dirt and waste (see Friedman and Lahiji 1997; Loos [1931]1987).

10. As Saarinen put it: "John Deere and Company is a sound, well established, successful farm machinery company, proud of its Midwestern farm-belt location. Farm machinery consists not of slick, shiney [sic] metal but of forged iron and steel in big, forceful shapes. The proper character for its headquarter's [sic] architecture should likewise not be a slick, precise, glittering glass and spindly metal building but a building which is bold and direct, using metal in a strong and basic way" (cited in Martin 2006, 73).

11. Kipnis was referring specifically to the early projects of Herzog and De Meuron, including their copper-clad and patinated Signal Box in Basel.

12. The *Bangkok Post* reported in March 2012: "An investigation has been launched into the structural integrity of remnants of the abandoned Hopewell concrete pilings after a massive slab measuring six by 50 meters collapsed 20 meters to the ground" (Ngamkham 2012).

13. Experiments such as this relate to work in material and building sciences, and more conventional biology, that has examined the ways in which materials—such as metals, alloys, ceramics and, most promisingly, concrete—might be designed to be "self-healing" through the application of naturally occurring bacteria (Ghosh 2009; Jonkers 2007).

6 OBSOLESCENCE

1. Reports on such developments can be found in Al Jazeera (2009), Balston (2010), Barboza (2010), and Bill Powell (2010).

2. They are also known as eyesores. Anthropologist Mélanie van der Hoorn (2009) has shown how people living with such architectural eyesores can acquire perverse affection for them and attachments to them.

3. Ghosttransmissions (Art Connection) was a 2005 sound and video installation by Building Transmission exhibited in H Gallery Bangkok, June 16–30, 2005, which used materials from a visit to Sathorn Unique.

4. For example, in England in 1951, in the context of the decline of the local coal fields, the Durham County Development Plan classified entire villages as "D-settlements," meaning no future development would be permitted, and property would be acquired and demolished. Mining is notorious for both bringing settlements into being and then letting them down. In Australia the coal town of Leigh Creek was built, fully relocated, then entirely demolished, over the course of half a century.

5. As economic historians note, the development of the skyscraper and the improved fortunes of the steel industry went hand in hand. After the stagnation of the rail market in the 1880s, the industry's survival depended on opening out to other markets.

Bethlehem Steel, under the risk-taking leadership of Charles M. Schwab, began fabricating in steel Henry Grey's wide-flange I-beams, then H-beams specifically for use in tall-building construction (Hogan 1971; Rogers 2009, 44).

6. In 1967, a year before Red Road was completed, an inquiry was established into the overspend on its construction. The inquiry found that Bunton produced a proposal that was in no way a "natural outgrowth" of the original brief, which was to devise a standard high-rise typology for Glasgow (Baird Smith et al. 1969, 21). Instead, Bunton developed a "novel," "unprecedented," "experimental," "speculative," "singular" project, whose claims to be efficient and economical were "illusory" (Baird Smith et al. 1969, 42, 49, 31, 33, 53, 60). Red Road was, the inquiry concluded, produced in a costly "atmosphere of improvisation" (1969, 30).

7. In one of their publications (Schmidt et al. 2011) they cite Paduart et al.'s finding (2009) that new construction, maintenance, and renovation of buildings contribute 45 percent of European waste.

8. For further discussion of this, see also van Hoogstraten and Vos (2000).

9. In chapter 9 we note the rapid pace of demolition and construction in Japanese cities like Tokyo.

10. According to Eguchi et al. (2011, 75) Japan's 2006 Basic Plan for Housing proposed a new housing policy known as the "200-year housing," in an attempt to promote the construction of more durable houses with easier and less costly maintenance demands.

11. The list of such studies is long, and by way of example we might think here merely of the more influential: Pearl Jephcott's relatively early study of the high-rise housing of Glasgow (1971); Lee Rainwater's (1973) and William L. Yancey's (1978) studies of Pruitt-Igoe; Oscar Newman's (1972) study of New York's public housing; and, belatedly, Alice Coleman's (1985) "trial" of British public housing estates. For the role of such scholarship in urban science and housing policy, more generally, see Jacobs and Lees (2013); Strebel and Jacobs (in press).

7 DISASTER

1. The hut referred to in Isaiah's passage is variously translated as "tent," "cottage," "shack," "lodge," or "hammock."

2. Such criticism can be found in T.G. (2005), Freudenburg et al. (2009), Gotham (2007), and Brym (2011).

3. See <www.christchurchquakemap.co.nz>.

4. Benjamin Mountfort was subsequently appointed as the supervising architect of Christchurch Cathedral from 1873. Frederick Stouts replaced Crisp as architect for St. Michael's.

5. As Lochhead notes, stone parish churches were "the exception rather than the rule throughout the nineteenth century, although most of the city's more modest timber churches were replaced during the course of the twentieth century" (Lochhead 2012, 4).

6. It is estimated that more than 4,000 mostly British, but also French, German, and American, foreign advisors worked in Japan, on three-year contracts typically, during this period (1874–1899) (Cybriwsky 2011, 272).

7. Waters recommended replacing the stone with brick in the cathedral spire. Ironically, most of the brick buildings were destroyed in the Great Kanto Earthquake of 1923 (Cybriwsky 2011, 80).

8. The seeming fit between structure and stone medium did not stop speculations as to the timber origins of Gothic architecture. These principally rest on the experiments and historical conjecture of Scottish geologist James Hall. Hall, observing the rustic utilitarian timber buildings of northern Europe, conducted an experiment in which he "re-enacted" a kind of archaeology to show that the typical characteristics of Gothic architecture—"the pointed arch, clustered column, and the branching roof"—were derived from timber origins (cited in Rykwert 1981a, 85). Rykwert also notes that it was also fashionable among philosophers—Goethe, Hegel, Coleridge—to regard the Gothic as emanating from a wood or forest (Rykwert 1981a, 93).

9. See Cairns (2004, 24) for a discussion of Ban's not inconsiderable efforts to have his proposal for a "paper-tube" building accepted by the Takatori church community. See also Elizabeth Farrelly's (2011) opinion piece on the "gimmicky" quality of Ban's Christchurch proposal.

8 RUIN

1. Salmon (2000, 27) argues that these architectural visits were sufficiently different in purpose and in practice to be distinguished from the "Grand Tour." They were skill-based, and those undertaking the trips were economically different to those undertaking Grand Tours. Often the itineraries followed and the lengths of stay were different. His detailed descriptions of such study tours also suggest that those on them were far more than dilettantes. Similarly, archaeologist Christopher Evans has noted that John Soane was very aware of excavation practices (Evans 2000, 349).

2. Angela Schönberger has argued that this "theory of ruin value," which legitimized the use of natural stone without any iron reinforcements, was in fact a euphemism which hid the real reason why this building technique was preferred: the economic necessity to minimize the use of iron, which was urgently needed for the armament program (Schönberger 1981, 168–169).

3. According to Hell (2010, 186), Speer even produced a "Romantic drawing" of the Zeppelin Field's Grandstand as a future ruin, much in the style of Joseph Gandy's painting of the Bank of England in ruins.

4. Rem Koolhaas has referred to the first essay as "one of the most interesting texts written by an architect"; Isozaki describes the essays as "science fiction." When the first of the essays went to its publisher, The Japan Architect, the editor found it so perplexing that, in Isozaki's words, "he buried the essay at the back of the advertising pages," consigning it to "a decade of posteriority" (Koolhaas and Obrist 2011, 49).

5. As James S. Ackerman (1974, 299) put it, modern public housing projects embodied an ambition to design space thoroughly and prescriptively, but they produced a lesser quality of life than that provided by "the old and decayed dwellings they replaced." Ackerman threaded this specifically through his own variant of a theory of value. While modernist housing designed in "use value," it designed out the possibilities for "surplus value," such as neighborliness, a sense of community and belonging. See also Jacobs and Lee for an account of the relationship between Newman's and Coleman's work (2013).

6. Gordon Matta-Clark's work is well documented in Lee (2000), Diserens (2003), and Walker (2009).

7. Guides on urban exploring include Deyo and Leibowitz (2003), and Ninjalicious (2005). Tim Edensor (2005a) puts this practice into theoretically informed account of ruins, politics, and aesthetics. Variations on urban exploration such as bunkerology are accounted for by Bennett (2011) and Garrett (2011a, 2011b).

8. Eschatological accounts of the city include Davis (2002), Abbott (2006), and Page (2008). Detroit's demise is recorded in Austin (2010), Gallagher (2010), Levine and Moore (2010), Marchand and Meffre (2011), and Brooke (2012). For discussion of more general conditions of shrinking, including design and planning responses, see Bowman and Pagano (2004), Oswalt (2005), Oswalt and Rieniets (2006), Langner and Endlicher (2007), Haase (2008), Gallagher (2010), and Ryan (2012). Those questioning whether it is time to move beyond ruin porn and "Detroitism" include Leary (2011), Binelli (2012), and Piiparinen (2012).

9. We are grateful to Hanna Göbel (2012), who has allowed us to draw on her unpublished research in this area.

10. Of course a similar, but by some decades earlier, process of cultural creatives (artists, architects, and designers) taking up and revaluing abandoned city buildings was charted by Sharon Zukin (1982) in her study of New York City's loft living.

11. This aesthetic is evident, for example, in E-Werk on Wilhelmstraße in the central Mitte district, Berlin.

12. Willis (2009, 403) distinguishes between squatting (where land is occupied illegally), shanty-towns (defined largely on the basis of the flimsy construction of buildings), and informal settlements (a more general term to designate areas of dubious land tenure).

13. In other disciplines concerned with the built environment, notably urban studies and planning, such a comparative and postcolonial revision is well underway. Jennifer Robinson's (2006) project of building theory through ordinary cities, and Ananya Roy's (2007) interest in locating the production of planning theory in the informalities of the developing world, offer templates for this.

14. An organization like Slum/Shack Dwellers International, which offers a global network for mobilization and problem-solving advocacy, is an example of the political creativity that has attached to informal settlements. For discussion on informal infrastructures generally, see De Soto (1989, 2000), Roy and AlSayyad (2004), Simone (2004), Gandy (2006), Roy (2007), and McFarlane (2008).

15. Another well-known project is Michel Ecochard's urban quarter in Casablanca, which was not designed for incremental addition but was extended anyway.

16. Two projects were excluded on the grounds of technical and material complexity.

17. For García-Huidobro, Torres Torriti, and Tugas (2011, 31), in their contemporary study of PREVI, the ideal growth scenario culminated in a "hyperhouse" which was capable of supporting a multigenerational social group and diverse income-generating opportunities.

9 DEMOLITION

1. Page's source here is "The Building of New York," *Architecture* 56 [December 1927], 324.

2. These statistics were presented in Bognar (1997).

3. Scapegoat theory was forwarded by psychologists Hovland and Sears (1940), and later Zawadzki (1948).

4. Deleuze and Guattari use the relationship between the destruction of the Temple and the Jewish flight to advocate the need to break free of what they describe as the "signifying regime" in order to move toward the deterritorializing possibilities of what they call the "subjective regime." In an ironic way, given the emphasis in postmodern architecture on signification and language (sign), this is exactly what architecture's embrace of the demolition of Pruitt-Igoe seeks to do. As it was, the radically deterritorialized potentials of this move were virtually impossible to realize in the conservative and expressive variants of architecture advocated by that first wave of postmodernism. As Deleuze and Guattari note, lines of flight from despotic regimes are relative: some achieve deterritorialization of the "signifying regime," whereas others simply stay within it, talking back in a "countersigning semiotic" (1987, 135). This they refer to as only a "relative deterritorialization" (1987, 145). There is a far more radical and deterritorialized architecture that can be, and is, anticipated in Deleuzian thinking. This is an architecture that is shaped not by expressive language (the sign), but by the deconstructive potentialities of the diagram. A diagrammatic architecture is a derivative of what Deleuze and Guattari call the "abstract machine," wherein there is no longer "a sign-to-sign circularity," but what they describe as a "linear proceeding into which the sign is swept away" (1987, 127). This is a deterritorialized architecture yet to come.

5. Metzstein worked for the Scottish firm Gillespie Kidd & Coia, and during the period when he was a creative force the firm produced noteworthy modernist buildings, a number of them brutalist in style.

6. Hodder's statement is in a report on the demolition on The Rubble Club's website. See Hodder (2009).

7. In an 8-page X-Listing Manifesto, both the procedure for X-listing and the criteria are specified. Procedurally, anyone could nominate a building for X-listing; a nominated jury would then determine a short list from the nominees, and then a panel of "experts" (expertise unspecified) would make the final decision. Once served with a notice of X-listing, those responsible for the building would be obliged to seek out a fast-track route to demolition or radical remodeling. A building would be X-listed only if it met three criteria: (1) it must have no aesthetic or architectural merit; (2) it must have a demonstrable "anti-social" effect; (3) it must be an economic failure.

10 ECOLOGICAL HORIZONS

1. Braungart and McDonough developed the cradle-to-cradle approach into a full-fledged Certified Products Program that rates products across a range of five criteria—material health, material reutilization, energy required for production, water used and discharge quality, social responsibility, including labor practices—and promotes best practice through a system of awards.

2. Guggenheim (2011, 25) concludes that architecture needs to enrich its conceptual frame for building conversion, and adopt a "processual view of buildings … based on the convergence of technological, semiotic, and sociological perspectives." We would note that Guggenheim's critique of architectural discourses and practices with respect to conversion focuses on a relatively conservative vein of thinking, and ignores more radical event-generated architecture imaginaries such as those of Bernard Tschumi (see chapter 3).

3. Colin May (2009) notes that this popular view of King Canute is not supported by historical evidence. Rather, the Canute narrative is a complex and subtle account in which human, political, and environmental agencies are negotiated. For example, one lesser-known interpretation of the narrative is that "[a]lthough ostensibly designed to demonstrate his boundless authority, the public spectacle that he stages is in fact a symbolic and strategic demonstration of his limited powers and his all-too-human frailties" (May 2009, 261).

4. See Marc Angélil and Cary Siress's (2010) essay "Re: Going Around in Circles: Regimes of Waste" for a detailed account of the recent history of diagramming and conceptualizing metabolic and recycling loops of various kinds.

5. Žižek's observations were made with a specific reference to that commonplace architectural touchstone, Bentham's Panopticon. Apparently everything in the building, up to and including the prisoners' excrement and urine, was to be put to further use. "Regarding urine," Žižek reports, "Bentham proposed the following ingenious solution: the external walls of the cell should not be fully vertical, but lightly curved inside, so that, when the prisoners urinated on the wall, the liquid would drip downward, keeping the cells warm in winter" (Žižek 2011, 35).

BIBLIOGRAPHY

Abbott, Carl. 2006. The Light on the Horizon: Imagining the Death of American Cities. *Journal of Urban History* 32:175–196.

Abbott, Charles F. 1930. Obsolescence and the Passing of High-Pressure Salesmanship. In *A Philosophy of Production: A Symposium*, ed. George Frederick, 153–156. New York: Business Bourse.

Abramson, Daniel M. 1999. The Bank of England. In *John Soane, Architect: Master of Light and Space*, ed. Margaret Richardson and Mary-Anne Stevens, 208–251. London: Royal Academy of Arts.

Abramson, Daniel M. 2003. Obsolescence: Notes towards a History. *Praxis: Journal of Writing and Building* 5:106–112.

Abramson, Daniel M. 2009. Obsolescence: Notes towards a History. In *Building Systems: Design Technology and Society*, ed. Kiel Moe and Ryan E. Smith, 159–170. London: Routledge.

Abramson, Daniel M. 2010. Obsolescence and the Fate of Zlín. In *Autopia of Modernity: Zlín*, ed. Katrin Klingan with Kerstin Gust, 157–169. Berlin: Jovis Verlag.

Abramson, Daniel M. 2012. Boston's West End: Urban Obsolescence in Mid-Twentieth-Century America. In *Governing by Design: Architecture, Economy and Politics in the Twentieth-Century*, ed. Aggregate: Architectural History Collaborative, 47–69. Pittsburgh: University of Pittsburgh Press.

Abujidi, Nurhan. 2010. *Spaces of Oppression and Resilience: State of Exception, Urbicide and Beyond; the Palestinian Case*. Beirut: Institute for Palestine Studies.

Ackerman, James S. 1974. Transactions in Architectural Design. *Critical Inquiry* 1 (2):229–243.

Adams, Cassandra. 1998. Japan's Ise Shrine and Its Thirteen-Hundred-Year-Old Reconstruction Tradition. *Journal of Architectural Education* 52 (1):49–60.

Adams, Nicholas. 1993. Architecture as the Target. *Journal of the Society of Architectural Historians* 52 (4):389–390.

Adamson, Glenn, ed. 2010. *The Craft Reader*. London: Berg.

Addis, Bill. 2006. *Building with Reclaimed Components and Materials: A Design Handbook for Reuse and Recycling*. London: Earthscan.

Agrest, Diana I. 1988. Architecture from Without: Body, Logic, Sex. *Assemblage* 7 (October):28–41.

Al Jazeera. 2009. China's Empty City. Documentary video, 10 November. http://www. youtube.com/watch?v=0h7V3Twb-Qk (accessed 10 July 2012).

Alter, Lloyd. 2013. Beware Brutalism: Concrete-Eating Robot "Literally Erases Buildings." Treehugger, July 16. http://www.treehugger.com/green-architecture/beware-brutalism-concrete-eating-robot-literally-erases-buildings.html (accessed 8 August 2013).

Ama, Toshimaro. 2005. *Why Are the Japanese Non-religious? Japanese Spirituality: Being Non-religious in a Religious Culture*. Lanham, MD: University of America Press.

Angélil, Marc, and Cary Siress. 2010. Re: Going Around in Circles: Regimes of Waste. In *Re-inventing Construction*, ed. Ilka and Andreas Ruby, 248–264. Berlin: Ruby Press.

Anon. 2009. The Rubble Club. *Architect: Official Journal of the Kamra Tal-Periti* 49 (July):6.

Anon. N.d. From Cradle to Cradle—ein Leben ohne Müll. http://www.kultur-kreative.de/2010/07/from-cradle-to-cradle-ein-leben-ohne-muell/ (accessed 12 January 2013).

Aravena, Alejandro, and Andrés Iacobelli. 2012. *Elemental: Incremental Housing and Participatory Design Manual*. Ostfildern: Hatje Cantz.

Arendt, Hannah. 1958. *The Human Condition*. Chicago: University of Chicago Press.

Ariès, Philippe. 1974. *Western Attitudes toward Death: From the Middle Ages to the Present*. Baltimore: Johns Hopkins University Press.

Armstrong, Rachel. 2009. Living Buildings: Plectic Systems Architecture. *Technoetic Arts: A Journal of Speculative Research* 7 (2): 79–94.

Armstrong, Rachel. 2010. Self-Repairing Architecture. *Next Nature*. http://www. nextnature.net/2010/06/self-repairing-architecture/ (accessed 27 May 2012).

Armstrong, Rachel. 2012. *Living Architecture: How Synthetic Biology Can Remake Our Cities and Reshape Our Lives*. TED Books.

Arnheim, Rudolf. 1971. *Entropy and Art: An Essay on Order and Disorder*. Berkeley: University of California Press.

Ashworth, Gregory. 1991. *War and the City*. London: Routledge.

Auer, Gerhard. 1995. Building Materials Are Artificial by Nature. *Daidalos* 56:56–65.

Austin, Dan. 2010. *Lost Detroit: Stories behind Motor City's Majestic Ruins*. Charleston, SC: History Press.

Bacon, Mardges. 2003. *Le Corbusier in America: Travels in the Land of the Timid*. Cambridge, MA: MIT Press.

Bahamón, Alejandro, and Maria Camila Sanjinés. 2008. *Rematerial: From Waste to Architecture*. New York: W. W. Norton.

Bailey, George. 2009. Originality. In *A Companion to Aesthetics*, ed. Stephen Davies, Kathleen Marie Higgins, Robert Hopkins, Robert Stecker, and David E. Cooper, 457–459. Chichester: Wiley-Blackwell.

Bainbridge, David A. 2011. *Passive Solar Architecture: Heating, Cooling, Ventilation, Day-lighting, and More Using Natural Flows*. White River Junction, VT: Chelsea Green Publishing.

Baird Smith, James H., William Sinclair Gauldie, and James Shankley. 1969. *Red Road Inquiry: Report of the Committee Appointed by the Corporation of Glasgow*. Glasgow: Corporation of Glasgow.

Baldwin, Geoff, Richard I. Kitney, Paul Travis Bayer, S. Freemont, Tom Ellis, Karen Polizzi, and Stan Guy-Bart, eds. 2012. *Synthetic Biology: A Primer*. London: Imperial College Press.

Balston, Andrew. 2010. Revisiting China's "Empty City" of Ordos. *Wall Street Journal* (12 May). http://blogs.wsj.com/chinarealtime/2010/05/12/revisiting-chinas-empty-city-of-ordos/ (accessed 12 July 2012).

Ban, Shigeru. 1999. *Shigeru Ban: Projects In Process to Japanese Pavilion, Expo 2000 Hannover*. Tokyo: Mitsuo Kawago.

Banham, Reyner. 1989. *A Concrete Atlantis: U.S. Industrial Building and European Modern Architecture, 1900–1925*. Cambridge, MA: MIT Press.

Banham, Reyner. 1999. *A Critic Writes: Selected Essays*. Cambridge, MA: MIT Press.

Bankoff, Greg, Georg Frerks, and Dorothea Hilhorst, eds. 2004. *Mapping Vulnerability: Disasters, Development and People*. Sterling, VA: Earthscan.

Barasch, Moshe. 1990. *Modern Theories of Art, 1: From Winckelmann to Baudelaire*. New York: New York University Press.

Barboza, David. 2010. Chinese City Has Many Buildings, but Few People. *New York Times* (19 October). http://www.nytimes.com/2010/10/20/business/global/20ghost.html?pagewanted=all (accessed 12 July 2012).

Barras, Richard, and Paul Clark. 1996. Obsolescence and Performance in the Central London Office Market. *Journal of Property Valuation and Investment* 14 (4):63–78.

Barry, Ellen. 1999. How Vijecnica Was Lost. *Metropolis Magazine* 18 (9):108–113.

Barta, Patrick. 2007. High-Rise Relics: Ghost Structures Haunt Bangkok. *Wall Street Journal* (27 July).

Barthes, Roland. [1967] 1988. Semiotics and Urbanism. In *The Semiotic Challenge*, trans. Richard Howard, 191–201. New York: Hill and Wang.

Bastéa, Eleni, ed. 2004. *Memory and Architecture*. Albuquerque: University of New Mexico Press.

Bataille, Georges. 1985. The Notion of Expenditure. In Bataille, *Visions of Excess: Selected Writings, 1927–1939*, ed. Allan Stoekl, trans. Allan Stoekl et al., 116–129. Minneapolis, University of Minnesota Press.

Bataille, Georges. 1988. *The Accursed Share*. Vol. 1. New York: Zone Books.

Bataille, Georges. 1991. *The Accursed Share: An Essay on General Economy*. Vols. 2–3. New York: Zone Books.

Bataille, Georges, et al. 1995. *Enclycopaedia Acephalica*. London: Atlas Press.

Baudrillard, Jean. 1993. *Symbolic Exchange and Death*. Thousand Oaks, CA: Sage.

Baudrillard, Jean. 1994. The Beaubourg Effect: Implosion and Deterrence. In Baudrillard, *Simulacra and Simulation*, trans. Sheila Faria Glaser, 61–74. Michigan: University of Michigan Press.

249

Baudrillard, Jean. 1998. *The Consumer Society: Myths and Structures*. Thousand Oaks, CA: Sage.

Bauer, Catherine. 1952. Low Buildings? Catherine Bauer Questions Mr. Yamasaki's Arguments. *Journal of Housing* 9 (July):227.

Baum, Martina, and Kees Christiaanse, eds. 2013. *City as Loft: Adaptive Reuse as a Resource for Sustainable Urban Development*. Zurich: GTA Publishers.

Bauman, Zygmunt. 1992. *Mortality, Immortality and Other Life Strategies*. Stanford: Stanford University Press.

Beauregard, Robert A. 1993. *Voices of Decline: The Postwar Fate of US Cities*. Oxford: Blackwell.

Bedau, Mark A., and Emily C. Parks. 2009. Introduction to the Ethics of Protocells. In *The Ethics of Protocells: Moral and Social Implications of Creating Life in the Laboratory*, ed. Mark A. Bedau and Emily C. Parks, 1–16. Cambridge, MA: MIT Press.

Beesley, Philip. 2010. Introduction: Liminal Responsive Architecture. In Beesley, *Hylozoic Ground: Liminal Responsive Architecture*, ed. Pernilla Ohrstedt and Hayley Issacs, 12–40. Cambridge, Ontario: Riverside Architectural Press.

Benjamin, Walter. 1983. *Charles Baudelaire: A Lyric Poet in the Era of High Capitalism*. London: Verso.

Benjamin, Walter. [1928] 1998. *The Origin of German Tragic Drama*. Trans. John Osborne. London: Verso.

Benjamin, Walter. 1999a. *The Arcades Project*. Ed. Rolf Tiedemann. Cambridge, MA: Belknap Press.

Benjamin, Walter. 1999b. *Illuminations*. London: Pimlico.

Benjamin, Walter. 1999c. *Selected Writings 1931–1934*. Ed. Michael William Jennings and Marcus Paul Bullock. Cambridge, MA: Harvard University Press.

Bennett, Jane. 2010. *Vibrant Matter: A Political Ecology of Things*. Durham: Duke University Press.

Bennett, Luke. 2011. Bunkerology—A Case Study in the Theory and Practice of Urban Exploration. *Environment and Planning D: Society and Space* 29:421–434.

Berger, Alan. 2006. *Drosscape: Wasting Urban Land in America*. New York: Princeton Architectural Press.

Berman, Marshall. 1982. *All That Is Solid Melts into Air: The Experience of Modernity*. New York: Verso.

Berman, Marshall. 1987. Among the Ruins. *New Internationalist* 178 (December):1–3.

Berman, Marshall. 1996. Falling Towers: City Life after Urbicide. In *Geography and Identity*, ed. Dennis Crow, 172–192. Washington, DC: Maisonneuve Press.

Bermúdez, José Roberto, and Ramon Bermúdez. 2008. Dismantled City. In *Rematerial: From Waste to Architecture*, ed. Alejandro Bahamón and Maria Camila Sanjinés, 84–89. New York: W. W. Norton.

Berns, Gregory. 2010. *Iconoclast: A Neuroscientist Reveals How to Think Differently*. Cambridge, MA: Harvard Business School Publishing.

Bevan, Robert. 2006. *The Destruction of Memory: Architecture at War*. London: Reaktion.

Binelli, Mark. 2012. How Detroit Became the World Capital of Staring at Abandoned Old Buildings. *New York Times* (9 November).

Binney, Marcus, and Max Hannah. 1979. *Preservation Pays: The Economic Benefit of Preserving Historic Buildings*. London: Save Britain's Heritage.

Birksted, Jan Kenneth. 2007. The Politics of Copying: Le Corbusier's "Immaculate Conceptions." *Oxford Art Journal* 30 (2):305–326.

Blake, Peter. 1964. *God's Own Junkyard: The Planned Deterioration of America's Landscape*. New York: Holt, Rinehart and Winston.

Blau, Judith. 1987. *Architects and Firms: A Sociological Perspective on Architectural Practice*. Cambridge, MA: MIT Press.

Blier, Suzanne Preston. 1987. *The Anatomy of Architecture: Ontology and Metaphor in Batammaliba Architectural Expression*. Cambridge: Cambridge University Press.

Bloomer, Kent, and Charles Moore. 1977. *Body, Memory and Architecture*. Cambridge, MA: MIT Press.

Boden, Margaret. 1994. What is Creativity? In *Dimensions of Creativity*, ed. Margaret Boden, 75–117. Cambridge, MA: MIT Press.

Boden, Margaret. 2004. *The Creative Mind: Myths and Mechanisms*. London: Routledge.

Bogdanovic, Bogdan. 1993. Murder of the City. *New York Review of Books* 40 (10):10.

Bognar, Botond. 1997. What Goes Up Must Come Down: Recent Urban Architecture in Japan. *Harvard Design Magazine* 3 (Fall):1–8.

Bois, Yves-Alain, and Rosalind Krauss. 1997. *Formless: A User's Guide*. New York: Zone Books.

Bosanquet, Bernard. [1892] 2005. *A History of Aesthetic*. New York: Cosimo.

Botar, Oliver, and Isabel Wünsche, eds. 2011. *Biocentrism and Modernism*. Farnham: Ashgate.

Bougdah, Hocine, and Stephen Sharples. 2010. *Environment, Technology and Sustainability*. New York: Taylor and Francis.

Boukema, Esther, and Philippe Vélez McIntyre, eds. 2002. *Louis G. Le Roy: Nature Culture Fusion*. Rotterdam: NAi Publishers.

Boustead, Ian, and George F. Hancock. 1979. *Handbook of Industrial Energy Analysis*. Halsted Press.

Bowman, Ann, and Michael Pagano. 2004. *Terra Incognita: Vacant Land and Urban Strategies*. Washington, DC: Georgetown University Press.

Brand, Stewart. 1995. *How Buildings Learn: What Happens after They're Built*. London: Penguin.

Brandsetter, Gabriele, Hortensia Völckers, Bruce Mau, and André Lepecki, eds. 2000. *ReMembering the Body*. Ostfildern: Hatje Cantz.

Braungart, Michael, and William McDonough. [2002] 2009. *Cradle to Cradle: Remaking the Way We Make Things*. London: Vintage Books.

251

Brodey, Inger Sigrun. 2008. *Ruined by Design: Shaping Novels and Gardens in the Culture of Sensibility*. London: Routledge.

Brook, Pete. 2012. Photos of Detroit Need to Move beyond Ruin Porn. *Wired Magazine: Raw File* (Website). http://www.wired.com/rawfile/2012/06/photos-of-detroit-need-to-move-beyond-ruin-porn/ (accessed 3 July 2012).

BRS. 1964a. Design and Appearance—1. *Building Research Station Digest* 46 (April):1–5.

BRS. 1964b. Design and Appearance—2. *Building Research Station Digest* 46 (May): 1–4.

Brym, Robert J. 2011. Hurricane Katrina and the Myth of Natural Disasters. In Brym, *Sociology as a Life or Death Issue*. Belmont, CA: Wadsworth Publishing.

Buchanan, Andrew, David Carradine, and Justin Jordan. 2011. Performance of Engineered Timber Structures in the Canterbury Earthquakes. *Bulletin of the New Zealand Society for Earthquake Engineering* 44 (4):394–401.

Buchli, Victor, and Gavin Lucas, eds. 2001. *Archaeologies of the Contemporary Past*. London: Routledge.

Buck-Morss, Susan. 1989. *The Dialectics of Seeing: Walter Benjamin and the Arcades Project*. Cambridge, MA: MIT Press.

Bunton, Sam. 1963a. Letter to the Editor. *Glasgow Herald* (8 February).

Bunton, Sam. 1963b. Letter to the Editor. *Glasgow Herald* (19 February).

Burns, Jennifer. 2009. *Goddess of the Market: Ayn Rand and the American Right*. New York: Oxford University Press.

Butler, Judith. 2004. *Precarious Life: The Powers of Mourning and Violence*. London: Verso.

Byles, Jeff. 2005. *Rubble: Unearthing the History of Demolition*. New York: Broadway Books.

Cairns, Stephen, ed. 2004. *Drifting: Architecture and Migrancy*. London: Routledge.

Callenbach, Ernest. 2002. The Gleaners and I (Les glaneurs et la glaneuse). *Film Quarterly* 56 (2):46–49.

Campkin, Ben, and Rosie Cox, eds. 2007. *Dirt: New Geographies of Cleanliness and Contamination*. London: I. B. Tauris.

Camuffo, Dario. 1995. Physical Weathering of Stones. *Science of the Total Environment* 167 (1–3):1–14.

Canguilhem, Georges. 1991. *On the Normal and the Pathological*. Trans. Carolyn Fawcett. New York: Zone Books.

Carlson, Allen. 1994. Existence, Location, and Function: The Appreciation of Architecture. In *Philosophy and Architecture*, ed. Michael H. Mitias, 141–164. Amsterdam: Rodopi.

Caruso, Adam. 1998. Tyranny of the New. *Blueprint* 150 (May):24–25.

Carvalho, John. 2009. Creativity in Philosophy and the Arts. In *The Idea of Creativity*, ed. Michael Krausz, Denis Dutton, and Karen Bardsley, 313–330. Leiden: Brill.

Charlesworth, Esther. 2006. *Architects without Frontiers: War, Reconstruction and Design Responsibility*. London: Architectural Press.

Chau, Adam Yuet. 2008. An Awful Mark. *Visual Studies* 23 (3):195.

Chen, David. 2009a. The House the Quake Built. *Taipei Times* (26 September): 16. http://www.taipeitimes.com/News/feat/archives/2009/09/26/2003454503 (accessed 20 November 2011).

Chen, David. 2009b. Greener and Wiser. *Taipei Times* (20 September): 13. http://www.taipeitimes.com/News/feat/archives/2009/09/20/2003454035 (accessed 23 November 2011).

Cho, Minsuk, and Mass Studies. 2010. Best Used Before: The Asian City and the Quest for a Time-Specific Architecture. In *Re-inventing Construction*, ed. Ilka and Andreas Ruby, 201–216. Berlin: Ruby Press.

Choay, Françoise. 1997. *The Rule and the Model: On the Theory of Architecture and Urbanism*. Ed. Denise Bratton. Cambridge, MA: MIT Press.

Christchurch Cathedral. 2012. Transitional Cathedral: A Symbol of Hope for the Future. Media release.

Clancey, Gregory. 2004. Towards a Spatial History of Emergence: Notes from Singapore. In *Beyond Description: Singapore Space Historicity*, ed. Ryan Bishop, John Phillips, and Wei-Wei Yeo, 30–59. London: Routledge.

Clancey, Gregory. 2006. *Earthquake Nation: The Cultural Politics of Japanese Seismicity, 1868–1930*. Berkeley: University of California Press.

Clark, Eric. 1995. The Rent Gap Re-examined. *Urban Studies* 32 (9):1489–1504.

Clark, Kenneth. [1928] 1964. *The Gothic Revival*. London: Pelican.

Clark, T. J. 2006. *The Sight of Death: An Experiment in Art Writing*. New Haven: Yale University Press.

Clément, Gilles, and Philippe Rahm. 2006. *Environmental Approaches for Tomorrow*. Montreal: Canadian Centre of Architecture.

Coaldrake, William. 1996. *Architecture and Authority in Japan*. London: Routledge.

Cohen, Adam, and Elizabeth Taylor. 2000. *American Pharaoh: Mayor Richard J. Daley. His Battle for Chicago and the Nation*. Boston: Little Brown.

Cohen, Stanley. 1973. Property Destruction: Motives and Meanings. In *Vandalism*, ed. Colin Ward, 23–53. London: Architectural Press.

Colean, Miles. 1953. *Renewing Our Cities*. New York: Twentieth Century Fund.

Coleman, Alice. 1980. The Death of the Inner City: Cause and Cure. *London Journal* 6:3–22.

Coleman, Alice. 1985. *Utopia on Trial: Vision and Reality in Planned Housing*. London: H. Shipman.

Coles, Alex, and Mark Dion, eds. 1999. *Mark Dion: Archaeology*. London: Black Dog.

Colley March, H. 1889. The Meaning of Ornament, or Its Archaeology and Its Psychology. *Transactions of the Lancashire and Cheshire Antiquarian Society* 7:160–192.

Colloredo-Mansfield, Rudi. 2003. Introduction: Matter Unbound. *Journal of Material Culture* 8 (3):245–254.

Colomina, Beatriz. 2000. *Privacy and Publicity: Modern Architecture as Mass Media*. Cambridge, MA: MIT Press.

253

Connor, Steven. 1992. *Theory and Cultural Value*. Oxford: Blackwell.

Cooper, Frederick, and Tomeu Ramis. 2012. Local Background. *Digital Architectural Papers* 9 (4 June). http://www.architecturalpapers.ch/index.php?ID=95 (accessed 24 September 2012).

Copley, Stephen, and Peter Garside, eds. 1994. *The Politics of the Picturesque: Literature, Landscape and Aesthetics since 1770*. Cambridge: Cambridge University Press.

Corvalán, Juan Pablo. 2007. The Return of Previ. http://the-return-of-the-previ.blogspot.sg/?m=1 (accessed 23 August 2011).

Coward, Martin. 2004. Urbicide in Bosnia. In *Cities, War, and Terrorism: Towards an Urban Geopolitics*, ed. Stephen Graham, 154–171. Oxford: Blackwell.

Coward, Martin. 2008. *Urbicide: The Politics of Urban Destruction*. London: Taylor & Francis.

Cresswell, Tim. 1996. *In Place/Out of Place: Geography, Ideology and Transgression*. Minneapolis: University of Minnesota Press.

Cronin, Leroy. 2011. Defining New Architectural Design Principles with "Living" Inorganic Materials. *Architectural Design* 112 (March/April):35–44.

Cros, Caroline. 2006. *Marcel Duchamp*. London: Reaktion.

Crowther, Paul. 1991. Creativity and Originality in Art. *British Journal of Aesthetics* 31:301–309.

Cuff, Dana. 1991. *Architecture: The Story of Practice*. Cambridge, MA: MIT Press.

Curl, James Stevens. 1993. *A Celebration of Death: An Introduction to Some of the Buildings, Monuments, and Settings of Funerary Architecture in the Western European Tradition*. London: B. T. Batsford.

Curl, James Stevens. 2002. *Death and Architecture*. Stroud: Sutton Publishing.

Cybriwsky, Roman A. 2011. *Historical Dictionary of Tokyo*. Lanham, MD: Scarecrow Press.

Daily Southern Cross. 1869. All Stone and Brick Buildings in Town Were More or Less Damaged. St. John's Church Was Split. *Daily Southern Cross* 25 (3712) (11 June): 3.

Damisch, Hubert. 1985. The Drawings of Carlo Scarpa. In *Carlo Scarpa: The Complete Works*, ed. Francesco Dal Co and Giuseppe Mazzariol, 209–213. Milan: Electa.

DAS-SABIH. 1994. *Urbicide Sarajevo*. Bordeaux: Arc en Rêve Centre d'Architecture/ Sarajevo: DAS-SABIH Association of Architects.

Davies, John. 1995. Dirt, Death, Decay and Dissolution: American Denial and British Avoidance. In *Contemporary Issues in the Sociology of Death, Dying and Disposal*, ed. Glennys Howarth and Peter C. Jupp, 60–71. London: Palgrave Macmillan.

Davis, Mike. 1999. *Ecology of Fear: Los Angeles and the Imagination of Disaster*. New York: Vintage Books.

Davis, Mike. 2002. *Dead Cities, and Other Tales*. New York: New Press.

Davis, Mike. 2006. *Planet of Slums*. London: Verso.

Deam, B. L. 1997. Seismic Ratings for Residential Timber Buildings. Building Research Association of New Zealand (BRANZ), Study Report SR (73). Wellington.

De Landa, Manuel. 1997. Immanence and Transcendence in the Genesis of Form. *South Atlantic Quarterly* 96 (3):499–514.

De Landa, Manuel. 1998. Deleuze, Diagrams, and the Genesis of Form. *ANY* 23 (June):30–34.

De Landa, Manuel. 2006. *A New Philosophy of Society: Assemblage Theory and Social Complexity*. London: Continuum.

Deleuze, Gilles. 1989. *Cinema 2: The Time-Image*. Trans. Hugh Tomlinson and Robert Galeta. London: Athlone Press.

Deleuze, Gilles. 1992. *The Fold: Leibniz and the Baroque*. Trans. Tom Conley. Minneapolis: University of Minnesota Press.

Deleuze, Gilles. 2003. *Francis Bacon: The Logic of Sensation*. London: Continuum.

Deleuze, Gilles, and Félix Guattari. 1983. *Anti-Oedipus: Capitalism and Schizophrenia*. Trans. Robert Hurley, Mark Seem, and Helen R. Lane. Minneapolis: University of Minnesota Press.

Deleuze, Gilles, and Félix Guattari. 1986. *Kafka: Toward a Minor Literature*. Trans. Dana Polan. Minneapolis: University of Minnesota Press.

Deleuze, Gilles, and Félix Guattari. 1987. *A Thousand Plateaus: Capitalism and Schizophrenia*. Trans. Brian Massumi. Minneapolis: University of Minnesota Press.

Demers, Joanna. 2010. *Listening through the Noise: The Aesthetics of Experimental Electronic Music*. Oxford: Oxford University Press.

Derrida, Jacques. 1990. Letter to Peter Eisenman. *Assemblage* 12:7–13.

Derrida, Jacques. 1994. Letter to Peter Eisenman. In *Critical Architecture and Contemporary Culture*, ed. William J. Lillyman, Marilyn F. Moriarty, and David J. Neuman, 20–28. Oxford: Oxford University Press.

De Silvey, Caitlin. 2006. Observed Decay: Telling Stories with Mutable Things. *Journal of Material Culture* 11 (3):317–337.

De Soto, Hernando. 1989. *The Other Path: The Invisible Revolution in the Third World*. London: I. B. Tauris.

De Soto, Hernando. 2000. *The Mystery of Capital: Why Capitalism Triumphs in the West and Fails Everywhere Else*. New York: Basic Books.

Desrochers, Brigitte. 2000. Ruins Revisited: Modernist Conceptions of Heritage. *Journal of Architecture* 5 (1):35–46.

Devine, James. 2001. Utopia. In *Encyclopedia of Political Economy*, ed. Phillip Anthony O'Hara, 2:1214–1216. London: Routledge.

Deyo, L. B., and David Leibowitz. 2003 *Invisible Frontier: Exploring the Tunnels, Ruins, and Rooftops of Hidden New York*. New York: Three Rivers Press.

Dickens, Charles. 1842. *American Notes for General Circulation*. Vol. 1. London: Chapman and Hall.

Diserens, Corinne, ed. 2003. *Gordon Matta-Clark*. London: Phaidon.

Dizdarević, Zlatko. 1993. *Sarajevo: A War Journal*. New York: Fromm International.

Dollimore, Jonathan. 2001. *Death, Desire and Loss in Western Culture*. London: Routledge.

255

Dolske, Donald A. 1995. Deposition of Atmospheric Pollutants to Monuments, Statues and Buildings. *Science of the Total Environment* 167 (1–3):15–31.

Douglas, Mary. [1966] 1970. *Purity and Danger: An Analysis of Concepts of Pollution and Taboo*. London: Penguin.

Drucker, Johanna. 2004. Affectivity and Entropy: Production Aesthetics in Contemporary Sculpture. In *The Craft Reader*, ed. Glenn Adamson, 588–595. Oxford: Berg.

Duffy, Francis. 1990. Measuring Building Performance. *Facilities* 8 (5):17–20.

Dunham-Jones, Ellen, and June Williamson. 2011. *Retrofitting Suburbia: Urban Design Solutions for Redesigning Suburbs*. Hoboken: John Wiley.

Dunleavy, Patrick. 1981. *The Politics of Mass Housing in Britain, 1945–1975: A Study of Corporate Power and Professional Influence in the Welfare State*. Oxford: Clarendon Press.

Easterling, Keller. 2003. Subtraction. *Perspecta* 34:80–83, 86–90.

Easterling, Keller. 2005. *Enduring Innocence: Global Architecture and Its Political Masquerades*. Cambridge, MA: MIT Press.

Eco, Umberto. 1980. Function and Sign: The Semiotics of Architecture. In *Signs, Symbols and Architecture*, ed. Geoffrey Broadbent, Richard Bunt, and Charles Jencks, 33–67. London: John Wiley and Sons.

Eco, Umberto. 1996. From the Internet to Gutenberg. Lecture at Columbia University, Italian Academy for Advanced Studies in America, 12 November. http://www.umbertoeco.com/en/from-internet-to-gutenberg-1996.html (accessed 12 March 2012).

Edensor, Tim. 2005a. *Industrial Ruins: Aesthetics, Materiality and Memory*. Oxford: Berg.

Edensor, Tim. 2005b. The Ghosts of Industrial Ruins: Ordering and Disordering Memory in Excessive Space. *Environment and Planning D: Society and Space* 23 (6):829–849.

Edensor, Tim. 2005c. Waste Matter: The Debris of Industrial Ruins and the Disordering of the Material World. *Journal of Material Culture* 10 (3):311–332.

Eguchi, Toru, Robert Schmidt III, Andrew Dainty, Simon Austin, and Alistair Gibb. 2011. The Cultivation of Adaptability in Japan. *Open House International* 36 (1):73–85.

Eisenstein, Elizabeth L. 1979. *The Printing Press as an Agent of Change*. Cambridge: Cambridge University Press.

Elfassy, Natanel, and François Roche. 2010. Stuttering. *New Territories*. http://www.new-territories.com/blog/?p=457 (accessed 23 November 2010).

Engels, Friedrich. [1892] 1987. *The Condition of the Working Class in England*. London: Penguin.

Engler, Mira. 2004. *Designing America's Waste Landscapes*. Baltimore: Johns Hopkins University Press.

English Standard Bible. 2007. Good News Publishers.

Enwezor, Okwui. 2003. Terminal Modernity: Rem Koolhaas' Discourse on Entropy. In *What Is OMA: Considering Rem Koolhaas and the Office for Metropolitan Architecture*, ed. Véronique Patteeuw, 105–117. Rotterdam: NAi Publishers.

Erikson, Kai T. 1976. *Everything in Its Path: Destruction of Community in the Buffalo Creek Flood*. New York: Simon and Schuster.

Evans, Christopher. 2000. Megalithic Follies: Soane's "Druidic Remains" and the Display of Monuments. *Journal of Material Culture* 4 (3):347–367.

Eysenck, Hans J. 1994. The Measurement of Creativity. In *Dimensions of Creativity*, ed. Margaret A. Boden, 199–241. Cambridge, MA: MIT Press.

Farrar, C. H. 1972. Control of Lichens, Moulds and Similar Growths. *Building Research Station Digest* 139 (March):1–4.

Farrelly, Elizabeth. 2011. Victims Need Art Like a Hole in the Head. *Sydney Morning Herald* (22 September). http://www.smh.com.au/opinion/society-and-culture/victims-need-art-like-a-hole-in-the-head-20110921-1kl4m.html#ixzz22xVKhV7j (accessed 8 January 2012).

Fernández-Galiano, Luis. 2000. *Fire and Memory: On Architecture and Energy*. Trans. Gina Cariño. Cambridge, MA: MIT Press.

Feuerstein, Günther, ed. 2002. *Biomorphic Architecture: Human and Animal Forms in Architecture*. Berlin: Axel Menges.

Filarete [Antonio Averlino]. 1965. *Trattato d'architettura (1461–63). Treatise on Architecture*. 2 vols. Trans. John R. Spencer. New Haven: Yale University Press.

Fletcher, Banister. 1872. *Dilapidations*. London: E. & F. N. Spon.

Fletcher, Banister. 1897. *A History of Architecture*. London: B. T. Batsford.

Ford, Edward. 1997. The Theory and Practice of Impermanence: The Illusion of Durability. *Harvard Design Magazine* 3:12–18.

Forty, Adrian. 2004. *Words and Buildings: A Vocabulary of Modern Architecture*. London: Thames and Hudson.

Forty, Adrian. 2013. *Concrete and Culture: A Material History*. London: Reaktion Books.

Foster, Hal. 1996. Who's Afraid of the Neo-Avant-Garde? In Foster, *The Return of the Real*, 20–32. Cambridge, MA: MIT Press.

Foucault, Michel. 1980. *Power/Knowledge: Selected Interviews and Other Writings, 1972–1977*. Ed. Colin Gordon. New York: Pantheon Books.

Frampton, Kenneth. 1991. Post-Metabolism and the Dissolution of Architecture: Amplification and Neutrality 1960–75. *GA 6* (July): 120–127.

Frampton, Kenneth. 1995. *Studies in Tectonic Culture: The Poetics of Construction in Nineteenth and Twentieth Century Architecture*. Cambridge, MA: MIT Press.

Franck, Karen, and Quentin Stevens, eds. 2007. *Loose Space: Possibility and Diversity in Urban Life*. London: Routledge.

Frascari, Marco. 1999. Architectural Traces of an Admirable Cipher: Eleven in the Opus of Carlo Scarpa. *Nexus Network Journal* 1 (1–2):7–22.

Frascari, Marco. 2003. Architectural Synaesthesia: A Hypothesis on the Makeup of Scarpa's Modernist Architectural Drawings. http://art3idea.psu.edu/synesthesia/documents/synesthesia_frascari.html (accessed 5 October 2011).

Fraser, Craig, photographer. 2003. *Shack Chic: Innovation in the Shack-Lands of South Africa*. London: Thames and Hudson.

Freud, Sigmund. 1957. *The Standard Edition of the Complete Psychological Works of Sigmund Freud*. Vol. 14. Trans. James Strachey. London: Hogarth Press.

257

Freudenburg, William R., Robert B. Gramling, Shirley Laska, and Kai Erikson. 2009. *Catastrophe in the Making: The Engineering of Katrina and the Disasters of Tomorrow*. Washington, DC: Island Press.

Frichot, Hélène. 2005. Stealing into Gilles Deleuze's Baroque House. In *Deleuze and Space*, ed. Ian Buchanan and Gregg Lambert, 61–79. Edinburgh: Edinburgh University Press.

Fried, Michael. 2008. *Why Photography Matters as Art as Never Before*. New Haven: Yale University Press.

Friedman, Daniel S., and Nadir Lahiji. 1997. At the Sink: Architecture in Abjection. In *Plumbing: Sounding Modern Architecture*, ed. Daniel S. Friedman and Nadir Lahiji, 35–55. New York: Princeton Architectural Press.

Frow, John. 2002. Invidious Distinction: Waste, Difference, and Classy Stuff. In *Culture and Waste: The Creation and Destruction of Value*, ed. Gay Hawkins and Stephen Meucke, 25–38. Lanham, MD: Rowman and Littlefield.

Gallagher, John. 2010. *Reimagining Detroit: Opportunities for Redefining an American City*. Detroit: Wayne State University Press.

Gamboni, Dario. 1997. *The Destruction of Art: Iconoclasm and Vandalism since the French Revolution*. London: Reaktion.

Gamboni, Dario. 2002. Image to Destroy, Indestructible Image. In *Iconoclash: Beyond the Image Wars in Science, Religion and Art*, ed. Bruno Latour and Peter Weibel, 87–135. Karlsruhe: Centre for Art and Media.

Gandy, Matthew. 2003. Landscapes of Deliquescence in Michelangelo Antonioni's Red Desert. *Transactions of the Institute of British Geographers* 19:218–237.

Gandy, Matthew. 2006. Planning, Anti-planning and the Infrastructure Crisis Facing Metropolitan Lagos. *Urban Studies* 43 (2):371–396.

Gans, Deborah. 1987. *The Le Corbusier Guide*. New York: Princeton Architectural Press.

García-Huidobro, Fernando, Diego Torres Torriti, and Nicolás Tugas. 2008. *¡El Tiempo Construye! Time Builds! The Experimental Housing Project (PREVI), Lima: Genesis and Outcome*. Barcelona: Gustavo Gili.

García-Huidobro, Fernando, Diego Torres Torriti, and Nicolás Tugas. 2011. The Experimental Housing Project (PREVI), Lima: The Making of a Neighbourhood. *Architectural Design* 81 (3):26–31.

Gargiani, Roberto, and Anna Rosellini. 2011. *Le Corbusier: Béton Brut and Ineffable Space, 1940–1965: Surface Materials and the Psychophysiology of Vision*. Lausanne: EPFL Press.

Garrett, Bradley. L. 2011a. Assaying History: Creating Temporal Junctions through Urban Exploration. *Environment and Planning D: Society and Space* 29:1048–1067.

Garrett, Bradley L. 2011b. Shallow Excavation, a Response to Bunkerology. *Environment and Planning D: Society and Space*. http://societyandspace.com/2011/06/10/shallow-excavation-a-response-to-bunkerology-by-bradley-l-garrett/ (accessed 21 July 2012).

Gaut, Berys. 2009. Creativity. In *A Companion to Aesthetics*, ed. Stephen Davies, Kathleen Marie Higgins, Robert Hopkins, Robert Stecker, and David E. Cooper, 207–210. Chichester: Wiley-Blackwell.

Gettens, Rutherford J. 1970. Patina: Noble and Vile. In *Art and Technology: A Symposium on Classical Bronzes*, ed. Suzannah F Doeringer, David Gordon Mitten, and Arthur Richard Steinberg, 57–72. Cambridge, MA: MIT Press.

GHA (Glasgow Housing Association). 2004. Letter to Occupants. 19 May.

Ghosh, Swapan Kumar, ed. 2009. *Self-Healing Materials: Fundamentals, Design Strategies, and Applications*. Weinheim: Wiley-VCH.

Giblett, Rob. 2009. *Landscapes of Culture and Nature*. London: Palgrave Macmillan.

Gibson-Graham, J. K. 2006. *A Postcapitalist Politics*. Minneapolis: University of Minnesota Press.

Gieryn, Tom F. 2002. Three Truth-Spots. *Journal of the History of the Behavioral Sciences* 38 (2):113–132.

Gigon, Annette, and Petra Hagen Hodgson. 2007. Materials and Colours. In *The Architect, the Cook, and Good Taste*, ed. Rolf Toyka and Petra Hagen Hodgson, 38–49. Berlin: Birkhäuser.

Ginsberg, Robert. [1970] 2004. *The Aesthetics of Ruins*. Amsterdam: Rodopi.

Girard, René. 1986. *The Scapegoat*. London: Althone Press.

Gissen, David. 2009a. Debris. *AA Files* 58:8–11.

Gissen, David. 2009b. *Subnature: Architecture's Other Environments*. New York: Princeton Architectural Press.

Glasgow Herald. 1963. North-east Coast and Scottish Heavy Steel Makers. Advertisement. *Glasgow Herald* (11 March).

Glass, Ruth. 1964. Introduction: Aspects of Change. In *London: Aspects of Change*, ed. Centre for Urban Studies, xiii–xlii. London: MacKibbon and Kee.

Glendinning, Miles. 1992. "Public Building": Sam Bunton and Scotland's Modern Housing Revolution. *Planning History* 14 (3):13–22.

Glendinning, Miles, and Stefan Muthesius. 1994. *Tower Block: Modern Public Housing in England, Scotland, Wales and Northern Ireland*. New Haven: Yale University Press.

Göbel, Hanna. 2012. Practicing Urban Atmospheres: The Re-use of Ruins in the Cultural-ized City. PhD diss., Universität Konstanz.

Goldschmitt, Gabriela. 1999. Design. In *The Encyclopedia of Creativity*, ed. Mark A. Runco and Steven R. Pritzker, 1:525–535. London: Academic Press.

Goldstein, Carl. 1996. *Teaching Art: Academies and Schools from Vasari to Albers*. Cambridge: Cambridge University Press.

Goldstein, Walter. 2010. *Sick Building Syndrome and Related Illness*. Boca Raton: CLC Press.

Gombrich, Ernst. 1960. *Art and Illusion: A Study in the Psychology of Pictorial Representation*. London: Phaidon Press.

Gorman, Thomas, Ronnie Johnston, Arthur McIvor, and Andrew Watterson. 2004. Asbestos in Scotland. *International Journal of Occupational Health* 10:183–192.

Gotham, Kevin Fox. 2007. Critical Theory and Katrina: Disaster, Spectacle and Immanent Critique. *City* 11 (1):81–99.

259

Gould, Stephen J., and Richard C. Lewontin. 1979. The Spandrels of San Marco and the Panglossian Paradigm: A Critique of the Adaptionist Programme. *Proceedings of the Royal Society of London (Series B)* 205 (1161): 581–598.

Graham, Peter. 2006. *Environment Design Guide*. Sydney: Royal Institute of Australian Architects.

Graham, Stephen. 2002. Clean Territory: Urbicide in the West Bank. http://www.geography.dur.ac.uk/information/staff/personal/graham/pdf_files/12.pdf (accessed 12 June 2011).

Graham, Stephen. 2003. Lessons in Urbicide. *New Left Review* 19:63–77.

Graham, Stephen. 2004a. Cities, Warfare, and States of Emergency. In *Cities, War, and Terrorism: Towards an Urban Geopolitics*, ed. Stephen Graham, 1–25. Oxford: Blackwell.

Graham, Stephen. 2004b. Postmortem city: Towards an Urban Geopolitics. *City* 8 (2):165–196.

Graham, Stephen. 2011. *Cities under Siege: The New Military Urbanism*. London: Verso.

Greco, Joann. 2012. The Psychology of Ruin Porn. *Atlantic Cities: Place Matters* (6 January). http://www.theatlanticcities.com/design/2012/01/psychology-ruin-porn/886/ (accessed 10 July 2012).

Gregson, Nicky, and Louise Crewe. 2003. *Second-hand Cultures*. Oxford: Berg.

Griffiths, Hugh, Alfred Pugsley, and Owen Saunders. 1968. *Report of the Inquiry into the Collapse of Flats at Ronan Point, Canning Town*. London: HMSO, Ministry of Housing and Local Government.

Groák, Steven. 1992. *The Idea of a Building: Thought and Action in the Design and Production of Buildings*. London: E. & F. N. Spon.

Gross, David. 2002. Objects from the Past. In *Waste-Site Stories: The Recycling of Memory*, ed. Brian Neville and Johanne Villeneuve, 29–37. Albany: State University of New York Press.

Grosz, Elizabeth. 2001. *Architecture from the Outside: Essays on Virtual and Real Space*. Cambridge, MA: MIT Press.

Gruber, Petra. 2011. *Biomimetics in Architecture: Architecture of Life and Buildings*. Vienna: Springer.

Guattari, Félix. [1989] 2000. *The Three Ecologies*. Trans. Ian Pindar and Paul Sutton. London: Athlone.

Guggenheim, Michael. 2009. Mutable Immobiles: Change of Use of Buildings as a Problem of Quasi-technologies. In *Urban Assemblages: How Actor-Network Theory Changes Urban Studies*, ed. Thomas Bender and Ignacio Farías, 161–178. London: Routledge.

Guggenheim, Michael. 2011. Formless Discourse: The Impossible Knowledge of Change of Use. *Candide: Journal for Architectural Knowledge* 4 (7):9–36.

Guillitte, Olivier. 1995. Bioreceptivity: A New Concept for Building Ecology Studies. *Science of the Total Environment* 167 (1–3):215–220.

Guyer, Paul. 2003. Exemplary Orginality: Genius, Universality and Individuality. In *The Creation of Art: New Essays in Philosophical Aesthetics*, ed. Berys Nigel Gaut and Paisley Livingston, 116–137. Cambridge: Cambridge University Press.

Haase, Dagmar. 2008. Urban Ecology of Shrinking Cities: An Unrecognized Opportunity? *Nature and Culture* 3 (1):1–8.

Habraken, N. John. 1972. *Supports: An Alternative to Mass Housing*. Trans. B. Valkenburg. London: Architectural Press.

Hagedorn, John M., and Brigid Rauch. 2004. *Variations in Urban Homicide: Chicago, New York City, and Global Urban Policy*. Chicago: UIC Great Cities Institute.

Hall, Peter, and Ulrich Pfeiffer. 2000. *Urban Future 21: A Global Agenda for 21st Century Cities*. London: E. & F. N. Spon.

Hamon, Philippe. 1992. *Expositions: Literature and Architecture in Nineteenth-Century France*. Trans. Katia Sainson-Frank and Lisa Maguire. Berkeley: University of California Press.

Hanczyc, Martin. 2009. Introduction. In *Protocells: Bridging Nonliving and Living Matter*, ed. Steen Rasmussen, Mark A. Bedau, Liaohai Chen, David Deamer, David C. Krakauer, Norman H. Packard, and Peter F. Stadler, xv–xx. Cambridge, MA: MIT Press.

Hanczyc, Martin. 2011. Structure and the Synthesis of Life. *Architectural Design* 112 (March/April):26–33.

Hanczyc, Martin, and T. Ikegami. 2009. Protocells as Smart Agents for Architectural Design. *Technoetic Arts: A Journal of Speculative Research* 7 (2): 117–120.

Hanley, Lynsey. 2006. *Estates: An Intimate History*. London: Granta.

Harbison, Robert. 1977. *Eccentric Spaces*. London: Deutsch.

Harbison, Robert. 1991. *The Built, the Unbuilt and the Unbuildable: In Pursuit of Architectural Meaning*. London: Thames and Hudson.

Hare, John. 2012. *Preliminary Observations from the Christchurch Earthquakes*, 1–17. Christchurch: Canterbury Earthquakes Royal Commission.

Harries, Karsten. 1998. *The Ethical Function of Architecture*. Cambridge, MA: MIT Press.

Harris, Neil. 1999. *Building Lives: Constructing Rites and Passages*. New Haven: Yale University Press.

Harris, Steven, and Deborah Berke, eds. 1997. *Architecture of the Everyday*. New York: Princeton Architectural Press.

Harvey, David. 1975. The Political Economy of Urbanization in Advanced Capitalist Societies: The Case of the United States. In *The Social Economy of the City*, ed. Gary Gappert and Harold M. Rose, 119–164. Beverly Hills: Sage Urban Affairs Annual Review 9.

Harvey, David. 1996. *Justice, Nature and the Geography of Difference*. Cambridge, MA: Blackwell Publishers.

Harvey, John. 1972. *The Medieval Architect*. London: Wayland.

Hasegawa, Nyozekan. 1965. *The Japanese Character: A Cultural Profile*. Trans. John Bestor. Tokyo: Kodansha International.

Hauser, Sussane. 2002. Waste into Heritage: Remarks on Materials in the Arts, on Memories and the Museum. In *Waste-Site Stories: The Recycling of Memory*, ed. Brian Neville and Johanne Villeneuve, 39–54. Albany: State University of New York Press.

Hawkins, Gay. 2002. Documentary Affect: Filming Rubbish. *Australian Humanities Review* 27 (September–December).

Hawkins, Gay. 2005. *The Ethics of Waste: How We Relate to Rubbish*. Lanham, MD: Rowman and Littlefield.

Hawkins, Gay, and Stephen Muecke, eds. 2003. *Culture and Waste: The Creation and Destruction of Value*. Lanham, MD: Rowman and Littlefield.

Hazard, Leland. 1964. Revitalizing the Older City: The Challenges of Urban Obsolescence. Sperry and Hutchinson Lecture, University of Pittsburgh.

Heathcott, Joseph. 2002. The City Remade: Public Housing and the Urban Landscape in St. Louis, 1900–1960. PhD diss., Indiana University.

Heathcott, Joseph. 2004. Vertical City: Public Housing in the Life of an American City. Exhibition, October 18, 2003–January 17, 2004. Bernoudy Gallery of Architecture.

Hecker, Tim. 2010. The Slum Pastoral: Helicopter Visuality and Koolhaas's Lagos. *Space and Culture* 13 (3):256–269.

Hegel, G. W. F. [1837] 1956. *Philosophy of History*. Trans. J. Sibree. New York: Dover.

Hegel, G. W. F. 1977. *Phenomenology of Spirit*. Trans. A. V. Miller. Oxford: Oxford University Press.

Heilman, Kenneth. 2005. *Creativity and the Brain*. London: Taylor and Francis.

Hell, Julia. 2010. Imperial Ruin Gazers, or Why Did Scripo Weep? In *Ruins of Modernity*, ed. Julia Hell and Andreas Schölne, 169–192. Durham: Duke University Press.

Hellman, Gerben, and Frank Wassenberg. 2004. The Renewal of What Was Tomorrow's Idealistic City: Amsterdam's Bijlmermeer High-Rise. *Cities* (London, England) 21 (1):3–17.

Heron, Katharine. 2007. Potteries Thinkbelt. In *Cedric Price: Potteries Thinkbelt: Supercrit #1*, ed. Samantha Hardingham and Kester Rattenbury. Abingdon: Routledge.

Herrmann, Wolfgang. 1962. *Laugier and Eighteenth Century French Theory*. London: A. Zwemmer.

Herscher, Andrew. 2006. American Urbicide. *Journal of Architectural Education* 60 (1):18–20.

Hersey, George. 1989. *The Lost Meaning of Classical Architecture: Speculations on Ornament from Vitruvius to Venturi*. Cambridge, MA: MIT Press.

262   Hersey, George. 1999. *The Monumental Impulse: Architecture's Biological Roots*. Cambridge, MA: MIT Press.

Herzog & De Meuron. 2002. Just Waste. In *Herzog & De Meuron: Natural History*, ed. Philip Ursprung, 74–77. Baden: Lars Müller.

Hetherington, Kevin. 1997. *The Badlands of Modernity: Heterotopia and Social Ordering*. London: Routledge.

Hetherington, Kevin. 2004. Second-handedness: Consumption, Disposal and Absent Presence. *Environment and Planning D: Society and Space 22* (1):157–173.

Hetherington, Kevin. 2010. The Ruin Revisited. In *Trash Cultures: Objects and Obsolescence in Cultural Perspective*, ed. Gillian Pye, 13–37. Oxford: Peter Lang.

Hewitson, Robert. 1987. *The Heritage Industry: Britain in a Climate of Decline*. London: Methuen.

Heynen, Nik, Maria Kaika, and Erik Swyngedouw. 2006. Urban Political Ecology. In *Urban Political Ecology and the Politics of Urban Metabolism*, ed. Nik Heynan, Maria Kaika, and Erik Swyngadouw, 1–19. London: Routledge.

Hilhorst, Dorothea, and Greg Bankoff. 2004. Introduction: Mapping Vulnerability. In *Mapping Vulnerability: Disasters, Development and People*, ed. Greg Bankoff, Georg Frerks, and Dorothea Hilhorst, 1–9. Sterling, VA: Earthscan.

Hill, Jonathan. 2003. *Actions of Architecture: Architects and Creative Users*. London: Routledge.

Hill, Jonathan. 2006. *Immaterial Architecture*. London: Routledge.

Hill, Jonathan. 2012. *Weather Architecture*. London: Routledge.

Historic Places Trust. 2012. Church of St. Michael and All Angels (Anglican). www.historic.org.nz/TheRegister (accessed 29 April 2012).

Hobhouse, Hermione. 1971. *Lost London: A Century of Demolition and Decay*. London: Macmillan.

Hodder, Stephen. 2009. Berners Pool—Hodders Associates, Cumbria. *The Rubble Club*. http://www.therubbleclub.com/2009/05/berners-pool-hodders-associates-cumbri/ (accessed 12 November 2011).

Hoffman, Alexander von. 2000. Why They Built Pruitt-Igoe. In *From Tenement to the Taylor Homes: In Search of an Urban Housing Policy in Twentieth-Century America*, ed. John F. Bauman, Roger Biles, and Kirstin M. Szylvian, 180–205. State College: Pennsylvania State University Press.

Hogan, William T. 1971. *Economic History of the Iron and Steel Industry in the United States*. Lexington: D. C. Heath.

Hollier, Denis. 1989. *Against Architecture: The Writings of Georges Bataille*. Trans. Betsy Wing. Cambridge, MA: MIT Press.

Hollis, Edward. 2009. *The Secret Lives of Buildings: From the Ruins of the Parthenon to the Wailing Wall in Thirteen Stories*. London: Portobello.

Hommels, Anique. 2008. *Unbuilding Cities: Obduracy in Sociotechnical Change*. Cambridge, MA: MIT Press.

Honeyborne, D. B. 1971. Changes in the Appearance of Concrete on Exposure. *Building Research Station Digest* 126 (February):1–7.

Horn, Christian. 2005. Paris Air Terminal Collapse Report. *Architecture Week*, N1.1. http://www.ArchitectureWeek.com/2005/0427/news_1-1.html (accessed 23 November 2011).

Horne, Ralph E., Tim Grant, and Karli L. Verghese. 2009. *Life Cycle Assessment: Principles, Practice and Prospects*. Melbourne: CSIRO Publishing.

Horsey, Miles. 1982. The Story of Red Road Flats. *Town and Country Planning* (July–August):177–179.

Hovland, Carl Iver, and Robert R. Sears. 1940. Minor Studies of Aggression: VI. Correlation of Lynchings with Economic Indices. *Journal of Psychology* 9 (2):301–310.

Hsing, You-tien. 2010. *The Great Urban Transformation: Politics of Land and Property in China*. Oxford: Oxford University Press.

263

Hubert, Henri, and Marcel Mauss. [1898] 1964. *Sacrifice: Its Nature and Function*. Chicago: University of Chicago Press.

Hughes, Anthony. 1986. An "Academy for Doing" I: The *Accademia del Disegno*, the Guilds and the Principate in Sixteenth-Century Florence. *Oxford Art Journal* 9 (1):3–10.

Hugo, Victor. [1831] 2001. *Notre-Dame de Paris*. Trans. Isabel F. Hapgood. New York: F. M. Lupton.

Hui, Andrew. 2009. Poetics of Ruins in Renaissance Poetry. PhD diss., Princeton University.

Humphrey, Caroline. 2002. *The Unmaking of Soviet Life: Everyday Economies after Socialism*. Ithaca: Cornell University Press.

Hung, Wu. 2005. Ruins, Fragmentation and the Chinese Modern/Postmodern. In *Theory in Contemporary Art since 1985*, ed. Zoya Kocur and Simon Leung, 309–317. Malden, MA: Blackwell.

Hunt, John Dixon. 1992. *Gardens and the Picturesque: Studies in the History of Landscape Architecture*. Cambridge, MA: MIT Press.

Huyssen, Andreas. 2006. Nostalgia for Ruins. *Grey Room* 23 (Spring):6–21.

Huyssen, Andreas. 2010. Authentic Ruins: Products of Modernity. In *Ruins of Modernity*, ed. Julia Hell and Andreas Schölne, 17–28. Durham: Duke University Press.

ICTY. 2003. Transcripts Milosović Case (IT-02-54) "Kosovo, Croatia, Bosnia and Herzegovina." Session 9 July 2003. http://www.un.org/icty/transe54/030709IT.htm (accessed 4 November 2011).

Imrie, Rob, and Emma Street. 2011. *Architectural Design and Regulation*. Chichester: Wiley.

Ingraham, Catherine. 2006. *Architecture, Animal, Human: The Asymmetrical Condition*. London: Routledge.

Ingraham, Catherine. Forthcoming. *Architecture's Claim: On Property*. Princeton: Princeton University Press.

Inskip, Peter. 1972. Letter to Editor. *Times* (9 September).

Isozaki, Arata. 2006. *Japan-ness in Architecture*. Cambridge, MA: MIT Press.

Isozaki, Arata. 2007a. City Demolition Industry, Inc. *South Atlantic Quarterly* 106 (4):853–858.

Isozaki, Arata. 2007b. Rumor City. *South Atlantic Quarterly* 106 (4):859–869.

Issacs, Warwick. 2011. Demolition of Your Building at 100 Cathedral Square—Christchurch Cathedral. *CERA: Canterbury Earthquake Recovery Authority* (September).

Ito, Toyo, Sophie Roulet, and Sophie Soulie. 1991. Towards a Postephemeral Architecture. In *Toyo Ito*, ed. Sophie Roulet and Sophie Soulie, 74–76. Paris: Éditions Moniteur.

Itōh, Teiji, Tanaka Ikkō, and Sesoko Tsune, eds. 1993. *Wabi, sabi, suki: The Essence of Japanese Beauty*, trans. Lynne E. Riggs. Hiroshima: Mazda.

Jackson, John Brinckerhoff. 1980. *The Necessity for Ruins, and Other Topics*. Amherst: University of Massachusetts Press.

Jacobs, Henry. 1863. Cathedral Commission. *Lyttelton Times* 20 (1113; 11 July): 10.

Jacobs, Henry, R. J. S. Harman, and H. J. Ainger. 1870. Subscriptions for the Building of the New Church of St. Michael and All Angels. *Star* 544 (16 February): 1.

Jacobs, Jane M. 2006. A Geography of Big Things. *Cultural Geographies* 13 (1):1–27.

Jacobs, Jane M., Stephen Cairns, and Ignaz Strebel. 2006. "A Tall Story ... but, a Fact Just the Same": The Red Road Highrise as a Black Box. *Urban Studies* 44 (3):609–629.

Jacobs, Jane M., and Loretta Lees. 2013. Defensible Space on the Move: Revisiting the Urban Geography of Alice Coleman. *International Journal of Urban and Regional Research* 37 (5):1559–1583.

Jamaković, S., ed. 1993. *Warchitecture*. Sarajevo: ARH: Magazine for Architecture, Town Planning and Design.

Jameson, Fredric. 1994. *The Seeds of Time*. New York: Columbia University Press.

Jameson, Fredric. 2003. Future City. *New Left Review* 21 (May–June):65–79.

Jameson, Fredric. 2007. Introduction to Isozaki Arata's "City Demolition Industry, Inc." and "Rumor City." *South Atlantic Quarterly* 106 (4):849–852.

Jencks, Charles. 1977. *The Language of Postmodern Architecture*. New York: Rizzoli.

Jencks, Charles, and Karl Kropf, eds. 1997. *Theories and Manifestoes of Contemporary Architecture*. London: Academy Press.

Jephcott, Pearl. 1971. *Homes in High Flats: Some of the Human Problems Involved in Multi-storey Housing*. Edinburgh: Oliver & Boyd.

Jokilehto, Jukka. 2002. *A History of Architectural Conservation*. Oxford: Butterworth-Heinemann.

Jonkers, Henk. 2007. Self-Healing Concrete: A Biological Approach. In *Self-Healing Materials: An Alternative Approach to 20 Centuries of Materials Science*, ed. Sybrand van der Zwaag, 195–204. Dordrecht: Springer.

Juniper, Andrew. 2003. *Wabi sabi: The Japanese Art of Impermanence*. Boston: Tuttle.

Kagan, Shelly. 2012. *Death*. New Haven: Yale University Press.

Kahatt, Sharif S. 2011. PREVI-Lima's Time: Positioning Proyecto Experimental de Vivenda in Peru's Modern Project. *Architectural Design* 81 (3):22–25.

Kant, Immanuel. [1790] 1987. *Critique of Judgment*. Trans. Werner S. Pluhar. Indianapolis: Hackett.

Kaufmann, Edgar, Jr. 1961. *Creation Is a Patient Search*, by Le Corbusier [book review]. *Saturday Review*, January 28:20.

Kaufmann, Emil. 1955. *Architecture in the Age of Reason: Baroque and Post-Baroque in England, Italy, France*. New York: Dover.

Keeler, Marian, and Bill Burke. 2009. *Fundamentals of Integrated Design for Sustainable Building*. Hoboken: John Wiley and Sons.

Kendall, Stephen. 1999. Open Building: An Approach to Sustainable Architecture. *Journal of Urban Technology* 6 (3):1–16.

Kendell, Stuart. 2007. *Georges Bataille*. London: Reaktion.

Khushuf, George. 2009. Open Evolution and Human Agency: The Pragmatics of Upstream Ethics in the Design of Artificial Life. In *The Ethics of Protocells: Moral and Social Implications of Creating Life in the Laboratory*, ed. Mark Bedau and Emily C. Parks, 223–262. Cambridge, MA: MIT Press.

Kikutake, Kiyonori. 1964. The Approach of Kiyonori Kikutake. *Architectural Design* 34:507–509.

Kintrea, Keith. 2006. Housing Aspirations and Obsolescence in Britain: Understanding the Relationship. Paper presented at the ENHR conference "Housing in an Expanded Europe: Theory, Policy, Participation and Implementation," Ljubljana, Slovenia.

Kipfer, Stefan, and Kanishka Goonewardena. 2007. Colonization and the New Imperialism: On the Meaning of Urbicide Today. *Theory and Event* 30 (2):1–26.

Kipnis, Jeffrey. 1997. The Cunning of Cosmetics. *El Croquis* 84:22–28.

Kirby, David A. 1971. The Interwar Council Dwelling: A Study of Residential Obsolescence and Decay. *Town Planning Review* 42 (3):250–268.

Klassen, Helmut. 1994. Michelangelo: The Image of the Human Body, Artifice, and Architecture. In *Chora: Intervals in the Philosophy of Architecture*, ed. Alberto Pérez-Gómez and Stephen Parcell, 57–82. Montreal: McGill-Queens University Press.

Klett, Mark, et al. 2006. *After the Ruins, 1906 and 2006: Rephotographing the San Francisco Earthquake and Fire*. Berkeley: University of California Press.

Knechtel, John, ed. 2007. *Trash*. Cambridge, MA: MIT Press.

Koolhaas, Rem. 2002. Junkspace. In *Guide to Shopping, Harvard Design School Project on the City*, ed. Chuihua Judy Chung, Jeffrey Inaba, Rem Koolhaas, and Sze Tsung Leong, 408–421. Cologne: Taschen.

Koolhaas, Rem, and Bruce Mau. 1995. *S, M, L, XL: Small, Medium, Large, Extra-Large*. Ed. Jennifer Siegler. New York: Monacelli Press.

Koolhaas, Rem, and Hans Ulrich Obrist. 2011. *Project Japan: Metabolism Talks*. Ed. Kayoko Ota with James Westcott. Cologne: Taschen.

Körbes, Jan. 2008. A World without a Manual. In *Rematerial: From Waste to Architecture*, ed. Alejandro Bahamón and Maria Camila Sanjinés, 182–189. New York: W. W. Norton.

Kōshirō, Haga. 1995. The Wabi Aesthetic through the Ages. In *Japanese Aesthetics and Culture: A Reader*, ed. Nancy G. Hume, 254–276. Albany: SUNY Press.

Kostof, Spiro. 1977. *The Architect: Chapters in the History of the Profession*. New York: Oxford University Press.

Kozák, Jan, and Vladimír Cermák. 2010. *The Illustrated History of Natural Disasters*. Dordrecht: Springer.

Kozbelt, Aaron, Ronald A. Beghetto, and Mark A. Runco. 2010. Theories of Creativity. In *The Cambridge Handbook of Creativity*, ed. James C. Kaufman and Robert J. Sternberg, 20–47. Cambridge: Cambridge University Press.

Krauss, Rosalind E. 1986. *The Originality of the Avant-Garde and Other Modernist Myths*. Cambridge, MA: MIT Press.

Krauss, Rosalind E. 1997. "… And Then Turn Away?" An Essay on James Coleman. *October* 81 (Summer):5–33.

Krauss, Rosalind E. 1999a. *A Voyage on the North Sea: Art in the Age of the Post-Medium Condition*. New York: Thames and Hudson.

Krauss, Rosalind. 1999b. Reinventing the Medium (Art and Photography). *Critical Inquiry* 25 (2):289–305.

Krell, David Farrell. 1995. *Architecture: Ecstasies of Space, Time, and the Human Body*. Albany: State University of New York Press.

Kristeller, Paul Oskar. 1951a. The Modern System of the Arts: A Study in the History of Aesthetics. Part I. *Journal of the History of Ideas* 12 (4):496–527.

Kristeller, Paul Oskar. 1951b. The Modern System of the Arts: A Study in the History of Aesthetics. Part II. *Journal of the History of Ideas* 13 (1):17–46.

Krstic, Vladimir. 1985. A Life Act and Urban Scenography: Supraphysical Concept of Urban Form in the Core of the Japanese City. Master's thesis, Kyoto University.

Kruft, Hanno-Walter. 1994. *A History of Architectural Theory: From Vitruvius to the Present*. New York: Princeton Architectural Press.

Krumbein, Wolfgang E. 2003. Patina and Cultural Heritage: A Geomicrobiologist's Perspective. Proceedings of the 5th European Commission Conference "Cultural Heritage Research: A Pan European Challenge," ed. R. Kozlowski, 39–47. Cracow, May 16–18, 2002.

Kuniichi, Uno. 1998. The Enemy of Architecture. *D (Columbia Documents in Architecture and Theory)* 6: 101–105.

Lacan, Jacques. 1981. *The Four Fundamental Concepts of Psychoanalysis. The Seminar of Jacques Lacan,* Book XI, ed. Jacques-Alain Miller, trans. Alan Sheridan. New York: W. W. Norton.

Lambourne, Nicola. 2001. *War Damage in Western Europe: The Destruction of Historic Monuments During the Second World War*. Edinburgh: Edinburgh University Press.

Land, Peter. 2008. The Experimental Housing Project (PREVI), Lima: Antecedents and Ideas. In Fernando García-Huidobro, Diego Torres Torriti, and Nicolás Tugas, *¡El Tiempo Construye! Time Builds! The Experimental Housing Project (PREVI), Lima: Genesis and Outcome,* 10–25. Barcelona: Gustavo Gili.

Landis, Amy E. 2010. Cradle to Gate Environmental Footprint and Life Cycle Assessment of Poly(Lactic Acid). In *Poly(lactic acid): Synthesis, Structures, Properties, Processing, and Application*, ed. Rafael A. Auras, Loong-Tak Lim, Susan E. M. Selke, and Hideto Tsuji, 431–442. Hoboken: John Wiley and Sons.

Lang, Peter. 1997. *Mortal City*. Princeton: Princeton University Press.

Langewiesche, William. 2003. *American Ground: Unbuilding the World Trade Center*. New York: Farrar, Straus and Giroux.

Langner, Marcel, and Wilfried Endlicher, eds. 2007. *Shrinking Cities: Effects on Urban Ecology and Challenges for Urban Development*. New York: Peter Lang.

Latour, Bruno. 2002. What Is Iconoclash? Or Is There a World beyond the Image Wars? In Iconoclash: Beyond the Image Wars in Science, Religion and Art, ed. Bruno Latour and Peter Weibel, 13–38. Karlsruhe: Centre for Art and Media.

Latour, Bruno. 2005. *Reassembling the Social: An Introduction to Actor-Network-Theory*. Oxford: Oxford University Press.

267

Latour, Bruno. 2009. A Cautious Prometheus? A Few Steps toward a Philosophy of Design (with Special Attention to Peter Sloterdijk). In Proceedings of the 2008 Annual International Conference of the Design History Society—Falmouth, 3–6 September, ed. Fiona Hackney, Jonathan Glynne, and Viv Minto, 2–10. e-books, Universal Publishers.

Latour, Bruno, and Emilie Hermant. 1998. *Paris ville invisible / Paris: Invisible City*. Trans. Liz Carey-Libbrecht. Paris: La Découverte.

Latour, Bruno, and Albena Yaneva. 2008. Give Me a Gun and I Will Make All Buildings Move. In *Explorations in Architecture: Teaching, Design, Research*, ed. Reto Geiser, 80–89. Basel: Birkhäuser.

Law, John. 2003. Ladbroke Grove, or How to Think about Failing Systems. On-line paper, Centre for Science Studies, Ladbroke Grove.

Law, Jonathan, and Elizabeth A. Martin. 2009. *A Dictionary of Law*. Oxford: Oxford University Press.

Leach, Neil. 2002. Vitruvius Crucifixus: Architecture, Mimesis and the Death Instinct. In *Body and Building: Essays on the Changing Relation of Body and Architecture*, ed. George Dodds and Robert Tavernor, 210–225. Cambridge, MA: MIT Press.

Leary, John Patrick. 2011. Detroitism. *Guernica: A Magazine of Art and Politics* (15 January). http://www.guernicamag.com/features/leary_1_15_11/ (accessed 4 July 2012).

Leatherbarrow, David. 2000. *Uncommon Ground: Architecture, Technology, and Topography*. Cambridge, MA: MIT Press.

Le Corbusier. [1937] 1947. *When the Cathedrals Were White: Journey to the Country of Timid People*. Trans. Frances E. Hyslop. New York: Reynal and Hitchcock.

Le Corbusier. [1925] 2008. The Decorative Art of Today. In *Raumplan versus Plan Libre: Adolf Loos [and] Le Corbusier*, ed. Max Risselada, 178–181. Rotterdam: 010 Publishers.

Le Corbusier, Anthony Eardley, Kenneth Frampton, and Silvia Kolbowski. 1981. Le Corbusier's Firminy Church: An Exhibition. Exhibition, 29 April–3 June 1981, Institute for Architecture and Urban Studies, Cooper Union for the Advancement of Science and Art, School of Architecture.

Lee, Pamela M. 2000. *Object to Be Destroyed: The Work of Gordon Matta-Clark*. Cambridge, MA: MIT Press.

Lefaivre, Liane. 1989. Dirty Realism in European Architecture Today. *Design Book Review* 17: 17–20.

Lentzos, Filippa, Caitlin Cockerton, Susanna Finlay, R. Alexander Hamilton, Joy Yueyue Zhand, and Nikolas Rose. 2012. The Societal Impact of Synthetic Biology. In *Synthetic Biology: A Primer*, ed. Geoff Baldwin, Paul Travis Bayer, S. Freemont, Richard I. Kitney, Robert Dickinson, Tom Ellis, Karen Polizzi, and Guy-Bart Stan, 131–150. London: Imperial College Press.

Lerup, Lars. 2000. *After the City*. Cambridge, MA: MIT Press.

Leupen, Bernard, René Heijne, and Jasper van Zwol, eds. 2005. *Time-Based Architecture*. Rotterdam: 010 Publishers.

Le Vine, V. T. 1997. On the Victims of Terrorism and Their Innocence. *Terrorism and Political Violence* 9 (3):55–62.

Lilienfeld, Robert, and William Rathje. 1998. *Use Less Stuff: Environmental Solutions for Who We Really Are*. New York: Ballantine Books.

Linethal, Edward Tabor. 2001. *The Unfinished Bombing: Oklahoma City in the American Memory*. New York: Oxford University Press.

Lingis, Alphonso. 1989. *Deathbound Subjectivity*. Bloomington: Indiana University Press.

Lipovetsky, Gilles. 1994. *The Empire of Fashion*. Trans. Catherine Porter. Princeton: Princeton University Press.

Liss, Helene. 2000. *Demolition: The Art of Demolishing, Dismantling, Imploding, Toppling and Razing*. New York: Black Dog & Leventhal Publishers.

Lochhead, Ian. 1999. *Dreams of Spires: Benjamin Mountfort and the Gothic Revival*. Christchurch: Canterbury University Press.

Lochhead, Ian. 2012. A Gothic Revival City in a Seismic Zone: The Rise and Fall of Christchurch, New Zealand. Paper presented at "New Directions in Gothic Revival Studies Worldwide: The 2012 A. W. N. Pugin Bicentennial Conference," University of Kent, 13–14 July, 1–8.

Locke, John. 1993. *Political Writings*. Ed. David Wootton. Indianapolis: Hackett.

Locke, John. [1689] 1996. *An Essay Concerning Human Understanding*. Indianapolis: Hackett.

Locke, John. [1690] 2002. *The Second Treatise of Government and A Letter Concerning Toleration*. London: Courier Dover Publications.

Loos, Adolf. [1910] 1975. Architecture. In *Architecture and Design, 1890–1939: An International Anthology of Original Articles*, ed. Tim Benton, Charlotte Benton, and Dennis Sharp, 45. New York: Whitney Library of Design.

Loos, Adolf. 1987. Plumbers. In Loos, *Spoken into the Void*, 49. Cambridge, MA: MIT Press.

Lopes, Dominic McIver. 2007. Shikinen Sengu and the Ontology of Architecture in Japan. *Journal of Aesthetics and Art Criticism* 65 (1):77–84.

Lowenthal, David. 1985. *The Past Is a Foreign Country*. Cambridge: Cambridge University Press.

Lucas, Gavin. 2002. Disposability and Dispossession in the Twentieth Century. *Journal of Material Culture* 7 (1):5–22.

Luna, Ian, and Lauren A. Gould, eds. 2009. *Shigeru Ban: Paper in Architecture*. New York: Rizzoli.

Lynch, Kevin. 1960. *Image of the City*. Cambridge, MA: MIT Press.

Lynch, Kevin. 1990. *Wasting Away*. San Francisco: Sierra Club Books.

Lyon, David. 2006. *Theorizing Surveillance: The Panopticon and Beyond*. Portland, OR: Willan Publishing.

Lyotard, Jean-François. 1991. *The Inhuman: Reflections on Time*. Trans. Geoffrey Bennington and Rachel Bowlby. Stanford: Stanford University Press.

Macarthur, John. 2007. *The Picturesque: Architecture, Disgust and Other Irregularities*. London: Routledge.

Macaulay, Rose. 1953. *Pleasure of Ruins*. London: Weidenfeld and Nicolson.

269

MacKinnon, Donald W. 1965. Personality and the Realization of Creative Potential. *American Psychologist* 20:273–281.

MacKinnon, Donald W. 1970. The Personality Correlates of Creativity: A Study of American Architects. In *Creativity*, ed. Philip E. Vernon, 289–311. Harmondsworth: Penguin.

Maclagan, Robert. 2012. Quakes Leave Wooden St Michael's Undaunted. *Christchurch Press* (17 April). http://www.stuff.co.nz/the-press/opinion/perspective/6754192/Quakes-leave-wooden-St-Michaels-undaunted (accessed 12 March 2012).

Mallgrave, Harry Francis, ed. 2005. *Modern Architectural Theory: A Historical Survey, 1673–1968*. Cambridge: Cambridge University Press.

Mallgrave, Harry Francis, ed. 2006. *Architectural Theory: An Anthology from Vitruvius to 1870*. London: Wiley-Blackwell.

Mallgrave, Harry Francis. 2010. *The Architect's Brain: Neuroscience, Creativity, and Architecture*. Chichester: Wiley.

Manaugh, Geoff. 2010. Synthetic Geology: Landscape Remediation in an Age of Benign Geotextiles. In *Hylozoic Ground: Liminal Responsive Architecture: Philip Beesley*, ed. Pernilla Ohrstedt and Hayley Issacs, 42–49. Cambridge, Ontario: Riverside Architectural Press.

Marcavage, Michael. 2005. Hurricane Katrina Destroys New Orleans Days before "Southern Decadence" (August 31). http://www.repentamerica.com/pr_hurricanekatrina.html (accessed 16 May 2012).

Marchand, Yves, and Romain Meffre. 2011. *The Ruins of Detroit*. Innovative Logistics.

Mars, Neville, and Adrian Hornsby, eds. 2008. *The Chinese Dream: A Society Under Construction*. Rotterdam: 010 Publishers.

Martin, Reinhold. 2006. What Is a Material? In *Eero Saarinen: Shaping the Future*, ed. Eeva-Liisa Pelkonen and Donald Albrecht, 69–81. New Haven: Yale University Press.

Masco, Joseph. 2008. Survival Is Your Business: Engineering Ruins and Affect in Nuclear America. *Cultural Anthropology* 23 (2):361–398.

Mateo, Josep Lluís. 2012. PREVI Experience. *Digital Architectural Papers* 9 (13 June). http://www.architecturalpapers.ch/index.php?ID=96 (accessed 2 December 2012)

Mathews, Stanley. 2006. The Fun Palace as Virtual Architecture: Cedric Price and the Practices of Indeterminacy. *Journal of Architectural Education* 59 (3):39–48.

Matta-Clark, Gordon. 2003. *Gordon Matta-Clark*. Ed. Corinne Diserens. London: Phaidon.

Matthews, Philip. 2011. Christchurch Earthquake: Act of God? *Stuff* (26 March). http://www.stuff.co.nz/national/christchurch-earthquake/4813735/Christchurch-earthquake-act-of-God (accessed 22 June 2012).

Matthews, Robert C. O. 1959. *The Trade Cycle*. Cambridge: Cambridge University Press.

Mauss, Marcel. 1967. *The Gift: Forms and Functions of Exchange in Archaic Societies*. Trans. Ian Cunnison. New York: W. W. Norton.

May, Colin. 2009. King Canute and the "Problem" of Structure and Agency: On Times, Tides and Heresthetics. *Political Studies* 57 (2):260–279.

Mayer, Jürgen, and Neeraj Bhatia, eds. 2010. *Arium: Weather + Architecture*. Ostfildern: Hatje Cantz.

270

Maynard, Jessica. 2005. Revolutionist Consumers: The Application of Sacrifice in Ruskin, Bataille and Henry James. In *Metaphors of Economy*, ed. Nicole Bracker and Stefan Herbrechter, 135–146. Amsterdam: Rodopi.

McFarland, Thomas. 1981. *Romanticism and the Forms of Ruin: Wordsworth, Coleridge, and Modalities of Fragmentation*. Princeton: Princeton University Press.

McFarlane, Colin. 2008. Urban Shadows: Materiality, the "Southern City" and Urban Theory. *Geography Compass* 2 (2):340–358.

McGuirk, Justin. 2011. PREVI: The Metabolist Utopia. *Domus*. http://www.domusweb.it/en/architecture/2011/04/21/previ-the-metabolist-utopia.html (accessed 20 July 2013).

McKee, David L. 1991. *Schumpeter and the Political Economy of Change*. New York: Praeger.

McLeod, Mary. 1994. Undressing Architecture: Fashion, Gender and Modernity. In *Architecture in Fashion*, ed. Deborah Fausch, Paulette Singley, Rodolphe El-Khoury, and Zvi Efrat, 38–123. New York: Princeton Architectural Press.

McLuhan, Marshall. 1962. *The Gutenberg Galaxy*. Toronto: University of Toronto Press.

Melvin, Jeremy. 2005. Value: Culture and Commerce. *Architectural Review* 218 (1302):87–94.

Menghini, Anna Bruna. 2002. The City as Form and Structure: The Urban Project in Italy from the 1920s to the 1980s. *Urban Morphology* 6 (2):75–86.

Menin, Sarah, and Flora Samuel. 2003. *Nature and Space: Aalto and Le Corbusier*. London: Routledge.

Metzstein, Isi. 2008. Isi Metzstein: Architect at Home. *Architects' Journal* (16 September). http://www.architectsjournal.co.uk/isi-metzstein-architect-at-home/1852024 (accessed 4 April 2012).

Millard, Bill. 2003. Violence against Architecture: Quixote Comes of Age in Sarajevo. In *Content*, ed. Rem Koolhaas, Brendan McGetrick, Simon Brown, and Jon Link, 38–43. Cologne: Taschen.

Mitchell, Andrew. 2010. *Heidegger among the Sculptors: Body, Space, and the Art of Dwelling*. Palo Alto: Stanford University Press.

Mitchell, C. Thomas. 1992. *Redefining Designing: From Form to Experience*. New York: Van Nostrand Reinhold.

Mittig, Hans-Ernst. 1993. Dauerhaftigkeit, einst Denkmalargument. In *Mo(nu)mente: Formen und Funktionen ephemerer Denkmäler*, ed. M. Diers, 11–34. Berlin: Akademie-Verlag.

Miyake, Riichi. 1987. Pursuit for Internal Microcosms. *Japan Architect* 357 (January–April): 6.

Miyake, Riichi. 2009. The Birth of Paper Tube Architecture. In *Shigeru Ban: Paper in Architecture*, ed. Ian Luna and Lauren A. Gould, 19–23. New York: Rizzoli.

Modell, Arnold. 2003. *Creativity and the Meaningful Brain*. Cambridge, MA: MIT Press.

Moore, Andrew, and Philip Levine. 2010. *Detroit Disassembled*. Bologna: Damiani/Akron Art Museum.

271

Moran, Joe. 2005. *Reading the Everyday*. London: Taylor and Francis.

Morawicki, Rubén O. 2012. *Handbook of Sustainability for the Food Sciences*. Chichester: John Wiley and Sons.

Morris, William. [1888] 1902. The Revival of Handicraft. In Morris, *Architecture, Industry and Wealth: Collected Papers*, 198–213. London: Longmans, Green.

Moser, Walter. 2002. The Acculturation of Waste. In *Waste-Site Stories: The Recycling of Memory*, ed. Brian Neville and Johanne Villeneuve, 85–105. Albany: State University of New York Press.

Mostafavi, Mohsen, and David Leatherbarrow. 1993. *On Weathering: The Life of Buildings in Time*. Cambridge, MA: MIT Press.

Mullin, Stephen. 2007. Potteries Thinkbelt. In *Cedric Price: Potteries Thinkbelt*, ed. Samantha Hardingham and Kester Rattenbury. London: Routledge.

Mumford, Lewis. 1931. *Sticks and Stones: A Study of American Architecture and Civilization*. New York: Horace Liveright.

Murdoch, Jonathan. 2006. *Post-structuralist Geography: A Guide to Relational Space*. London: Sage.

Murphy, Daniel V., Elizabeth A. Stockdale, Philip C. Brookes, and Keith W. T. Goulding. 2007. Impact of Microorganisms on Chemical Transformations in Soil. In *Soil Biological Fertility: A Key to Sustainable Land Use in Agriculture*, ed. Lynette K. Abbott and Daniel V. Murphy, 37–60. Dordrecht: Springer.

Murphy, Michelle. 2006. *Sick Building Syndrome and the Problem of Uncertainty: Environmental Politics, Technoscience, and Women Workers*. Durham: Duke University Press.

Murray, James. 2011. Dean Beck: Quake Not an Act of God. *3 News* (25 February). http://www.3news.co.nz/Dean-Beck-Quake-not-an-act-of-God/tabid/423/articleID/199760/Default.aspx (accessed 23 June 2012).

Mustafić, S. 1993. Destruction of Cultural Heritage in Bosnia and Herzegovina. In *Warchitecture*, ed. S. Jamaković. Sarajevo: ARH: Magazine for Architecture, Town Planning and Design.

Myers, Garth. 2005. *Disposable Cities: Garbage Governance and Sustainable Development in Urban Africa*. Burlington: Ashgate.

Nabarro, Rupert, and David Richards with Honor Chapman. 1980. Wasteland, a Thames Television Report. Thames Television.

Neilsen, Tom. 2002. The Return of the Excessive: Superfluous Landscapes. *Space and Culture* 5 (1):553–562.

Nesbitt, Kate, ed. 1996. *Theorizing a New Agenda for Architecture: An Anthology of Architectural Theory 1965–1995*. New York: Princeton Architectural Press.

Neville, Brian, and Johanne Villeneuve, eds. 2002. *Waste-Site Stories: The Recycling of Memory*. Albany: State University of New York Press.

Newman, Oscar. 1972. *Defensible Space: Crime Prevention through Urban Design*. New York: Macmillan.

New Yorker. 1931. The Talk of the Town: Wrecker's Reminiscences. *New Yorker* 6 (51) (7 February): 12.

Ngamkham, Wassayos. 2012. Hopewell Collapse Sparks Probe: Passing Train Narrowly Escapes Platform Plunge. *Bangkok Post* (2 March). http://www.bangkokpost.com/news/local/282425/hopewell-collapse-sparks-probe (accessed 5 May 2012).

Nietzsche, Friedrich. 1968. *Thus Spoke Zarathustra*. Trans. W. Kaufmann. London: Penguin.

Ninjalicious. 2005 *Access All Areas: A User's Guide to the Art of Urban Exploration*. Toronto: Infilpress.

Nochlin, Linda. 1994. *The Body in Pieces: The Fragment as a Metaphor of Modernity*. London: Thames and Hudson.

Noever, Peter. 1997. Gordon Matta-Clark's Penetration of Space. In *Anarchitecture: Worlds by Gordon Matta-Clark*, ed. Peter Noever, 5–6. Vienna: MAK.

Nute, Kevin. 2004. *Place, Time, and Being in Japanese Architecture*. London: Routledge.

Nutt, Bev. 1976. *Obsolescence in Housing*. Fairborough: Saxon House.

NZPA. 2011. Christchurch Quake: People Likely to Be Trapped in Cathedral. *New Zealand Herald* (22 February). http://www.nzherald.co.nz/christchurch-earthquake/news/article.cfm?c_id=1502981&objectid=10708016 (accessed 23 June 2012).

Olasky, Marvin N. 2006. *The Politics of Disaster: Katrina, Big Government, and a New Strategy for Future Disasters*. Nashville: W Publishing.

OMA. 1991. Mission Grand Axe, La Défense, France, Paris: Transforming an Existing Urban Fabric. OMA. http://oma.eu/projects/1991/mission-grand-axe-la-défense (accessed 15 May 2012).

OMA. 2012. Available from: http://www.oma.eu/ (accessed 29 August 2012).

ONE News. 2011. Cardboard Option for Christchurch Cathedral. ONE News (31 July). http://tvnz.co.nz/national-news/cardboard-option-chch-cathedral-4333995/video?vid=4334000 (accessed 27 April 2012).

Onians, John. 1971. Alberti and Filarete: A Study in Their Sources. *Journal of the Warburg and Courtauld Institutes* 34:96–114.

Onians, John. 1988. *Bearers of Meaning: The Classical Orders in Antiquity, the Middle Ages, and the Renaissance*. Princeton: Princeton University Press.

Oppenheimer, Dean, Andrea Hursley, and Timothy Hursley. 2002. *Rural Studio: Samuel Mockbee and an Architecture of Decency*. New York: Princeton Architectural Press.

Oswalt, Philipp, ed. 2005. *Shrinking Cities*. Ostfildern: Hatje Cantz.

Oswalt, Philipp, and Tim Rieniets, eds. 2006. *Atlas of Shrinking Cities*. Stuttgart: Hatje Cantz.

Otero-Paillos, Jorge. 2006. Conservation Cleaning/Cleaning Conservation. *Futur Antérieur* 4 (1):1–8.

Ourousoff, Nicolai. 2009. Future Vision Banished to the Past. *New York Times* (6 July).

Paduart, A., W. Debacker, C. Henrotay, N. D. Temmerman, W. P. Wilde, and H. Hendtrickx. 2009. Transforming Cities: Introducing Adaptability in Existing Residential Buildings through Reuse and Disassembly Strategies for Retrofitting. In *Lifecycle Design of Buildings, Systems and Materials*, 18–23. Enschede: Construction Materials Stewardship.

273

Page, Max. 2001. *Creative Destruction of Manhattan, 1900–1940*. Chicago: University of Chicago Press.

Page, Max. 2008. *The City's End: Two Centuries of Fantasies, Fears, and Premonitions of New York's Destruction*. New Haven: Yale University Press.

Page, Max, and Randall Mason. 2004. *Giving Preservation a History*. London: Routledge.

Pallasmaa, Juhani. 1994. An Architecture of the Seven Senses. In *Questions of Perception: Phenomenology of Architecture*, ed. Steven Holl, Juhani Pallasmaa, and Alberto Pérez-Goméz, 27–37. Toyko: A+U Publishing.

Palma, Cristóbal, dir. 2011. *PREVI, Proyecto Experimental Vivienda, Various Architects, 1973-Ongoing, Lima, Peru*. Film. http://www.domusweb.it/en/architecture/2011/04/21/previ-the-metabolist-utopia.html (accessed 20 July 2013).

Panofsky, Erwin. [1936] 1963. Et in Arcadia Ego: On the Conception of Transience in Poussin and Watteau. In *Philosophy and History: Essays Presented to Ernst Cassirer*, ed. Raymond Klibansky and H. J. Paton, 223–254. New York: Harper and Row.

Papanek, Victor J. 1972. *Design for the Real World: Human Ecology and Social Change*. New York: Pantheon Books.

Pauly, Danièle. 1997. *Le Corbusier: La chapelle de Ronchamp*. Basel: Birkhäuser.

Pelkmans, M. 2003. The Social Life of Empty Buildings: Imagining the Transition in Post-Soviet Ajaria. *Focaal: European Journal of Anthropology* 41:121–135.

Pelling, Mark. 2003. *The Vulnerability of Cities: Natural Disasters and Social Resilience*. Sterling, VA: Earthscan.

Perera, Daniel. 2008. Dry Toilets and Green Roof Terraces. In *Rematerial: From Waste to Architecture*, ed. Alejandro Bahamón and Maria Camila Sanjinés, 240–243. New York: W. W. Norton.

Pérez-Gómez, Alberto. 1983. *Architecture and the Crisis of Modern Science*. Cambridge, MA: MIT Press.

Perisić, S. 1993. Historical Reminder. In *Warchitecture*, ed. S. Jamaković, 66–67. Sarajevo: ARH: Magazine for Architecture, Town Planning and Design.

Pevsner, Nikolaus. 1940. *Academies of Art, Past and Present*. Cambridge: Cambridge University Press.

Phillips, Tom. 2006. Brazil's Roofless Reclaim the Cities. *Guardian* (23 January).

Pick, Daniel. 1993. *Faces of Degeneration: A European Disorder c. 1848–c. 1918*. Cambridge: Cambridge University Press.

Picon, Antoine. 1992. *French Architects and Engineers in the Age of Enlightenment*. Trans. Martin Thom. Cambridge: Cambridge University Press.

Picon, Antoine. 2000. Anxious Landscapes: From the Ruin to Rust. *Grey Room* 1 (Fall):64–83.

Piiparinen, Richey. 2012. Ruin Porn: As Dirty as You Need It to Be. *Huffington Post* (22 June). http://www.huffingtonpost.com/richey-piiparinen/ruin-porn-photography-detroit_b_1613871.html (accessed 5 July 2012).

Piper, John. 1948. Pleasing Decay. In Piper, *Buildings and Prospects*, 89–116. Westminster: Architectural Press.

Pireddi, Nicoletta. 2002. Gabriele D'Annunzio: The Art of Squandering and the Economy of Sacrifice. In *The Question of the Gift: Essays across Disciplines*, ed. Mark Osteen, 172–190. London: Routledge.

Pohlad, Mark. 2005. The Appreciation of Ruins in Blitz-Era London. *London Journal* 30 (2):1–24.

Porteous, W. A. 1992. Classifying Building Failure by Cause: New Approach to Identifying the Causes of Building Failure Avoiding Involvement with Issues of Blame. *Building Research and Information* 20 (6):350–356.

Porter, Roy. 1990. *The Enlightenment*. Basingstoke: Macmillan Education.

Powell, Bill. 2010. Inside China's Runaway Building Boom. *Time* (5 April). http://www.time.com/time/magazine/article/0,9171,1975336,00.html (accessed 9 July 2012).

Powell, Richard R. 2004. *Wabi Sabi Simple*. Avon, MA: Adams Media.

Prakash, Gyan, ed. 2010. *Noir Urbanisms: Dystopic Images of the Modern City*. Princeton: Princeton University Press.

Press. 1862. The Cathedral. *Press* 3 (78; 25 October): 1.

Press. 1863. The Cathedral. *Press* 3 (119; 18 March): 1.

Press. 1864. The Cathedral Commission. *Press* 4 (404; 15 Feburary): 2.

Press. 1865. The Cathedral. *Press* 7 (703; 30 January): 3.

Press. 1870. Church of St. Michaels and All Angels. *Press* 17 (2320; 30 September): 2.

Press. 1901. Previous Damage to the Spire. *Press* 58 (11125; 18 November): 5.

Price, Cedric. 1960. PTb Potteries Thinkbelt. *Architectural Design* (October): 433.

Price, Cedric. 1966. Potteries Thinkbelt: A Plan for an Advanced Educational Industry in North Staffordshire. *Architectural Design* 36 (October):484–497.

Prigmaier, Elke. 2012. Alternative Economic and Social Concepts. In "Growth in Transition," conference proceedings. Vienna: Sustainable Europe Research Institute.

Proll, Astrid, Sacha Craddock, and Walter Schönauer. 2010. *Goodbye to London: Radical Art and Politics in the Seventies*. Ostfildern: Hatje Cantz.

Pugin, Augustus Welby Northmore. 1853. *The True Principles of Pointed or Christian Architecture: Set Forth in Two Lectures Delivered at St. Marie's, Oscott*. London: Henry G. Bohn.

Quinejure, Michel. 2006. *Shigeru Ban: An Architect for Emergencies*. Documentary film. Brooklyn: First Run/Icarus Films.

Quiviger, François. 2002. Renaissance Art Theories. In *Companion to Art Theory*, ed. Paul Smith and Carolyn Widle, 49–60. Oxford: Blackwell.

Rainwater, Lee. 1973. *Behind Ghetto Walls*. Chicago: Aldine.

Ramis, Tomeu. 2012. What Is PREVI? *Digital Architectural Papers* 9 (4 June). http://www.architecturalpapers.ch/index.php?ID=91 (accessed 2 December 2012).

Rand, Ayn. [1943] 2007. *The Fountainhead*. London: Penguin Books.

Rathje, William L. 2001. Integrated Archaeology: A Garbage Paradigm. In *Archaeologies of the Contemporary Past*, ed. Victor Buchli and Gavin Lucas, 63–76. London: Routledge.

275

Rathje, William L., and Cullen Murphy. 1992. *Rubbish! The Archaeology of Garbage*. New York: HarperCollins.

Ray, Nicholas. 2005. *Architecture and Its Ethical Dilemmas*. London: Taylor & Francis.

Réau, Louis. [1958] 1994. *Histoire du vandalisme: Les monuments détruits de l'art français*. Édition augmentée par Michel Fleury et Guy-Michel Leproux. Paris: Robert Laffont.

Red Road Resident Interview 2. 2005. High-rise Project Digital Archive. April. Arts and Humanities Research Council, London.

Red Road Resident Interview 5. 2005. High-rise Project Digital Archive. April. Arts and Humanities Research Council, London.

Reinert, Hugo and Erik S. Reinert. 2006. Creative Destruction in Economics: Nietzsche, Sombart, Schumpeter. In *Friedrich Nietzsche 1844–2000: Economy and Society*, ed. Jürgen Backhaus and Wolfgang Drechsler, 55–85. Boston: Kluwer.

Rendell, Jane. 2006. *Art and Architecture: A Place in Between*. London: I. B. Tauris.

RIBA. 2003a. Role of Historic Buildings in Urban Regeneration. RIBA comments submitted to the Office of the Deputy Prime Minister's Housing, Planning, Local Government and the Regions Committee. London: RIBA.

RIBA. 2003b. Protecting Our Historic Environment: Making the System Work Better. RIBA comments submitted to the Department of Culture, Media and Sport's heritage review consultation paper. London: RIBA.

Rice, Shelley. 1999. *Parisian Views*. Cambridge, MA: MIT Press.

Richie, Donald. 2007. *A Tractate on Japanese Aesthetics*. Berkeley: Stone Bridge Press.

Riedlmayer, Andras J. 2002. *Destruction of Cultural Heritage in Bosnia-Herzegovina 1992–1996: A Post-war Survey of Selected Municipalities*. The Hague: Report Commissioned by the International Criminal Tribunal for the Former Yugoslavia.

Riegl, Alois. [1903] 1996. The Modern Cult of Monuments: Its Character and Origin. In *Historical and Philosophical Issues in the Conservation of Cultural Heritage*, ed. Nicholas Stanley Price, Mansfield Kirby Talley, and Alessandra Melucco Vaccaro, 69–83. Los Angeles: Getty Conservation Institute.

Rieniets, Tim, Jennifer Sigler, and Kees Christiaanse, eds. 2009. *Open City: Designing Coexistence*. Amsterdam: Sun Publishers.

Ritter, Harry. 1986. *Dictionary of Concepts in History*. Westport: Greenwood Press.

Rivett, Geoffrey. 1998. *From Cradle to Grave: Fifty Years of the NHS*. London: King's Fund, National Health Service.

Robben, Antonius C. G. M. 2004. Death and Anthropology: An Introduction. In *Death, Mourning, and Burial: A Cross-Cultural Reader*, ed. Antonius C. G. M. Robben, 1–16. Malden, MA: Blackwell.

Robbins, David. 1990. *Independent Group: Postwar Britain and the Aesthetics of Plenty*. Cambridge, MA: MIT Press.

Robinson, Jennifer. 2006. *Ordinary Cities: Between Modernity and Development*. London: Routledge.

Roche, François. 2012. Interview. Stephen Cairns, 9 May, Singapore.

276

Roche, François, and Stéphanie Lavaux. 2004. Dusty Relief/B_mu: Bangkok, Thailand, 2002: Design of a Contemporary Art Museum. In François Roche et al., *Spoiled Climate: R&Sie, Architects*, 137–138. Basel: Birkhäuser.

Roche, François, Stéphanie Lavaux, Jean Navarro, and Pascal Bertholio. 2005. *Corrupted Biotopes*. Seoul: Damdi Publishing.

Rodriguez, Luis. 2012. The Impact of PREVI on Lima. *Digital Architectural Papers* 9 (4 June). http://www.architecturalpapers.ch/index.php?ID=92 (accessed 3 December 2012).

Rogers, Robert P. 2009. *An Economic History of the American Steel Industry*. New York: Taylor & Francis.

Rosefeldt, Julian, and Piero Steinle. 1996. *Detonation Deutschland: Sprengbilder einer Nation*. Munich: Peschke.

Rosen, Christine Meisner. 1986. *The Limits of Power: Great Fires and the Process of City Growth in America*. Cambridge: Cambridge University Press.

Rossi, Aldo. 1981. *A Scientific Autobiography*. Trans. Lawrence Venuti. Cambridge, MA: MIT Press.

Roth, M. S. 1997. Irresistible Decay: Ruins Reclaimed. In *Irresistible Decay: Ruins Reclaimed*, ed. M. S. Roth, C. Lyons, and C. Merewether, 1–23. Los Angeles: Getty Research Institute.

Rowe, Colin, and Fred Koetter. 1978. *Collage City*. Cambridge, MA: MIT Press.

Roy, Ananya. 2005. Urban Informality: Toward an Epistemology of Planning. *Journal of the American Planning Association* 71 (2):147–158.

Roy, Ananya, and Nezar AlSayyad, eds. 2004. *Urban Informality: Transnational Perspectives from the Middle East, Latin America, and South Asia*. Lanham: Lexington Books.

Ruby, Andreas. 2004. Hyper-locality: On the Archaeology of the Here and Now in the Architecture of R&Sie. In *Spoiled Climate: R&Sie, Architects*, ed. François Roche et al., 64–70. Basel: Birkhäuser.

Ruskin, John. 1857. *Modern Painters, Part V: Of Mountain Beauty*. New York: Wiley & Halsted.

Ruskin, John. [1849] 1996. The Lamp of Memory. In *Historical and Philosophical Issues in the Conservation of Cultural Heritage*, ed. N. S. Price, M. K. Talley, Jr., and A. M. Vaccaro, 42–43, 322–323. Los Angeles: Getty Conservation Institute.

Ryan, Brent D. 2012. *Design after Decline: How America Rebuilds Shrinking Cities*. Philadelphia: University of Pennsylvania Press.

Rykwert, Joseph. 1981a. *On Adam's House in Paradise: The Idea of the Primitive Hut in Architectural History*. Cambridge, MA: MIT Press.

Rykwert, Joseph. 1981b. On an (Egyptian?) Misreading by Francesco di Giorgio. *Res: Anthropology and Aesthetics* 1 (Spring): 78–83.

Rykwert, Joseph. 1990. Semper's "Morphology." *Rassegna* 12 (41/1) (March): 40–47.

Rykwert, Joseph. 1996. *The Dancing Column: On Order in Architecture*. Cambridge, MA: MIT Press.

SafeDem. 2012. http://www.safedem.co.uk (accessed 12 November 2012).

Saint, Andrew. 1985. *The Image of the Architect*. New Haven: Yale University Press.

Saint, Andrew. 2007. *Architect and Engineer: A Study in Sibling Rivalry*. New Haven: Yale University Press.

Salas, Julian, and Patricia Lucas. 2012. The Validity of PREVI, Lima, Peru, 40 Years On. *Open House International* 37 (1):6–15.

Salmon, Frank. 2000. *Building on Ruins: The Rediscovery of Rome and English Architecture*. Burlington: Ashgate.

Salvadori, Ornella, and A. Elena Charola. 2011. Methods to Prevent Biocolonization and Recolonization: An Overview of Current Research for Architectural and Archaeological Heritage. In *Biocolonization of Stone: Control and Preventive Methods,* proceedings from the MCI Workshop Series, ed. A. Elena Charola, Christopher McNamara, and Robert J. Koestler, 37–51. Washington, DC: Smithsonian Institution Scholarly Press.

Sam Bunton and Associates. 1966. Balornock Glasgow Red Road Development. *International Asbestos Cement Review* 44 (October):20–25.

Samuel, Flora. 2004. *Le Corbusier: Architect and Feminist*. London: Academy Press.

Sanjinés, Daniela. 2008. Chandigarh, between Utopia and Garbage. In *Rematerial: From Waste to Architecture*, ed. Alejandro Bahamón and Maria Camila Sanjinés, 288–291. New York: W. W. Norton.

Saunders, Christi L., Amy E. Landis, Laurel P. Mecca, Alex K. Jones, Laura A. Schaefer, and Melissa M. Bilek. 2013. Analyzing the Practice of Life Cycle Assessment: Focus on the Building Sector. *Journal of Industrial Ecology* 17 (5):777–788.

Savatier, T., and F. Raynaud. 2001. Zone-Tour: Database of Urban Exploration. http://www.zone-tour.com (accessed 12 April 2012).

Sawislak, Karen. 1995. *Smoldering City: Chicagoans and the Great Fire, 1867–1874*. Chicago: University of Chicago Press.

Sbriglio, Jacques. 1999. *Le Corbusier: La Villa Savoye, the Villa Savoye*. Paris. Fondation Le Corbusier; Basel: Birkhäuser.

Scanlan, John A. 2005. *On Garbage*. London: Reaktion.

Scheuer, Chris, Gregory A. Keoleian, and Peter Reppe. 2003. Life Cycle Energy and Environmental Performance of a New University Building: Modeling Challenges and Design Implications. *Energy and Buildings* 35 (10):1049–1064.

Schlegel, Moritz-Caspar, Adnan Sarfraz, Urs Müller, Ulrich Panne, and Franziska Emmerling. 2012. First Seconds in a Building's Life: In-Situ Synchrotron X-Ray Diffraction Study of Cement Hydration on the Millisecond Timescale. *Angewandte Chemie* [International Edition] 51 (20):4993–4996.

Schmidt, Robert, III, T. Eguchi, Simon Austin, and Alistair Gibb. 2010. A Critical Look at the Meaning of Adaptability in the Building Industry. CIB W104 16th International Conference "Open and Sustainable Building," Bilbao. www.adaptablefutures.com (accessed 28 June 2012).

Schmidt, Robert, III, T. Eguchi, Simon Austin, and Alistair Gibb. 2011. Understanding Adaptability through Layer Dependencies. Paper presented at the International Conference on Engineering Design ICED11, 15–18 August 2011. http://adaptablefutures.com/wp-content/uploads/2011/11/Schmidt-et-al.-2011.pdf (accessed 28 June 2012).

Schmidt-Bleek, Friedrich. 1999. The Factor 10/MIPS-Concept: Bridging Ecological, Economic, and Social Dimensions with Sustainability Indicators. Paper presented at United Nations University, Zero Emissions Forum. Tokyo and Berlin.

Schmidt-Bleek, Friedrich. 2009. *The Earth: Natural Resources and Human Intervention*. Trans. Sandra Lustig. London: Haus Publishing.

Schmitt, Cannon. 2004. Introduction: Materia Media. *Criticism* 46 (1):11–15.

Schneekloth, Lynda H. 1998. U[n]redeemably Utopian: Architecture and Making/Unmaking the World. *Utopian Studies* 9 (1):1–25.

Schneider, Jane, and Ida Susser, eds. 2003. *Wounded Cities: Destruction and Reconstruction in a Globalized World*. Oxford: Berg.

Schönberger, Angela. 1981. *Die neue Reichskanzlei von Albert Speer. Zum Zusammenhang von nationalsozialistischer Ideologie und Architektur*. Berlin: Gebr. Mann.

Schrödinger, Erwin. 1967. *What Is Life? The Physical Aspect of the Living Cell*. Cambridge: Cambridge University Press.

Schumpeter, Joseph A. [1942] 1975. *Capitalism, Socialism and Democracy*. New York: Harper.

Schwanhäußer, Anja. 2010. *Kosmonauten des Underground : Ethnografie einer Berliner Szene*. Frankfurt: Campus Verlag.

Scobie, Alex. 1990. *Hitler's State Architecture: The Impact of Classical Antiquity*. University Park: Pennsylvania State University Press.

Seelig, Michael Y., ed. 1978. *The Architecture of Self-Help Communities: The First International Competition for the Urban Environment of Developing Countries*. New York: Architectural Record Books.

Seery, John E. 1996. *Political Theory for Mortals: Shades of Justice, Images of Death*. Ithaca: Cornell University Press.

Semper, Gottfried. 1989. *The Four Elements of Architecture and Other Writings*. Trans. Harry Francis Mallgrave and Wolfgang Herrmann. Cambridge: Cambridge University Press.

Serres, Michel. 1995. *The Natural Contract*. Ann Arbor: University of Michigan Press.

Serres, Michel. 2011. *Malfeasance: Appropriation through Pollution?* Trans. Anne-Marie Feenberg-Dibon. Stanford: Stanford University Press.

Shaw, Martin. 2004. New Wars of the City: "Urbicide" and "Genocide." In *Cities, War, and Terrorism: Towards an Urban Geopolitics*, ed. Stephen Graham, 141–153. London: Blackwell.

Shinbunsha, Asahi, Kenzō Tange, and Noboru Kawazoe. 1965. *Ise: Prototype of Japanese Architecture*. Cambridge, MA: MIT Press.

Sibley, David. 1995. *Geographies of Exclusion: Society and Difference in the West*. New York: Routledge.

Silver, Nathan. 1997. *The Making of Beaubourg: A Building Biography of the Centre Pompidou, Paris*. Cambridge, MA: MIT Press.

Simmel, Georg. 1959. The Ruin. In *Georg Simmel*, ed. K. Wolff, 259–266. Columbus: Ohio State University Press.

Simone, Abdoumaliq. 2004. People as Infrastructure: Intersecting Fragments in Johannesburg. *Public Culture* 16 (3):407–429.

Simson, Otto von. 1956. *The Gothic Cathedral: The Origins of Gothic Architecture and the Medieval Concept of Order*. London: Routledge and Kegan Paul.

Sinopoli, James. 2010. *Smart Buildings Systems for Architects, Owners and Builders*. Burlington: Elsevier.

Sir John Soane's Museum. 1999. *Visions of Ruin: Architectural Fantasies and Designs for Garden Follies*. Exh. cat. London: Sir John Soane's Museum.

Smith, Barbara Herrnstein. 1988. *Contingencies of Value: Alternative Perspectives for Critical Theory*. Cambridge, MA: Harvard University Press.

Smith, George. 1971. Steel Fit for the Countryside. *New Scientist* 23 (December):211–213.

Smith, Neil. 1982. Gentrification and Uneven Development. *Economic Geography* 58 (2):139–155.

Smithson, Robert. 1979. Entropy Made Visible. In *The Writings of Robert Smithson*, ed. Nancy Holt. New York: New York University Press.

Smithson, Robert. 1996. Entropy and the New Monuments. In *Robert Smithson: The Collected Writings*, ed. Jack Flam, 10–23. Berkeley: University of California Press.

Snaffler, Hank, Jr. 2011. Sathorn Unique. Abandoned Journey: Journey through Abandoned Buildings from around the World with Dr. Hank Snaffler Jr. (15 June). http://www.abandonedjourney.com/ (accessed 25 June 2012).

Solomon, Yuki. 2007. Kurokawa's Capsule Tower to Be Razed. *Architectural Record* 195 (6): 10.

Sorkin, Michael, and Sharon Zukin, eds. 2002. *After the World Trade Center: Rethinking New York City*. New York: Routledge.

Spalding, David. 2002. Ghosts among the Ruins: Urban Transformation in Contemporary Chinese Art. MA thesis, California College of Arts.

Speer, Albert. 1970. *Inside the Third Reich*. London: Weidenfeld and Nicolson.

Speer, Albert. 1985. Foreword. In *Albert Speer Architecture 1932–1942*, ed. Leon Krier, 213–214. Brussels: Archives d'Architecture Moderne.

Spiller, Neil, and Rachel Armstrong. 2011. It's a Brand New Morning. *Architectural Design* 81 (2):14–23.

Star. 1869. St. Michael and All Angels. *Star* 493 (December 15): 2.

Star. 1870. The New Church of St. Michael and All Angels. *Star* 735 (30 September): 2.

Stead, Naomi. 2000. The Ruins of History: Allegories of Destruction in Daniel Libeskind's Jewish Museum. *Open Museum Journal* 2 (August). http://archive.amol.org.au/omj/volume2/stead.pdf (accessed 10 July 2011).

Steadman, Philip. 1979. The Evolution of Decoration. In Steadman, *The Evolution of Designs: Biological Analogy in Architecture and the Applied Arts*, 101–123. Cambridge: Cambridge University Press.

Steinberg, Ted. 2006. *Acts of God: The Unnatural History of Natural Disaster in America*. New York: Oxford University Press.

Stirling, James. 1956. Ronchamp: Le Corbusier's Chapel and the Crisis of Rationalism. *Architectural Review* 119 (March):155–161.

Stoler, Ann Laura. 2008. Imperial Debris: Reflections on Ruins and Ruination. *Cultural Anthropology* 23 (2):191–219.

Stoppani, Teresa. 2007. Dust Revolutions: Dust, *informe*, Architecture (Notes for a Reading of Dust in Bataille). *Journal of Architecture* 12 (4):437–447.

Stout, David. 2005. Bush Rules Out Tax Increases to Pay for Hurricane Recovery. *New York Times* (16 September). http://www.nytimes.com/2005/09/16/national/nationalspecial/16cnd-bush.html (accessed 22 April 2012).

Strasser, Susan. 1999. *Waste and Want: A Social History of Trash*. New York: Metropolitan Books.

Straus, Ivan. 1994. *Sarajevo, l'architecte et les barbares*. Paris: Éditions du Linteau.

Strebel, Ignaz. 2011. The Living Building: Towards a Geography of Maintenance Work. *Social and Cultural Geography* 12 (3):243–262.

Strebel, Ignaz, and Jane M. Jacobs. In press. Houses of Experiment: High-rise Housing and the Will to Laboratorization. *International Journal of Urban and Regional Research*.

Stroud, Gregory. 2006. The Past in Common: Modern Ruins as a Shared Urban Experience of Revolution-Era Moscow. *Slavic Review* 65 (4):712–735.

Sudjic, Deyan. 2005. Celebratory Demolition? The Whole Idea Stinks. *Observer* (2 January).

Sully, Nicole. 2009. Modern Architecture and Complaints about the Weather, or, "Dear Monsieur Le Corbusier, It Is Still Raining in Our Garage." *M/C Journal* 12 (4): 1–10.

Summerson, John. [1949] 1998. *Heavenly Mansions and Other Essays on Architecture*. London: W. W. Norton.

Sweeney, Marvin Alan. 1996. *Isaiah 1–39: With an Introduction to Prophetic Literature*. Cambridge: Eerdmans Publishing.

T. G. 2005. It's All God's Fault. *Salon* (17 September). http://www.salon.com/2005/09/16/god_5/ (accessed 15 March 2012).

Tafuri, Manfredo. 1976. *Theories and Histories of Architecture*. New York: Harper & Row.

Taki, Koji. 1999. Maturity and Freedom. In *Toyo Ito: Blurring Architecture*, 35–47. Exh. cat. Milan: Charta.

Tamura, Yōshirō. 2000. *Japanese Buddhism: A Cultural History*. Tokyo: Kosei Publishing.

Taussig, Michael. 1999. *Defacement*. Stanford: Stanford University Press.

Taylor, Robert R. 1974. *The Word in Stone: The Role of Architecture in the National Socialist Ideology*. Berkeley: University of California Press.

Thackara, John. 1991. In Tokyo They Shimmer, Chatter and Vanish. *Independent* (25 September).

Thompson, D'Arcy Wentworth. 1961. *On Growth and Form*. Cambridge: Cambridge University Press.

Thompson, Michael. 1979. *Rubbish Theory: The Creation and Destruction of Value*. Oxford: Oxford University Press.

281

Thorndike, Edward. 1921. *The Psychology of Learning*. New York: Teachers College Press.

Thrift, Nigel. 2005. But Malice Aforethought: Cities and the Natural History of Hatred. *Transactions of the Institute of British Geographers* 30 (2):133–150.

Till, Jeremy. 2009. *Architecture Depends*. Cambridge, MA: MIT Press.

Tobler, Konrad. 2007. Built in a Void. In *White Elephants*, photographs by Christian Helme with an essay by Konrad Tobler, 5–13. Berlin: Jovis.

Tobriner, Stephen. 2006. *Bracing for Disaster: Earthquake-Resistant Architecture and Engineering in San Francisco, 1838–1933*. Berkeley: Heyday Books.

Tokyo Metropolitan Government. 1994. *Tokyo Metropolis: Facts and Data*. Tokyo: Tokyo Metropolitan Government.

Tonkins and Taylor. 2011. *Christchurch Earthquake Recovery Geotechnical Factual Report St Albans*. Christchurch: Tonkins and Taylor.

Toone, Michael. 1972. Letter to Editor. *Sunday Times* (10 September).

Trigg, Dylan. 2006. *The Aesthetics of Decay*. New York: Peter Lang.

Tschumi, Bernard. 1981. *Manhattan Transcripts*. London: Academy Editions.

Tschumi, Bernard. 1996. *Architecture and Disjunction*. Cambridge, MA: MIT Press.

Tsukada, Nobuhiro. 1999. Reproduktion / Reproduction. In *Toyo Ito: Blurring Architecture*, 80–85. Exh. cat. Milan: Charta.

Turner, Barry A. 1978. *Man-Made Disasters*. London: Wykeham Publications.

Turner, John. 1972. *Freedom to Build: Dweller Control of the Housing Process*. New York: Macmillan.

Turner, John. 1976. *Housing by People: Towards Autonomy in Building Environments*. London: Marion Boyars.

Turner, Victor. 1969. *The Ritual Process: Structure and Anti-Structure.* Chicago: W. Aldine.

United Nations Human Settlements Programme (Habitat). 2003. *The Challenge of Slums: Global Report on Human Settlements*. London: Earthscan.

Urban Exploration London. 2004. Exploration in London Ontario and Surrounding Areas. http://uel.minimanga.com (accessed 12 February 2011).

van Beek, Gosewijn. 1996. On Materiality. *Etnofoor* 9 (1):5–24.

Vanderbilt, Tom. 2002. *Survival City: Adventures among the Ruins of Atomic America*. Princeton: Princeton Architectural Press.

van der Hoorn, Mélanie. 2009. *Indispensable Eyesores: An Anthropology of Undesired Buildings*. Oxford: Berghahn Books.

van Hoogstraten, Dorine, and Martijn Vos. 2000. *Housing for the Millions: John Habraken and the SAR (1960–2000)*. Rotterdam: NAi Publishers.

Varda, Agnes. 2000. *The Gleaners and I (Les glaneurs et la glaneuse)*. Documentary film. Paris: Ciné Tamaris.

Vasari, Giorgio. [1550] 1991. *The Lives of the Artists*. Trans. Julia Conaway Bondanella and Peter Bondanella. Oxford: Oxford University Press.

Veblen, Thorstein. [1899] 1965. *The Theory of the Leisure Class*. New York: A. M. Kelley.

Veblen, Thorstein. 1990. *The Place of Science in Modern Civilization*. Piscataway: Transaction Publishers.

Venkatesh, Sudhir Alladi. 2000. *American Project: The Rise and Fall of a Modern Ghetto*. Cambridge, MA: Harvard University Press.

Venturi, Robert, Denise Scott Brown, and Steven Izenour. [1972] 1977. *Learning from Las Vegas: The Forgotten Symbolism of Architectural Form*. Cambridge, MA: MIT Press.

Verdery, Katherine. 1999. *The Political Life of Dead Bodies: Reburial and Postsocialist Change*. New York: Columbia University Press.

Vergara, Camilo J. 1999. *American Ruins*. New York: Monacelli Press.

Vesely, Dalibor. 2004. *Architecture in the Age of Divided Representation: The Question of Creativity in the Shadow of Production*. Cambridge, MA: MIT Press.

Vichit-Vadakan, Nuntavarn, Nitaya Vajanapoom, and Bart Ostro. 2008. The Public Health and Air Pollution in Asia (PAPA) Project: Estimating the Mortality Effects of Particulate Matter in Bangkok, Thailand. *Environmental Health Perspectives* 116 (9):1179–1182.

Vidler, Anthony. 1977. The Idea of Type: The Transformation of the Academic Ideal, 1750–1830. *Oppositions* 8 (Spring):95–115.

Vidler, Anthony. 1981. The Hut and the Body: The "Nature" of Architecture from Laugier to Quatremère de Quincy. *Lotus International* 33: 102–111.

Vidler, Anthony. 1987. *The Writing of the Walls: Architectural Theory in the Late Enlightenment*. New York: Princeton Architectural Press.

Vidler, Anthony. 1990. The Building in Pain: The Body and Architecture in Post-modern Culture. *AA Files* 19 (Spring):3–10.

Vidler, Anthony. 1992. *The Architectural Uncanny: Essays in the Modern Unhomely*. Cambridge, MA: MIT Press.

Virilio, Paul. [1975] 1994a. *Bunker Archaeology.* New York: Princeton Architectural Press.

Virilio, Paul. 1994b. *The Vision Machine*. Bloomington: Indiana University Press.

Virilio, Paul. 2003. *Unknown Quantity*. London: Thames and Hudson.

Vitruvius Pollio, Marcus. 1960. *The Ten Books on Architecture*. Trans. Morris Hicky Morgan. New York: Dover.

Vroege, Bas, Frits Gierstberg, and Jacqueline Hagman, eds. 1992. *Wasteland: Landscape from Now On*. Rotterdam: 010 Publishers.

Walker, Paul. 1992. Shaky Ground. *Interstices* 2:25–44.

Walker, Stephen. 2009. *Gordon Matta-Clark: Art, Architecture and the Attack on Modernism*. New York: I. B. Tauris.

Wang, Bing, dir. 2003. *Tie Xi Qu: West of the Tracks*. Film.

Wang, Jinsong. 1999. *One Hundred Signs of the Demolition.* Chromogenic print. New York: Metropolitan Museum of Art.

Ward, Colin, ed. 1973 *Vandalism*. London: Architectural Press.

Weber, Rachel. 2002. Extracting Value from the City: Neoliberalism and Urban Redevelopment. *Antipode* 34 (3):519–540.

283

Weber, Rachel. 2006. Tearing the City Down: Understanding Demolition Activity in Gentrifying Neighbourhoods. *Journal of Urban Affairs* 28 (1):19–41.

Webster, George. 2011. "Living" Buildings Could Inhale City Carbon Emissions. CNN. http: //edition.cnn.com/2011/10/14/tech/innovation/living-buildings-carbon/index.html (accessed 19 May 2012).

Weinstein, Liza, and Xuefei Ren. 2009. The Changing Right to the City: Urban Renewal and Housing Rights in Globalizing Shanghai and Mumbai. *City and Community* 8 (4):407–432.

Weinstock, Michael. 2010. *The Architecture of Emergence: The Evolution of Form in Nature and Civilisation*. London: Wiley.

Weizman, Eyal. 2007. *Hollow Land: Israel's Architecture of Occupation*. London: Verso.

Weizman, Eyal. 2012. *Forensic Architecture*. dOCUMENTA 13 Notebook. Ostfildern: Hatje Cantz.

Werner, Frank. 2000. *Covering + Exposing: The Architecture of Coop Himmeb[l]au*. Trans. Michael Robinson. Basel: Birkhäuser.

Whitehead, Alfred North. 1920. *The Concept of Nature*. Cambridge: Cambridge University Press.

Whyte, Iain Boyd, ed. 2003. *Modernism and the Spirit of the City*. London: Routledge.

Wiebel, Peter, ed. 2005. *Beyond Art: A Third Culture: A Comparative Study in Cultures, Art and Science in 20th Century Austria and Hungary*. Vienna: Springer.

Wiener, Norbert. 1950. *The Human Use of Human Beings: Cybernetics and Society*. Boston: Houghton Mifflin.

Wigley, Mark. 1994. White Out: Fashioning the Modern. In *Architecture in Fashion*, ed. Deborah Fausch, Paulette Singley, Rodolphe El-Khoury, and Zvi Efrat, 149–268. New York: Princeton Architectural Press.

Wigley, Mark. 1995a. *The Architecture of Deconstruction: Derrida's Haunt*. Cambridge, MA: MIT Press.

Wigley, Mark. 1995b. Terrorising Architecture. In *AD Profile* 114 (The Power of Architecture) 65 (3–4): 42–45. London: Academy Editions.

Wilkinson, Catherine. 1977. The New Professionalism in the Renaissance. In *The Architect: Chapters in the History of the Profession*, ed. Spiro Kostof, 124–160. Oxford: Oxford University Press.

Williams, Raymond. 1976. *Keywords: A Vocabulary of Culture and Society*. London: Fontana Press.

Williams, Raymond. 1989. Politics of the Avant-Garde. In Williams, *Politics of Modernism*. London: Verso.

Willis, Katie. 2009. Squatter Settlements. In *International Encyclopedia of Human Geography*, ed. Rob Kitchen and Nigel Thrift, 403–408. Oxford: Elsevier.

Wilson, Asa. 2003. Bangkok: Bubble City. In *Wounded Cities*, ed. Jane Schneider and Ida Susser, 203–226. London: Berg.

Wilson, James Q., and George L. Kelling. 1982. Broken Windows. *Atlantic Monthly* 249 (3):29–38.

Wisner, Ben, Piers Blaikie, Terry Cannon, and Ian Davis. 2004. *At Risk: Natural Hazards, People's Vulnerability and Disasters*. London: Routledge.

Wittkower, Rudolf. 1971. *Architectural Principles in the Age of Humanism*. New York: W. W. Norton.

Wood, John George. 1875. *Homes without Hands*. London: Longmans, Green.

Woods, David D., Sidney Dekker, Richard Cook, Leila Johannesen, and Nadine Sarter. 2010. *Behind Human Error*. Farnham: Ashgate.

Words and Phrases. Vol. 2. St. Paul, MN: Thomson/West.

Worringer, Wilhelm. 1920. *Form Problems of the Gothic*. New York: G. E. Stechert.

Wu, Nan-wei, and Liang-ping Yen. 2012. Interview with Meei-Ya Chen, Deputy Director of the Newhomeland Foundation. Paper Dome, Puli, Taiwan, 13 August 2012.

Yamasaki, Minoru. 1952. High Buildings for Public Housing? *Journal of Housing* 9:226.

Yancey, William L. 1974. Architecture, Interaction and Social Control: The Case of a Large-Scale Housing Project. In *Crowding and Behavior*, ed. Chalsa M. Loo, 68–79. New York: Arno Press.

Yancey, William L. 1978. Architecture, Interaction and Social Control. In *Humanscape: Environments for People*, ed. Stephen Kaplan and Rachel Kaplan, 293–307. North Scituate, MA: Duxbury Press.

Yashiro, Tomonari. 2009. Overview of Building Stock Management in Japan. In *Stock Management for Sustainable Urban Regeneration*, ed. Y. Fugino and T. Noguchi, 15–32. Tokyo: Springer Japan.

Yau, J. 1997. The Anarchitectural Vision of Gordon Matta-Clark (1943–1978). In *Anarchitecture: Works by Gordon Matta-Clark*, ed. Peter Noever, 7–13. Vienna: MAK.

Zaera-Polo, Alejandro. 2005. Alchemical Brothers. In *Herzog & De Meuron: Natural History*, ed. Philip Ursprung, 179–183. Baden: Lars Müller.

Zaugg, Rémy, and Herzog & De Meuron. 1996. *Herzog & De Meuron: An Exhibition*. Basel: Hatje Cantz.

Zawadzki, Bohan. 1948. The Limitations of the Scapegoat Theory of Prejudice. *Journal of Abnormal and Social Psychology* 43:127–141.

Zhang, Yan, and Ke Fang. 2004. Is History Repeating Itself? From Urban Renewal in the United States to Inner-City Redevelopment in China. *Journal of Planning Education and Research* 23 (3):286–298.

Zhao Xudong, and Duran Bell. 2005. Destroying the Remembered and Recovering the Forgotten in Chai: Between Traditionalism and Modernity in Beijing. *China Information* 19:489.

Zimmerman, Howard L. N. Forensic Architecture: The Art of Understanding a Building's Unwritten History. *Building Business* 1 (1).

Žižek, Slavoj. 2003a. *The Fragile Absolute: Or, Why Is the Christian Legacy Worth Fighting For?* London: Verso.

Žižek, Slavoj. 2003b. Not a Desire to Have Him, but to Be Like Him. *London Review of Books* 25 (6):13–14.

Žižek, Slavoj. 2011. *Living in the End Times*. London: Verso.

Zoloth, Laurie. 2009. Second Life: Some Ethical Issues in Synthetic Biology and the Recapitulation of Evolution. In *The Ethics of Protocells: Moral and Social Implications of Creating Life in the Laboratory*, ed. Mark A. Bedau and Emily C. Parks, 143–164. Cambridge, MA: MIT Press.

Zukin, Sharon. 1982. *Loft Living: Culture and Capital in Urban Change*. Baltimore: Johns Hopkins University Press.

Zukin, Sharon. 1996. Space and Symbols in an Age of Decline. In *Re-presenting the City: Ethnicity, Capital and Culture in the 21st Century Metropolis*, ed. A. D. King, 43–59. Basingstoke: Macmillan.

Zulaika, Joseba, and William A. Douglass. 1996. *Terror and Taboo: The Follies, Fables and Faces of Terrorism*. New York: Routledge.

INDEX

287

INDEX

289

291

INDEX